MAJESTY AND HUMANITY

Majesty and Humanity

*Kings and Their Doubles in the Political
Drama of the Spanish Golden Age*

Alban K. Forcione

Yale University Press

New Haven & London

Published with assistance from Princeton University, Department of Hispanic Languages and Culture, University Committee on Research in the Humanities and the Social Sciences, and the Program for Cultural Cooperation between Spain's Ministry of Culture and United States Universities.

Set in Electra and Trajan types by Tseng Information Systems, Inc.
Printed in the United States of America.

Library of Congress Cataloging-in-Publication Data
Forcione, Alban K., 1938–
Majesty and Humanity : kings and their doubles in the political drama of the Spanish Golden Age / Alban K. Forcione.
p. cm.
Includes bibliographical references and index.
ISBN 978-0-300-13440-7 (cloth : alk. paper)
1. Spanish drama—Classical period, 1500–1700—History and criticism.
2. Political plays, Spanish—History and criticism. 3. Kings and rulers in literature.
4. Vega, Lope de, 1562–1635. Villano en su rincón. 5. Vega, Lope de, 1562–1635.
Rey Don Pedro en Madrid. I. Title.
PQ6105.F67 2009
862'.3093581—dc22
2008035069

A catalogue record for this book is available from the British Library.

This paper meets the requirements of ANSI/NISO Z39.48-1992 (Permanence of Paper). It contains 30 percent postconsumer waste (PCW) and is certified by the Forest Stewardship Council (FSC).

10 9 8 7 6 5 4 3 2 1

For Suzanne and Bogey,
compañeros de caminos estrellados

CONTENTS

Preface and Acknowledgments

The research and writing of this book were for me something of an adventure. It confronted me with unknown paths, poorly understood detours, unforeseen challenges and risks, as well as a continuing experience of ordeal, frustration, and doubt. One of its rewards was a resigned recognition of how much there will always be still to know and how many ways untaken will never reveal their secrets. The book grew out of a large general project on Baroque literary forms and values I had undertaken in the late 1980s, itself an outgrowth of my previous studies of European humanism and the place of Cervantes's fiction within it. I quickly realized that the Baroque was forcing me into unfamiliar and at times uncongenial territory—political theory and history, the prominence of the public art of the theater in the seventeenth century, and, more specifically, the challenging philosophical and literary worlds of Baltasar Gracián. At some point it occurred to me that a play I had admired and taught for several years, Lope de Vega's *El villano en su rincón*, might provide a link among these three contexts. In its unusual integration of classical values and philosophy, its concern with political culture and the ascendance of monarchy, and its imaginative exploration and resolution of conflicts connected with the social origins of the modern state, it seemed to offer a sharply drawn focus through which I could approach and perhaps control what had grown into a nearly unmanageable mass of readings connected with numerous aspects of Baroque culture and its relation to early modernity. Moreover, here was a dramatic work of considerable power and beauty that called into question the view prevailing in Spanish cultural history that the literary worlds of Cervantes and Lope de Vega are best understood as sharply oppositional. The book began as an essay on Lope's play, which I presented in an abridged version in lectures at the University of Colorado, Harvard, Miami University, and Stanford in 1996 and 1997. Encouraged by the interest, suggestions, and provocations of my audiences, I decided to develop the project in various directions.

I am especially grateful to my friend and colleague David Quint, whose writings about political issues and the literary imagination are exemplary in their analytical subtlety and erudition. He read the entire manuscript carefully and generously offered knowledge and criticisms, as well as the encouragement I needed to find my way on a very circuitous course. I would also like to thank Diana de Armas Wilson, who read the completed manuscript, graciously shared with me her considerable knowledge of Spanish Golden Age literature and the critical writing in the field, and offered several specific suggestions for improvements.

I have benefited from the presence of numerous colleagues and friends who have taken an interest in my work and have always been available with advice, critical dialogue, and encouragement: the late Edmund L. King, Jorge Checa, Joachim Coelho, Marsha Collins, Lionel Gossman, Margaret Greer, Patricia Grieve, Robert Hollander, Raymond Keck, John Logan, Luis Murillo, Suzanne Nash, Thomas Pavel, Michael Predmore, François Rigolot, Stephen Rupp, Gonzalo Sobejano, and Ronald Surtz.

Special thanks are due to Hall Bjørnstad and Hilaire Kallendorf, whose impressive knowledge of seventeenth-century political and theological culture, combined with a remarkable command of computer technology, made their various efforts to come to the rescue of my periodically derailed journey seem like providential interventions from a world far beyond my reach.

Finally, I would express my gratitude to the students who participated in my seminars on these subjects over the years at Princeton, Stanford, and Columbia. They have welcomed my ideas, challenged my arguments, expected clarity, and always offered support. They enlivened lonely hours of thinking and cheered moments of confusion and lost direction. They are far too many to name here, but I would mention those who have made specific contributions to this project: Belén Atienza, Laura Bass, Ariadna García-Bryce, Christina Lee, William Nowak, Maria Teresa Robertson, Michael Scham, and Rachel Schmidt.

I wish to thank the Guggenheim Foundation for a grant that enabled me to explore the literature and culture of the European Baroque; Columbia University for providing funds for research, travel, and copying; and Princeton University for a subvention that made possible the publication of this book.

To assist my readers, I have provided English translations for quotations in foreign languages. Unless otherwise indicated, all translations are my own.

Majesty and Humanity

INTRODUCTION:
REMOVING THE ROYAL FRAME:
GHOSTLY IMAGES OR STATELY ILLUSIONS?

Historians routinely designate the seventeenth century the Age of Absolutism, the greatest age of kings. It was a period of grandiose expansions of the royal figure—splendid palaces, courts, and royal stages for his display; monumental statues and paintings depicting his royal image and regalia; epics, panegyrics, and dramas celebrating his achievements and the providential movement of history toward the establishment of his glorious rule; and voluminous political theories reasserting in the most elaborate terms traditional conceptions of his suprahuman, even divine, identity. This study aims at identifying a countercurrent in the political and literary culture of the period and clarifying the complexities of its interactions with the dominant conceptions of rulers and states that founded so much of the public art of the Age of Absolutism. In all the works that it considers one can discern a critical awareness of the constructed character of monarchy and a reflection on a loss of humanness—in kings and citizens—that is the price of the rise of the absolutist state and its expansion of the royal institution. The old precept that the king must on occasion "descend to his humanity" and remove his royal robes took on a new kind of intensity and range of political and philosophical implications in the continuing magnification of the new governing apparatus and its metamorphosis into the Leviathan of the modern machine state. What had been a mere abstraction in the medieval *speculum principis* tradition, the real educable body of the monarch, seamlessly transferable to its royal dignity, became a preoccupation and paradoxically a source of anxiety in its glorious elevation to the suprapersonal and immortal majesty. In the plays that I have chosen to examine, one discovers a striking preoccupation with the "disrobing of the king." All turn out to be concerned not only with what it means to be king, but also, and more fundamentally, what it means to be human. In this age of spectacular coronations and royal displays and portraits, these plays oddly achieve their most powerful dramatic effects through a process that we might describe as *un-kinging* or *un-portraiting*—an abdication that involves a stepping out of the royal frame in search of a humanness that has been lost. By the same token we might describe the fulfillment of the process as a *recrowning* of a recovered humanity.

Before turning to the theater, I would briefly examine two non-dramatic works that provide concentrated insights into the kind of denuding and refractive processes that I find in the plays to be discussed. The works are the creations of two of Spain's greatest artists, who rediscovered an unrecognized "royalty" in the real human being at this transitional moment in the history of Western society, art, and political thought. The perspectives from which they made their discoveries could hardly be more different: one, Diego Velázquez, a successful and highly honored artist, comfortably established at the center of the most powerful and luxurious court in the world; the other, Miguel de Cervantes, an outsider whose adventures and wanderings had taken him to the borders of the Spanish Empire, the prisons of its enemies, and the underworlds of its cities and had left him for much of his life a retired, disabled soldier in a condition of poverty, neglect, "invisibility," and frustration.

VELÁZQUEZ'S MIRROR: AN ALTERNATE ROYALTY

Velázquez was of course the major painter of the official, public "portrait of the king" in Spain. His most interesting image of Philip IV, however, is not to be found in the splendid equestrian figures that so imposingly represent his sovereign body controlling, dominating, and ordering the chaos of the political and instinctual worlds with royal skill, courage, power, and charisma. It is rather a strange, oblique, ironic, and perplexing image of the king. *Las Meninas* is, as is immediately evident to any viewer, not really about kings but rather—perhaps— about "ladies in waiting," the most serviceable title that history subsequently could come up with to designate its provocative refusal to be about kings (see figure 1). Its location was the private study of Philip IV, a setting neither grandiose nor even public. Yet within its domestic scene, slightly off center, there is a portrait of kings, seemingly hanging, as it were, amid various other paintings. In the illusionistic "mirror-portrait's" images the king and queen *dim out*—the viewer looks in vain for the customary radiance of royal portraiture; the regalia lose all power of electrification; everywhere around it artistic forms are menaced by shadows; and everywhere framing devices break. A ghostliness haunts the figures themselves, who hover in their "mirror-portrait" like intrusive apparitions visiting from somewhere else, from some mysterious order of being that is alien

Fig. 1. Velázquez, *Las Meninas* (Madrid, Museo del Prado).
(Erich Lessing/Art Resource, NY.)

to a world that, by contrast, is intensely alive.[1] We are not in the monumental world of the throne and public encounter but rather in the private chamber of a father, a mother, a child, family attendants, a dog, etc., a space animated not by the aura of the symbolic regalia and the frozen poses of majesty but rather by a vigorous, inconclusive gestural language of the quotidian—bodies extending and turning in the offer and reception of a drink, expressing the unsettling, undirected energy of play, exchanging and perhaps disregarding fragments of passing conversation, a fleeting "encounter" of subjectivities—an "encounter" that is decisively non-framed and non-posed. We appear to be witnessing some random, shadowy event disclosing the spontaneity, uncenteredness, and inter-ruptedness of non-ceremonial life and present time in its continuous flowing. Considering our co-presence among the participants of the scene in spatial terms, we find ourselves at the opposite extreme from a world framed out, con-ventionally ordered, and reassuringly distanced, as in the Hercules depictions that embellish the Hall of Realms in the Retiro Palace and imaginatively lift the human being who must wear the royal robes and regalia into the familiar supra-human spheres of idealization and myth.[2]

It is worth considering in greater detail how Velázquez invests with a special kind of dignity this alternate human order within the palace and in the presence of a majestic royal figure. As has been frequently noted, *Las Meninas* brings us also into the world of the atelier and the artist, who is revealed at work amid a swirling, unbounded chaos and in the presence of the ungraspable inward-ness of individuality—elusive, perhaps capricious, but in any event ultimately unreachable. As indicated by the organization of the perspective, Velázquez is completing a portrait of the king and queen, its hidden surface revealed by a reflection in a mirror. The royal couple may or may not be present, posing for the artist and "joining" us as spectators before the unposed scene of private life. Focal points emerge amid the flow of uncontained space in the glances of the depicted human beings, glances that have nothing to do with the choreographed relational gazes and interchanges of the rituals of power (the *arcana imperii*) and court etiquette or with their portraited displays and evocations in the spectators outside the paintings. One might contrast, for example, the riveting gaze elicited in the spectator of Rigaud's quintessential Baroque images of potentates and their institutional power. Here the spectator himself is invited to enter the enig-matic consciousnesses of figures who, like himself, inhabit a space that is sub-stantialized and vitalized as self-consciously and self-assertively *non-artistic*—that is, as "ordinary," as non-official, non-framed, non-bounded, non-distanced, and non-scripted. Whatever this space is, in its elusiveness, it is primarily, defi-antly *not that*; its significance lies paradoxically in its non-significance. Its "list of negations"—to recall Steinberg's illuminating analysis[3]—ranges from the dog's indifference and the boyish dwarf's extemporaneous, personally motivated play, to the courtier's enigmatic valediction (or is it a salutation?) at an opened door in the background, to the shadows enveloping the images of the incorporated paintings, and, most strikingly, to the "massive No" of the contained canvas, which outrageously turns its back to us and leaves us with a mass of emptiness. It is the crowning image of *Las Meninas*' denial of resolution and its pervasive interruption of composition, a negation that poignantly and paradoxically brings about an eruption of human intimacy. One might recall the Cervantine characters and editors that refuse to cooperate in their inclusion and fixation in the conventional literary worlds to which an author would appear to assign them—from the heroine's protests in the opening pages of *La Galatea*, Cervantes's early pastoral romance, to Alvaro Tarfe's disavowals and self-assertion at the end of *Don Quixote*. In effect we find ourselves confronting a reality that we are compelled to grasp for in vain—*individuum ineffabile est*—the "elsewhere" of another human being, the insinuation of an unseen inwardness and, at the same time, an unsettling hint that its ungraspable formlessness is mysteriously more substantial than the coherent "form" whose lines would endow it with a meaning or dignity that can be realized only at the expense of its inner substance. It is the arresting point at which we can perhaps see most clearly the common ground shared by Velázquez and Spain's greatest writer. Cervantes is anything but a political writer or a celebrant of kings, but it is certainly relevant to the age's discovery of the "concealing" portraiture of the royal figure that his most defiantly unbounded individual and his spokesman for a new literary image of man, Sancho Panza, should, in his most memorable act of self-realization, cast off the royal robes of a ruler and enter a world thoroughly *humanus* and ordinary, with its animals; its society of naked pilgrims; its flight from official worlds, nations, and religions; and its determination to forget all epic conquests, empires, robings, and rituals—the empty dreams of humanity.[4]

Velázquez's artist is at work portraiting the king, presumably bringing the latter's monumental order into existence on the unseen side of a canvas, an object as fragile, delicate, and depthless as the sumptuous decorative clothing worn by dwarfs, duenas, children, nuns, and attendants. In the dim mirror, the regalia of sovereignty and majesty are imperceptible, and without the testimony of the painting's earliest extensive description, in Antonio Palomino's biography of Velázquez in 1724, it would be difficult to recognize the reflected couple as monarchs and assume that their ghostly figures have taken substantial form on the far side of the canvas. Or do they in fact stand in a virtual space that Velázquez's total painting, as it were, projects forward beyond the boundaries of its own "frame" to envelop us and the monarchs of Spain in 1656 in a phantasmagoric encounter? The confusing effects of the *trompe-l'oeil* may be brief, as the spectator copes with the oscillations between the illusionistic center of the painting in the mirror image and the true geometrical center around which its perspective is organized, the illuminated space beneath the extended arm of José Nieto, whose figure appears enigmatically at a threshold in the back of the room.[5] Is he entering or exiting? Is he, in performing his ordinary duties as *aposentador* of the queen, opening the door to enable her departure from a session of posing before the court artist?[6] Standing at the border between inside and outside, the *aposentador* breaks the containing plane of the back wall, just as the mirror, with its projected images and their confusing location, has broken the "front wall," the surface separating the "real world" of the spectator and the depicted world he beholds. The unbinding of ceremonial space in the restless recessive and projective composition is compounded by the depiction from a low perspective of the huge, encroaching shadowy spaces of the ceiling and the empty, towering back side of the canvas of the artist at work. The instability rising from the picture's emphatic rejection of spatial determinacy is intensified by its multiplication and dispersion of "centers of attention"—princess, mirror, *aposentador*, artist, and projected spectator.[7] Amid the shadows all might appear to be competing on equal terms for our attention. The phantasmal, oscillating movement between canvas images and the "real space" of the palace room is perhaps most noticeably concentrated in the asymmetry of the depiction of body and glance in the princess Margarita, the figure dominating the painting's foreground and suggesting to some recent interpreters that the original intention of the work was simply the formal, public unveiling of a royal heir.[8]

Far closer to the displaced hieratic emblems of coherent monarchy is the cross of Santiago, which emblazons the breast of the painter, who, in an ingenious strategy of self-portraiture, has brilliantly turned the disintegrating portrait of the king into the unambiguous portrait of the artist.[9] But in fact, one must wonder, is the most radiant survivor of the vanishing world of majesty, alive here in the artist's cross—the emblem of a dignity that in fact the man Velázquez did not yet possess[10]—any more substantial and immune to the dimming powers of time, change, and disintegration than the royal arcana? As Velázquez allows the expression of his own dreams and the implementations of his strategies for their realization to superimpose themselves on the celebration of majesty and to appropriate subjectively the alleged aura of its most venerated symbols and distinctions, we find that, as is so often the case, the central question of the Baroque refuses to be silenced amid its most imposing art. Is the portraiting of a king in reality any more substantial than the game of a dwarf and a dog paralleling it at the opposite side of the canvas? One might note that such provocative equivalences assert themselves in less radical and less artistically self-reflexive versions in Velázquez's paintings—for example, in his earlier depiction of Philip's first heir, the prince Baltasar Carlos, in the company of a dwarf who holds a rattle and an apple in a perfect balance with the prince's icons, the scepter and the sword. Even in a hypothetical early version of *Las Meninas* as a celebrative work, one would note that the attendant's act of homage, the genuflection highlighting the central cynosure, is mirrored inversely by the playful kick of the dwarf bestirring a tranquil dog to break out of his "pose." Such unsettling doublings, unveilings, and interrogations are never far from the foreground of the greatest art of the period. One might recall Don Quixote's vision of the hero's rotting heart in the Cave of Montesinos, King Lear's hallucinatory accusations in his "authentic" royal tribunal on the heath, or Segismundo's revelations in his tower on awakening from the dream world of the court—the universal skeleton concealed beneath the splendid clothing of the world. Perhaps more to the point of the following argument, one might note Diego de Saavedra Fajardo's conclusion of his extensive *speculum principis*: after robing the prince in his splendid regalia and powers for hundreds of pages, he thrusts a crowned skull at his reader on its final page. It is a riddle that inspires kings' most authentic and challenging literary progresses in the period, the descending quests toward the nothingness on which the majesty rests. The chilling recesses that lurk in man's most extravagant theaters and palaces are not to be overlooked, and the most grandiose creations of human culture must be recognized as little more than the luminous spaces surrounding flickering candles brilliantly, perhaps magnificently, but vainly attempting to stave off the surrounding shadows and postpone their ultimate moment of triumph.

Traditional positivist celebrations of Velázquez's and Cervantes's *verismo* are certainly justified, but what is not so commonly recognized is the degree to which their distinctive kind of realism draws its imaginative power from the negation or emptying out of the constructed forms of human culture and the simultaneous dramatization of their own efforts as artists at recovering a resistant and appealing unofficial reality and investing it with a mystery and an aesthetic value that are thoroughly human. In the temporal and spatial indeterminacy, the "in-betweenness" of Velázquez's scene—life and art, society and self, monarch and man, public and private, inside and outside, closed and open, then and now—the released energies of a powerfully assertive life-world freely flow beneath reminders of culture's immobilizations and frozen forms. The artist's efforts at construction are interrupted, the pose of his objects relaxes, and the non-constituted reality both in front of and behind the scene thrusts forth in shadows and liberated spaces of background and foreground. The discontinuities of canvas and canvas assert themselves, and the brush pauses above the formless blobs of color on his palette. The painter's efforts to impose determinate form on his canvases are suspended. Momentarily life would appear to have its way and, as the artist watches intently, gazing into a space that surely contains his models and includes his spectators, runs its course beyond the stabilizing grasp of all cultural constructions—aesthetic, decorative, political, or social. A sovereign genius of uncreation is paradoxically at work, creating, or recovering, a lost humanness.[11] One thinks of Cervantes, poised in suspense at his desk, struggling to give the final touches to his manuscript, reflecting on and discarding the models of the official literary culture around him and leaving us with nothing more than the colorful residues of a deconstructed monumental world.

CERVANTES: DISMANTLING MAJESTY'S MONUMENT

> ¡Voto a Dios, que me espanta esta grandeza
> y que diera un doblón por describilla!

(I vow to God that the grandeur of it terrifies me/And I would give a doubloon to be able to describe it!)

—Cervantes

Given the phantasmic, ephemeral quality of the royal figures in Velázquez's "mirror of kings," it is useful to look briefly at another ghostly conjuration of the majesty in the non-dramatic art of the period. While in its relative simplicity it offers nothing to dignify an alternate world evacuated by the quasi-divine royal creatures, in its disintegrative power it incorporates the entire "cult of the majesty" with which the following studies are directly concerned.

As a commentator on monarchy, Cervantes is most effective and memorable when writing as an iconoclast. He of course served his king faithfully, but his few efforts in the rhetoric of royal panegyric—for example, the heroic ode exhorting King Philip as redeemer, as a new Moses, to rally the dispersed Spanish forces of the great Armada; his *décimas* honoring the memory of the deceased Philip II ("la mejor flor de la tierra") in 1598; and the various prophecies of his epic narrative, *El Persiles*—strike one as particularly bland and formulaic when considered beside the poem that circulated widely in manuscript and that he subsequently, in his late artistic testament, *The Journey to Parnassus*, described as the "honra principal de mis escritos."[12] It is a comically distorted sonnet expressing the reactions of one of the thousands of citizens who visited the cathedral of Seville during the months of ceremonial mourning following Philip II's death. Standing before a gigantic simulacrum replicating Philip's tomb in San Lorenzo del Real in El Escorial, the local population could mourn and honor the memory of their lost king and gaze on an imposing visual recreation of his majesty and the myths that would honor his historical memory. The cult of the king, so delicately and ironically echoed in the private world of Velázquez's domestic portrait, appears here as a communal creative project and the performance of a public ritual. The

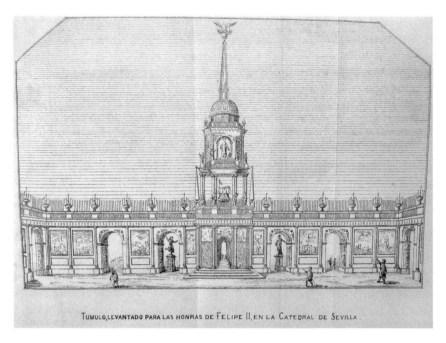

TUMULO,LEVANTADO PARA LAS HONRAS DE FELIPE II, EN LA CATEDRAL DE SEVILLA

Fig. 2. Catafalque for the honoring of the deceased Philip II in the Cathedral of Seville (from F. G. Collado, *Descripción del túmulo*, ed. Sociedad de Bibliófilas Andaluces [Seville, 1869]). (Photograph courtesy Hilaire Kallendorf.)

ritual proclaims the immortality of the lost leader in a monumental setting conceived on the most prodigious scale imaginable (see figure 2).

Sponsored by the city government of Seville and erected in fifty-two days by numerous architects, painters, and sculptors of the region, including the renowned Francisco de Pacheco, Velázquez's father-in-law and mentor, the structure stood as a spectacular monument to the king's majesty—to what I shall refer to in the following chapters as the monarch's official identity or body, the suprahuman, charismatic creature that represents and administers the political power that, according to St. Paul, God confers on earthly rulers. It offered an impressive assembly of the royal regalia, the symbols, the myths, and the historical narratives that manifest and are animated by that power as it descends from above. One hundred and forty feet above the floor, at the pinnacle of an obelisk that nearly touches the cathedral vault, the rainbow colored Phoenix, a traditional symbol of both the glorified, transformed soul of the Christian and the uniqueness and perpetuity of the official monarch, struggles amid flames and ashes to be reborn. Descending to the base of the obelisk, the viewer's eye discovers, at the middle level of the three-tiered monument, the imposing effigy of St. Lawrence, the saint of El Escorial, a church and palace itself modeled on the temple of King Solomon. The elevated figure is crowned by a cupola and an octagonal lantern, the sides of which are inscribed at the four points of the compass with four Biblical pronouncements announcing renewal and salvation. Below the saint, the royal casket is visible, bearing on top a scarlet cushion and a golden crown studded with jewels. On the lower level the numerous surfaces between arches and columns are covered with allegorical figures (for example, the virtues), along with emblems, insignias, hieroglyphics, symbols, and banners, all emphasizing aspects of rule and mysteriously revealing the qualities and continuing presence of the deceased king.

Who is the awesome figure metaphorically displayed in the multitude of images? Like Virgil's Aeneas, Philip II is the sturdy oak tree, standing the course with *constantia* amid the raging winds of the mountains; in his unwavering commitment to justice he is the evergreen palm; his perfectly structured kingdom matches the pomegranate in its neat containment of a multitude of identical seeds. In his exemplary temperance he resembles the marvelous giant turtle of the Nile. Just as the beast anticipates the moment and calculates the reach of the river's seasonal floodings and prudently withdraws to safety, the tactful monarch knows how to "pesar las cosas, y medir las fuerzas de sus vasallos, y el gobierno, con el tiempo" (assess situations and measure the strengths of his vassals and to decide on the acts of rule at the proper time).[13] Numerous paintings depict the grand historical events and achievements that mark the life and reign of Philip II, from his Catholic marriage to Mary Tudor of England in the early period of religious schism; to his assumption of the imperial throne of his father, Charles V ("pintado, con tanto injenio y perfeccion, que no se puede encarecer, admirando a todos los que vieron este cuadro la propiedad de los rostros del Emperador y el Rey nuestro Señor, sacados muy al vivo de sus mejores retratos"; painted with so much ingeniousness and perfection that it cannot be sufficiently praised, the naturalness of the faces of the Emperor and the King our Lord, taken lifelike from their best portraits, bringing wonder to all who looked upon this painting); to the great military triumph at Lepanto; to the pious death of a Christian ruler, who is likened to the sun, serenely following its brilliant course westward.

The majesty of the king is on display everywhere. The principal regalia of robe, scepter, sword, and orb shine forth, proclaiming his power, his justice, and his ubiquity. The royal figure is continually depicted as an exemplar, an embodiment of moral ideals to be imitated by his subjects. Allegory, symbol, and myth crowd into all available spaces in this process of political "transubstantiation."

The king is Hercules, dominating the hydra of chaos and sedition and holding the world on his shoulders. He places chains on the cringing figures of Jewish heresy and Mohammedan idolatry. Under his rule Astrea, the goddess of justice, returns to the world, and he applies a balance and a measuring ruler to bring equity and consistency to his individual acts of justice. He masters the equestrian art, grasping the reins firmly in order to restrain the fury of the wild horses of civic disorder. Amid the cornucopia of panegyric ornamentation, we discover an enchained crocodile with the motto "Violence is subjected by law." The motto is followed by the venerable verses of Virgil—the "blason del Senado y pueblo romano"—describing his hero's underworld vision of the unimaginable glories yet to come. The Virgilian moment was omnipresent in Renaissance exaltations of rulers, and, as we shall see below, its words will sound at the climactic epiphany of *El Rey Don Pedro en Madrid* and associate the Castilian state-builder with the glories of the Roman imperial destiny to replace barbarity with civilization and to bring justice to the entire earth: "Haec tibi erant artes magna virtute, Philippe,/Parcere subjectis et debellare superbos" (These were your arts, Philip, by great strength to spare the conquered and to overthrow the proud).[14]

Like the benign and spectacular god of the contemporary hexameral epics, the "solar" king of this monument has remained ever within the confines of the zodiac, a visible sign of universal order, law, and divine presence for his worshippers below. The order he maintains is represented in the precisely painted details of a standing clock, in which all parts move according to "number, weight, law, and measure" (cuncta movet, numero, pondere, lege, modo). Here too the monarch is assimilated to conceptions of cosmic rationality familiar in hexameral and scholastic traditions. The overall effect of this carefully designed monument for the public expression of grief is to be one of national celebration and political, historical, and cosmic reassurance for the multitudes of witnesses. The innumerable frames of the geometrically balanced monument include many epitaphs that echo the conventional consolatory sentiments concerning the death of kings; the disparity between ashes and earthly splendors, dust and diamonds; and the ultimate superiority of the truer crown above.

In transcribing the verses of the epitaphs, F. Gerónimo Collado notes that one of them employs the mode of the "coloquio, a quien el griego llama dialojismo, que es plática entre dos" (colloquy, which in Greek is called dialoguism, a chat between two speakers). Through the give and take of its dialoguing voices the poem asserts the superiority of Philip to the greatest and most famous princes and Caesars. When one of the voices expresses fear and wonder ("se espanta y admira") at the realization that so small an urn can contain the remains of such a grand monarch, his interlocutor piously reassures him that one must realize that "la muerte todo ese imperio tiene sobre los Reyes y Emperadores, y ansí los suele aniquilar como a hombres mortales que son" (death holds its absolute rule over Kings and Emperors, and is wont to annihilate them as the mortal men that they are).[15]

Cervantes's sonnet is also a dialogue of spectators, but it depicts a shocking disruption in the ritual of honoring, memorializing, and mourning the dead king. The elegiac tone of the occasion, its exhilarating sense of a meaningful ending, are in fact crudely and comically shattered. As an interruption the moment has none of the subtlety of the scene that unexpectedly suspends Velázquez's task before the portrait of his monarchs. The wonder and awe to which Collado repeatedly refers in the reactions of the participating spectators in this culminating ceremony of the cult of the king are distorted in the offensive and vulgar enthusiasms, hyperboles, and swearings of a visiting soldier, a spectator, as it were, gazing on the portrait of his king.

> ¡Voto a Dios, que me espanta esta grandeza
> y que diera un doblón por describilla!;
> porque ¿a quién no sorprende y maravilla
> esta máquina insigne, esta riqueza?
> ¡Por Jesucristo vivo! Cada pieza
> vale más de un millón, y que es mancilla
> que esto no dure un siglo, ¡oh, gran Sevilla!,
> Roma triunfante en ánimo y nobleza!
> Apostaré que el ánima del muerto
> por gozar este sitio hoy ha dejado
> la gloria donde vive eternamente.
> esto oyó un valentón, y dijo: "es cierto
> cuanto dice voacé, señor soldado.
> Y el que dijere lo contrario, miente."
> Y luego, incontinente,
> caló el chapeo, requirió la espada,
> miró al soslayo, fuése, y no hubo nada.

(I vow to God that the grandeur of it terrifies me and I would give a doubloon to be able to describe it. For who does this celebrated construction, this splendor, not astonish and amaze? By the body of the living Christ, each piece of it is worth a million or more, and what a shame it is that all this will not last a century, oh great Seville, a Rome triumphant in your spirit and nobility. I'll wager that the soul of the deceased to enjoy this place has today left the paradise where it spends eternity. All this a braggart overheard, who said: "All you say is right, Sir Soldier, and whoso'er denies it lies." And then, without more ado, he jammed on his hat, adjusted his sword, gave a sideways glance, departed—and then there was nothing.)[16]

The pointed, conclusive form of the epitaph poetry offered on the monument itself is parodied in the collapse of the movement of the sonnet toward its anticipated climactic closure. Unexpectedly a new speaker intrudes in the concluding tercet and requires accommodation in an added stanza. The so-called *estrambote* of the comic sonnet works its customary hilarious effects of anticlimax and deflation. As if to defy and ridicule the multiple forms of containment framed and completed individually within the larger frame of the gigantic enclosing monument, the colorful little poem decisively breaks all borders and releases a force that refuses to be contained; overflows all appropriate, ceremonially drawn margins; and menaces the entire order affirmed and celebrated in the *túmulo* with a collapse into chaos and absurdity. What seems initially to be a tightly focused sonnet turns into an overheard, fragmentary comic dialogue, reminiscent of satirical narratives (for example, those of Francisco de Quevedo and Baltasar Gracián) and the small dramatic form of the *entremés*, which, as Lope emphasized in his *Arte nuevo de hacer comedias en nuestro tiempo*, is inappropriate for the depiction of kings. The overheard voices express wonder not at the virtue and glory of the dead, but rather at the extravagance of his tomb and its sensational display of wealth and power. Admiration becomes the absurdly inflated magnification of conventional satire. Accompanying such magnification is a deflationary movement resulting from the intrusion of incongruous codes of economic value and calculation, low-life language, and the stylized criminal characterization and gesture of picaresque literature.[17]

What is most interesting in terms of the issues that I am considering in this study is the sonnet's iconoclastic reduction of the official identity of the monarch, as well as the discourse, the cult, and the ceremony of majesty, to pure illusion. The genius of the little poem lies in its achievement of the kind of alienating, phantasmic effects that we associate with the satiric discourse of the greatest scoffer at human vanity and the grandiose forms by which human beings honor their "greatness": Lucian. In his bluster of admiration at the splendor of the tomb, the soldier appears to conjure forth the dead spirit, Philip II, who presumably shares his scandalous enthusiasms. "Apostaré que el ánima del muerto/por gozar este sitio hoy ha dejado/la gloria donde vive eternamente" (I'll wager that the soul of the deceased to enjoy this place has today left the paradise where it spends eternity).[18] The voice of the stylized criminal figure who intrudes at this moment appears to answer an implied invitation. Like a spirit, he takes shape from nowhere, voices a boisterous challenge to all present, and vanishes into the shadows. Is this a ghostly visitation of the king? Is the monumental creation of the king and the majesty little more than an immense culturally sanctioned act of empty braggadocio? In any event, all that remains of this little ceremony of royal adoration and mourning is nothingness—"fuése, y no hubo nada."[19] The immense spectacle of majesty seems no less ephemeral than the images in a mirror. Cervantes's "coloquio" for the occasion might be taken in fact as a burlesque epitaph, and its insights into the hollowness of the official framing and exalting creation of the monarch—its doctrines, its complex symbology and allegory, its constructions of history—are devastating.

THE DRAMA OF SPAIN'S GOLDEN AGE: A KING'S THEATER?

> Cuando levantan los Reyes
> A quien quieren, desde el suelo
> A las estrellas del cielo,
> ¿Con qué razón, con qué leyes
> Más que ser su voluntad?
> ¿Que disculpa dan, si es culpa?
> No dan los Reyes disculpa,
> Que es libre la Majestad;
> Y hacer hombres de la tierra
> Es en lo que imita el Rey
> A Dios.

(When Kings raise whom they wish from the earth to the heavenly stars, with what reason, with what laws do they do so beyond their own will? What justification do they give if it is an offense? Kings do not give excuses, for the Majesty is free. And it is in creating men from the earth that the King imitates God.)

—*Lope de Vega*, Del mal lo menos[20]

If Velázquez's *Meninas* is surely far more subtle and interesting in its view of the mysteries of monarchy than his imposing equestrian portraits; if, in fact, the painting points to new insights into contemporary political thinking regarding the representational and institutional aspects of the absolutist state; and if, in its most general frame of reference, it records a radically new consciousness in the individual's conception of his divided identity and *distanced* relations to the surrounding social, political, and objective worlds, we might wonder whether we can find analogous explorations of monarchy in the contemporary theater, the most flourishing public art of the period and the location for the showing forth of numerous dramatic portraits of rulers.[21]

At the outset it might seem unlikely. A commonplace of Spanish literary history that only recently has been challenged and subjected to necessary modification is the simplicity and uniformity of the hundreds of depictions of kings in the public theater of the Golden Age, figures enveloped in an institutional aura— royal, theological, mythical—that shines blindingly from the icons, arcana, and suprahuman physical traits assembled in the "man." Such kings stand close to the Baroque grand style of Rigaud's royal portraiture and have little to do with such exceptional and memorable figures of European drama as King Lear and Prince Hamlet, whose discomfort with their royal robes exposes the illusory basis of all royal mythography. Lope de Vega, the principal architect of the new theater, can certainly be characterized, like Velázquez, as an artist of the official royal gaze and a master of the conventions of dramatic royal portraiture. One need only think of the radiant monarchs whose brief intervention in the celebrated peasant honor plays brings instantaneous deliverance and restoration, or of his new world plays, which conclude with the hieratic ceremonial display of the portrait of the king in a climax celebrating the power and ubiquity of the royal will to carry out the providential historical mission of God's elect, the Spanish nation.

One might mention at this point Lope's carefully wrought, popular dramatization of the education of the king, *El príncipe perfecto*, which begins with the image of a prince dressing, passes to his education concerning the cosmic order of things, and at the climactic moment celebrates the arrival of Vasco de Gama and the establishment of the global hegemony of an emperor. Framing and embracing the Spanish-Portuguese empire and its sovereign as if in the center of a dramatic portrait are the metaphysical order, the terrestrial world, and the neat movement of history toward its utopian climax. In the ritual scene of the prince's robing, we hear the music that the contemporary political theorist Mariana recommended for the proper education of a king, harmonies that instill in the young prince the rationality, proportionality, prudence, and moral perfection of the macrocosm—aside from God himself, the monarch's most exalted model. At the opening of the second act, Lope directly situates his work within the field of royal portraiture. The Portuguese ambassador, figuratively "draws aside the curtain of his portrait" and offers the Spanish queen nearly three hundred verses detailing King Juan's charismatic physical features, moral perfections, and grand achievements. We are told of the *gravedad* of the royal face, immediately recognizable amid one thousand men as that of a king; the heavenly blue of his eyes when content; the glance that instantly inspires fear; the beauties of his eques-

Fig. 3. Velázquez, *Philip IV on Horseback* (Madrid, Museo del Prado).
(Erich Lessing/Art Resource, NY.)

trian exercises and poses, compelling all to see him and love him; his godlike
acts of justice; his respect for and willing subjection to the law; his Solomonic
adjudications and distributions of favors; his heroic deeds "in the conquest of the
Moor, the Indian, and the Negro"; and his courtly refinement and social graces.
Recalling the most influential classical model of the *speculum principis* tradition, the ambassador laments that his talent cannot match that of Xenophon in
the painting of the "new Christian Cyrus" (see figure 3).[22]

   In an influential essay in 1959, Arnold Reichenberger argued that the Spanish *comedia* must be recognized as unique among the national dramas of the
modern European states and that it requires comprehension in its own terms.
Its distinctive features are to be accounted for in the circumstances of its origin
as a public institution dedicated to a great extent to the narration, glorification,

and mythification of Spanish history. Its cultural and political function was akin to that of the populist art of the *romancero* in its reassuring fictionalized images of national traditions, values, protagonists, and enemies.[23] This view was inspired to a great extent by Karl Vossler's classical study of Lope de Vega in 1932, *Lope de Vega und sein Zeitalter*, and it found support in works of numerous leading scholars of Golden Age drama in the following three decades.[24]

According to this account, the monarchy was envisioned in the Spanish theater as an unshakable pillar sustaining a state system, itself founded by divine authority. Kings were the anointed vicars of God, and their decrees represented God's unquestionable, at times inscrutable and apparently capricious, will and power. To call attention to troubling possibilities for conflict in their paradoxical reality as immortal institution and individual human being or to focus on their falls and failures could only interfere with the fulfillment of its primary purposes. Karl Vossler, for admittedly personal reasons, found himself drawn to Lope's *comedia* as a communal art, a celebrative vision of identification, inclusion, and spiritual unification for all members of its society, at the same time an inspiring counter-vision to the images of individuation, separation, materialism, and alienation that he found characteristic of modern hermetic, novelistic, and satirical literature. Vossler's historical reconstruction of the rise of the *comedia* was almost immediately translated into Spanish, and the appeal of its portrayal of Lope de Vega as a "genio de la adecuación" (genius of adaptation) is registered in an enthusiastic review by Amado Alonso in 1933.

In another essay Alonso intensified his insight in an elegant comparison of two exemplary writers whose gigantic literary worlds embraced the entire Spanish nation: Galdós and Lope de Vega.

> Lope was—as Vossler recognized—the unsurpassed genius of communion, creating his dramas within a situation of stable equilibrium. But Lope's Spain was very different from that of Galdós. Lope could make the identification unilaterally, he could give himself over, abandon himself with no reservations to the sociopolitical disposition of the Spaniards of the time, for Lope found functioning a constellation of ideals and of living and operating institutions, all supporting triumphantly the life of the nation. Religion; the monarchy; the military might; the incredible overseas empire; the coincident abundance of great captains, conquistadors, painters, saints, writers—in summary, the entire national grandeur lay before the Spaniards of the time in evident cohesion, and the sentiment of national unity was identified with it. And Lope, with his unproblematic nature, could embrace all the values of the patriotic communion joyously, euphorically. And the work of that poet of conformity was the expression of the unanimous, multitudinous soul of a century.

In an often repeated generalization, offered by Alonso in a study of the dramatist's use of sources, Lope de Vega should in fact be seen as Spain's "greatest poet
of conformity."[25]

With the socioeconomic and political literary study adopted by José Antonio
Maravall and the generation of Hispanists he profoundly influenced, the view of
Lope's *comedia* as celebrative, conformist, and communal took a new direction,
achieved a much sharper formulation, and led to commonplaces and simplifications of a far different and far less romantic type. The Spanish national theater
should be understood not primarily as expressing and representing historically
developing beliefs and values rooted in the distinctive realities of Spanish history
and the specific character—the *índole*—of the culture it had created, from the
Reconquista to the Habsburg Empire, but rather as a highly effective machine of
propaganda and indoctrination manipulated by the power elite of the absolutist
state to impose on a docile population a cultural life dictated by, serving, and
legitimizing its own interests.[26] In an essay on Quevedo's political philosophy,
Maravall describes the monarchism of the Spanish theater, in its uncompromising endorsement of royal power and its celebrative view of kings, as sharply
distinguishable from the more modernist and enlightened, pragmatist, and neo-
scholastic political philosophers of the period.[27] Clearly such conceptions of the
all-controlling absolutist state, its monolithic culture, and its manipulation of
its submissive, homogeneous audience have been influenced to some extent
by the realities of twentieth-century totalitarianism. Despite historians' and political philosophers' developing insight into the complexities of sixteenth- and
seventeenth-century statism, its historical "necessity" and function in the development of modern forms of social and political organization, and the numerous
limitations on its allegedly centralized or "monopolized" power, from R. Mousnier to J. Elliott, B. Kriegel, and P. Kléber Monod, traditional opinions regarding
the monolithic, "totalitarian" character of Lope's Spain and the claustrophobic
nature of the *comedia* within it continued, in their simplicity, to appeal to historians.[28] "Our seventeenth-century playwrights employ unsurpassable terms in
the affirmation of the absolute character of the king's sovereignty and of the
impossibility of resisting it. . . . Lope develops in *La estrella de Sevilla* or in *El
duque de Viseo* the same conception of the cruel grandeur of monarchist absolutism, which, as Vossler observes, does not permit any rebelliousness or even the
slightest protest against injustice."[29]

The prevailing view of the Spanish drama of the Golden Age that followed
Maravall's historical interpretation was called into question in a brief, thoughtful essay by Charlotte Stern in 1982, "Lope de Vega, Propagandist?,"[30] but it
continued to be widely accepted until a major revision that the current genera-

tion of Hispanists began some fifteen years ago. In two articles (1993 and 1994), Melveena McKendrick challenged the "Maravallian orthodoxy" and called for a new approach to the role of the royal dignity in Lope's theater: "Lope . . . has emerged from the doctrinaire accusations of recent years as the consummate propagandist of the Spanish theater, a cosmic conservative—anti-change, anti-intellectual, anti-individuality—an unreflective believer in the ideal of God, king, and country, a conscious procreator of insolent myths."[31]

McKendrick subsequently developed her insights in an important book on Lope's theater, *Playing the King: Lope de Vega and the Limits of Conformity* (2000). Through careful textual analysis, supported by an impressive control of Lope's vast dramatic output and broad knowledge of the field of Spanish drama, she in effect reverses the reductive conception of Lope as royal propagandist. Focusing on the moral misbehavior of his numerous kings in their relations to favorites, rivals, and subjects, she argues that Lope frequently uses the conventional rhetoric of royal celebration "as a way of constructing absolutism in order to combat it"; that the vast majority of his kings "are dysfunctional both as kings and as human beings"; and that readers have been blind to the fact that when Lope displays the behavior characteristic of a tyrant—capriciousness, brutality, injustice, and self-involvement—he is neither, as Maravall and his followers have suggested, displaying the hypothetical outer limits of obedience that the Spanish establishment uncompromisingly demands, nor sanctioning an authoritarian politics that in the twenty-first century we can only find repugnant. McKendrick points out that Lope's drama was far from innocent in its continual allusiveness to the political topics and agents of contemporary Madrid; that the thin veils of its satirical references were easily penetrable by the highly informed urban and courtly populace that constituted its audience; that, for all its alleged conformity, it was frequently under attack by moralists and ecclesiastical critics; and that its advocates recognized that in fulfilling its responsibilities to offer "mirrors of kings" to its royal audience, it could justifiably compel its lord to look "into a mirror" and discover the "imperfection of his conduct" and to erase, like a good painter, "the defect and the ugly feature in order to free himself of the blemish that dishonors him." In a striking rejection of Maravall's thesis, McKendrick concludes that Lope should be understood as carrying out a "relentless demystification of the monarchy" and a "campaign to counteract the growing move, if only within the court, towards absolutism and quasi-divinization."[32]

In another important work in the current recuperation of dimensions of the *comedia* that had been overlooked in the narrow perspective on the Spanish theater initiated by Vossler and climaxing in Maravall and his school, Enrique García Santo-Tomás has exploited recent advances in reader/audience reception theory to refute any conception of the Spanish Golden Age theater as "mono-lithic." In a chapter focusing on probably the most widely known and successful of Spain's Golden Age dramas, *Fuenteovejuna*, he points to the variations in the meaning of the play effected in the historical life of its productions and argues that they reflect not only historical changes in ideological, cultural, and social history, but also the complexities and potentialities of the drama itself.[33] According to Santo-Tomás, *Fuenteovejuna* should not be viewed reductively as a cele-bration of either monarchy or revolution, but rather as a "space of debate" that brings about a deepened and nuanced understanding of the political issues that it raises.

In the following study I hope to show through close analysis how two of the major plays of the Spanish Golden Age, *El villano en su rincón* and *El Rey Don Pedro en Madrid o El Infanzón de Illescas*, which have been held up frequently by Maravall and others as exemplary works of celebratory monarchism and con-formist propaganda, should in fact be understood as "spaces of debate," compel-ling their audiences to reflect critically on the foundations and implications of established political doctrines and commonplaces. In general terms the study fol-lows the revisionist directions taken by McKendrick, Santo-Tomás, and others.[34] In its focus on early modern political theory and the striking ways in which the plays develop political issues through paradoxical and "dialogical" exposition, it provides a distinctive perspective in the ongoing recovery of Spain's Golden Age theater after nearly a century of ideological interpretation dominated by such powerful critics and historians as Marcelino Menéndez y Pelayo, Vossler, Américo Castro, and Maravall.

Each of the plays that I have chosen reaches its most profound—and pro-gressive—insights while subjecting the traditional doubleness of the monarch—majesty and man, institution and individual—to a subtle dramatic analysis.[35] To recall the achievements of Velázquez and Cervantes, such works are marked by an impulse to *disrobe the king*—to rediscover the king's humanity hidden by his institutional garb and in his public role as sovereign and to look within it for a source of value that must refound his regal majesty, reinvest his official body, and reanimate his royal crown.

As Philip IV put it, there is a time when a king must provisionally cast off his divinity and find and cultivate the human in himself. The following argument is not concerned with humanness primarily as a locus of frailty, inadequacy, fail-ure, or sinfulness, although it is worth mentioning that there are certainly many more dramatic depictions of corrupt and sinful monarchs in the Spanish the-ater than both its celebrants and its critics have realized. Philosophers have fre-quently approached humanity as a quality or a dignity, a precious locus of value continually under threat of destruction by its inhabitants. Humanity (*humanitas*) has been located in courage and justice, wisdom and honesty, suffering and love, humility and self-abnegation—experiences accessible to all and offering a majesty entirely of their own order. The plays on which I focus my analysis represent very different perspectives on the humanity of a king—incorporating the values of different cultural traditions and different conceptions of individual dignity in the face of the rising statism, its expanding institutionalization of man's activities and aspirations, its rationalization of the sociopolitical organization of life, and its fundamental reorientation of man's perspectives toward human identity and relationship. Such matters as privacy, individuality, political power, class identity, community binding, self-restraint, and civic responsibility thrust themselves to the forefront of human consciousness with a new urgency.

In the period of absolutism the king was frequently viewed mystically as a new *corpus mysticum*—the state. To recall Díez Borque's phrase, he was an entity that existed "beyond human limits." But for the philosophically inclined, the king could also be the paradigmatic human being transformed and burdened by an inescapable new consciousness of his identity as a divided being. If with the state's monopoly of power the official body of the king was expanded and mythified as never before, by the same token the king could become, for thoughtful observers of the changing conditions of society and human relationships, paradigmatic for the loss of self in the new dominant spaces of public performance and political interaction—the city and the court. The "misery of kings" and the "loneliness of kings" became fascinating themes, from Shakespeare's imaginative resurrection of the battlefield of Agincourt in London's Globe Theater, to Giovanni Botero's practical counsels in a political handbook for princes in the Habsburg court of Madrid (the *Detti*; discussed further in chapter 1 below), to Pascal's solitary ruminations in Port Royal on the emptiness menacing the human identity and its alleged grandeur beneath the veils of compliment, flattery, honor, and reputation. Only kings, it would seem, really know how chilling and empty silence can be when masks are removed and the human comedies of role and rule are suspended.

In the two plays that I analyze in detail, as well as in a number of others that I consider briefly in notes and in an epilogue, kings are depicted who choose or are compelled to remove their masks, to depart from the space of absolutism and its political agendas in search of something that is missing, to test the grounds, as it were, on which it is founded, to expose something that it has denied—manliness, tranquility, moral autonomy, self-knowledge, saintliness, caritas—and to return to it renewed by contact with a lost or forgotten other that becomes paradoxically a source of true royal power. In each case the play is constructed as a complex interaction of doubles, and the king is drawn toward an alienating confrontation with an enigmatic and challenging stranger—a dramatic engagement that can be as sophisticated as the dialectic argumentation of two stubborn philosophers, as primitive as the brute "chivalric" contest of the individual wills of two warrior aristocrats, or as subtle as the intuitive and ironically understated communication of lovers of different cultures and religions.

The circumstances surrounding the encounter of doubles differ widely in the plays I examine, and they are generally clarified as belonging to very different types of drama. One is a romantic comedy set in an imagined kingdom of France and centering in a utopian pastoral space where the reconciliation and resolution of various philosophical, political, and moral problems can be imaginatively achieved and lyrically orchestrated. Another is a somber historical drama set in the fourteenth-century period of Spain's civil wars and feudal anarchy and bordering on tragedy in its depiction of the costly, blood-soaked triumphs of the legendary king Pedro el Cruel. A third, discussed briefly at the conclusion of the study, is a hagiographic drama depicting a saintly prince who sacrifices himself in the heroic crusades of Portugal to spread the faith and found its empire in the fifteenth century. Their focus on the nature and the mysteries of monarchy, their concern with the ambiguities of worldly power, and their fascination with a surplus humanness that resists easy incorporation in the royal figure—the forgotten real body of the king—provide a revealing nexus linking these very different plays and pointing to the dramatic power and complexities latent in the theme of monarchy in the period.

The order I have chosen for my discussions of the plays is, I think, appropriate historically in that it traces a decline in the prominence and effectiveness of the humanness of a king—from the early "prince-state" of the Renaissance and its theoretical, optimistic approaches to man's political and civic experience in the humanistic traditions of the *speculum principis*; to the machine-state of law, awe-inspiring majesty, and empowered bureaucracy of the Baroque absolutist monarchy; to the eclipse of the royal figure beneath the ascendant theocentrism and political pessimism of the Counter-Reformation.[36]

The trajectory begins in a humanist utopia envisioning politics as an agenda that is moral and centering on the king as model man and citizen, an arboreal creature who exercises proper control of power and instinct through moral discipline and whose kingdom, to recall Dante's foundational vision of this ideal in the recovered terrestrial paradise of a recrowned Adam, is a place of "forestry" with the king a "woodsman" (*silvano*) who "rules" beneath a "royal" purple that gleams in the four stars of the classical or cardinal virtues visible above.[37] From the utopian abstractions and musical harmonies of romantic comedy I turn in the second study to the ambiguous, tragic world of human history and a much darker exploration of political realities. Undoubtedly the most remote and puzzling of the works I have chosen, *El Rey Don Pedro en Madrid o El Infanzón de Illescas* is concretely concerned with the origins of the Spanish monarchy and one of the major figures in its triumphant emergence from the turmoil of the anarchy of medieval feudalism and aristocratic oligarchy, Pedro el Cruel. In its bizarre struggle of a calculating king and a titanic figure of lawlessness, one sees most clearly in this play the great historical tasks of the absolutist state: the sublimation and juridification of the human being's attachment to heroic violence and the proper direction of a vast constraining power—monopolized and concentrated in the hands of a central authority and its rule of law as never before since the Roman Empire. The study concludes with a brief look at a dark hagiographic tragi-comedy, a powerful and pessimistic renunciation of the entire order of earthly politics, states, and kings and a recovery by a suffering prince of a royalty that is not to be realized in the fallen world of the earth and its City of Man. The authentic coronation of kings can only be elsewhere. But it is a coronation that is available to all human beings, and its most haunting image is the pitiful sacrificial human body of a king.

KING AND PHILOSOPHER:
EL VILLANO EN SU RINCÓN

Una misa del poder que es
un ceremonial de corte.

—*Marcel Bataillon*

The various studies that exist on Lope de Vega's *El villano en su rincón*, one of his most puzzling political plays, have focused on its confrontation of king and peasant-philosopher in a way that fails to do justice to the complexity of its engagement with the problematics of royal power. They have seen the play as a kind of ritual, a static enactment of power, or, in Marcel Bataillon's words, a "political mass"—"a Mass of power that is a court ceremonial"—a "morality play dedicated to the glory of the monarchy," and a "lesson in monarchical devotion."[1] They have emphasized the king's triumphant and "punitive" resolution of his conflict with the peasant, who stubbornly refuses to come to the court to gaze upon his sovereign, and the dramatic power in the climactic banquet in the palace—its display of the immense expanses of the royal domains to the *villano*, who is so content within his *rincón*, suddenly dramatically shrunken by comparison; its brilliant unveiling of the awesome emblems of regal authority; and its concern to reveal the terror that they strike in their beholders.

El villano en su rincón is, among other things, a play about the *fearsome* character of royal power; its uncompromising demands for obedience; its unquestionable enactments of justice; its control of its subjects through a ceremonial of fear; and its inescapable presence in the ubiquitous icons, emblems, and regalia of the charismatic king. At the end of Act I, as the disguised king prepares to enter the secluded world of the *villano* (Juan Labrador), shielded as it were from the electrifying field of royal charisma, Finardo, a gentleman of the court, expresses his amazement at the "barbaric" *villano's* apparent defiance. "¡A un Rey de tanto valor/que tiemblan sus flores de oro/el scita, el turco feroz!" (a king of such might/that the Scythian and the fierce Turk/tremble before his golden fleurs de lis!).[2] For José de Valdivielso, Lope's friend who subsequently rewrote the play as a religious *auto sacramental*, the process of divinization and the concentration of all the frightening aspects of the epiphany of authority in the allegorical figure of Rigor, God's justice, who demands the harshest of punishments for a recalcitrant *villano*, a rebellious "rey pequeño de sus labradores" (small king of his farmhands) symbolically transformed into the fallen Christian Everyman, obstinately incapable of raising his gaze from the enthralling *visibilia* of this world to look upon his Creator's face, were all too easy.[3]

The play's ceremonial character and its easy adaptability to the untroubled schemas of representation and mystification of the religious *autos* and their theological master text are deceptive.[4] In the climactic scene the monarch tells another frightened witness to his theatrical activities, this time an aristocrat, "Nunca al poder tengas miedo/cuando es discreto el poder" (Never be afraid of power/when power is wise) (194). The fleeting comment resonates oddly and elusively amid the events of the rapidly unfolding spectacle of absolutism's authority, but the possibility of a challenge that it raises is impossible to overlook. Does it perhaps point to a qualification of royal power? Is it an admonition to king and subject alike? Might it in fact represent an admonition to understand the spirit lying beneath its representations, whether in the king's official body — the universally vivifying face of monarchism — or in his frightening insignia? Is the play a "lesson in monarchical devotion" that in its critical disclosures was perhaps far more profound and reflective than Bataillon and his numerous followers realized? The fact is that although *El villano en su rincón* concludes with a theater of power — a theatrical spectacle put on by the king himself — I would argue that it is itself not a spectacle of power. The play is obsessed with seeing and probing the dynamics of royal visibility in the theatrically constructed absolutist state. But its deeper purpose is to bring its audience to reflect critically on and truly understand what it is that it is seeing.[5]

THE SOURCE: A LOST KING

At this point it is useful to consider the familiar historical-folkloric anecdote that appears to have given Lope the idea for his plot. It describes Francis I of France losing his way while hunting and at nightfall finding shelter in the forest hut of a peasant — a charcoal burner — who fails to recognize him but generously offers him his hospitality. According to a Spanish version written by Antonio de Torquemada in his pastoral dialogues between "dos caballeros llamados Leandro y Florián y un pastor Amintas sobre los excelencias de la vida pastoril" (two gentlemen, named Leandro and Florián, and a shepherd Amintas concerning the excellences of the pastoral life),[6] the peasant is a model of courtesy, insisting both that his guest must occupy the place of honor at the head of the table and that he, as "king of his own house," has the power to compel him to do so. The peasant is later rewarded for his exemplary courtesy when the king reveals his identity, invites his host to share his table in the palace, marries the latter's two daughters to gentlemen of the court, and in a culminating act of magnanimity exempts all charcoal burners from royal taxation.

Bataillon argues that Torquemada's account "beyond any doubt inspired" the creation of Lope's figure of the *villano* and his encounter with the king. This may well have been the case, but there is, in fact, more to the story than Torquemada's version reveals, and Renaissance moralists and political philosophers could easily invest this "historical" confrontation of the orders of artifice and nature with other ranges of significance. Another version of the story is extremely suggestive, and it casts an interesting light on dimensions of the play that Bataillon does not care to integrate into his monarchist interpretation. It is articulated by a man who, unlike Torquemada's courtly shepherds, whose dialogue frames the anecdote, is fascinated above all else with the realities of power and with courtesy only insofar as it is a strategy for the successful enactment of power: the cold and brilliant Baroque moralist Baltasar Gracián. In his analytical panegyric of the model political man, Fernando el Católico, Gracián emphasizes a king's difficulty in achieving self-knowledge ("no tiene espejo un rey"—a king does not have a mirror) and praises the intelligence of leaders, such as Tacitus's Germanicus, who in disguise solicited the judgments and criticisms of their subordinates. As an example he describes Francis I's encounter with the anonymous peasant subject.

> Perdido en la caza Francisco Primero de Francia, desde entonces Grande, hizo noche en casa de la sencillez, y, entre unos villanos, le amaneció el sol de la verdad; y solía repetir el discretísimo príncipe: "yo me gané perdido, porque mudé de rumbo."

> (Having lost his way in the hunt, Francis the First of France, henceforth known as Francis the Great, spent the night in a house of simplicity, and among several peasants the sun of truth dawned and awakened him. And this most discreet of princes was, from that moment on, accustomed to repeat: "Having lost myself, I won myself, because I changed my course.")[7]

In Gracián's depiction of the event, the focus is entirely on the king's experience—a moment of crisis, an awakening to truth and *discreción*, a profound alteration in the direction of his life; a discovery of an authentic self that had been lost (the discovery of a mirror); a paradoxical victory in defeat, the decisive moment in his development—"desde entonces Grande." The philosophical direction is even clearer in Gracián's great philosophical narrative *El criticón*. Here his protagonists, the questing pilgrims Critilo and Andrenio, are granted an allegorical vision of the spectacle of political power—an unchanging circle of men capriciously tossing the world, a ball stuffed with rags and air, from one to another. Gracián's characteristic epiphany of nothingness culminates with the discovery of an empty throne, abandoned by a man who would truly be king. The pilgrims suspect that "se habría perdido en la caza (que no será el primero), que en casa de algún villano habría hecho noche, despertando de su gran *sueño* y cenando *desengaños* el que tan ayuno vivía de *verdades*" ([that] he probably lost his way in the hunt [for he would not be the first to have done so], that he spent the night in the house of some peasant, and that he who had lived fasting, abstaining from all truths, awakened from his deep sleep and feasted on *desengaños* [disenchantments]). They are amazed when they discover that he has departed to seek the only possible monarchy, *that over oneself,* and wonder "como un príncipe de tan alto genio ha podido *humanarse* a conversar con tan *vil canalla*" (how a prince of such an exalted nature has been able to descend to the human level [*humanarse*] to converse with such base canaille).[8] The encounter with the *villano* is recast as an awakening to truth; a recognition of the insubstantial nature of the nocturnal world of the court, power, the affairs of state, and the ceremonial reality of royalty; and a discovery of one's humanity and, of course, one's mortality. As a vision of *desengaño*, it might recall the age's most memorable depiction of a fruitful encounter of a lost king—one who as yet "but slenderly knows himself"—and a philosophical "peasant": *King Lear.*

In his appropriation of the historical anecdote, Gracián, it must be said, fails to individualize the peasants or to define the alterity of their world in any specific or extensive philosophical or moral terms that would elicit critical reflection on the world that they oppose. His interest lies entirely in the king's experience of *desengaño*, humility, self-discovery as a mortal human being (*humanarse*), and conversion—an experience that he describes in the conventional metaphors of sleeping, dreaming, and suddenly awakening to reality. The experience and the metaphors were, as is well known, ubiquitous in the literature of the seventeenth century. The most familiar comic version is, of course, Sancho Panza's sleep and awakening to self-knowledge; his renunciation of his throne; his solemn processional entry, in the *silentium mysticum* of court ceremony, into the stable to embrace his ass and gaze on his most reliable mirror of self-knowledge; his return to his vineyards; and his repossession of his authentic being.[9]

Certainly less familiar to the modern reader are the resonances that the term *humanarse* had in seventeenth-century writings on the "double" nature of the monarch. Philip IV himself provides an interesting commentary on the implications of Gracián's perception of the originary anecdote and on the experience of descent, transformation, and education of Lope's French king in the other world of Juan Labrador. In justifying his modest efforts to translate Guicciardini's *History of Italy,* he reminds his reader that kings too are subject to human ignorance and other limitations ("comunes a todos los otros hombres") and that they should occasionally divest themselves of their divine being in order to educate themselves morally and philosophically. He notes that the laws themselves exempt the king from such "humanity," assuming that he is privy to the most arcane truths through the mysterious powers of his royal dignity:

> humanidad de que hasta las mismas leyes nos excusan, presumiéndonos sabios de lo más escondido por sola la dignidad y carácter real. No llegando decir que sé, sino que voy sabiendo, desnudándome de la divinidad por afectar más la filosofía y moderación y sobre todo la rectitud y verdad.

> (the humanity from which the very laws excuse us, presuming us, through the royal dignity and character alone, to be wise concerning things that are most hidden. Without going so far as to say that I know, but only that I am beginning to know, taking off my robes of divinity in order to pursue more intensely philosophy and moderation and above all rectitude and truth.)[10]

Applied to the mystery that Gracián discerns at the root of the parable of the lost king and his peasant host, Philip's words might suggest that the issues raised by the king's transformation in the forest are far more profound than the simple lessons in respect, courtesy, precedence, and refined social sensitivity that Torquemada's version expounds. More revealing, however, is the nature of his elaboration of the process of a king's humanization: on the one hand, the descent from a divine order above; on the other hand, the metaphorical conception of that descent in terms of the concrete rituals of robing and disrobing that were so essential to a monarch's existence, from the ceremonies of crowning to the daily awakenings and the endless ceremonial activities of rule, a process continuing until the final veiling in the constructed effigies of the royal body at death. From the opening scenes, where we learn that a "seraphim" has chosen to "humanarse en una aldea"—"become human in a village"—to the king's concluding display of his quasi-divine regalia, we discover that the world of *El villano en su rincón* is one of restless movement upward and downward and that the action is marked by continuous changes of clothing. At the heart of movement and counter-movement, disrobing and rerobing, laying aside and recovering—uncrowning and recrowning—is a process of authentication of the monarch through his education in humanist values and his imaginative assimilation to the classical sage.

GENRE: ROMANTIC COMEDY

It is perhaps worth noting that of the four plays by Lope that Gracián praised in his *Agudeza y arte de ingenio*, one was *El villano en su rincón*, a work that he described as a "moral fable." Whether he found in it a dramatic articulation of the insights that he was to condense into the laconic antitheses of his version of Francis I's encounter with the peasants is impossible to know, but two things are clear: The play emphasizes the *desengaño* of the French king at the conclusion of his nocturnal experience in the other world. Moreover, it depicts a decisive and astonishing change in his speech and actions following his return to the palace. It is also worth noting that whatever Gracián may have meant by the designation *fábula*, Lope, as so often was the case, designed his drama according to the conventions of romantic comedy. The work has far more in common with the folktale than with a historical or political drama or with a hypothetical theatrical celebration of the specific historical circumstances to which Bataillon links its genesis, the double royal marriage, in 1612, of Louis XIII of France and Philip III of Spain, and the contemporary political ambitions of Lope's patron, the Duke of Sessa.[11]

In its action and imaginative frame of reference, magical metamorphoses of the type insinuated by its folkloric germ proliferate. Kings become philosophers, peasants become nobles; a princess appears to possess a double identity of the historical princesses of Spain (Ana) and France (Isabel). Olive trees strangely mingle with acorn and hazelnut trees in what is presumably a French landscape. The trees themselves are metaphorically transmuted into trees of glittering gems, which through intertextual allusion in turn assume the forms of beautiful enchanted maidens. In its continuing imaginative evocations, radiant Moorish youths emerge as if by magic to woo them and assist them in their harvesting activities in a world that is momentarily illuminated by an exotic light that might conjure up in its seventeenth-century audience romantic visions of medieval Granada. Musical harmonies and the universalizing dream language so prominent in folk songs embellish the proceedings with a kind of lyrical intensity discernible in none of Lope's other "political" plays. In fact, as Alfredo Rodríguez has pointed out, the quantity of sung verses is matched by only nine—

nearly all religious in subject—of the hundreds of other *comedias* by Lope.[12] Such elements are particularly pronounced in the arboreal world of Act II, in which the king's visit to Juan's house, near his hunting estates in Belflor (an imaginary location that characteristically at another point of the play turns into Miraflor—familiar to Lope's audience as the delightful site of the castle near London where Amadís de Gaula and Oriana secretly consummate their love) suggests a mysterious initiatory passage into a world of confusion, erotic pursuit, lost identity, disguises, dreamlike encounters of doubles, fateful thresholds, and dangerous metamorphoses.[13]

As I have suggested above, the central transformation in the wondrous world of this romantic comedy is the metamorphosis of the king, which he himself describes as a miracle that has unfolded in his nocturnal dialogue with Juan Labrador. In the following I would like to make some sense of this alleged miracle, reexamining the relationship of king and peasant in Lope's play; revisiting the mysterious other world of their encounter; and reconsidering the elliptical, suggestive doubling in their presentation in the light of certain traditional doctrines concerning the mysteries of the monarch—his inherent doubleness and the denuding experience involved in his necessary humanization.[14]

THE SUPRAHUMAN KING AND HIS CULT

> Mira al Rey, Juan Labrador;
> que no hay rincón tan pequeño
> adonde no alcance el sol.
> Rey es el sol.

(Look upon thy King, Juan Labrador; for there is no corner so small that the sun cannot reach it. The King is the sun.)

— *The King of France*

In order to understand both the preoccupation of *El villano en su rincón* with the king's identity and the paradoxical process of doubling that marks Lope's dramatic development of the king's relationship with the strange peasant, Juan Labrador, it is useful to turn to some of the voluminous writings of the period dealing with monarchy, regal authority and responsibility, and the rise of the new nation-states. Lope was, of course, writing in the period of absolutism, and he is generally viewed as a monarchist, if not an enthusiastic ideologue of the ascendant state and its central institutions. In the *Arte nuevo de hacer comedias en nuestro tiempo,* he reminds us that kings have no place in the world of low comedy (the *entremés*), and in an address to an audience in Toledo at a literary festival honoring the recent birth of Philip IV, he even suggests that the elevation of the monarch to his earthly "divinity" is a miracle brought about by the mediating powers of the poet.

> ¿ Quién duda que naciendo humanos Príncipes
> Será justo alabarlos con los versos? . . .
> Que los Reyes son Dioses de la tierra.

(Who doubts that, as Princes are born human, it will be just to praise them with verses? . . . For Kings are Gods of the earth.)[15]

In other words the "human side of the king," so abundantly recognized in writings concerning the drudgery, the exhaustion, the discomforts, the endless administrative banalities, and the petty conflicts and trivial political decisions that plagued the day-to-day existence of the rulers of the increasingly expansive, costly, and disorderly national states, is to be veiled and adorned by the poets' imaginative construction of a "divine" majesty.[16] The literary process in a sense replicates or echoes imaginatively the robing and transformative rituals of traditional coronation ceremonies that in such influential depictions of monarchs as Lope's *El príncipe perfecto* and Calderón's *La vida es sueño* (not to mention Shakespeare's great dramas of kings) are occasionally visible in the background.

In political-philosophical terms the construction of the suprahuman figure represents a celebration of the institutional, the "undying," aspect of the monarch and of the monarchy itself as an incarnate perpetuity. As Ernst Kantorowicz revealed in his classic study of the historical life of this figure, from its origins in the theological culture of transcendence in the late Middle Ages to its peculiar elaboration as a legal myth in sixteenth-century England to its most expansive spectacular development in the Age of Absolutism, the variations in its metaphorical and symbolic procedures and mythic associations and the determining conceptual contexts of its personifications—sacramental, liturgical, political, scholastic, legalistic—were rich and complex, and they constituted an imposing and serviceable heritage for the seventeenth-century celebrants of the absolute monarchs and their "pontifical" proclamations of "mysteries of state."[17]

As the verses above indicate, Lope de Vega would appear to endorse the project of creating the awe-inspiring, suprahuman figure of the king, and had he limited himself to carrying it out, he would certainly be the doctrinaire royal propagandist that many historians have found him to be.[18] *El villano en su rincón*, I would suggest, reveals that the most interesting aspect of Lope's monarchism lies in his effort to escape the radical dualism underlying the traditional conception of the monarch as a "geminated" or "two-bodied" figure, split irreconcilably between divine and human identities. In his careful elaboration of a doubling procedure linking a peasant and a king, Lope is in fact reversing the directions of royal portraiture and ceremony. Disrobing, uncrowning, unframing, casting his charismatic monarch into the shadows of an unknown, "unofficial" world, he succeeds in recovering *lo humano* by taking seriously the possibilities for moral perfection and exemplification in an ethically sensitive, fruitfully educated ordinary human being and ultimately reanimating and redefining the charismatic, "divine" royal figure in terms of the perfections attainable by his modest philosophical double. The royal hybrid—the geminated figure so central to European traditions of mysterious monarchy—survives in Lope's tranformations but only after it has been demystified and radically humanized. The *dignitas* aligns itself closely and literally with the *humanitas* in which it is in fact now founded.

The root of the humanistic approach to the new awareness of the complexities and inescapable ambiguities of the political life is to be found in the *speculum principis* tradition and, behind it, the traditions of political virtue; civil law; and Aristotelian, Ciceronian, and Senecan conceptions regarding the interdependence of individual and civic fulfillment.[19] Lope's play, at one level, can be seen as dramatizing a conflict between contemporary political agendas for the exaltation of the suprahuman figure of the king and the traditional moral approach to the proper understanding of the political context of human life. The peculiar power of its relatively static plot derives to a great extent from its dramatization of the crisis faced by the suprahuman king, who must lay aside his crown, step out of his ritualized world, and confront a deep challenge to his understanding of his *dignitas*. To heighten the intensity of what is in essence an intellectual and non-dramatic conflict, Lope gives considerable attention to the splendors of the royal frame, which contains the "portraited" king of France. To understand this, it is necessary to look more closely at the cult of the official king in Lope's Spain.

One of the reasons that *El villano en su rincón* can be so easily read as a straightforward celebration of monarchy is that it incorporates so many of the most fundamental doctrines and symbols of the ideology of absolutism and culminates in the supreme ritual in the contemporary cult of the king. The very source of its dramatic energy—Juan Labrador's refusal to look at the king, whom he nevertheless adores and to whose court he is willing to send his children—is in fact incomprehensible if we are unaware of absolutism's conception of the monarch as ubiquitous, a universally present figure whose face or image incorporates the multitudinous spaces and individuals of the kingdom into harmonious interaction as members of a body politic and whose gaze endows them with being. In this imaginative vision the king is, like the bountiful, self-revealing God of the contemporary hexameral epics, literally everywhere, and, by the same token, everywhere, animated and individuated by the creative effulgence of the regal mirror and its store of archetypes, is where the king is. Like the creating deity, the king is the supreme cartographer.[20] There can be no realities beyond his gaze and his map, no hidden retreats, no protective nooks or pockets—*rincones*—no spaces for somebody who, for whatever incomprehensible reason, would passionately exclude himself from the celebrations of this collective body and the identity conferred by its undeniable beneficence. Such scandalous behavior might in fact be compared to the creature's unthinkable repudiation of the creator, a preference for the shadowy nothingness that preceded his creation.

> El magnífico poder
> del Rey es Sol; los demás
> sombras son, y donde estás
> (que Sol del mundo te nombras),
> No pueden estar las sombras.

(The magnificent power of the King is the Sun; the rest are shadows, and where you are, shadows cannot be [for you are named Sun of the world]).[21]

As I shall argue below, one of the most interesting implications of Juan Labrador's "perversity" is his obsessive demand for a human space beyond such metaphysical and political circumscription, a space beyond the confines of any map. In one of the central conceits of absolutist political theory, Diego de Saavedra Fajardo writes of the universality of majesty, present in its animating energy throughout the organism of the state: "Y sepan que, como en el cuerpo humano, así en el del reino está en todo él y en cada una de sus partes entera el alma de la majestad" (and may they [the king's subjects] know that just as the soul within the human body, so the soul of majesty is in the whole body of the kingdom and in the entirety of each one of its parts).[22] As for the monarch as the power of integration, Saavedra Fajardo resurrects Pythagorean metaphysical conceptions of political power and declares that the state is like a harp, its various strings representing the different estates and the numerous regions, cities, and villages and emitting a beautiful harmony of majesty when all are played by the single ruling hand of the prudent king.[23] Just as God adorns himself in the splendors of light, the king should display his grandeur and "ilustrar" his royal persona or majesty with radiant public ceremonies that arouse "wonder and respect" in the populace.[24] His kingdom is held together, like the universe it images, by the bonds of love, reciprocally exerted through all the divisions of its hierarchical structure, and since only the God who is not concealed is loved, the king, as God's vicar, must show himself, opening the door of his temple, knowing that "por los ojos y por los oídos entra el amor al corazón" (through one's eyes and ears love enters the heart).[25] The radiance of the royal gaze has the miraculous power to lift its objects out of the subhuman condition of barbarity and to invest their interactions with the society-building virtues of civility and politesse.

The doctrine is formulated with striking precision in a contemporary English treatise, Edward Forsett's A Comparative Discourse on the Bodies Natural and Politique. Forsett emphasizes the perfection that one beholds in the person of the prince, "whereon we doe seldom gaze enough," and likens the splendor of the immortal majesty residing in his mortal body to the "sun shining in glass," which "dazzleth the eyes of all beholders" and like a "magnum naturae miraculum transforms savageness into civility."[26] Such beliefs underlie the comic repetition of the motif of Juan Labrador's "savagery" (the "Scythian," the cannibal, the monster "que injuria la misma naturaleza" [that affronts nature itself]; the "bárbaro que ni aun hombre mereció ser" [the barbarian who did not even deserve to be a man]); its disturbing effects on both the king and his own children, who covet the beneficence of the royal gaze; its ultimate paradoxical transvaluation as the uncompromising philosophical and moral integrity of the "primitive" Diogenes; and its miraculous transformative effects on the disguised king. The anxieties aroused in Juan Labrador's accusers seem to go well beyond the frustrated ambitions of his children and undoubtedly have something to do with a scandalous calling into question of the fundamental axiom of the dominant political philosophy of the age—that man is in fact by nature a political animal and fulfills his distinctively human purposes as a participating member in his rationally constructed community. Perhaps nothing illustrates absolutism's desire to bring the presence of the king and the "civilizing" royal gaze to every rincón of its spreading empire more directly than Lope's New World plays, which climax with the hieratic display of the portrait of the Spanish king.[27]

As Saavedra Fajardo's suggestion of the numinous character of the revealed monarch makes clear, absolutism's conception of the gaze binding monarch and subject—in both awe and love—has obvious connections with religious experience and the contemporary cult of the image. In its most extreme development, wherein the subject's very being is conceived as dependent on the animating glance of his godlike lord, described in the metaphor of the vivifying sun, it might be understood as a striking secularization of traditional notions in a mystical theology that underscores the absolute dependence of the created being for his concrete existence on the presence of a creator in whose essence he participates and articulates such dependence in a drastic accentuation of the conventional solar analogy: "When the sun withdraws, its rays disappear; likewise, if God were to withdraw from the creature, the creature would vanish."[28]

When we take into consideration such conceptions of the monarch and his relation to his subjects, the extravagant compulsions and anxieties that mark Lope's characters and the stakes involved in the dramatic conflicts of both primary and secondary plots become suddenly quite comprehensible and far more serious than is immediately evident. The recognition of conventional comedic stereotypes, caricatures, and conflicts (for example, the free-spirited daughter, the smitten *galán*, and the stubborn, "blocking" father) is of little help in providing an adequate explanation of all that is being implied by this play. If, however, we bear in mind the peculiarities of the royal cult, we can account for Lisarda's (Juan's daughter) irresistible desire to place herself close to the king, to risk scandal in her disguises and impersonations, to expose herself to the destructive powers of his "divine light," and above all to seek a new identity as if she were a cloud—dominated, gilded, and menaced with disintegration by the searing rays of the charismatic royal face. At the same time, we realize that the scandalous, seemingly hysterical behavior of the cranky Juan Labrador conceals something highly serious in its psychological and social implications. One senses in his discomfort in exposing himself to the "royal light" a refusal to yield his authentic self and let go of his own "rival form of monarchy" in the rituals of subjection and circumscription demanded by the structure of dependencies constituting the new cosmos of the court, with its unprecedented social determination of the individual human being.

In the contrapuntal interactions of his protagonists and their respective worlds, it is clear that Lope endows his "alternate king" with a wondrous light of his own. The luminosity that bathes Juan Labrador's children as they thrill to the king's radiant procession is in fact preceded by a light that flows through nature and glows warmly in a gift of grapes that Juan prepares ritualistically to bestow on his neighbor. It is of course the primary light, and its source is the divine creator.

> Tú, Fileto, alcanza
> la más blanca y limpia cesta,
> y de unas uvas doradas
> que se vengan a los ojos,
> y estén sus racimos rojos,
> por las mañanas heladas,
> descubriendo con el sol
> el puro color del oro,
> la llena, y lleva a Peloro. . . .

Los pámpanos, de manera
unos en otros asidos,
con clavellinas tejidos,
que vayan cayendo afuera;
que juntas hojas y flores
parece, se están lozanos,
sus hojas paños de manos
y los claveles labores.

("You, Fileto, take the whitest and cleanest basket. Fill it for Peloro with golden grapes, whose red clusters in the morning frost are gleaming like the sun with the pure color of gold. . . . The vine shoots, interlaced and interwoven with carnations in such a way that they seem in their luxuriance to be spilling over their containers, in their mingling of leaves and flowers, appear to be, the former hand cloths, the latter embroidered decorations.") (101–102)

The emphasis on benevolence, authenticity, and the beautiful colors of "natural regalia" and their juxtaposition to the dazzling spectacle of the royal hunt and its luxuries that immediately follows introduce already at this point, early in the play, suggestions of secondariness, artificiality, and even the counterfeit in the cult of the king and in its primary myth of royal ubiquity. The opposition will be developed in various permutations. One of its most concentrated manifestations will be in the encounter of Diogenes, the philosopher of the true light, and the brilliant emperor Alexander, who provide the paradigm for the transformative experience of Lope's king of France.

A look at the actual behavior inspired by the cult of the king and its program of sacralization and philosophical elevation of the office brings us even closer to the imaginative and thematic center of Lope's mysterious work. A famous witness is the French observer of manners Jean de La Bruyère. If Spanish drama frequently depicts the anxiety of loss of self that a subject can feel when threatened with the withdrawn glance or turned back of the monarch, La Bruyère's well-known description of the court of France suggests the degree to which such sensitivities actually affected the lives of the subjects of the period: "Whoever will consider that a king's presence constitutes the entire happiness of courtiers, that their sole occupation and satisfaction during the whole course of their lives is to see and be seen by him, will in some measure understand how to behold God may constitute the glory and felicity of the saints."[29]

If we find it puzzling that Lope's entire dramatic conflict in the primary action of the *Villano* hinges on the fact that a subject's adoration of his monarch and self-sacrifice on his behalf apparently count for nothing if he is unwilling to *look upon him* (a number of critics have preferred to disregard the challenge of the phrase by erroneously concluding that Juan Labrador's failure is "castigated" as a simple refusal of service), we might recall La Bruyère's bemused description of the Mass in the royal chapel of Versailles, where the courtiers turn their backs on the altar and the holy mysteries in order to gaze on the face of their king as he worships God. The scene, of course, literally enacts one of the royal cult's imaginative conceptions of the ruler, who is not only analogized with God, but is also simultaneously viewed as a quasi-divine intermediary between Him and this world—"el vicario de Dios." In its Christocentric evocations, the conception harks back to the "magical" sacramental identifications in which the "two-body" mythification originated.[30]

Within Lope's dramatic world, the implications and the power of Juan Labrador's defiant attitude toward the ritualized "seeing" that is the mark of the courtly world can be better understood if he is compared to another of the dramatist's idealized peasant heroes, Peribáñez, in his ennobling act of pilgrimage to Toledo to gaze on the quasi-divine monarchs as they gaze on the holy image of the Virgin. Here the refusal to look upon the king is in fact a degrading act of the villainous antagonist, the aristocratic Comendador, who participates in the holy festivity with his eyes idolatrously fixed on the object and image of his sexual desires, Casilda. Perhaps the most shocking moment in the dramatization of Juan Labrador's eccentric attitudes toward such cultic behavior is his refusal, shortly after piously acknowledging the sacrality of kings, "guarded by angels night and day," to hear Mass in the church where the king is simultaneously offering his visible majesty to the villagers.

> Feliciano: . . . está
> desde que al Rey ha sentido,
> o encerrado o escondido.
> Lisarda: Pues ¿a misa no saldrá?
> Feliciano: Perderála por no ver
> la Corte, el Rey ni las damas.
> Lisarda: Y ¿bárbaro no le llamas?
> Feliciano: Ni aun hombre mereció ser.

(Feliciano: Since he has been aware of the king's presence, he is either locked up or hidden. Lisarda: Will he not come to Mass? Feliciano: He will miss it in order not to see the court, the king, and the ladies. Lisarda: And you do not call him a barbarian? Feliciano: He doesn't even deserve to be called a human being.) (113)

Several historical studies of the past twenty-five years have confirmed Maravall's conclusions concerning the spectacular character of political life in the Spain of the Habsburgs and specifically the importance of the visible monarch in maintaining a centralizing and stabilizing focus for a nation of considerable local diversity and demographic instability. In his description of the cult of the monarch and its repressive political agenda, C. Lisón Tolosana emphasizes the overwhelming power of the elaborately choreographed epiphanies of the ruler to "circumvent the cognitive faculties" of the multitudes assembled, to stifle any impulses toward rational detachment, and to bring about a pleasurable immersion of self in the harmonies and splendors of the spectacle.[31] Describing the "lavish spectacles in the gardens of the Royal Palace, with their costumes, scenic stage effects, music, song, dance, and three-dimensional settings," he suggests that their effects "must have created an entire world of fantasy and illusion, of grandeur and superpower, in the astonished throngs of Madrid, who witnessed scenes that by themselves alone invited their viewers to leave behind the world of quotidian reality and enter the realms of imagination and desire." The general similarities with the liturgical ritual and its mysterious effects are unmistakable. In short, seeing the king—the commandment that provokes the spectacular anxiety of Lope's *villano*—is "a visual experience which, like religious liturgy, conveyed an existential understanding both of the practical dimension of the monarchy and of the sacred aspect of royalty, but everything within a limbo or an ambiguous universe, a symbiosis of the exotic and the familiar."[32] The compulsion *to see* becomes extraordinary. When Philip IV died, throngs of people demanded to see his body and forced their way past corps of guards at the *capilla ardiente* (funeral chapel); "the authorities, in agreement with the people's wishes, decided to extend the period of public viewing." Hundreds of churches throughout the peninsula created a visual spectacle so that all Spaniards could, at this moment of passage and reconnection, gaze on the figure of their king.[33]

Probably the most splendid displays of the sacred body of the king were in the numerous processionals, the kind of triumphant passage that provides the epiphany of royalty in the first act of *El villano en su rincón* and touches off its principal dramatic conflict. In emphasizing the importance of the majestic entry by the king into the cities of his kingdom, J. de Santa María writes: "Esta es visita que conviene a los Reyes, porque son las cabezas de sus Republicas, y para ella se han de reservar los negocios mas graves de su pueblo, que es razon que los vean (como dizen) con sus propios ojos. Para esto se ordenan las visitas, y entradas que los Reyes suelen hazer en las ciudades y Provincias de sus Reynos" (This is a visit that is appropriate for Kings, because they are the heads of their Republics, and the most serious affairs of the people must be reserved for it; for it is right that they see them [as is said] with their own eyes. For this reason the visits and entries that monarchs are accustomed to making in the cities and provinces of their kingdoms are ordained).[34] The entry culminates in the measured, stately passage of the radiant royal figure at the head of his brightly colored cortege through the center of the town, where balconies, windows, roofs, and terraces, as well as *miradores* (observation platforms), specially constructed for the occasion, are packed with the throngs of loyal subjects who have gathered to gaze on their king: "effervescent, ecstatic, transcendent moments, moments of legitimization for the monarchy and divinization for the royalty . . . active participation by the masses, generating a solidarity among the citizens and a communion joining them and their king. To see and to be seen in pomp and magnificence; to see is to create an image; to see is to believe in a divinity."[35] Statues, effigies, royal portraits, the crowned image of a *dignitas* . . . a *dignitas* that can never die.

THE HUMAN KING AND HIS LIMITATIONS:
THE FASCINATION OF THE TYRANT

> Salvano: ¿Este es el rey?
> Fileto: Aquel mancebo rojo.
> Salvano: ¡Válgame Dios! Los reyes ¿tienen barbas?
> Fileto: Pues ¿cómo piensas tú que son los reyes?
> Salvano: Yo he visto en un jardín pintado al César,
> A Tito, a Vespasiano y a Trajano;
> Pero estaban rapados como frailes.

(Salvano: Is this the king? Fileto: That red-bearded youth. Salvano: God help us! Do kings have beards? Fileto: Well, what do you think kings are like? Salvano: Once I saw painted in a garden Caesar, Titus, Vespasian, and Trajan, but they were clean shaven like friars.)

> —*El villano en su rincón*

No piensen que son Reyes solamente de nombre y representación, que no estan obligados a mas de hazerse adorar, y representar muy bien la persona Real, y aquella soberana dignidad. . . . No ay cosa mas muerta, y de menos sustancia, que una imagen de sombra.

(Do not think that kings are kings in name and representation alone, that they are not obligated to anything beyond making themselves adored and representing effectively the royal person and that sovereign dignity. . . . Nothing is more dead and less substantial than an image of a shadow.)

—*Fray Juan de Santa María*

Before turning to the complex interaction of king and peasant in *El villano en su rincón*, we should look at one more aspect of the contemporary conception of the royal figure. Here the elevating process carried out by political theorists, philosophers, poets, and dramatists does not, strictly speaking, conform to the demands of Lope's injunction to the dramatists that I cited above. It is not, in fact, one of divinization. Its focus is rather on the other side of the traditionally geminated figure—the human king—the side that, to recall Kantorowicz's studies, absolutism, given its project to magnify the official body, tended to veil or ritualistically cover in the dress and regalia of power and immortality, from the elaborate ceremonies of awakening, dressing, and morning toilette through the punctiliously maintained routines of a day of official duties—audiences, receptions, decisions on matters of state, banquets, masques, and other carefully scripted activities. Throughout the period the king was presented not only as a numinous object, a "consecrated idol" before which the adoring subject prostrated himself, but also, and paradoxically, as a mirror, a model on which his subjects should look to find an ideal they could emulate in their individual lives—a "mere" human being, to be sure, but a morally perfected human being. Although they could freely invoke the traditional aggrandizing doctrines and myths surrounding the royal figure, the spokesmen for this tradition were not primarily concerned with hypostatizing a singular human being distinguished by divine or magical blood, by a Phoenix-like capacity to rise renewed and immortal from the very embers of his funeral pyre, by an abstract unicity as the genus above the species, or by a metaphysical identification with an Aristotelian unmoved mover or a Platonic universal form or mirror animating a variegated matter.

The king as a real human being standing as moral exemplar—simply the best of men—before his subjects, co-equals as fellow human beings, was a central feature of the humanistic tradition of the *speculum principis*, from Aegidius's widely read *De regimine principum* (1285?) to its numerous Renaissance descendants such as Patrizi's late-fifteenth-century *De regno et regis institutione* and Erasmus's *De institutione principis christiani* (1515). Here the center of man's political life lies in the moral perfectioning of his society. Rulers, republics, and citizens exist to promote the virtues—the cardinal, the princely, and the godly.

As Erasmus put it in his influential treatise, the duty of the ruler must be to serve as the embodiment of "virtue in its highest and purest form." He is a model who exemplifies, a teacher who enlightens his fellow citizens. In the words of Pontano's De principe, the ruler's offering to his subjects is "'the most splendid thing in the world,' more magnificent even than the sun, for 'the blind cannot see the sun' whereas 'even they can see virtus as plainly as possible.'"[36] In his treatise on the Christian prince, Pedro de Ribadeneira writes that the monarch is "the mirror in which all things are reflected." To his court lords and knights send their sons "to observe and be educated" by the royal model. "The example of the Prince can better persuade the others to virtue than all the laws and diligence that they exercise without it. Also commonly the great lords and knights of the realm see themselves, as in a mirror, in the Prince; and they try to imitate him and from them is derived the good and the ill in the remainder."[37] In developing the reiterated solar imagery beyond its customary metaphysical directions, Saavedra Fajardo likens the subjects of the state to sunflowers, constantly turning about the sun of their sovereign, "mirando y imitando al príncipe," attentive to every expression and movement of his face. The prince must be an unstained mirror, the perfect image in which his vassals can look upon themselves in an ideal form.[38]

Saavedra Fajardo's association of the process of gazing on the royal mirror with edification and with the fulfillment of the monarch's responsibility to bring harmony to the "música del gobierno" might be compared to Lope's display of the mirror in the final scene of the Villano and his philosophical king's instruction of the frightened peasant concerning the authentic significance of what he sees in the royal spectacle—a theater of royal power that he has so carefully arranged, arbitrarily but rationally, for the purpose of education and the harmonious integration of his kingdom. Representing in his behavior all the virtues "dignas del imperio," upholding the written laws of the land wherein lie the rational foundations of sovereignty, the king becomes the moral exemplar for the citizen, who "se compone" in the royal mirror: "Vasallo que no se mira/en el Rey, esté muy cierto/que sin concierto ha vivido,/y que vive descompuesto" (It is certain that the vassal who does not look upon himself in the king has lived in disorder and that he will continue to live in confusion).[39]

The awareness of the importance of the human "half" of the traditionally geminated monarch, however, had another consequence in the political writings of the period, and it is important to recognize it if we are to fathom the ambiguities in the doubling of king and peasant in Lope's play and the fundamental fact that the play dramatizes a reciprocal education. Despite the prominence of the cult of the king, citizens, politicians, and theorists of the state and the institution of monarchy did not hesitate to confront the dangers in absolute regal power and to enjoin limitations and caution in its use.

Perhaps it is well to recall at this point that while the ideology of absolutism and its ruler cults generally stressed the immense power of the monarch as head of the corporate body of the state and invoked the divine origin of his sovereignty, the ruler's freedom of action was in actual fact curtailed by an increasingly complex system of centralized "statist" institutions, as well as by numerous regional and local governing bodies and deeply entrenched systems of customary laws (for example, the Spanish *fueros*). Whether stemming from bureaucratic rivalries and obstructionism, local constitutional resistance to impositions from the central government, or rebellions by provinces in defense of traditional rights, disobedience was, contrary to current assumptions about the effectiveness of absolutism as a totalitarian machine of governance, a common feature of the political experience of the early modern nation-states. More relevant for Lope's *Villano en su rincón*, however, was the fact that according to contemporary political theory, the royal will was in a very fundamental way limited by constraints of divine and natural law.[40] Traditional theories of governing had stressed that both laws manifested themselves in the rule of reason,[41] and it was characteristic of contemporary treatises on statecraft to emphasize the king's need for a sense of rational restraint and obligation, which he could acquire only through education and the refining processes of culture.[42]

Amid the pessimistic diatribes of his evangelical *regimen principis*, *Política de Dios*, Quevedo reminds his readers that the cries of the midwife attending to the birth of the royal infant are hardly proclamations of the advent of a fully perfected divine creature.[43] Governing itself is viewed as an "arte," and it is characteristically visualized in such emblems as the cultivation of nature and the orderly pruning (*podar*) of its abundant and potentially chaotic growth. Saavedra Fajardo invokes an "agricultural model," which might recall Juan Labrador's stewardship of nature and the royal palace. He notes: "Princes were born powerful, but they were not born educated." They must flee bad counsel and learn the *true* "razón de Estado." "Aquélla solamente es cierta, fija y sólida, que usa en el gobierno de las cosas vegetativas y vivientes, y principalmente la que por medio de la razón dicta a cada uno de los hombres en su oficio, y particularmente a los pastores y labradores para la conservación y aumento del ganado y de la cultura. De donde quizá los reyes que del cayado o del arado pasaron al ceptro supieron mejor gobernar sus pueblos" (Alone that statecraft is certain, fixed, and solid which is used in the governing of vegetative and living things, and principally that which through reason gives instructions to each man in his occupation, and particularly to shepherds and farmers for the conservation and increase of their livestock and agricultural produce. Perhaps this is the reason why the kings who rose from the shepherd's staff and the plow to the scepter knew best how to govern their peoples).[44]

Majesty might be eternal and unchanging in its splendor, but the mortal individual in whose body it inheres must be perfected. If he fails to look into the "mirrors" of his ancestry and of past and hypothetical future events and therein learn to look at things with lucid judgment and maintain his activities within the "bounds of reason," he will stand as an empty idol, "de culto y no de efecto," receiving adoration that masks contempt. In words that, by contrast, illuminate the emblematic climaxes of *El villano en su rincón* and its concern to align reason with the fearsome insignia of power and the king with the shepherd-philosopher, Saavedra Fajardo writes: "Por esto llamó ídolo el profeta Zacarías al príncipe que no atiende a su obligación, semejante al pastor que desampara su ganado; porque es una estatua quien representa y no exercita la majestad" (For this reason the prophet Zechariah called the prince who fails to attend to his duty, like the shepherd who abandons his flock, an idol; because he is a statue who represents but does not exercise the majesty).[45]

In this essay—a commentary on an emblem depicting a serpent, the symbol of prudence, twined about a scepter above an hourglass flanked by two mirrors, representing past and future history—Saavedra Fajardo is writing as a Tacitist, and his concern is with the restraints of rationality understood as prudence, the pragmatic art of governing based on the ruler's learned capacity to study scientifically and to "anatomize" the past, and to develop a viable political policy according to its lessons. In other essays he exalts rationality as a constraint on royal power in traditional moral terms, and his arguments are more directly applicable to the dynamics of Lope's play and its presentation of the king's momentary loss of control at its moment of crisis. As I shall point out below, it is the moment when the play engages most directly with the great obsession of the contemporary political culture—the figure of the tyrant.

Saavedra Fajardo's discussion of the hidden thorns of responsibility concealed behind the splendid jewels of the royal crown makes it clear that the king's rule is more an "oficio" than a "dignidad," that "la dominación es gobierno, y no poder absoluto, y los vasallos, subditos y no esclavos," and that a king is bound to his subjects as a father to his children, a point that is perhaps echoed in the final act of *El villano* when, following his conversion, Lope's king stresses his bond with Juan Labrador as members of a single family.

In the more ethically oriented, explicitly anti-Machiavellian treatise of Pedro de Ribadeneira, we observe an even greater concern for the necessary restraint in the prince and a characteristic emphasis on the figure of the tyrant and all that distinguishes him from the true king. The latter is "subject to the laws of God and nature"; he is the soul of the body of the commonwealth, the father of each one of his subjects, and he seeks out the best among them to honor them with responsibilities and duties. The former "holds to no other law than his own wish"; he is the knife and the executioner of his people, and he considers himself absolute owner of the estates of his subjects.[46] Like most contemporary analysts of tyranny, Ribadeneira gives a good deal of attention to the devastating consequences of lust, the sin that most vividly emblematizes the fundamental perversion that tyranny represents, the violation of rational law and the loss of rational control: "Dishonest love is heedlessness of reason, brother of folly, enemy of the soul." Throughout history it has brought indescribable depravity, disorder, and destruction to commonwealths. Since in his position of power the prince is constantly subject to temptation, he must "bridle his impulses and in his chastity shine forth and take great pains to be considered above mortal in the land," to inspire by his example the ordinary people, to rein in the sensual appetites they so readily allow to enslave them. The properly integrated character of the prince brings proper integration to the state, and Ribadeneira, citing the words of Isocrates' classical mirror of the king, exhorts the ruler to the heroic act of self-governance: "You will command yourself no less than the others, and you should think nothing so regal as to serve no carnal appetite and to rule your passions and appetites more than your subjects."[47]

The writings on kingship, then, were very much concerned with the rational restraints on power that are inculcated through proper moral education and are based on the sovereign's constant awareness that beneath the royal dignity he is an ordinary man and subject to all the ills and temptations that afflict the human condition. Admonitions to know oneself and lessons in humility were recurrent features of their educational programs for the young prince. The ultimate wisdom becomes precisely the continuing recollection of the mortality of the being who wears the crown. At this point we reach the most profound implications of Gracián's commentary on the parable underlying Lope's play. What in fact is the recognition that rewards the king's accidental tumble into the lower world of the forest and his fruitful experience of abjection, humanization, and *desengaño* amid its mirrors of truth? Why is a true king not to be sought at a throne, the customary site of his magnificent display?

A hint can be found in the writings of a well-known French jurist and theorist of monarchy. In his *De republica libri sex* (1578) Pierre Grégoire insists that the prince must remember that he is "of the same substance as the rest of men." His duty (*munus*) to rule and his royal persona are imposed on him by God, and he must act out his required role in this earthly drama (*fabula*) of the great theater of this world, subject as it is to corruption. However, beneath the external majesty he remains the human being, his will free to choose good and evil, and in the case of its failure, the royal majesty is no different from empty idols such as the hollow colossi described by Lucian. The prince must, then, know himself; he must become human (*humanare*) and, "disdaining nothing that is human," descend from the heights of his exalted power to the level of his subjects.[48]

In a passage that is particularly revealing in relation to *El villano en su rincón* with its emphasis on the visibility and ceremonial display of royal power, Grégoire writes of the royal "insignia," which, while they have *numen* (a supernatural aura), do not remove the human nature of the king. They do not release him, under the pretext of the dignity, from restraint in his human actions; they do not relax (*laxant*) the reins that hold him in check and strengthen his will to resist the temptations to evil conduct (*ad deteriora*). Grégoire details the vices of numerous unbridled rulers, and he concludes that all the disasters that consumed their kingdoms came about because they did not know themselves and the responsibilities of the *office* to which they were called. The remedy lies in education. Since the "greatest regal virtue is the proper governance of oneself," the king must be educated "first to know himself, afterwards to know the dignity which he fulfills (*gerit*)." "*Nam ipse non est dignitas; sed agit personam dignitatis*; praeceptum illud e coelo natum est . . . nosce teipsum."

In discovering himself, the king discovers that by nature he and his subjects are equal; they are nourished by the same elements, spring from the same seed, live beneath the same heaven ("fruuntor eodem caelo"), alike live and die. How must the king avoid confusing his true, human self with his insignia and his royal persona? He must, first of all, think of death and his ultimate resting place. Here Grégoire offers an anecdote that casts an interesting light on the importance of Juan Labrador's grave as one of the sage's dwellings and as the object that provokes the king's philosophical agitation and his "descent" into the world of his double, a descent that becomes, as I shall argue below, a recollection or a repossession of his authentic self—a kind of ritual of "rekinging." The most prudent of kings, Charles V, at the height of his power and amid the "maxima negotia regni sui," constructed a portable grave and secretly kept it with him in his presence wherever he would go, so that he might have before his eyes a perpetual reminder of death and of the consequent necessity of doing good. Grégoire's conclusion is relevant: the king is in fact the royal dignity, the consecrated model being; he is looked upon by all as the ideal mirror that illuminates the commonwealth by his example. Yet he can ascend to the exalted level of his being only after accepting, understanding, and perfecting his mortal self. The same sequence is essential in the primary action of Lope's play in its depiction of the development of a king: a passage from fallen mortal or tyrant (see below), to perfected mortal or sage, and finally to immortal majesty (that is, the letter of the regalia now properly spiritualized or morally "consecrated") manifest in the displayed insignia of his climactic theater of power and governance.

A descent amid funerary motifs, tombs, epitaphs, and lugubrious philosophical speculations is a familiar feature of absolutism's great dramatizations of the mysteries of monarchy and the new insights into the most challenging realities of political power and violence. It is important to note that the awakening of Lope's king and his philosophical quest toward *desengaño* begin at the moment of his first appearance, when, on discovering the tombs of a village church, he engages in a discussion with his attendants of the "notables cosas" inscribed "en los sepulcros." Here he immediately learns that Darius discovered, on opening Semiramis's magnificent tomb, that the wealth she offered was in fact "las cenizas de los muertos" (the ashes of the dead).[49] To recall the words of Richard II, one of the blindest of kings, there is a time when rulers must "talk of graves, of worms, and epitaphs . . . and tell sad stories of the death of kings" (III, ii). But what is striking in Lope's articulation of the pattern when compared with the more memorable and disturbing versions (for example, in the drama of Shakespeare and Calderón) is its philosophical and moral optimism, its humanistic resolution, and its comedic construction.

The contrast with some of the most famous contemporary figures who tread the same dark path toward the unveiling of a king's hidden humanity is instructive. One might recall the denuding and abjection of Calderón's young "príncipe constante" and the revulsion of the political, materialistic, self-absorbed, and hedonistic Arab world around him at the smell of his decaying body, or Segismundo's discovery of the phantasmic character of the monarch, whose royal robes, like a flickering candle, merely conceal for a few brief moments the surrounding darkness, the implacable skeleton within, and the inherited human inclination to evil and tyranny—the failed Adam of Augustine's somber vision of man's political capacities.[50] The most grotesque and ultimately tragic development of these conceptions lies, of course, in Shakespeare's bleak political worlds. In *King Lear*, a descent leads through chaos and madness to the discovery that a king's flesh "stinks of mortality." Hamlet, the "naked," shipwrecked prince, wanders in graveyards, contemplates the skulls of his ultimate nudity, and reminds his ruler that the final royal progress bears the king's august body through the guts of a beggar. In the work most directly concerned with the issues raised by Lope's analytical examination of the royal cult and the royal body, the deposed Richard II gazes into his mirror; contemplates his "unkinged," disrobed image; and wonders whether, having lost his royal face, "washed away his balm," and "undecked the pompous body of a king," he is in fact no more than nothing. "Was this the face/That, like the sun, did make beholders wink? . . . For I must nothing be" (IV, i).

In summary, to understand the strange obsession of *El villano en su rincón* with seeing and the complicated interaction of its protagonists, who appear to be motivated by a dynamics of ritualistically looking upon one another, it is necessary to bear in mind that the gaze binding the subject with the monarch was understood in the period both as a passive process of surrender of self, the self-subjugation through awe before the sublimity of an omnipotent, suprahuman majesty, and as an active process of self-formation through imitation of a morally exemplary human being.[51] In either case the individual realizes his identity in the presence of the image of his monarch, whether through the honoring glance bestowed by the latter or through his own contemplative process of measuring himself beside the ideal being and founding his emulation according to its moral perfections. The ambiguities lurking in the obsession with seeing are evidenced throughout the literature of princes—the prince as mirror of majesty and the prince as mirror of emulation, the suprahuman and the all too human, the model for subjection and the model for independence—and *El villano en su rincón*, with its compelling reiteration of its protagonist's anxieties about leaving his philosophically constructed *rincón*—a kind of fortress of the self—and his ultimate transformation into a mirror of emulation for his troubled prince should be understood as an intricate, paradoxical elaboration of the two positions in the dramatic exchanges of a reciprocal education.

EL VILLANO EN SU RINCÓN, I: THE CEREMONIAL KING

> ¡Qué la púrpura real
> no cause veneración
> a un villano en su rincón
> que viste pardo sayal!

(That the royal purple does not arouse veneration in a peasant in his corner who dresses in coarse brown homespun!)

> —*The King of France*

If we bear in mind absolutism's "deep mysteries of monarchy"—in the words of one of their most enthusiastic and widely read celebrants, James I—we might understand more clearly that puzzling fascination and agitation (*desasosiego*) that Lope's king of France suddenly feels when he enters the church and gazes on the tomb of Juan Labrador, a man who not only has refused to look upon the majesty of a king, but who also has insisted on having his tomb, his eternal home, constantly at his side while he lives. The doubling process, the confusions of identity, motivating the frequently criticized "non-plot" of the play and leading to an increasingly rich and enigmatic series of exchanges between the two figures, begins at this instant as a kind of call to the king to recall himself, to *humanarse*, to descend to his human condition. To amplify Gracián's figure, one might say that the king is provoked to find a mirror of truth and self-knowledge rather than a distorting mirror of majesty.[52]

The fact is that until his entry into the other world of Juan Labrador's *rincón*, a world that we might characterize as defiantly *humanus*, unceremonial, and unofficial, Lope's king appears to exist, or at least to understand himself, only as majesty. In the first act we see him in the world of ceremony—the splendid festivity, the colors, the ornament, the clothing, the hunt, the brilliant games of the royal procession. We are told of their thrilling effects on his beholders and might note that the monarch is carrying out perfectly the precepts of such pragmatic contemporary theorists of regal power as Saavedra Fajardo, who writes that the king must ostentatiously display his grandeur, *ilustrando* his majesty with brilliant public ceremonies that arouse "admiración y repeto, porque el pueblo se deja llevar de lo exterior, no consultándose menos el corazón *con los ojos que con el entendimiento*" (wonder and respect, because the common people let themselves be carried away by externals, judging in their hearts no less by their eyes than by their minds).[53]

Recalling the dazzling effects of the royal display, Juan's son turns to the most extravagant conceits of royal panegyric to capture his reactions. The monarch's family displaces the cosmos and nature; pages in white sashes are "rayos del sol" that illuminate the thick forest and threaten to penetrate the defenses of Juan Labrador's "rincón." The king and his sister are sun and moon, surrounded by the stars of his entourage.

> Ven, porque todo el camino
> se cubre de más señores
> que tienen los campos flores
> y fruta aquel verde pino.
> Ven a ver cuán envidioso
> está el sol de los caballos,
> porque quisiera roballos
> para su carro famoso.
> Verás tanto paje hermoso

que el pecho tierno atraviesa
con banda blanca francesa,
opuesta al rojo español,
ir como rayos del sol
por esa arboleda espesa.

(Come, for our entire lane is covered by more lords than there are flowers in
the fields and cones in that green pine tree. Come to see how envious the sun
is of the horses, because he would like to steal them for his famous chariot.
You will see so many beautiful pages, their gentle breasts crossed by the white
French sash, the opposite of the Spanish scarlet, all moving like beams of sunlight through that thick grove of trees.) (106–107)[54]

We then observe the king's solemn entry into the village church to hear mass,
a spectacle to which all the local inhabitants flock, only to find themselves so
alarmed (*turbados*) by the approach of the numenous figure that Otón has to
calm them by reminding them of his humanity: "¿Cómo turbar? ¿No veis cuán
apacible,/cuán humano es el Rey?" (Why be frightened? Don't you see how
gentle, how human the king is?) (118). As in La Bruyère's description of Louis
XIV's courtiers attending mass with their eyes riveted on the sovereign as he
faced the altar, the scene suggests a displacement of the divinity and a ceremony
of royal devotion.

At this point it becomes impossible to overlook the setting that Lope chooses
for the opening scene of his play: Lisarda passes from the palace world of Paris
to the pastoral retreat of Belflor. The threshold of her crossover is the gate and
village of St. Denis, where she stops at an inn to change clothing and identity.
One of many parallels that Lope establishes between the two worlds and plots
of his play, the scene anticipates the church and tombs of Juan Labrador's forest
kingdom and associates their enigmas with the Abbey of St. Denis, the most holy
of France's royal shrines, the necropolis of its kings, and the custodian of its royal
insignia and the effigies bearing witness to the undying identity of the figures
whose skeletons lie beneath them.[55] Crowning and burial, the major rituals in
the lives of the kings of France, loom imaginatively in the background of Lope's
tale of kings, philosophers, peasants, disrobings, and recrownings.

The powerful effects of royal charisma are acknowledged in other ways in
Act I. Juan Labrador's children, who are eager to enter the glamorous court
society, speak of their intense desire to see and to be seen by the king, to be
given life and selfhood by the animating glance of the charismatic monarch—
the "miracle" pursued by the ambitious and insecure members described in La

Bruyère's analysis of the French court society. Juan Labrador himself joins the chorus of the celebrants of monarchy. Echoing the traditional commonplaces of the theorists of royal absolutism, he praises the king as God's vicar and describes him as the "hombre perfecto que Dios singular crió" (the perfect man whom God created as singular) (108).[56] He notes that this perfect being is protected by two guardian angels, a conception intimately connected with the belief that the king is a two-bodied creature, human and suprahuman:

> El cura nos predicó
> que dos ángeles tenía
> que le guardan noche y día.

(The priest preached to us that he had two angels who watch over him night and day.) (108)[57]

To sum up, by the end of Act I the king has taken shape only as his official self and primarily as theatrical spectacle and effect, and as he issues the order that the apparently defiant Juan Labrador must see him—must situate himself within the field of ceremonial connection—he is speaking as that self. Appropriately his final apparition is emblematic and fearsome: "¡A un rey de tanto valor, que tiemblan sus flores de oro, el scita, el turco feroz!" (A king of such might that the Scythian and the fierce Turk tremble before his golden fleurs-de-lis!) (125).

One might expect the act to end here. But such is not the case; a curtain, so to speak, does not fall. Lope instead presents a remarkable coda—a glimpse of the *rincón*—a mysterious kingdom shadowed by a forest of towering trees and veiled by the smoke rising from its dwellers' fires. In verses that perhaps echo Góngora's *Soledades* and recall its pilgrim's ascent from the darkness and chaos of the stormy sea to the distant fires of a radiant world of pastoral perfection, Lope describes the *rincón* as a refuge beckoning to lost wanderers, who, crossing its magical threshold, find their way to its center and the alluring figure of its shepherd-king, seated on an earthly throne beneath a canopy of sheltering oaks, surrounded by a circle of mastiffs gazing on him as their lord. The unsettling effect of the non-conclusion is compounded by the uncanny variant on the endlessly repeated motif of gazing on the king.[58] The ballad drifts toward the imaginative space of the fairy tale and a kingdom far different from the man-made monarchies of contemporary Europe. Might a dreamlike projection and identification of doubles be taking place? The contrapuntal, musical design of Act I, with its continuing shifts in place, theme, and motif between the two worlds of the play, is suspended with a challenging riddle and the insinuation of a folkloric quest. Before we move on to Act II, we suspect that the mysterious passage of an initiation, a loss of direction, a reorientation, a rediscovery of the way, might lie before the omnipotent and frightening king of France, whose luminous image strikes terror in those who behold him.

EL VILLANO EN SU RINCÓN, II: THE FOREST KINGDOM

> Aunque alto y bajo estén, mira
> que aunque son tan desiguales
> como la noche y el día,
> aquella unión y armonía
> los hace en su acento iguales;
> que el alto en un punto suena
> con el bajo siempre igual.

(Look, although they may be high and low, although they are even as different as night and day, that union and harmony make them in their sound equals; for the high, conjoined in one point with the low, sounds always as its equal.)

—*Costanza*

At the beginning of the second act, the king of France admits that since his discovery of the tomb of Juan Labrador, he lives in anxiety (*desasosiego*), disturbed by the peasant's independence and absolute indifference to his royal presence. It is clear that at this point he still understands his identity entirely in terms of his public self—his dignity—and he may be approaching the insight that the king who is no more than the majesty is nothing at all when the confirming gaze of his subjects is withdrawn. One might recall Pascal's famous observation: "Leave a king entirely alone with no company or diversion . . . and . . . we will see that a king without diversion is a man full of misery."[59] In attempting to comprehend his unhappiness, he continually refers to himself as the majesty, and he confesses that he is baffled by the fact that his "consecrated identity" does not compel his subject's worship, that his "royal purple does not arouse veneration." He laments that while thousands of people go on pilgrimages to look upon the "majesty" of cities, he, the king, must endure the pain of looking upon a man who is "opposed to his own majesty."

Faced with the possible emptiness of the ceremonial world and the phantasmal nature of its ritualized seeing, in a sudden reversal that is characteristic of the symbolic economy of this strange play, he begins to fear the *villano* and to envy him his immunity to desire.

¡Que tenga el alma segura,
y el cuerpo en tanto descanso!
Pero ¿para qué me canso?
Digo que es envidia pura,
y que le tengo de ver.

(That he is so secure in his soul and so at peace in his body! But why do I exhaust myself? I confess that it is pure envy, and that I must see him.) (128)

While the abrupt turn would appear to make little sense in terms of psychological plausibility, it is perfectly consistent with the conventions of folktale that are so prominent in the work.[60]

Failing to find consolation in the lessons of traditional moral philosophy, the king falls victim to a compulsive, tormenting desire to gaze on the man whose withdrawn gaze threatens him with deprivation of being. He rejects Solon's and Aristotle's speculations regarding the nature of human happiness as inapplicable to his case, and he insists that his unprecedented misery should be accounted for among the monstrous exceptions to the natural order that delighted skeptic philosophers of the age—for example, the lion's fear of the creaking sounds of a turning wheel and the horse's panic at the sight of a small bird known as the *floro*.[61]

In what might be viewed as a reversal of Machiavellian precepts on rule, the subject has aroused the fear and reverence of the prince. The laconic, proverbial rhetoric of Juan Labrador's tombstone threatens to disclose the emptiness of all courtly and political rhetoric. Charisma has shifted from ruler to ruled. The master has become the slave. Lope's paradoxical, reflective, and ultimately enlightening play with traditional hierarchies of value has begun. The burden of Valdivielso's religious rewriting of the play as an *auto* will be to recapture this "wayward," secular charisma and displace it onto the figure of Christ, who replaces Lope's king as unrecognized guest at the forest banquet table.

At this point, disguised as a hunter, the king crosses over into the *villano's* world, evidently seeking something far more fundamental than the quarry pursued by his numerous folkloric ancestors of the hunt, the erotic figures who appear over and over again in Lope's dramatic worlds. The entire act occurs at night in the forest world of the *labrador*. The atmosphere is charged with erotic intensity. The colorful, artificial pageantry of the king's equestrian passage of Act I is displaced by the peasants' festival, centering on the elm tree, where lovers secretly meet; sing; dance; exchange riddles, jests, and festive parodies; and philosophically discourse on love, virtue, harmony, and music. The protective elm tree, hovering over the dances in the night, suggests folkloric tree cults and fertility rites—for example, the midsummer festivals and circular maypole dances of northern Europe—all of which are imaginatively preserved in the erotic metaphors of elm and vine running through traditional epithalamic poetry. Here too Shakespeare's dramatic world offers interesting similarities—for example, the forest world of A *Midsummer Night's Dream*, where mysterious erotic unions are brought about as if by magic and "the female ivy so enrings the barky fingers of the elm."[62]

Lope's scene is deeply marked by the spirit of the pastoral symposium. It presents a striking image of community integration, celebrating the power of love and friendship to "concertar voluntades," to overcome differences of age, sex, and class, affirming the seriousness of marriage, and imaginatively exalting such convergences in the musical analogies common in the Renaissance Neo-Platonic metaphysics of love. To understand the play's dialectical alignment of palace and country, as well as its political themes, it is important to note that such analogies appeared frequently in the political theories on the integrative design of the absolutist state and perhaps reflected the influence of remote Hellenistic treatises on monarchy—rediscovered and transmitted in Stobaeus's widely read anthology (*Sententiae, ex thesauris Graecorum delectae*). Under the impact of Pythagorean doctrines, such treatises stressed the divinely created, harmonious design of the cosmos; envisioned its replication in the state, society, *policé*, and *civilitée*; and conceived of the king as a sage whose acts in creating living, rational laws and assuring justice could be likened to the tuning of a lyre and the elevation of the souls of his subjects through the sounds of his music.[63] The contemporary theorist of absolutism, Saavedra Fajardo may well have had such doctrines in mind when he described the king's obligations to order and maintain his state in the image of the musician tuning and playing his harp.[64] In any event the metaphysical analogies elevating the forest symposium of Lope's play certainly prefigure the most spectacular convergences of the drama—the concluding bonding of king and peasant at the climactic banquet with its multiple marriages and its accompanying musical harmonies.

At this moment the disguised king, lurking in the woods, enters Juan Labrador's house, again referring to himself as the *corona* and the *majestad*, and we witness the central scene in his "education" as king and the crucial scene in his self-discovery, the *humanarse* or "descent to the human," and his identification with his peasant *Doppelgänger*. As they sit facing each other in the candlelight of the dinner table, Juan Labrador offers his unrecognized guest a systematic description of his way of life—a life of piety, simplicity, industry, humility, and moderation, devoted to the honest toil of farming and raising a family, closely guided by the rhythms of nature, the earth, and the real human body. He speaks eloquently of the rewards of such an existence—tranquility of mind; independence; the happiness that moral fulfillment brings; and a condition of spiritual, interior royalty. He is king over himself and his *rincón*, and as he points out, his life is notably free from the distinctive torments of the court society—ambition; restlessness; envy; *negotia*; social and ceremonial responsibilities; and the kind of self-regarding eroticism that founds itself in lust, power relations, egotism, and intrigue. The image of perfection that Juan Labrador offers the disguised king in an emblematic form—the sequence of concrete scenes of his described life and his moral commentary on each—is, as has often been pointed out, modeled on classical philosophy, and, as in several other ritualistic scenes presented in this play about witnessing, its visual effects are underscored by musical accompaniment. At its climax a chorus offers a hymn based on the Horatian *beatus ille*, with its celebration of the kind of inner perfectioning and felicity that one can enjoy only if one flees the pressures of society and the *negotia* of the court.[65]

As the scene develops, the king's admiration for his host's wisdom steadily increases. He acclaims the encounter as a "convite real"—a philosophical symposium: "¡Oh, filósofo villano! Mucho más te envidio agora" (Oh, philosopher-peasant! Much more do I envy you now) (153). He is amazed to have heard "tan notables desengaños" from the mouth of "aqueste villano sabio" (163). The act closes with his exclamation to Otón: "Tu sabrás que milagro/me trujo adonde he venido/a ver, siendo rey tan alto, el villano en su rincón" (You shall know what miracle brought me, so lofty a king, to where I have come to see the lowly *villano* in his humble corner). His words underscore the crucial importance of the encounter—a miracle and a *desengaño*—as well as the fruitful paradoxicality of the entire confrontation—a paradoxicality that is consistent with the fundamental traditions of Stoic philosophy that underlie the ethical ideal that the king has here assimilated from the sage.[66] At the same time they should be seen as a manifestation of a paradoxicality that is latent in the entire political tradition of the king's twofold identity, a tradition that lies behind the monarchist conception of the play and animates its complex development of the archetypal literary convention of the double. High has become low, and low, high—the king's education is a humanization that involves descending from the sublimity of the majesty to the human self. The familiar misery of the king is paradoxically found to lie rooted in the sublimity of his exalted royal identity.

To understand Lope's conception of the *rincón*, as well as his pride in his achievement as creator of this mythical space and its philosophical inhabitant,[67] it is well to bear in mind that the word *rincón* is etymologically connected with the concepts of shelter, defense, and protection[68] and that in the early seventeenth century it was being assimilated as an effective metaphor in the precepts for self-integration, social positioning, and ethical fulfillment in the influential contemporary elaborations of Neo-Stoic ideals and discourse. It appears several times with these positive connotations in Lope's correspondence.[69] For example, in a letter to the Duke of Sessa, he describes his garden retreat in Madrid as a "rinconcillo," where his patron has heard him "tantas vezes . . . disputar esta philosophía del vivir quieto." More revealingly the philosopher Antonio López de Vega, whose *Paradoxas racionales* constitute one of the major testimonies to the appeal of Neo-Stoic doctrines in Spain, described his philosophical ideal in the following terms:

> Yo en el rincón de mi sucinta casa
> mi Eráclito i Demócrito examino,
> i lloro i río mi fortuna escasa.
> Borro, i enmiendo, i poco determino;
> que como sólo de ocuparme trato,
> no trato de llegar, amo el camino.

(In the corner of my sturdy little house I ponder my Heraclitus and Democritus, And I weep and laugh over my meager fortune. I blot and I emend, and I conclude little; for since I am concerned only with keeping busy, I do not try to arrive; I love the journey.)[70]

From the opening of the third act to the climactic banquet at its conclusion, the king speaks with an entirely new voice—the philosophical voice of the classical sage. He likens his nocturnal experience with Juan Labrador to the encounter of Alexander and Diogenes, an encounter in which the most powerful man in the world, a ruler whose life furnished examples both of heroism and wisdom and of the most frightening tyrannical failures, discovered a model being who, in his contentment with his *rincón*; the benefits of nature; and the rewards of inner fulfillment, personal autonomy, and moral integrity, appeared to represent the opposite of everything to which he as conqueror and pursuer of glory aspired. The anecdote was frequently recalled in humanist discussions of princes and politics, and one can easily imagine that the philosopher's famous rebuke of the emperor who stood between him and his sunlight had a particularly ironic appeal in an age noted for its spectacular solar metaphorics of royal aggrandizement. Like his descendant in Lope's stubborn peasant, Diogenes is in fact sublimely indifferent to the power of the principal myth of absolutism and eloquently aware of the fraudulence of its attractions and claims.

The primary action of *El villano en su rincón* can be viewed as a dramatic expansion of the classical anecdote. Whatever the psychological motives might be that one chooses to impute to Lope's troubled king, it is obvious that his irritation with Juan Labrador's refusal to make the effort to see him, his determination to visit the seemingly irascible and aloof rustic sage, his admiration for the philosophical wisdom in the *villano*'s indifference to regal power and glory, and his majestic display of the enormous dimensions of his kingdom in contrast to the shrunken spaces of the philosopher's *rincón* are all elements that evoke the legendary confrontation of Alexander and Diogenes. When, at the beginning of Act III, we note that the king, following his emergence from the *rincón*, has experienced an astonishing conversion and appropriated the discourse and the ideal of the sage—by "touching with his hand the gold of his value"—we recognize that Lope's work has in fact successfully articulated the classical anecdote's most elliptically insinuated but most fascinating aspect—the fusion of emperor and beggar, ruler and philosopher. From this moment on it becomes increasingly clear that the doubling process that has marked the relations of Juan Labrador and the king of France from the beginning will be a transference and ultimately an identification. The king recalls the mysterious encounter, his metamorphosis, and his bonding with the challenging double:

> Cuando en su rincón le vi;
> que ya por él y por mí
> pudiera decir mejor
> lo que de Alejandro Griego
> y Diógenes: el día
> que le vio, cuando tenía
> casa estrecha, sol por fuego,
> dijo que holgara de ser
> Diógenes, si no fuera
> Alejandro; y yo pudiera
> esto mismo responder,
> y con ocasión mayor,
> porque, a no ser Rey de Francia,
> tuviera por más ganancia
> que fuera Juan Labrador.

(When I saw him in his corner; and it would be more appropriate to say of our encounter what was said of Alexander and Diogenes: the day that the former saw him, when he had a cramped house, the sun for his fire, he said that if he were not Alexander, he would like to be Diogenes; and I could give the same reply and with an even greater cause, for, if I were not King of France, I would hold it more profitable to be Juan Labrador.) (176)[71]

In an earlier play, politically far less sophisticated and very different in its engagement with the institution of monarchy, *La quinta de Florencia,* Lope again employs a philosophical double to highlight the duties and perfections of a king. Disguised as a hunter, Alexander of the Medici secretly visits a "filósofo labrador," whose daughter Laura has been raped by one of his most beloved retainers, a victim of melancholy and erotic madness. The *villano* entertains him with an evening symposium in the "humilde cabaña" of his mill; vies with him in acts of courtesy; and offers, in a riddling interchange, several principles, each coordinated with a specific dish of the banquet and concerning just rule, virtue, and humility. The lessons in governing are accompanied by a chorus of peasants singing of the Roman heroine Lucrecia's legendary chastity and suicide and indirectly appealing to the "guest" for justice against tyranny. Like Juan Labrador's *rincón,* the pastoral kingdom is associated with cosmic harmony, as the "cítara del molino," the turning mill wheels, and the falling water produce a music that is echoed by birds, leaves, wind, and forest in the "divino acento" of a harmonious "contrapunto." In this utopian setting, the duke compares his experience with the classical encounter of Diogenes and Alexander and acknowledges that he needs to be educated by his host. The interaction of peasant-philosopher and idealized king is, however, basically celebrative rather than critical or philosophically dialectical. The latter remains a *retrato,* a portrait of perfection; an *espejo,* a mirror of exemplarity; and a splendid figure appearing in an equestrian portrait in the Medici palace. The "suprahuman" king, he dwells in a beautiful palace symbolizing justice and protection of the weak. He needs no instruction in order to recognize that the white flour "ornamenting" the doors of the run-down mill is purer ("más limpia") than the gold shining on the gates of César's *villa.* In its focus on aristocratic villainy, pride, rape, and the abuse of the lower class, *La quinta de Florencia* belongs to Lope's melodramatic, tightly focused, and swiftly plotted honor plays and is in fact fundamentally different from the subsequent *Villano en su rincón,* despite its resemblances in design and character relations. As such, it climaxes with the restoration of lost honor by a magnanimous ruler, whose lofty and somewhat abstract majesty is humanized through the discovery that the mistreatment of a daughter causes a pain that equalizes a peasant and a king. It is perfectly consistent with its positive approach to monarchy that, at another point, it celebrates the Medicean Alexander by attributing to him one of the most illustrious of the deeds of the Macedonian Alexander: the offer of Campaspe, the woman he loves, to the enthralled and suffering portraitist Apelles.[72]

In *El villano en su rincón,* immediately after his encounter with Juan Labrador, the transformed king goes on to make his most striking philosophical pronouncements. Citing Philemon, "filósofo de gran nombre," who expressed his wonder "al ver tan diferente el hombre," he reverses the accentuation of his earlier arguments maintaining the naturalness of the institution of monarchy and the cultic reverence for the royal figure as evidenced in the hierarchies of the animal world (the beasts naturally revere the lion as their ruler; the birds, the eagle), an argument universally proclaimed in medieval and Renaissance political treatises and familiar to all young princes (for example, Hamlet and Calderón's Constant Prince). Man is now celebrated as radically different from the beasts in his possession of "divine reason" and in his capacities for the free exercise of his will, moral differentiation, and—most interestingly in view of the nature of Juan Labrador's rejection of social conformity—individuality.[73] Intensely preoccupied up to this point with the distinctions of class, etiquette, and ceremony, he appears to have learned that what truly distinguishes human beings is quality of character and that a "labrador tan honrado" is in no way "unequal" to a well-intentioned marshal of France. His optimistic philosophy of man culminates in a sonnet celebrating the virtues of inner peace and freedom and denouncing *negotium*, the defining feature of the courtly world according to the conventional antithesis of court–country on which his confrontation of the peasant is founded. The sonnet is a close paraphrase of a philosophical fragment by Epictetus.

> La vida humana, Sócrates decía
> cuando estaba en negocios ocupada,
> que era un arroyo en tempestad airada,
> que turbio y momentáneo discurría.
> Y que la vida del que en paz vivía
> era como una fuente sosegada,
> que, sonora, apacible y adornada
> de varias flores, sin cesar corría.
> ¡Oh vida de los hombres diferente,
> cuya felicidad estima el bueno,
> cuando la libertad del alma siente!
> Negocios a la vista son veneno.
> ¡Dichoso aquel que vive como fuente,
> manso, tranquilo, y de turbarse ajeno!

(Socrates said that man's life, when it was spent in worldly business, was like a stream in a wild tempest, rushing turbidly and fitfully from moment to moment. And that the life of him who lived in peace was like a placid spring, which, sonorous, peaceful, and adorned by a variety of flowers, flowed continuously and evenly. Oh, how different is the life of men and the happiness that the good man holds in high esteem when he feels the soul's freedom!

Worldly affairs are poisons on sight. Happy is the man who lives as a smooth-flowing spring, gentle, tranquil, and free from all turbulence!) (178)[74]

The convergence of king, *villano*, and the Stoic philosophical tradition is particularly striking at this moment. Moreover, the sudden orchestration of fundamental Stoic doctrines and images — concerning, for example, tranquility, clarity of vision, spiritual freedom, divine reason, and the equality of human beings in virtue — makes it clear that the portrayal of the king's development in the play should be understood in the tradition of Stoic ethics and (to draw on Martha Nussbaum's recent work) its therapy of self-scrutiny and "awakening" of the soul and that the *rincón* of his spiritual cure should be recognized as having an imaginative connection with Seneca's famous description of the divine soul of a wise man as dwelling within a secluded forest, where the intertwining branches of towering ancient trees cast a shadowy, unfathomable veil of holiness about his existence and its rich inner depths.[75]

To recall Gracián's understanding of Francis I's experience in the world of the peasant, Lope's king has looked upon his double, the *villano*-sage, and, descending to the human level (*humanándose*), recovered the self and the clarity of vision that a king loses amid the splendor of his majesty and the turbulence of the *negotia* of the political realm.[76] From this moment on he displaces Juan Labrador as the controlling figure in the action, and his carefully planned acts can be understood as an effort to bring the world of the court and the awesome forces of regal authority into alignment with the ideal image of the peasant-sage and his pastoral order, which he has discovered in his sojourn in the other world. It is an order most notable for its underlying rationality, creatively controlled eros, and community integration. As a writer of pastoral, Lope is here finding his way to the deepest root of the pastoral literary tradition, the point at which its seemingly "alienated," "escapist" vision of perfection discloses itself paradoxically as in fact the ideal underlying its society's structures and an order that would represent the full realization of society's goals.[77]

THE KING'S DESCENT: A GLIMPSE OF TYRANNY

¿En qué laberinto he dado?

(In what labyrinth have I landed)?

—*The King of France*

At this point it is necessary to return to the second act and attempt to clarify another aspect of the king's descent into the other world of the *rincón*. It is to my mind the most difficult moment in a work that resists definitive interpretation in all sorts of ways. Anyone who involves himself in Lope scholarship quickly notes how unsatisfying the explanations have been. It seems that critical readers become reticent, uneasy, and standoffish when dealing with this disruptive moment.[78] At the same time it calls for commentary and clarification, because, quite simply, it forms the climax of the second act, and its kind of theatricality and violence is very intense—and very unusual in this philosophical and lyrical work. The shift of dramatic convention is more radical than in the surprising coda "appended" to Act I, which it parallels as a destabilizing, provocative conclusion. The scene is fleeting, as well as hallucinatory, and on a first viewing or reading, one's reaction may be to wonder whether it has actually occurred!

The entire sequence of scenes in Act II—with its initial dances beneath the erotically charged elm tree; its momentary, intense encounters of young lovers; its disguised king ("en cuerpo"), wandering and tying his horse in the dark woods; and its candlelight encounter of doubles—is suggestive of the dream world and its release of instinct. Situated in this context, the elliptical climactic scene might be viewed as a nightmarish plunge into the deepest reaches of the psyche, even as the action moves beyond all boundaries and differentiations into total darkness and chaos. In a hallucinatory atmosphere that appears to erode all firmly established formal divisions in the play, its two plots converge and effectively mingle and condense the erotic confusion of the developing *comedia de capa y espada* (cape and sword drama)—the secondary plot, centering on the ambitions and courtships of Juan Labrador's children—and the spiritual agitation that pervades the political-philosophical primary action.

The king startles us by unexpectedly crossing over generic boundaries—stepping, as it were, out of one literary system and into another, that designing the secondary plot—and assuming the role of the befuddled young courtly lover, the *galán*.[79] He discovers erotic rivals lurking amid the shadows, and he pursues a number of females, whose rapid, sequential appearance could easily be staged for surreal or phantasmic effects. They resist his advances disdainfully, insult him, and even threaten to slap him before vanishing into the darkness. As Juan Labrador's daughter Lisarda escapes from his grasp and angrily slams the door in his face, he finds himself trapped, blind, and disoriented in the total darkness of the labyrinths of an enchanted house. His words reveal a complete loss of control: "Aquesta ¿es casa encantada?/¿Qué es esto, Dios? ¿Dónde estamos?/¿Qué filosofía es ésa?/¿En qué laberinto he dado?/¿Cómo me he metido aquí?" (Is this an enchanted house? God, what is this? Where are we? What is this philosophy? In what labyrinth have I landed? How have I got myself here?) (161). One should of course note that in its fragmentary farcical elements, the scene represents a collapse of distinctions of tone separating the two generic systems of the play. To appreciate fully the peculiar humor in the girls' reaction of disgust at the disguised king of France's bedside manner and request that they pull off his boots—"Echese su porquería" (Go to bed with your boots on, you filthy pig [an amusing inversion of the form of polite address, "su señoría"])—one must understand that the play is in one sense a dramatic study—and quite a critical study—of the nature of royal charisma, etiquette, and the *arcana imperii*; that a contemporary political theorist such as Quevedo could actually write, "Majestad tienen los reyes hasta en los pies; digno es de reverencia su calzado" (Kings have majesty even in their feet; their footwear is worthy of reverence); and that, as Maravall points out, the figure of the king in the Spanish theater is generally a being who radiates "a supernatural effluvium that paralyzes any act of violence against [his person]."[80]

To recall once again Gracián's anecdote, Lope, in presenting the comic ineffectuality of the amorous advances of the king in the other world, emphasizes "lo humano," here literally dissociated from the official dressing and portraiting of the quasi-divine royal figure. As a seducer, the king makes his "all too human" moves in the gestural language of majesty. To appreciate the humor in Lisarda's recoil at the king's condensed, "ceremonial" sexual advances—the offer of the royal hand and the honor of removing his boots—one should recall the sacred aura of the monarch's feet, the shoes, the spurs, and the site of ritual homage and submission attested in traditional European coronation ceremonies. For example, an *ordo coronationis* of Louis VIII at Rheims Cathedral in 1246 reveals that before the central moment of unction and crowning, certain dignitaries administer a solemn rite of dubbing (*adoubement*). The grand chamberlain places the king's feet in the royal slippers—"les chausses de soie couleur d'hyacinthe entièrement brodées de lis d'or" (the hyacinth colored silk slippers entirely embroidered with golden lilies), which have been transported, with all the other regalia, from the Abbey of St. Denis—while the Duke of Burgundy attaches the golden spurs.[81] Like several other "all too human" aspects of the portrayal of the king in the first two acts—for example, the bearded "mancebo rojo," whom the incredulous peasants compare unfavorably to the bust of the Roman emperor—this intentional departure from the appropriate *gravedad* of "toda materia . . . cuando toca a la Majestad,"[82] is reversed in Act III, when Juan Labrador enters the palace and kneels at the feet of the monarch.

The effect of the king's sudden transformation becomes all the more startling and surreal as he unexpectedly steps into even another conventional role, that of the traditional "erotic hunter" of folklore, evoked in the peasants' song beneath the elm tree—the *serranilla*—earlier in the act and appears to violate the logic of plot by displacing Otón, the *capa y espada galán* of the secondary plot, who, lost in a "confused abyss and labyrinth of love," has been pursuing Lisarda and has made an appointment to meet with her secretly on this night. Our initial assimilation of Otón to the figure of the folksong's analogy is strengthened by the fact that both the hunter and the aristocrat refer to the object of their erotic pursuits as a *serafín* and that Lisarda rises to dance as the singer reaches the point of the *serrana*'s appearance in his narrative. The *serranilla* itself, with the characteristic concentrated dream imagery of folksong, presents a vision of hunting; violent sexual desire; betrayal; loss of self-control and direction; a search for shelter amid a dark, labyrinthine landscape; a forbidden world of transgressive eros; and a loss of identity in the complete surrender to desire. It is clear that the confusion that the king experiences in his descent into the night world of the "labyrinth" of the "enchanted house" of the *rincón* should be understood as reactualizing the condition of this dream double, the wayward knight, as he crosses the threshold in the crepuscular world of his illicit desire and his perdition.

> Olvidado se ha de sí;
> los perros siguen las sendas
> entre hayas y peñas mil.
> El caballo va a su gusto,
> que no le quiere regir.
>
> Perdido se han en el monte
> con la mucha oscuridad;
> al pie de una parda peña
> el alba aguardando están.

(He has forgotten himself, the dogs follow the trails. Among a thousand beech trees and crags his horse goes where it wishes to; for he does not wish to guide it. . . . They have got lost in the woods amid the increasing darkness; at the foot of a dark cliff they are waiting for the dawn.) (138–139)[83]

In conclusion, at this decisive moment in the play, when generic, formal, and tonal logic appear to be breaking down and the reader or viewer finds his control threatened by an entirely unexpected collapse into incoherence, the king—and the state, which he of course embodies so spectacularly through most of the play—are menaced with disintegration. It is the moment of crisis, as the king finds himself lost between the nocturnal world of lawless instinct and pure will of his dark double—the hunter—and the daylight world of rationality of Juan Labrador, the shepherd-gardener, the *mayordomo*, the "steward of God and nature"—the true self he has forgotten. At this point Lope's play is revealing, through the dream imagery of its songs and festivals—songs that have taken us from the protective elm tree of the forest village and the channeled, centered vitality of its dances and symposia to the forbidden landscape of the mountain wilderness and its disintegrative, centrifugal instinct—and through a corresponding dramatic action, the unbinding of a king from law. In doing so, it is affirming the commonplace notion of contemporary political theory that the ruler who is truly *ab-solutus*, released from all constraints and checks, is a tyrant.

Once again, as in so many other moments of this dense poetic drama, the doctrines, symbols, and emblems of contemporary absolutist political writings are visible in the background. One need only look to the official portraiture of the time—for example, in Velázquez's works—and its recurrent depictions of a ruler controlling and directing the powerful energies of the horse.[84] To take an example from celebrative courtly drama, one might mention Calderón's *Loa* to the *auto El nuevo palacio del Retiro*, where the figure of Philip IV is revealed, mounted triumphantly on a horse and analogized with the Old Testament God of Habakuk: "Thou didst ride upon these horses and thy chariots of salvation."[85]

More revealing for the effects of Lope's association of the king and horseman are the political theorist Saavedra Fajardo's discussions of rationality as a necessary constraint on royal power. He insists that the prince is obligated to "tame and bridle the young horse of power." In his elaborate development of the traditional conceit, he describes the figure of the tyrant as the ruler who incarnates the energy of pure will released (in this sense also *absolutus*) from the creative direction of instinct by reason. In vain does he attempt to control the energy of his horse with the "bit of the will." He is the victim of caprice, and his irrationality is condemned for its moral consequences and for its interferences in the proper functioning of the rationally ordered state.

> Menester es el *freno* de la razón, las *riendas* de la política, la *vara* de la justicia y la escuela del valor, *fijo siempre el príncipe sobre los estribos de la prudencia. No ha de ejecutar todo lo que le antoja, sino lo que conviene, y no ofende a la piedad.* . . . Ni ha de creer el príncipe que es absoluto su poder, sino sujeto al bien público y a los intereses de su Estado. Ni que es inmenso, sino limitado y expuesto a ligeros accidentes. . . . No está más seguro el príncipe que más puede, sino el que con más razón puede.

> (The *bridle* of reason is necessary, the *reins* of politics, the *staff* of justice, the school of bravery, the prince *firmly fixed always in the stirrups of prudence. He is not to enact whatever strikes his fancy, but rather whatever is proper and gives no offense to piety.* . . . The prince should not believe that his power is absolute but rather subordinate to the public good and to the interests of his state. That

it is not immense, but rather limited and exposed to the slightest of accidents.
. . . The most secure prince is not the one who is able to do the most, but rather
the one who is able to act with most reason.)[86]

In the light of such remote doctrines and preoccupations the most puzzling
elements of Lope's opaque climax of Act II become transparent—the unexpected, thoroughly *capricious* behavior of the king; the odd gestural language of
majesty in his sexual advances; the offer of the royal hand and the request that
the presumably honored and compliant object of his desire take off his boots;
the concentrated, emblematic character of the confrontation of master and subject; and the nearly instantaneous disintegration of the scene into darkness and
chaos. To draw on Blandine Kriegel's recent revisionist interpretation of the origins and historical role of the state, the king has suddenly violated the fundamental freedom that the absolutist state rose to protect—the right of a person
not to have his/her body appropriated by the sovereign power.[87] In *On Laws and
God the Lawgiver*, Francisco Suárez wrote: "In the nature of things all men are
born free; so that, consequently, no person has political jurisdiction over another
person, even as no person has dominion over another."[88]

As I have pointed out above, the obsession with tyranny in early modern political theory and dramatic representations of political situations and their frequent definitions of the tyrant as lustful and the archetypal despotic act as rape
are indications of this fundamental "statist" function.[89] The tyrant's act is a violation of the boundaries, laws, and rights dictated by rationality, and as such, it
plunges the state into lawlessness and threatens the universal rational order with
a return to chaos. At the same time, I would suggest that the obsession of the
contemporary imagination with the destructive effects of tyranny—evident, as
noted above, in the great political drama of Shakespeare and Calderón—reflects
an anxiety and a deep pessimism arising from a radical alteration in the foundations of sovereign power and its self-regulating laws—from a cosmic, *metaphysically* rational model given to man "from above" to a man-created "state," a flexible entity grounding itself in the adaptive resources of a purely *human* reason
and easily vulnerable to destabilization by the irrationality that is all too evident
in the human condition.[90]

From the depths of the lawless will (viz., the "fiera condición" of Calderón's
Segismundo, the "darker purposes" of Shakespeare's King Lear), the destructive
impulses of lust and wrath are ever ready to erupt and manifest themselves in
the paradigmatic tyrannical acts of rape, warfare, waste, capricious exercises of
power, and self-deification. Lope frequently associates the new "state reason"
and the fashionable political virtue "mixed prudence" with lust and treachery

in his dramatic world. In his *Comedia de Bamba*, the "prudent" usurper Paulo rises to challenge Lope's ideal king, the innocent *villano* Bamba, and introduces himself immediately as the tyrant: "No hay mayor *gusto* que ser/Señor solo y absoluto,/Que es grande cosa el poder" (There is no pleasure greater than to be Lord, alone and absolute, for power is a great thing). He issues his first command: "Vengan damas, que esto quiero; Gástese mi Estado entero/En deleites y placeres. . . . ¿Mujeres han de faltar? ¡Vayan un criado y coche,/Y podrá algunas buscar. . . . Andar, andar!" (Bring on ladies, for this is what I want; may the wealth of my entire state be spent in delights and pleasures. . . . Are there any women around? Send a servant and a coach to find some. . . . Go! Go!)[91]

As for a growing awareness of the *insubstantiality, theatricality,* and consequent *illegitimacy* of a man-created state and the anxieties rooted in this consciousness, one should note the increasing fascination in contemporary political theory, particularly that reflecting the impact of the Machiavellian tradition, with opinion, reputation, illusion, deceit, "mixed prudence," and rhetoric in the creation and successful maintenance of the state.[92] A revealing emblematic expression of this awareness can be found in Saavedra Fajardo's depiction of reputation as a marble Corinthian column sustaining, as its decorative capital, the royal crown and his discussion of the way in which the "foundational" column can easily reveal an inherent flimsiness and disintegrate unless firmed up by a "ligero espíritu encendido en la opinión de todos" (light spirit fired by public opinion). In the royal majesty nothing is more forceful than respect, which "nace de la admiración y del temor, y de ambos la obediencia" (is born of wonder and fear, and of both, obedience is born). If the latter is lacking, the "dignidad" of the ruler, founded as it is in the "opinión ajena," cannot survive, and "queda la púrpura real más como señal de burla que de grandeza" (the royal purple becomes a sign of ridicule rather than of grandeur).[93] A more striking hint of underlying emptiness is discernible in Saavedra Fajardo's representation of the king's power as a lion's skin, hung on a peg as if it were a disguise in a theater's dressing room.[94] The whole state is viewed as a theater of power, but there is a trace of anxiety that, as in a theater, a brilliant and imposing illusion might be momentarily creating order within an enveloping chaos before vanishing in the emptiness behind a fallen curtain.[95]

While Saavedra Fajardo ultimately remains true to the traditional commitments to a belief in metaphysical and cosmic foundationalism and moral absolutes in his incorporation of the age's new political science, such hints lose all ambiguity in the searing insights of Gracián's visions of political emptiness. The secretive prince rules through the dazzling public performance of his charlatan, Machiavelli, before an ecstatic mob, which he unites through the powerful manipulative effects of a drama of cruelty, the scapegoating of an outsider. Crouched behind the curtains of his palace window, he hides the coiling asymmetries and chaotic shapes of his real body and silently observes the spectacular successes of his "rhetorically constructed" state, until he is suddenly exposed in Artemia's mirror of truth.[96]

As I attempt to argue in the following pages, Lope's *Villano en su rincón* can be seen as a reaffirmation of the traditional conception of the state and its metaphysical foundations in a rationally constructed order of things, a "book of the world" to be read and imitated by its rational inhabitant. In keeping with his early role in the play, the king turns confidently to this book to offer Juan Labrador a lesson in reading its *visibilia:* the world of the creatures reveals the principle of hierarchy. Each genus has its "king"; the birds have the eagle; the animals, the lion, etc. Insofar as it introduces in its final act regal deceptiveness, manipulation, threatened cruelty, and "awesome" iconography and rhetoric as an educational process in the service of this ideal, *El villano en su rincón* can be said to incorporate Machiavellian insights—for example, "salutary cruelty" and dissimulation—into political experience and to dramatize their proper separation, as benign methods of governance, from the abuses that were so spectacularly displayed in the attacks, literary or direct, on Machiavelli and his "satanic" politics during the age.[97]

THE KING'S THEATER:
THE HUMANIZATION OF THE ROYAL CULT

No soy Diomedes: yo nunca convido
Para matar; que regalaros quiero.
¡Hola!, venga la mesa.

(I am not Diomedes: I never invite in order to kill; I wish to feast you. Come! Bring the table.)

—*The King of France*

In the economy of the drama's depiction of the formation of a king and a clarification of the nature of his power, the climax of the second act represents the monarch's most severe test, his crisis, and it terminates as abruptly and as unexpectedly as it begins—in a moment of awakening, a *desengaño*, as if he were returning from a world where, in the words of his interlocutor, Otón, "anda todo de revuelta" (everything is topsy-turvy) (164). He immediately announces that something miraculous—akin to an alchemical metamorphosis—has occurred in his encounter with the peasant ("toqué con la mano el oro de su valor,/cuando en su rincón le vi") (I touched with my hand the gold of his value, when I saw him in his corner) (176), and from this point on, throughout the final act, the voice of the sage is occasionally audible in his pronouncements. His opening speeches in Act III, which invoke the classical philosophers Philemon and Diogenes, reverse all his previous affirmations of the principle of hierarchy: the uniformity of the animal world in fact points up by contrast the striking variety of the human world, where the principle of individuality prevails and any differentiations in the value of its members are based on their free exercise of "la divina razón" in moral choice. There is a more fundamental hierarchy than that manifest in political and social divisions, and the possibility of ascent within it is available to all human beings. The point is driven home as the king, after acknowledging Juan Labrador's "honor" and equality with his marshal, proceeds to recall the encounter of Alexander the Great and Diogenes.

The turning point of the play is marked by an abrupt return from the night world of Act II and Juan Labrador's forest dwelling. Nearly all the following action takes place in the daylight world of the court. Like so many other elements in the play of parallels and reversals, the structure of Act III duplicates that of Act II, beginning with a rustic festival and concluding with an emblematic philosophical banquet providing enlightening nourishment for a guest in an alien world. The opening ceremony sets the tone for all that follows. It is a harvest festival centering on the olive tree and its fruit. The magical elm tree of erotic freedom of the preceding act and its vision of a chaotic wilderness of solitude and its song of unrestrained desire, impatient pursuit, and erotic consumation are replaced here by the olive grove; the daylight world of a community harvest; productive labor; the joy in the containment of nature's energy; the attuning of human life to its natural temporal rhythms; and a musical celebration of the beneficent fruit of civilization, peace, health, and ritual. "¡Ay, fortuna!/cógeme esta aceituna!" (Pray kind fortune! Pluck this olive for me!). As it turns out, the time is ripe for the harvest, even though the olive is a "fruta en madurar tan larga." And with the harvest, time offers itself for joy and pleasure. "Esténse las aceitunas/por un rato entre sus hojas,/y templemos las congojas/de algún disgusto importunas;/ansí Dios os dé placer" (Let the olives remain for a while among their leaves, and let us soften the sorrows of some misfortune that torments us; and so may God give you pleasure) (165–166). The chorus anticipates the spectacular comedic climax that will follow, with its multiple marriages, the announcement of Costanza's pregnancy—and, of course, the overcoming of the multiple oppositions articulated in action and theme throughout the work.

At this moment the king's role suddenly shifts noticeably toward center stage, where, stepping forth from the forest shadows and the distancing cover of his royal vestments, he displaces Juan Labrador as protagonist and preceptor, seizes control of the action, and spectacularly assumes the role of the dramaturgic king and hierophant of the absolutist state. If up to this point the play is primarily concerned with the education of the prince, from the moment of the monarch's unanticipated transformation at the conclusion of Act II, its dramatic movement abruptly reverses direction. It is now for the subject to learn and the prince to teach. The relation of doubles becomes reciprocal; a dialectic unfolds in an exchange of equals. The drama moves toward the establishment of an equilibrium rather than the celebration of a triumph. When it reaches its dramatic conclusion, all simple questions of masters and subalterns, all crude oppositions, will have been decisively transcended. At the same time the complexities increase noticeably, as the thematic focus shifts from the world of wisdom and morality to the world of power and politics, a world in which aristocrats, peasants, and "philosopher" find themselves baffled by the movements and ellipses of a secretive, manipulative, omnipotent, but ultimately benign and rational, king and state. The riddling exchange of emblems, beginning in the inscription that the king discovers on Juan Labrador's sepulcher in the village church early in the play, becomes more concentrated and more enigmatic, even as comprehension and explication shift from peasant to king. The metatheatrical constructs and effects, already prominent in Act II in Juan Labrador's "performance" before his masked spectator at his table, become more intricate and unsettling in what is clearly the king's act.

In its opening scenes the king begins enacting a play of his own composition, directed not only at us, but also at his palace audience, the other members of the play world he inhabits, none of whom appears to understand the exact nature of royal power. In other words, both the aristocrat Otón, who is in love with Lisarda, and the philosophical-peasant, Juan Labrador, suddenly reveal themselves as "unevolved" political subjects who think of state sovereignty in terms of archaic feudal, theocentric, and imperial conceptions of rule and obedience. The subject belongs as possession to his lord, whether emperor or suzerain—or tyrant. The will of the ruler regarding the subject's life, body, property, honor, or punishment is unquestionable. There are no limitations on his royal prerogatives and his imperial pleasure. Lope's play confronts the fundamental issue of the developing new political philosophy as it attempted to come to grips with the seemingly ineluctable striving of the nation-state to concentrate all of its enormous power in the will of the sovereign. As audience to the king's secretive machinations, we too are drawn along in the characters' frightening misinterpretations and share their unfounded expectations of catastrophe. All helpless spectators of the king's play fear the worst in what turns out to be no more than a thoroughly justifiable lesson concerning how royal power limits itself. It is certainly fitting in a play so obsessed with the act of gazing and reacting to visual imagery that it should climax in such striking interactions of audiences, performers, and dramatic illusions. The concluding "monarchical *auto*," the king's intentionally awesome theater of power, is in reality a subordinate part of the king's more profound educational theater of power, which includes as participants his manipulated spectators, Otón and Juan Labrador, each of whom must learn to reflect on what is being shone forth and to see beyond the letter. At the final remove of this theater within theater within theater is, of course, Lope's play, before which his contemporary (and modern) audiences view a spectacle that, among other things, is about how dramatic and rhetorical spectacles of monarchical authority are correctly and incorrectly to be viewed.

In itself Act III could easily justify a reading of the play such as Bataillon's: a "morality play dedicated to the glory of the monarchy." It is an impressive concentration of many of the fundamental conceptions and visual symbols of what I have referred to above as the cult and ideology of royal power. One is inclined to see it as an expanded dramatic articulation of the message and effect that the concluding ceremonial play, with its masked figures, its sequence of unveilings of icons and magical documents, and its participating king-hierophant, is to communicate instantaneously through symbolic condensation. In a play that thematizes the effects and powers of visibility in the epoch of the Counter-Reformation and absolutism, it is tempting to understand its mechanics and its message regarding the mysteries of the sovereign will in terms of Calderón's famous remark about the *auto*'s powers to communicate through visual representation realities that "razones no alcanzan a explicar ni comprender" (reasons do not manage to explain or comprehend) and his insistence that something seen has far more force than something heard.[98]

Like the omnipotent God of the Old Testament, Juan Labrador's king imposes mysterious trials on his subjects; arbitrarily demands sacrifices; intentionally provokes their fear; and ultimately rewards them for obedience, self-humiliation, pious adoration, and humility. Following the ordeal, he, like the sun, displays himself fully to every corner of the kingdom. In its triumphant injunction that the subject look upon the monarch, the play likens the latter to the God of mystic theology, endowing his worshippers with being itself. "¡Dichoso el que alcanza a ver/del sol del Rey solo un rayo! . . . Como sin el sol el hombre/no es hombre, es estatua, es piedra" (Happy is the man who manages to see a single ray from the sun that is the face of the king. As without such illumination he is not a man, he is no more than a lifeless statue, a stone) (190). Lisarda asks the king to fill her with his divine light in her wondrous metamorphosis into a lady of the court. In what appears to be an unintegrated scene, dictated by historical circumstances surrounding the play's composition and performance, the Admiral hails the king, as he arranges the royal wedding of his sister to an embattled king—clearly Philip IV of Spain—as a "príncipe perfecto."[99] On the surface the final act looks as if it might be more concerned with celebrating than with explaining, with overwhelming than with enlightening. It appears to be a kind of dramatic *exemplum,* a concrete representation of the message and effect that the climactic didactic masque and its iconic gifts are to communicate directly to the refractory subject. The regalia define the essentials of the official king—the scepter, the mirror, and the sword—an authority that binds vertically all strata of the kingdom, an exemplary model for all subjects who would perfect themselves morally, a power that is always guided and limited by justice.

While the "two theaters," as declarations of royal power, do in fact mutually reinforce one another, the nature of their interactions and parallels is ambiguous, disquieting, and oblique. The resulting explanations and qualifications of doctrines reach deeper into all that underlies them than the abstract formulations of doctrinaire political theorists. Lope's dramatic exploration of monarchy through the ingenuities of a double portrait leaves us with what is in effect a subtle and revealing refraction of the brilliant and blinding light of the mirror of majesty.

For all the power in its images of monarchic aggrandizement, the final act is, nevertheless, more striking for its numerous gestures and statements of fear and submission. Much of its dramatic tension is centered on questions of tyranny and rises from the puzzling movements of an inscrutable sovereign, whose mysterious machinations raise suspicions that we are in fact witnessing the unchecked will of a tyrant capriciously manipulating and frightening his subjects for personal profit and sexual gratification. As we eventually discover, the king's performative maneuvers are calculated to resolve the central problem of each of the two plots.

Shortly before the concluding *auto político* the king engages in a brief act for the benefit of Otón. The former has clearly been attracted by Lisarda's beauty, and he is aware that his marshal is in love with her and fears him as a rival. Without revealing his intentions to anybody, he summons Lisarda to the court to serve the *infanta,* announces his decision to bestow a title on her brother, and hints that he will reward her father for his *discreción* and *valor.* As Otón is stricken with pangs of jealousy, the king admits that he is playing a game with him, not unlike the one, as we later realize, that he has been playing with Juan Labrador throughout the final act. The point of the game, aside from the suspense, dramatic ironies, and ingenuities of a conventional *comedia de enredo* (comedy of intrigue) situation, is a lesson for character and audience alike about the necessary restraints on royal power, a lesson that recalls the contemporary political theorists' familiar distinction between king, bound by reason, and tyrant, "unbound" — *absolutus* — and free to act arbitrarily.

Otón appears to misunderstand everything, as he can only interpret the king's actions and words as indicating that he intends to enjoy Lisarda. He assumes that it is the king's prerogative to do whatever he wishes with his "possessions." Otón can find comfort only in the fact that the king's act, because of his unique rank in the hierarchy of honor, will bring him no infamy. Unknowingly, he poses one of the key questions that the play addresses: are there any limitations on the will of the absolute monarch?

> Que el Rey ¿por qué obligación
> No ha de procurar su gusto?

(As for the King, under what obligation is he not to take his pleasure?)

At this point the king finally enlightens the ingenuous aristocrat. There is never any ground for fear when power is guided by reason.

> Nunca al poder tengas miedo
> Cuando es discreto el poder. (193–194)

The words contain a precise definition of the limits of monarchical authority and anticipate the disclosure of the true meaning of the climactic spectacle, which follows immediately.[100]

Much more important in the king's theater of the third act is the extended interplay of the two protagonists of the primary plot. Initially Juan Labrador appears to be continuing in his role as preceptor, instructing his royal master as in Act II. An exemplary vassal, he offers him his wealth and his children, but as he does so, he includes an emblem, which appears to represent enigmatically the proper relation of subject to king: the sheep with a knife attached to its throat, offering itself to the shepherd. As in the scene in the church that begins the exchange of emblems, the king is once again puzzled by the riddles of the sylvan world: "Pues no es sin causa, algún sentido tiene" (There must be some cause for this, it must have a meaning).[101] The ruler seems to be testing the loyalty of his subject, and when the latter agrees to send his children to the court, succumbs to grief, and foresees the "decline of his days," it is evident that the dramatic action must at this point be understood in terms of Biblical sacrificial traditions, its paradigms of God and worshipper, and the virtues of self-dispossession, obedience, patient submission to an unquestionable divine will, and the kind of endurance and humility that contemporary Neo-Stoics and ascetic Christians celebrated in Job. "Aunque me mate, en él esperaré" (Although he may kill me, in Him shall I place my hope).[102] As a political being, Juan Labrador bases his conception of the relation of ruler and subject on the darkest models of Christian theological absolutism, Roman imperial theology, and the crudest practices of feudalism.[103] The unbound will of the supreme authority has the unquestionable power of life and death over the subject. The latter is in effect enslaved, his body and property to be disposed of at the pleasure of the master.[104]

The king appears to remain baffled by the riddle, and as he prepares his climactic theater of royal instruction for the peasant, he requests that the latter provide a clarifying exegesis. Juan explains that his symbolic gift expresses the obedience that the vassal owes his king and adds that the latter can "cut whenever it pleases him." The king shows no sign of understanding the offer's implications and instead proceeds to present the first of his climactic emblems of instruction, a panoramic description of his immense empire. In the enumeration of countries, cities, peoples, wealth, armies, and vassals, he reminds his guest that its territories—unlike Juan's *rincón*—are gigantic and that the responsibilities of governing them and overseeing them are endless. His philosophical antagonist immediately sees the point and assumes the worst—that he will receive an exemplary punishment. Once again he offers his throat to the royal blade:

> Señor, mi error conozco; digno he sido
> de la muerte; quitad a aquel cordero
> el cuchillo del cuello, al mío os pido
> que trasladéis el merecido acero.

(Lord, I recognize my error. I am worthy of death; I ask you to remove the knife from that lamb's neck and apply its steel blade to my own, which deserves it.) (198)

In the ambiguities of such elliptical, imagistic communication, the play momentarily evokes, in addition to disturbing sacrificial motifs of Old Testament Christianity, the darkest kind of theatrical strategies of arousing awe, suspense, stupefaction, and fear that one can find in the precepts of Machiavelli for effective governance.[105] The motif of fear continues to sound as Juan Labrador trembles before the opening of the symbolical plates of the king's banquet, and it is intensified in a chorus of peasants who give expression to their own terror at the prospect of royal cruelty. The figures of legendary tyrants and their unfortunate dinner guests loom in the background—Diomedes of Thrace feeding the latter to his ferocious horses, Dionysius seating Damocles beneath the dangling sword. Such images might support a reading of the play of the type we find in Valdivielso's recreation according to the schemas of divine retribution and theological absolutism. At this point it turns out that the king is a better interpreter of enigmas than Juan Labrador, disavowing any association with the classical tyrants and their demonic banquets, seating his guest of honor at the head of the table, and supervising the climaxes of both his and Lope's plays. In doing so, he rejects his antagonist's exegesis of the disturbing emblematic riddle.

Although the king is initially puzzled by Juan Labrador's enigma, the fact is that a very different meaning was available in numerous contemporary political theories and their emblematic representation. For example, Ribadeneira writes that the king is the law, the head, and the soul—the life-giver—of the commonwealth. The tyrant is its "knife, the executioner and tormenter." "The king seeks the best men of his realm, to give them the most honored responsibilities and duties." The tyrant "abhors nothing more than a serious, free, and virtuous man who can advise or criticize him." At the climax of his treatise, Ribadeneira invokes the figure of the shepherd as the model of the ruler and opposes him to the tyrant. His words recall Juan Labrador's riddling emblem and point to its most essential imaginative function in Lope's play—the identification of the king and the *villano:* "The duty of the true prince is the duty of the shepherd, to instruct, to govern, to defend, to fatten the flock, to shear them, and not to skin them."[106] The looming threat of bloodshed and violence that heightens the suspense of Lope's denouement is even clearer if we turn to Saavedra Fajardo's arguments. The true king is the responsible steward—the *mayordomo*—of the kingdom's resources, using them well; husbanding them prudently; and, despite his absolute power, exacting tribute with moderation. Close to nature and consequently in contact with the *true* "razón de estado," the shepherd heeds its rational directives and dedicates himself to "la conservación y aumento del ganado y de la cultura" (the conservation and increase of the flock). He too must approach his subjects with the knife, but he does so "con tal consideración, que ni le saca la sangre, ni le deja tan rasa la piel, que no pueda defenderse del frío y del calor" (with such consideration that he neither draws their blood nor leaves their skin so bare that it has no defense against the cold and heat).[107]

An indication of the familiarity of this image and the conception of monarchy that it represents is the fact that it had already achieved popularization through the emblem books of the period. The very enigma that, in Lope's contrived scene, initially baffles the king had appeared in Nicolaus Reusner's *Emblemata* (1581). It depicts a shepherd holding a knife at a lamb's throat beneath a motto declaring that the good shepherd shears but does not skin the sheep. Its commentary compares the shepherd with the good king, who strives to protect and enrich his subjects, knowing that he benefits from their prosperity.[108] In view of such doctrines, Juan Labrador's emblematic knife, presented innocently as a sign of abject submission, should be understood as the demonic inversion of the monarch's iconic sword of justice, displayed shortly thereafter at the concluding banquet. It becomes in fact the most powerful and the most dramatically articulated of the numerous motifs of tyranny sounding throughout Act III and leading suspensefully to its concluding comedic reversal and resolution.

A look at another of Lope's romantic comedies of kings and *villanos* is instructive at this point. *El rey por semejanza* presents the ideal portrait of a king as a systematic reversal of an initial concentrated dramatic anatomy of the tyrant—a metamorphosis from "Nero to Trajan." Here Lope similarly employs the strategy of the double—peasant and monarch—but he elaborates it in an imaginative development of the twins theme of traditional comedy. The play begins with three dense pages of abominable tyrannical acts. A frenzied king of Asiria, Antíoco, burns with lust for a servant woman, impatiently demands a horse for his hunt, abuses his servants and retainers, and beats his protesting queen. Lost in the deep forest while breathlessly pursuing a stag, he is slain by the queen's champion. At this point a *villano*, who happens to resemble the tyrant perfectly, emerges from the woods and expresses a desire to be king. The remainder of the play reviews the horrific political acts of the tyrant in a series of ceremonial scenes—for example, audiences, embassies, and tribunals. We discover corruption and collusion in the king's relations with the *privado*; excessive taxation of the grandees, who, in the despotic flow of power, in turn tax their vassals mercilessly; refusal to pay tithes to the church (Asiria is apparently a Christian kingdom); excommunication by the church; insensitivity and miserliness in the ruler's treatment of loyal and suffering veterans; the assertion of "absolute rule" in his rape of helpless virgins; and disastrous foreign policy decisions.

The *villano* king, the "new man," claims to be the real king, explaining that lost, he spent two nights in the forest hut of a peasant before finding his way back to the palace—an ingenious development of the conversion experience of Gracián's folkloric anecdote. He confronts all of "his" tyrannical failures and, as the wisest of kings, "corrects" each of them, crowning a series of glorious acts with an epically celebrated victory in war over the menacing Great Sultan of Egypt. Moreover, he "educates the young prince," who, spoiled by his tyrannical father, has been caught in bed with a palace lady. Despite the queen's pleading, he, as always, "does his duty" and, "as kings must always do," "obeys the law" and arrests the youth.[109] All of this is spiced with amusing theatrical moments in the *imbroglios* brought about by the twins theme. The queen is terribly confused as to whether the king is or is not her presumably dead husband, and as she finds herself falling in love with him in his goodness, she becomes victimized by a comic conflict between her desire that he be both the *villano* in his goodness and her former husband in his higher social class. In his mastery of theatrics and his skillful use of "salutary fear," the *villano* ruler resembles the king in *El villano en su rincón*. To educate the refractory grandees, spoiled by the tyrant that they supported, he erects a frightening scaffold and plans their execution. When they complain in fear, he tells them that he is using their own methods of terror to teach them how unjust they are in overtaxing their subjects and compelling their payments by holding "the knife to the throat" of their vassals (513).

As the king in *El villano en su rincón* assumes control of the theatrical elements of the plot, we begin to realize—with some relief—that the interaction of peasant and king at the heart of the play's dramatic design is becoming even more paradoxical than was evident at the conclusion of the second act; that the terms of the initial antithesis have reversed, so to speak; and that the king has now become the instructor of his subject in what is ultimately a complex and symmetrical exchange, an exercise in mutual enlightenment that is consistent with the theatrically orchestrated dissonances and harmonies of the denouement. In terms of the Stoic ethical doctrines and imaginative conceptions underlying the relationship, one can say that at this point it falls to the king-preceptor to remind the peasant, whom he now addresses repeatedly as *pariente* and *compañero*, that the firmly centered self of the autonomous human being is in fact the center of a series of concentric circles extending through immediate family and friends outwards to society, countrymen, and the entire human race and that the ethically mature individual strives to reduce the distances separating circles and to look upon himself as a member of a single universal family.[110] One might go so far as to say that the feudal, patriarchal conception of family—so frequently invoked as a foundational model by early theorists of the state—with its emphasis on power, dominion, and hierarchy, is superseded by the Stoic image of family as a body of equals united in friendship. Seneca's words have a particular appropriateness for the ultimate communitarian direction of Lope's dialectic: "Non sum uni angulo natus, patria mea totus hic mundus est" (I am not born for one corner, my country is this entire world).[111]

From this moment to the end, the king should be seen as the dramaturgic master of the theatrical politics of the absolutist state. However, we should note that his theater, in a departure from Saavedra Fajardo's recommendations and the pragmatic Machiavellian traditions behind them, exploits illusion—not to blind, overwhelm, or *turbar*, but rather to teach, illuminate, and enable its audience to see with renewed vision. In Act III the king is in full control of himself, and he assumes full control of Lope's play. As we have seen, he arranges a complex set of enigmas and metatheatrical constructions to enlighten his subjects—and, of course, the audience—precisely on the real meaning of the mysteries of monarchy, and he directs the drama toward its overcoming of the multiple oppositions articulated throughout the work: philosopher-king, peasant-king, commoner-aristocrat, poor-rich, young generation–old generation, French-Spanish, Moor-Christian, *aldea*-court, *rincón*-palace, private-public, individual-community, barbarity-civility, inner-outer, spirit-letter, and nature-artifice. The full clarification comes with the final scenes, where the king ceremoniously displays his nearly inconceivable power, considered in its concrete territorial extension, only to remind his terrified subject that the mightiest king labors under an obligation, that he is not free to pursue his *gusto*, and that power is never to be feared when it is founded in reason (*discreción*).

The climactic convocation of all subjects to the king's table turns out to be not a fearfully anticipated ritual of judgment or sacrifice, a demonic banquet of Diomedes of Thrace; it is not an intimidating imposition of a power through the idolatrous display of the insignia of the majesty. To use Juan Labrador's words, it is a ceremony not of blinding but rather of illumination—a distinction that is crucial in this play about seeing correctly. The festive sharing of food, drink, and song becomes a second philosophical symposium, compelling understanding through enigma, commentary, and philosophical song.

Bataillon insists on looking at this moment through the stabilizing focus of Valdivielso's theological reconstruction of the scene, where the protagonist observes a horrific equestrian figure of God's justice approaching his stuffed effigy as it dangles hopelessly above a pile of skulls. The grisly landscape of Golgotha displaces the luminous *rincón*. Like the good thief, Juan Labrador can do no more than helplessly await a redemptive gesture from the cross. The emphasis on his fear becomes nearly overwhelming: "Temo en el profundo abismo,/el verme forçado al remo,/Temo, ¿pero ¿qué no temo?/pues que me temo a mí mismo" (I fear to see myself a galley slave, punished at the oar in the deep abyss. I fear, but what don't I fear, since I am frightened even by myself?) The only hope in such a world of fear and diminished human agency lies in the mercy offered by an omnipotent divine will. For Bataillon, Lope's play is basically a political version of the theocratic *auto sacramental*, celebrating the omnipotence of the sovereign will, and its defiant *villano* can be saved only by a quasi-miraculous gift of grace bestowed on him by a quasi-divine king in the "asymmetrical" symposium of the *lord's* supper, a gift that, descending from above, is anything but an exchange between equals.[112] At this "symposium of the master," Juan Labrador finds himself on his knees at the king's table; blindness strikes his reason as he stares at the enigma of the unopened dish, observing a mystery of theological absolutism that he will never understand rationally. He can only shrug his shoulders helplessly, eat the body of his generous lord, and receive his new habit for his "palace life" as "muy otro"—no longer as Juan Labrador, whose human body of course has been transcended.

I would suggest that what is happening at the climax of Lope's play is most interesting when we recognize all that distinguishes it from Valdivielso's, that the *comedia* might be fruitfully viewed as the *reversal* of the subsequent *auto sacramental*. In its suppression of its model's most meaningful paradoxes and interrogations, the religious *auto* represents nothing less than a tyrannical exploitation and violation of Lope's work by his own admirers. As the appropriate conclusion of the processes of transference and transformation that we have followed through the work, the ritual fusion of king and peasant—scepter and plow—is in a fundamental way a demystification of the *corpus mysticum* of monarch and state. It is a metamorphosis downward, so to speak, a mysterious disrobing of a descent from the *arcana imperii* (which prove to be rather ineffective in the play) to an ideal for ruler and ruled rooted in *humanitas*. The ideal is most splendidly imaged in the thoroughly uncharismatic figure of Lope's earthy, stubborn, and occasionally farcical *villano*, who, as it were, displaces the Eucharist and the magical exchanges of the *auto's* elevated table. One might say that in Lope's play a cult of the simple human being supersedes the two great cults of the Counter-Reformation and Baroque state—those of the savior and the monarch.

Unlike many conservative dramas of the absolutist period, as well as numerous propagandistic proclamations, extremist political writings, and ritual celebrations—all of which would move the state, to recall Kantorowicz's argument on the developing conceptions of the king's suprahuman identity and role, back into the shadows of Holy Scripture, altar, sacrament, and liturgy in celebrating the sources of its legitimacy and guaranteeing the benevolence of the magical, theologically grounded powers of its unconstrained rulers—Lope's unusual play, far from being an exercise in propaganda or an embellishment of a palace occasion, takes its place in the progressive evolution of European political thought that Kantorowicz has traced from the theocentric and Christocentric doctrines of the Middle Ages to conceptions of sovereignty centered on rationality, law, ethics, and *humanitas* that were developed by political theorists, jurists, philosophers, and humanists from the thirteenth century on and were maintained, with increasing insight into changing historical conditions, through the period of absolutism. Lope's decisive alignment of *discreción* and Stoic rationality with power and power's representations points quite unenigmatically to the most enlightened political philosophy of his contemporaries, which conceived of the sovereign power of king and state as bound by an antecedent benevolent order of universal rationality and natural law, a power transferred to the specific sovereign from the people as community, wherein it resides, an order traditionally exemplified by the perfect community of Eden.[113]

At the same time Lope's complicated exchanges between the monarch and a classically drawn philosopher or sage can be seen as crowning a humanistic, secularizing approach to defining and conceiving the identity, powers, and obligations of the prince through the model of the classical sage. As Kantorowicz points out, the tradition reaches back to Dante's image of the emperor as actualizing a primarily human, terrestrial *dignitas* that manifested itself fully only in Eden, where the body natural of an individual man was the body corporate of MAN.[114] For Dante and his humanist descendants, the monarch strives to approximate this condition, and the path backward toward the recovery of forgotten and unspoiled *human* powers is illuminated by moral philosophy. The classical wise man, the Senecan sage or the Aristotelian *optimus homo* becomes the central figure in this tradition of political thinking and in its most characteristic form of expression—the *De regimine principum*. He stands as model preceptor in the necessary education of the ruler's human real self—an education emphasizing natural reason and the cardinal or natural virtues. More significant perhaps for an understanding of Lope's dramatic procedures of mirroring and doubling in the *Villano*, he stands as an ethical ideal—an image of *humanitas*, of a *dignitas hominis*—and as such, an ideal reality in which to mirror and legitimate the public universal body of the king.[115] The essence of "kingliness" is not to be sought in the various awesome archetypes of absolutism's self-portraits and its elaborate royal cults (Hercules, Alexander, Caesar, etc.) but rather in the unanointed, "disrobed," and modest figure of the "good man."

Considered in the light of such traditions, the fundamental lesson of the climactic banquet of *El villano en su rincón* is not really very different from the lesson that the king learned in the mysterious forest *rincón*. The brilliant palace spectacle turns out to be not the symmetrical displacement and "correction" of the shadowy sylvan theater of the peasant's self-presentation, which it recalls in such precise terms, but rather its *reconstitution*. The musical accompaniment of the king's banquet, the *contrafactura* of the Horatian *beatus ille* of pastoral tranquility sung at the peasant's table, is a fulfillment rather than an abrogation.

"Cuán bienaventurado/un hombre puede ser entre la gente" (How happy a man can be who lives among men). At this point we realize that the space of the *rincón* is in reality a moral order of being and a state of mind; that the legendary French king, here assuming direction of the play as Lope's own double, has imaginatively achieved its actualization in the Spanish state; and that the marvels of his comedic metamorphoses and triumphs have little to do with any mysteries of state or theology.

For most contemporary analysts of such mysteries — even those intent on denying the challenging insights of Machiavelli — political success and fear naturally go together. Botero argued that the stability of an effective king's rule was enhanced by his reputation and that reputation was achieved chiefly through "images of fear" (*spetie di timore*). Even the more traditional Saavedra Fajardo pointed out that for a successful king, "corta más el temor que la espada, y obra más la opinión que el valor" (fear cuts more effectively than the sword, and more is accomplished by reputation than by valor).[116] Fear, for Botero, establishes hierarchy, separates properly, makes unequal, and enables the majesty to arise from an underlying and threatening chaos and "restrain all the world." It is of course the opposite of love, which "conciliates, unites, and equalizes."[117] The dramatic monument to such political insights is, of course, Calderón's *La vida es sueño*, which ends with the reestablishment of hierarchy; the separation of rule from chaos; the banishment of the "deviant" to the frightening space of the tower; the renunciation of love; and, in what can be read as an inversion of Lope's ending, the triumph of an order of fear. In his last words even the perfected prince, Segismundo, announces that he reigns in dread: "Estoy temiendo en mis ansias." How different is Lope's climactic royal banquet, with its reconciliation of all oppositions, its universal inclusiveness, its ritualistic overcoming of fear, and its establishment of an open space accessible to all who are good. Its lesson is contained most concisely perhaps in a very simple admonition that is repeated over and over again as the king takes the secret sharer of his night in the forest into the palace as steward, *pariente*, *privado*, "true mirror," *compañero*, and friend:

> No temas, Juan Labrador;
> que nunca temen los buenos. (200)

In this imagined kingdom of the good, there is no longer any need for its citizens to live in fear and anxiety. Here there is a crown for each to wear, and its unseen radiance is of an order far different from the glow of the regalia of the world's most powerful monarchs.

BEYOND THE BOUNDARIES OF ROMANTIC COMEDY:
WHO IS JUAN LABRADOR?

But nobody can be one person except the wise man; the rest of us often shift our masks.

—*Seneca*

At a certain point in history men became individuals. . . . The individual looks into mirrors, larger and much brighter than those that were formerly held up to magistrates.

—*Lionel Trilling*

The striking assertion of the king's control—as ruler and dramatist—in the arbitrary turns and revelations of the action in the final act, the climactic theatrical spectacle of the contained ritual of absolutism, and the doctrinal commentary its political iconography elicits at the finale—all would validate a reading of *El villano en su rincón* as an emphatic celebration of the myths and institutions of the contemporary monarchy. Moreover, the congruence of its resolution of the symbiotic relationship of shepherd and king with the agricultural model for state and sovereign invoked by contemporary political theorists such as Ribadeneira (see above) would suggest that a utopian imaginative conception informs the play, that, to recall Northrop Frye's comments on Shakespearian romantic comedy, the *Villano en su rincón* fulfills the "archetypal function of literature in visualizing the world of desire, not as an escape from 'reality,' but as the genuine form of the world that human life tries to imitate."[118] So inclusive are the harmonious resolution and incorporation of the numerous conflicts and oppositions articulated in the course of the action that one might be tempted to say with Noël Salomon that "thanks to the monarchist sentiment and to the appearance of the royal figure at the denouement, the numerous problems that have been building up disappear. . . . They do not remain open but are closed as if by decree."[119]

In all its perfections the king's order is tightly and systematically closed. Two qualifying points might be easily reconciled with this view. The first is that the *Villano en su rincón* clearly suggests that the ceremonial of royal power and the ritual act of seeing the king must be based in the subject's understanding rather than in his awed submission and surrender of self. Another model for the kind of integration, unification, and closure achieved in the denouement is Costanza's musical chord—a figure that is philosophically linked with love, universal harmony, perfect communication, and spiritual and moral equality. The second is that the play carefully delineates the importance of restraint in the monarch, his limitation by ethical responsibility and rationality, and the necessity of the moral and philosophical education of the real man beneath the official body of the majesty. In this respect it can be seen as representing, although in an unconventional way, the popular Renaissance genre of the "education of the king." The king shares the fallibility of all other mortals, and the figure of his most catastrophic failure is the tyrant, a figure that the play envisions, if only in symbolic condensation and as a momentary and hypothetical possibility. Though recognized as the "singularly perfect being," the best "representative of his natural species," and the consecrated "vicar of God" whose power is linked with that of divine grace, the king is at the same time but a man, and that man, like any other human being, must be perfected. Perfecting involves a process of "descending" to the real self beneath the majesty and recognizing its mortality, its limitations, and its obligations, a process appropriately described as *humanarse*. The model—or mirror—for such perfectioning is the classical sage, and when the audience gazes on the doubles united at the banquet table, it sees in Juan Labrador not only the *pariente*, the *compañero*, and the obedient vassal of the king, but also the image of the king's mortal self perfected by education, philosophical insight, and classical wisdom.

At this point I would like to deal with a facet of the work that in fact stands in defiance of the neat scheme of closure that, according to Salomon, the dramaturgic king imposes, as if by decree, on its dramatic world. One important force appears to resist the dominant integrative movement converging on the palace theater of power and enlightenment and to linger as a subversive residue. Whether or not the author was aware of its disquieting effects, its presence is, in my opinion, undeniable, and it is also what ultimately lifts the play beyond its immediate doctrinal intentions and ideological functions, even when their sophistication, complexity, and enlightenment are recognized. The fact is that as a humanistic "education of a king" or a propagandistic celebration of the institution of monarchy, the play remains very unconventional. A restlessness continues to trouble the highly theatrical full stop of its dialectic in its concluding spectacle. One need only note the variety in its adaptations (*refundiciones*) and critical interpretations to be skeptical about any reductive explanations based on an alleged tight, teleologically ordered structure. Salomon's phrase "closure by decree" seems inappropriate for this play even when one acknowledges its monarchist foundations. As Bataillon himself admitted, there is something in the work that resists all interpretation and, of course, any collapse into propaganda.

To get at its unconventional aspect and the disquieting notes that trouble its
spectacular harmonies, I would like to return to its distinctive recreation of the
traditional confrontation of philosopher and king and to reconsider its strange
obsession with seeing and being seen—certainly one of its most remote and unconventional features. Above I have pointed out that a *locus classicus* for philosophical discussions of a king's moral education and obligation was Seneca's
De Beneficiis.[120] Here, in yet another of the legendary confrontations of emperor and philosopher that imaginatively loom behind, dignify, and invest with
significance Lope's encounter of king and peasant, we find Alexander pushing
beyond the bounds of nature, conquering the world, and yet failing to find contentment or to fill the inner emptiness that arouses a tormenting and insatiable
desire for power, glory, and self-aggrandizement. Commenting on the emperor's
encounter with Diogenes, Seneca observes that the true wise man lives in contentment within the safe retreat of his soul, free from ambition and the "great
anxieties that rack the mind." He knows that all that makes man better has been
placed "in plain sight or nearby." He scorns all accidents of fortune and rises to
the height of recognizing that death is not the source of any evil but rather the
end of many. Desiring nothing, he possesses everything, and he is in fact, paradoxically, the most powerful of men. "Like the immortal gods who govern their
realm without recourse to arms, and still from their serene and lofty heights
safeguard their own, so the wise man performs his duties, however far-reaching
they may be, without any turmoil, and, being the most powerful and best of
mankind, sees the whole human race beneath him."[121] Free from "all mental
disturbance," the sage finds the reward of his wisdom in "an evenness of joy," a
serenity that finds its most appropriate analogue in the tranquility of the trans-
lunary heavens. "Talis est sapientis animus, qualis mundus super lunam."[122] The
sage's contented survey of his vast possessions in nature is for Seneca a paradoxical metaphor for a state of mind: in the processes of his philosophical alchemy,
nothing in fact becomes everything.

It is not difficult to see how closely Lope's portrait of the good man conforms
to such Stoic principles. In praising his forest world, Juan Labrador emphasizes
its orderliness, its self-sufficiency, and the stability of its natural foundations and
boundaries—the groves of deeply rooted and straight trees beyond which he
has never found it necessary to venture. With his two well-defined dwellings,
the *rincón* and the tomb, Juan Labrador has apparently achieved the sense of
proportion that the Stoic derives from maintaining before his eyes an image of
the meaningful totality of his life and grasping its fundamental lesson: "Tota vita
discendum est mori" (The whole of life is learning how to die).[123] In full understanding of himself and in firm control of his existence, he has rendered himself

invulnerable to all the accidents and vicissitudes that plague human existence in the sublunary world where fortune holds sway. In a moment of envy—"conozco la envidia mía" (153)—the king recognizes the achievement of the forest sage in controlling his destiny: "A la fortuna los [grillos] pone/quien de esa manera vive" (The man who lives in this way puts fortune in shackles) (154).

While Lope's peasant-philosopher's estate and wealth are real, it is clear that his most prized possession is his state of mind, and it is clear that what torments the king with uncontrollable desire and envy following his discovery of the peasant's *rincón* is precisely the existence of that state of mind, a condition that in the *miseria* of his regal identity he could never hope to understand. Lope's relationship of doubles, then, is marked from the outset by the ambiguities of mimetic desire, and one of the most intriguing of its antithetical elements is that the object of desire and incitement to rivalry is the condition of freedom from desire. It is a philosophically rooted envy that stirs the most powerful monarch of Europe in his solitary, nocturnal adventure ("por la oscuridad extraña") into the deep woods, where a mysterious double holds the hidden "oro de su valor." In absolutism's great drama of kings, one might think of the lonely figure of Henry IV, sleepless in his palace, wistfully imagining the peaceful sleep of the lad in the storm-tossed crow's nest and reflecting on the inescapable obligations of the monarch in his life of ceremony and its alienations: "Uneasy lies the head that wears the crown."[124]

In view of his continuing characterization as the sage and the repeated emphasis on his contentment, Juan Labrador's uncontrollable anxiety about avoiding the king's image would appear to be a violent contradiction, and we might be initially tempted to see in it the kind of unmasking of impostors, hypocrites, fanatics, and pedants that has held a fundamental place in the repertory of comedy, from Aristophanes to the popular situation comedy of contemporary television. In some of its most bizarre expressions—for example, when Juan hides on hearing of the presence of the royal party in the area—it seems that Lope may be lapsing into the primitive conventions of farce, humor comedy, and satire and generating comic effects from the mechanical behavior of comic stereotypes and caricatures. Certainly as a tyrannical, stubborn father forbidding his children's contact with finer society and stifling their desires for incorporation within it through advantageous marriage, Juan fulfills one of the time-honored roles in the comedy of generational conflict. The problem, however, is that his unnatural, "monstrous," and "savage" opposition to the healthy desires of an attractive, intelligent, and energetic younger generation; his anti-courtly bluster; and his "panic attacks" at the approach of the royal party and the dreaded ritual of gazing on the monarch's face do not square very well with the admirable philosophical foundation on which they apparently rest, particularly when he turns out to be the wisest and most admired figure by everyone in the play, including the king of France. One might, of course, recall Lope's comfort with dramatic hybrids and inconsistencies (for example, "lo cómico y lo trágico mez-clado") and argue that he turned to a conventional secondary action in order to incorporate movement, conflict, and suspense in his philosophical drama and that its formula required some idiosyncratic behavior in his protagonist, who at times in the first act looks far more like an obstinate *senex iratus* of Plautine comedy than a Senecan wise man. As I suggested above in my discussion of the shocking incoherences of the bedroom scenes of Act II, Lope de Vega is a master of all traditional comic conventions, but he is strikingly unconventional in his free adaptation and combination of them.[125]

It should also be acknowledged that the comic treatment of the cult and the rites of monarchy—for example, the royal glance that annihilates, the aura that brings holy dread and loss of self-control, and the charisma that arouses an ir-resistible impulse to prostrate oneself—is not uncommon in the theater of the time. In *El villano en su rincón* we observe it, not only in the bedroom version of the "ritual of royal disrobing," but also in the peasant's awed reactions in the church and in the suspenseful denouement of the palace spectacle. It is consis-tent with Lope's interest in monarchy and the court that he should recast the ancient comic theme of identical twins—the "comedy of errors"—in monarchic terms. *El palacio confuso* is a hilarious *comedia de enredo*, offering an endless sequence of theatrically charged misperceptions based on the fact that there are two identical kings ruling in very different ways, despite the fact that everybody thinks that they are one. The play is full of light-hearted allusions to and exploi-tations of the philosophical, political, legal, and cultist conceptions of the mon-arch. For example, Duke Octavio reveals that he must abandon his betrothed, Porcia, immediately if the queen of Sicily should choose him as husband and king. Coronation lifts a man beyond the human species: "Subir a la Magestad/es dexar de ser humano,/y vn amago soberano/de la infinita deidad./Hombre, ado-rava su nombre;/mas diademas inmortales/de puntas piramidales/mudan la es-pecie del hombre" (To ascend to the Majesty is to cease to be human, and a sovereign sign of the infinite deity. As a man, I adored her name; but immortal diadems, tipped with pyramidal points, alter the species of the man). In one of its comic climaxes, a moment of anagnorisis is suspended because the guardian of the lost twin refuses to raise his eyes to look upon the king and experience the familiar terror: "Si éste es el Rey, yo me turbo. . . ./Los ojos pondré en la tierra,/no le tengo de mirar" (If this is the king, I would be alarmed and con-fused. . . . I shall fix my eyes on the earth, I will not have to look upon him). On being compelled to raise his eyes and discovering his "son"—who in reality happens to be the latter's unknown twin brother—clad in his royal attire, he amiably scolds him and orders him to "volver al aldea" (return to the village).[126]

More relevant to the serious issues raised in *El villano en su rincón* is the startling exploitation of the discourse of majesty in one of Lope's most bizarre *comedias de enredo*, *El servir con mala estrella*. Here a lustful, capricious, and manipulative king involves himself in an unsavory erotic adventure and cynically compels the courtly and valorous French knight, Rugero—like the Cid, a slayer of Moors and a victim of an ungrateful king—to serve his mistress and her bastard child in order to cover up his affair ("¡Oh, cuánto a un príncipe afea/una liviandad!"—Oh, how ugly does a lewd escapade make a prince!). Ignoring the heroic achievements of Rugero, the king refuses to find "un rincón" in Spain to bestow on him, and he frivolously distributes royal favors according to his gains or losses in a chess game with a captured Moorish king. When surprised by his mistress's honorable brother in a nocturnal assignation, he resourcefully exploits his "double identity" as the monarch, posing as a portrait commanding respect and instantaneously immobilizing his adversary, who in an illusionistic *coup de théâtre* rebukes the "absent" human king by praising, and hence reminding him of, the values of his "portraited" ideal identity. While yielding to the irresistible charisma and properly paying homage to the image, at the same time he manages to suggest that the iconology of the "portrait" on which he is gazing could be improved by replacing the garb of the king-*galán* with that of the king-warrior. The king literally turns into his double on stage, oscillating between human and suprahuman identities. It would be hard to imagine a more ingenious, "Baroque," manifestation of the doubleness of the king that Kantorowicz has traced through centuries of development and variation from the high Middle Ages to the period of absolutism.

The sophisticated parody of the cult of the king (and the conventions of the *comedia de enredo*) in *El servir con mala estrella* includes the doctrine of the king's ubiquity and visibility and the central metaphor of his solar identity. When his frightened mistress urges him to hide, his immediate response is: "¿Yo esconderme? . . . Nunca los reyes se esconden" (I hide? . . . Never are kings hidden). When she reminds him that the sun can be hidden by clouds, he replies: "El sol o el Rey, imagina/que no es posible." The deeper implications of her rejoinder—"Mas son/imágenes, que es razón/que tal vez tengan cortina" (But they are images, and so it is reasonable that they perhaps have a curtain)—are reinforced later, when the excitable, jealous Hipólita asserts that the perfections of the portrait of the king are in reality "flatterings," the inventions "de pinceles de pintores/y de plumas de poetas" (of painters' brushes and poets' pens). On the other hand, the comic dismantling of the discourse of monarchy is countered by the heroic Rugero, who, returning in disappointment to France, takes a portrait of the king, which he intends to unfold and contemplate whenever he has bad feelings about the misbehavior of the human king, who, as he puts it, bestows favors only on those who are already wealthy—in the manner of a horse that urinates only in a river.[127]

Such conventional and dramaturgic explanations of the playwright's intentions and strategies might be sufficient to account for the apparent inconsistencies and flaws in the total design of Lope's *El villano en su rincón*. However, I would like to conclude by suggesting that regardless of the determinations of comic plots, genres, types, conventions, traditions, and effects, Juan Labrador's great fascination as a character lies precisely in the resultant "inconsistencies," divisions, and exaggerations that mark his discourse and action in the play. These continue to resonate even after he is comfortably situated as court philosopher and *privado* of an enlightened king and his ultimate role in the play's design of mutual education is recognized.

There is a compelling force, an eloquent anxiety, that marks this man's life-long efforts to protect himself and his family against the irresistible dehumanizing forces of a new social order rising with the new nation-states and centering on the great courts of Europe. Once we recognize that Lope's play is really about the nature of state power, the relations of rulers and subjects, individual integrity, and the stakes involved in the necessary incorporation of the individual in a new social and political formation, we might suspect that Juan Labrador's bizarre preoccupation with the monarch's face conceals an anxiety that means much more than is immediately evident.[128] Although he inhabits a comic imaginative world and his conflicts end in reconciliation and celebration, Lope's peasant protagonist, in his phobia regarding hypocrisy, role playing, dressing, and disguising, should be seen as a comic relative in an impressive family of malcontents rising in early modern European literature to protest against the price in human authenticity exacted by the temptations and irresistible pleasures of the triumphant new sociability that would define the modern world. There is clearly something quite serious that he shares not only with his fellow *villano*, Sancho Panza, who solemnly walks out of the court, but also with his great philosophical contemporary, the alienated, uncompromising, and humorless Prince of Denmark, who simply does not want "to belong."

At this point it is necessary to return to the obsession with seeing and being seen that motivates the primary action of the play. Above I have noted that a fascination with visibility affected the courtly societies of the absolutist states in a variety of ways, manifesting itself not only in changing modes of consciousness and patterns of social behavior, but also, more specifically, in political organization, public ritual, codes of etiquette, and theories legitimizing power relations in the state. From Castiglione to La Bruyère and Gracián, one observes a deepening recognition of the social determination of man, the inescapable situation of the individual within a field of interacting images, and the fundamentally theatrical character of existence. From Castiglione's humane counsels for the proper projection of images in the beautiful "masked ball" that a civilized society can create to Gracián's strategies of "reading the faces of others," subjecting all spontaneous or authentic impulses to the tyrannical control of a practical, calculating reason, and perfecting the arts of manipulative dissimulation and casuistry in that theater of power that is human society, one can observe an increasing sense of the individual as a being necessarily implicated in a situation that demands self-division, a splitting apart and a creation of a persona, and the comfortable acknowledgment that the aims of the latter at times necessarily differ from those of a superior substantial, integrated, or constant underlying self.[129]

It is, of course, revealing that Gracián, the preceptor of self-fashioning at the moment of fullest self-awareness of the court societies of Europe, no longer writes of man's moral obligation to fashion himself as a man, but rather of his inescapable task of mastering—through carefully calculated tactics of attack and defense—the potentially hostile circumstances of his social environment by creating himself as a *persona* and, in effect, reassuring himself of his very existence by being seen by a spectator—"lo que no se ve es como si no fuese" (what is not seen, it is as if it does not exist).[130] In this order of mutually animating glances, the king is both supreme spectator and supreme spectacle, and his vivifying gaze and solar emanations (see above) are its central validating myths, just as the gaze conjoining king and subject is paradigmatic for all relations in the complex web of connections and dependencies that constitute society.

If the sensitivity to the inescapable visibility of man in his social arena accounts for the numerous cultural manifestations of the traditional theme of the world theater, it similarly accounts for the immense appeal in the age of the ancient Stoics, who conceived of man precisely in terms of this split; recognized its potential for tension; admitted the menace of dissolution or loss of self in the mask; and developed a philosophy for possessing or fortifying the inner, authentic self against an intrusive outside world of accidents and others.[131] As Groethuysen points out, one of Stoicism's great achievements was its conception of man as a *person*, an entity that can be viewed as a possession to be fortified amid inescapable situational or social circumstances that constantly confront it with a threat of appropriation and alienation, and it is hardly a coincidence that it developed in significant ways under the impact of Roman urbanization and political centralization and that it flourished in a period of absolutism.

The Stoics' insights into the risks that identification and compromise with society bring to a man of integrity lie behind a rich tradition of anti-court satirical writing in the Renaissance. A work that is particularly suggestive in terms of Lope's dramatic conception of Juan Labrador's defiance of his king in *El villano en su rincón* is Cervantes's early pastoral romance, *La Galatea* (1585). Here the dominant erotic concerns of the characters are momentarily interrupted by a philosophical interlude depicting, in the tradition of the Horatian *beatus ille*, the orderly life of Lauso, an aristocratic shepherd who has fled the court and the turning wheel of fortune. The sage's lifestyle, values, anxieties, and attitudes toward his king are remarkably similar to those of Juan Labrador.

> Reduce a poco espacio sus pisadas,
> del alto monte al apacible llano,
> desde la fresca fuente al claro río,
> sin que, por ver las tierras apartadas,
> las movibles campañas de Oceano
> are con loco antiguo desvarío.
> *No le levanta el brío*
> *saber que el gran monarca invicto vive*
> *bien cerca de su aldea,*
> *y aunque su bien desea,*
> *poco disgusto en no verle recibe;*
> *no como el ambicioso entremetido,*
> que con seso perdido
> anda tras el favor, tras la privanza. . . .
>
> *No su semblante o su color se muda*
> *porque mude color, mude semblante*
> *el señor a quien sirve, pues no tiene*
> señor que fuerce a que con lengua muda
> siga, cual Clicie a su dorado amante,
> el dulce o amargo gusto que le viene.
>
> No muestra en apariencia
> otro de lo que encierra el pecho sano:
> que la rústica ciencia
> no alcanza el falso trato cortesano.
> *¿Quién tendrá vida tal en menosprecio?*
> *¿Quién no dirá que aquella sola es vida*
> *que al sosiego del alma se encamina?*

(Within a circle small his footsteps wend/From the high mountain to the peaceful plain,/To the clear river from the fountain cold./Nor doth he plough, in madness without end/The heaving meadows of the ocean main/Desiring distant countries to behold./*It doth not make him bold/To learn that close beside his village lives/The great unconquered king,/And although he wishes him prosperity,/He feels no displeasure in not seeing him,/Not like the ambitious busybody/Who, having lost all balance, insanely/Runs after favor, and after a favorite's power. . . ./It is not for him to change his face or color/because the lord he serves changes color or face/*And forces him to follow him with mute tongue,/Just as Clytie hangs on the sweet or bitter pleasures of her golden lover./He does not show in appearance/Anything other than what his healthy breast holds within./*Who such a life as this will hold in scorn?/Who will not say that that alone is life/Which pursues the tranquility of the soul?*)[132]

If Cervantes's words elegantly disclose such familiar moral diseases of court life as hypocrisy, flattery, ambition, pretentiousness, and, above all, inauthenticity, the meditations of Lope's philosophical contemporary, López de Vega, take us even closer to the kind of derangement that threatens the stability of Juan Labrador's orderly existence. They reveal in very precise terms a recognition of the dangers of the individual's disintegrative appropriation by his society and the fragile character of an existence within a concentrated visual field where one's performance unfolds always under the surveillance of the others. It is the consciousness of the menacing character of a spectral social order that frequently gives the resurrected Stoicism of the early modern absolutist period—for example, in the works of Quevedo and Gracián—its distinctively *modern* accentuation.[133] Insisting that true happiness lies in the "tranquilidad del ánimo," López de Vega argues that it is a condition impossible to achieve under the gaze of the public: "Solo la vida privada se ha de buscar, que la pública sólo es buena para ser apuntado con el dedo, i esto basta para no poder uno usar de su libertad. Como se tenga lo preciso i suficiente para poder passar, el no ser visto ni oído viene a ser la mayor comodidad. . . . viva yo, pliegue a los Cielos, *ut nemo me vixisse sciat*" (Only the private life is to be sought after, for the only benefit of the public life is to be pointed at by the fingers of others; and that is enough to deprive a person of his freedom. As long as one possesses what is necessary and sufficient for getting by, not to be seen or heard become the greatest of goods. . . . May I live, if it please the Heavens, in such a way *that nobody might know that I have lived*). If compelled to exist in court society, López de Vega's sage looks upon its illusory distinctions, honors, and rites of courtesy as if he were witnessing a ridiculous "comedia de la humana vida," a theatrical spectacle in which the actors have persuaded themselves that they are in reality what they are merely representing. He will preserve his inner powers of recognizing and valuing the essential features that distinguish the human being from the animal—virtue and rationality—no matter how "degraded" by the absence of the varnished embellishments of "political" honors (*esmaltes políticos*).[134]

If we bear in mind such perceptions of the dispossessing power of the court society, Juan Labrador's "barbaric" and "ferocious" desire to hide when he suddenly hears the approach of the king's "trápala [commotion] y confusión" strikes us as more intelligible and certainly less farcical than at first glance. At this point we might notice that the theme of identity loss is registered in a variety of ways in this play of doubles, disguises, and complex crossovers. Most striking perhaps is its benign insinuation in the heroine's rewarded quest for a metamorphosis and transfer to the palace world. Belittling her unmannerly father's *villanaje*, she recalls how the elegant garments of her courtly attire once caught the eye of the crown prince and admits, with apparent pleasure, "Jamás a la Corte fui, que allá pareciese yo" (Never did I go to the court to appear there as myself) (112). A similar, and perhaps more subversive, ambiguity colors Juan Labrador's rebellious children's rhetoric amid the magical metamorphoses wrought by the king in the final scene. Celebrating the monarch in the conventional solar iconography, Feliciano, dressed now as a courtier, declares that if deprived of the animating rays of sunlight shining from the king's face, the human being "is not a man, he is a statue, he is a stone." Lisarda, the heroine of the fairy tale, rejoices in her "new being" and likens her transformed self to a cloud approaching the sun king and submitting to his domination and gilding power (190–193). The disturbing note of fragility and emptiness is somewhat more ominous in her sonnet, which parallels and reverses the king's earlier sonnet embracing the *via contemplativa* of the philosopher as the proper way to seek refuge from fortune's adversities. In another of the proliferating doublets that mark the thematic counterpoint of this operatic play, Lisarda expresses her determination to seize fortune, pursue her desires, and take the risk of ascending and "conquering greatness."[135] Acknowledging her vulnerability, she glances at the Icarus myth and the traditional fall of fortune of anti-court satire and, once again turning to the central solar metaphor, pleads with the fickle goddess to transform her into resistant glass rather than "weak ice" in her approach to the sun. Her highly artificial poem can be viewed as an ingenious "Baroque" elaboration of the fundamental conceits of contemporary political culture. As a display of wit it contrasts sharply with the conventional figuration of the king's philosophical sonnet.

No me permitas humillar al suelo;
si a tu cielo tu mano me llevare,

> hazme cristal al sol, no débil hielo.
> Agora es bien que tu piedad me ampare:
> que no es dicha volar hasta tu cielo,
> sin clavo firme que tu rueda pare.

(Do not let me fall to the earth; if your hand is bearing me upward to your Heaven, make me glass in facing the sun, not weak ice. Now it is right that your mercy come to my aid: For there can be no happiness in soaring toward your heaven, without a firm nail that stops your turning wheel.) (193)[136]

All of these references certainly intensify the prevailing atmosphere of the fairy tale that surrounds the magical exchanges at the conclusion of Lope's romantic comedy. One could in fact say that the double sonnets, celebrating *rincón* and *palacio*, crown a full and complex development of both motifs offered in Torquemada's primitive tale of the lost king—reflective descent into the self and triumphant return to society. At the same time their paradoxical appropriateness in the deepening satirical context of the work cannot be overlooked. Here their most interesting implications lie in their imaginative suggestion that there is something fundamentally spectral about the court and its society of reflected selves.

The play opens with a theatrical but thoroughly conventional scene of court satire. Men of the palace world pursue disguised ladies through the streets of Paris, speaking in the modish discourse of gallantry, arranging rendezvous, exchanging pledges, and sending servants to inquire secretly about the identities of the pursued. The conversation is spiced with cynical comments on the customs of court society, focusing on such traditional topics of moralist denunciations as venality, lust, duplicity, counterfeiting, and mendacity. It climaxes in a rhetorical *tour de force* by the predictably misogynistic *gracioso*, an ingeniously contrived diatribe against predatory ladies and prostitutes, figured grotesquely and comically differentiated as fisherwomen using a variety of hooks to land their victims. In the ugliness of its content, the formulaic character of its humor, and the crudity of its moral judgment, the passage belongs to a familiar tradition of aulic satire, cataloguing the *molestiae* of court life and extending back to such medieval critics of the court as John of Salisbury and Aeneas Sylvius Piccolomini.[137]

From the moment Juan Labrador enters the plot, we sense, however, that the social satire of the work is concerned with matters that are far more profound than the trivialities of formulaic *comedias de enredo* and *costumbres* and that its insights into human behavior are reaching into areas of anxiety that are those of a new age. The court seems far less menacing as a place of temptation to vice than as a threat to identity. Its ethos would appear to be based on a belief that, as Gracián's aphorism would suggest, one does not exist if one is not seen. But what lies behind the elaborately ritualized behavior it has devised for the projection of images? In Act III, Lope's peasants enter the palace and discover a strange world, hollowed out of all substance, lifeless in the mechanical movements of its inhabitants, empty of communication, and alienated from any sense of moral obligation. The fundamental inauthenticity and disintegration of its human relationships are effectively captured by the list of disconnected fragments constituting Fileto's advice to anybody who would be successful in the courtly performance:

> Cumplimientos extraños, ceremonias,
> reverencias, los cuerpos espetados,
> mucha parola, murmurar, donaires,
> risa falsa, no hacer por nadie nada,
> notable prometer, verdad ninguna,
> negar la edad y el beneficio hecho,
> deber, y otras cosas más sutiles.

(Strange compliments, ceremonies, bows, stiffened bodies and other acts of reverence, much chattering and gossiping, witticisms, false laughter, not doing anything for anybody, noteworthy promising, no holding to truth or to one's word, concealing one's age, and denying benefits received, being in debt, and other more subtle things.) (184)

Fileto's concentrated satirical description can be taken as an inversion of the Senecan ideal society, harmoniously bonded through mutual, freely offered benefits of its rational individual citizens. In its negations and defamiliarizations it has unmistakable affinities with such powerful contemporary anatomies of social breakdown and human alienation as Lazarillo de Tormes's encounter with the vanishing, ghostly courtier of Toledo and Gracián's nightmarish vision of an eclipsed palace banquet in which the courtiers' presence is revealed only by the glow of their rapacious hands.[138]

There is, however, in *El villano en su rincón*'s engagement with the insubstantiality of life at the court a distinctively personal and psychological element. It is concentrated primarily in the protagonist's exaggerated behavior and in the intensity of his children's desires. In its articulation we hear clear echoes of the age's most devastating and influential exposure of the threats posed by the rising court society to the maintenance of individual integrity, Antonio de Guevara's *Menosprecio de corte y alabanza de aldea* (Scorn for court life and praise of village life).

Guevara's diatribe registers already in 1539 the irresistible force of attraction exerted by the emerging absolutist courts and the alienating effects a sensitive individual could experience in their new social environment. Man finds himself helplessly swept into a vortex from which there is no escape. Its fascination resists all efforts at understanding. "Tiene la corte un no sé que, un no sé donde, un no sé como y un no te entiendo, que cada día hay que nos quexemos, que nos alteremos, que nos despidamos, y por otra parte, no nos da licencia para irnos. El yugo de la corte es muy duro" (The court has an I know not what, and an I know not where, and an I know not how, and an I know not how to understand you, so that everyday there is something we complain about, something that upsets us, so that we bid the court farewell but, on the other hand, find that it does not give us permission to leave. The yoke of the court is very hard).[139] Guevara's most powerful words are his climactic self-indictment, which describes his own experience in the court as that of a sick soul, poisoned not by sin, but by the venoms of a social pathology.

The most striking aspect of this confession is the kind of mental derangement that it reveals—that of an individual who is frightened at the loss of all control over his life and tormented by a sense of the continuing fragmentation of his identity. The stability and reassurances of an integrated self have been irrecoverably lost: "O quánto va de quien yo fuy a quien soy agora?" (Oh, how different am I now from the person I used to be?) Everywhere in the court one is watched; everywhere one must perform under the gaze of the others; everywhere one abandons oneself to their wishes. Above all, one must never remove one's mask and be "singular."[140] The dissociation can be frightening: "Yo mismo de mi mismo estoy espantado de verme que no en el que soy y no soy el que era" (I myself am frightened by myself on seeing in myself not the person I am and not the person I used to be). The healthy detachment of self-scrutiny of the Christian and classical moral traditions, the prophylactic self-division on the lines of public-private, have deserted the tormented soul and collapsed in a self-destructive, traumatic outpouring of sentiments of disorientation, anxiety, nausea, and self-loathing.[141] Life has become a continuing death. The *confesión* becomes a *confusión*. In recollection experiences assume the insubstantiality of incomprehensible dreams. The descriptions of the seductions and the enveloping powers of the court—its agitation, its ceaseless flow of novelties, and its oceanic unboundedness—are charged with a hallucinatory power. "La corte es un sueño que echa modorra, es un piélago que no tiene suelo, es una sombra que no tiene tomo, es una fantasma que está encantada y aun es un labirinto que no tiene salida, porque todos los que allí entran, o quedan allí perdidos o salen de allá assombrados" (The court is a sleep that leaves one numb and sluggish, it is a bottomless ocean, it is an ungraspable shadow without substance, it is a phantasm of an enchanted world, and it is a labyrinth that has no exit, because all who enter either remain lost within or come forth in a state of shock).[142]

In the midst of society the individual lives in isolation and anxious self-obsession and can find pleasure in nothing. Solitude has lost all of its traditional powers of restoration:

> En ninguna cosa tomo ya gusto y de mí más que todo estoy descontento. . . . Estando a solas, yo mismo conmigo mismo hablava. . . . Quanto oía en público y sabía en secreto hallava por mi cuenta que todo me dañava, de todo me pesava, todo me entristecía y aun con todo me podría. . . . La soledad poníame tristeza, y la mucha compañía importunidad. . . . Affirmo que muchas vezes me vi en la corte tan aborrido y yo mismo de mí mismo tan desabrido que ni ossava pedir la muerte, ni tomava gusto en la vida.

> (I no longer take pleasure in anything and most of all I am discontented with myself. . . . Alone with myself, I would speak with myself. . . . I judged that everything that I would hear in public and would learn in secret was detrimental to me, that everything weighed painfully on me, that everything saddened me and nauseated me. . . . Solitude brought sadness and company caused annoyance. . . . I swear that on many occasions in the court I found myself so bored, so embittered with myself, that I neither dared to cry out for death nor managed to take any pleasure in life.) (176–181)

The rhetoric of the helplessly addicted, despairing self, impotent in all its efforts to rise from a moral abyss, has, of course, a traditional Augustinian character, and it is no surprise that it concludes in a proclamation of ascetic renunciation of the world. It is consistent with its conclusive rejection of the court that at its climax it depicts the classical sages and wise rulers in flight—for example, Diogenes, Cato, Diocletian, Pericles, Seneca, and Plato—withdrawing from the world of palaces and politics, ambitions and hopes, to seek contentment and prepare for death in the pastoral world of the *aldea*. Guevara's praise of Scipio, who in eleven years of retirement to his village "ni torné a ver Roma," represents perfectly his own pessimistic determination to segregate decisively the court world from the "agricultural" models of self-fulfillment and self-perfectioning proposed in the contemplative traditions of classical moral philosophy.

However dominant traditional religious elements ultimately are in Guevara's conclusion, the kind of mental torment that he details and the undeniable pathos of his eloquence should be understood as responses to a social situation that is radically new, and one of the most interesting aspects of his oration and its universal appeal in the age lies in its representation of the changing social environment and the challenges to traditional values that it posed. Over and over again Guevara gives one the impression of disorientation, of an incapacity to understand the complexities that victimize him. One of the most interesting of his self-incriminations can be viewed as an early, if negative, manifestation of a new, socially rooted conception of the self as a being divided: "Fuí a la corte inocente y tornéme malicioso, fuí sincerísimo y tornéme doblado" (I went to the court innocent and I came back malicious, I went most sincere [upright], and I came back doubled [two-faced]) (177). For Guevara disguise of self in the complex interaction of society's members can only be understood as loss of self, morally evaluated as hypocrisy, and, as such, experienced as a source of guilt and anxiety.

In the intensity of its reiterated negations, Guevara's diatribe bears witness to what Norbert Elias has described as a decisive alteration in Western man's consciousness and linked with the rise of the court society. Elias argues that at the heart of this "comprehensive transformation of the human being" in his emergence within a new social configuration is a distancing of subject from object that aims at rational control of the self and the environment through detached observation and reflection—the mirroring of experience in abstraction—and, through suppression of affective, spontaneous impulses, the establishment of a controlled, predictable social environment shaped by ritualized behavior and the elaborate codes of etiquette prescribing it. Such distancing leads not only to the profound separation of the individual from the other members of his society, but also to a division within himself, as he learns to shape the self through mask, disguise, and imitative behavior as a strategy for social survival and success. While such mechanisms of social adaptation are to become integral elements in the human personality in modern society, Guevara is, as we have seen, driven to despair by that social persona he cannot avoid discovering and contemplating in himself, and he frequently decries the loneliness and life without trust that might appear to be inescapable consequences of the kind of rationalistic "individualization" that Elias views as essential to the development of civilization—where people "no longer experience themselves in the world simply as creatures among others, but more and more as isolated individuals each of whom is opposed, within his shell, to all other beings and things, including all other people, as something existing outside his shell and separated by it from his 'inner' self."[143]

Guevara's diatribe founded an oppositional discourse that was repeated ceaselessly throughout the period, and its undeniable conventionalization as a rhetorical set-piece and an encyclopedic arsenal of satirical topics, anecdotes, and ingenious turns of phrase should not blind us to the very real anxieties in which it was rooted; the profundity of its contestations; and the persuasiveness of its ultimate rejection of the possibility of reconciling court and country, politics and virtue, success and happiness, society and individual, persona and self.[144] Probably more insightfully than any one of the hundreds of works that it influenced, Guevara's *Menosprecio* exposed the human vulnerabilities that would be the price of the major social advancements of the following three centuries.

In a brilliant meditation on the darker consequences of the ascent of society and the inescapable "publicness" of the altered human environment, Lionel Trilling points out that from this historical point on the individual is "subject to the constant influence, the literal *in-flowing*, of the mental processes of others, which, in the degree that they stimulate or enlarge his consciousness, make it less his own." The "socialized" human being finds it ever "more difficult to know what his self is and what being true to it consists in."[145] If it is true, as Ramón Díaz Solís has suggested, that it was Guevara whom the alienated young prince Hamlet was reading as he wandered about a palace world phantasmagorically transformed by the inauthenticities of the social performances of its inhabitants, the coincidence could not have been more appropriate.[146] For one can say that Hamlet is the first great literary character representing the tragedy of authenticity in a world of incontestable and tyrannical inauthenticity. The young prince is the figure that everybody in the court of Denmark wants to gaze upon and admire as a mirror of perfection — "The glass of fashion and the mold of form,/The observed of all observers" (III,1,156–157) — but it is precisely the spectral, depthless character of this world that drives him ultimately to distraction. "I know not 'seems'/'Tis not alone my inky cloak . . . Together with all forms, modes, shapes of grief,/That can denote me truly. These indeed seem,/For they are actions that a man might play,/But I have that within which passes show" (I,2,75–86).[147] The inauthenticities of court life flow in an endless stream of hollow communications and expressions that are nothing but "words, words, words."

To return to *El villano en su rincón*, Juan Labrador's "savage" resistance, his "peasant stubbornness," his peculiar panic at the approach of the king, his exasperation at his children's addiction to the pleasures and excitements of court life, and the intensity of his satirical voice are all touched with the power of Guevara's discourse. Given Lope's reputation as one of the most worldly and conformist of Spain's great writers, it is tempting to conclude by insisting on the utopian resolutions of his romantic comedy and muting the dissonances of its satirical undertones. In this perspective the play would appear to manifest Lope's effort to incorporate Guevara's insights, respond to his contestations, and reconcile his powerfully orchestrated oppositions. In effect, Lope reverses the entire movement of the *Menosprecio*. In a moment of wishful thinking Guevara claims that the *aldea* should be brought to court. This is precisely what occurs in *El villano*. If Guevara's frustrated classical sages flee the halls of power, Lope's peasant-philosopher is transferred to the court, where he becomes the friend and honored adviser of the ruler, presumably bringing philosophical self-awareness and authenticity to a troubled human being hidden behind the "royal purple" of his official body.

For Guevara there can be no community in the atomized society of the court. In Lope's work, the peasant community and, within it, the family become the models for a purified palace world to which he returns.[148] If the *Menosprecio* displays the court world as a society of calculation and treachery, precariously held together through the predatory attachments generated by the common pursuit of power and profit and the fragile complicity of ambitious and envious, master and dependent, schemer and flatterer, *El villano en su rincón* celebrates the formation of a society in which love is the binding force and virtue is acknowledged to be a more substantial power of social differentiation than class or rank. If the *Menosprecio* leaves us with the display of the disintegrated consciousness and the two irreconcilable images of self that was and self that is, *El villano* culminates with the epiphany of a secular communion and a restored wholeness, as peasant and king, palace and *rincón*, unite in an imaginative perfectioning of the ruler in his two bodies—the majesty and the human—and in the establishment of a kingdom where those who are good need no longer live in fear.

While such a reading probably reflects Lope de Vega's intentions in *El Villano en su rincón*; certainly recognizes the dominating literary, ethical, and humanistic determinations of its design; and adequately describes its effects, one cannot deny that the fascination of Juan Labrador's opposition remains to trouble its neatness. As noted above, Bataillon conceded in his influential reading that there was something in the work that resisted any effort at conclusive interpretation. It is an ambiguity—a challenging "loose end"—that disappears entirely from the doctrinaire rewritings by Lope's contemporaries. The reliable formulas of romantic comedy do not quite work in their determination to contain the anxieties the work recognizes. The traditional humanist vision is not sufficient to deal with the threats to the human being that changing historical and social conditions are bringing. Both Lope and Guevara are among the most worldly of Spanish writers, and both could vividly capture the addictions and disturbances of the psyche that marked the new social experience of man in the court. The fact is that Lope's hostility to courtly life can be traced in his writings throughout his life, from minor pastoral lyrics in the Horatian tradition, episodes of retreat in such prose narratives as *La Arcadia* and *El peregrino en su patria*, and full-scale satirical denunciations of courtly values and corruptions in such dramas as *Con su pan se lo coma* to the profound anatomy of the Madrid social environment that he left to posterity in his "most beloved" work, *La Dorotea*, completed in 1632, three years before his death.

Of Lope's major literary works, his most personal is certainly the *Dorotea*, the retrospective recreation and "working through" of a disruptive crisis that decisively marked his coming of age as a poet in Madrid nearly fifty years earlier. A key to its unsparing, corrosive anatomy of life in the court, with its swarms of predatory, cynical courtiers, courtesans, pretenders, prostitutes, panderers, upstarts, flatterers, poets, and swindlers, is given early in the work in a confessional *romance* expressing a yearning for solitude. It is the only point in the autobiographical drama when Lope speaks explicitly in his own voice, and it reveals the kind of estrangement, spiritual weariness, awareness of being trapped, and sadness at one's own weaknesses and addictions that distinguish the unhappy consciousness of Guevara's self-scrutiny and that one might detect in the heartfelt anguish that momentarily deepens the comic exasperation of Lope's stubborn old peasant in *El villano en su rincón*. In all cases the human being's relations with others have become a source of torment. The old motif of "flight from the court" to the repose of the *aldea* is imaginatively transformed into the felicity of living in ignorance of who dwells next door; the *aurea mediocritas*, the classical condition of interior enrichment, is cynically reformulated as a life free from the compulsions created by the location of the self in a field of social hierarchies and dependencies and the resulting degradation of one's literary creativity in the quintessential forms of court writing—the flattery of panegyric and the rancor of satire. Anonymity appears to provide the only relief from the obsessions that continue to haunt the individual in his loneliness, but its satisfactions—the reassurances of *Schadenfreude*, resentment, and cynicism—grimly mock the inner fulfillment of the solitary sage, the Senecan wise man untroubled by the frivolities of society's game of masks, or the higher recognitions rewarding the self-dispossessions of quietist, ascetic, and mystic.

The reigning tyrants of the new order are *favor* and *dinero*. Pretence, hypocrisy, and inauthenticity are the foundations of its behavior. Truth has fled to heaven; virtue and philosophy wander about blindly in the rags of the beggar, weeping and attempting to console one another. Ominous signs of an approaching apocalypse are appearing: the world "sounds like broken glass"; madness is spreading everywhere. In a striking moment of imaginative insight the old Lope hears the tolling of bells and envisions the court of Madrid as a vast cemetery, the emblazoned crosses of its inhabitants' gaudy attire—the coveted emblems of membership in the prestigious military orders—metamorphosed in the marble images of their sepulchers, appropriate frames for the living dead. In the poet's exegesis of his vision a peculiar note of personal envy and class resentment supplements the conventional reminders of Baroque graveyard poetry concerning the inevitability of death and the insubstantiality of all earthly distinctions: "Blessed is the maker of the sepulchers," for he enjoys the satisfactions of revenge that the "pequeños" feel in the demise of the "grandes."

In effect, Lope's confessional ballad "A mis soledades" expresses a condition of spiritual fatigue, alienation, and disgust with oneself that recalls the darkest moments of Guevara's self-incrimination. Guevara makes no effort to contain and overcome the experience by turning to humanist values and their utopian imaginative constructs. As Francisco Márquez Villanueva has recently pointed out in an insightful study of the Franciscan's premodern consciousness, there is basically nothing in his rustic other world, his *aldea*, that stands as an ideal counterweight to his vision of social malaise and individual alienation. He is hopelessly attached to a flawed world that he deplores and that he understands very well. In the somber tones of his favorite work, the old Lope can approach such severity. One is perhaps tempted to find remnants of the discarded utopian aspiration of *El villano en su rincón* in his yearning for the life of those who,

> Sin ser pobres ni ser ricos,
> Tienen chimenea y huerto;
> No los despiertan cuidados,
> Ni pretensiones ni pleytos.
> Ni murmuraron del grande,
> Ni ofendieron al pequeño.

(Without being poor or rich,/They have a fireplace and an orchard;/They are not awakened by cares,/Or petitions or lawsuits;/They have neither gossiped of the great/Nor offended the small.)[149]

But considered in this context—as a recollection of Juan Labrador's courtly apotheosis nearly twenty years earlier—the words become simply one more ruin in the vast broken world of the life that the *Dorotea* attempts to account for, one more flash of recollection of the fleeting alternatives to the abiding emptiness of existence in the court that are briefly recovered before the expiration of Lope's flame. The recollections are summoned forth as fragments—experiences of intensity and happiness in unforgettable moments of erotic fulfillment, experiences of elation in the creative discoveries of a young poet, experiences of visionary piety and idealistic love of a converted priest and a middle-aged lover. Nothing but recollections, losses, shadows, and a bitter reminder—*memento mori*. No, Lope could never find much to recover beyond the frames of royalty and courtliness and the boundaries of their conventional utopian formulation.

It is perhaps not at all surprising that such an ambitious, worldly writer failed to find a happy response to the new awareness of the losses that humanity's "ascent to civilization" and its "golden cage" brought in its wake. Such a response would presuppose a sensitivity to the positive resources of the human being that are in fact left out when compromised by the new social formation and the alienating powers of the court model of human identity and interaction.

If Juan Labrador ultimately submits to participation in an order that fails to perceive and value the beauties lying in the abandoned residues of individuality, the "singularities" forbidden to Guevara's courtiers, the power of his protest and idiosyncrasies suggests that something else may remain for others to see. For a positive alternative that can be taken as a fulfillment of Juan Labrador's protest and its insinuation of a new awareness of loss and limitation in the new socialization of the human being, one must in fact look to another satirical depiction of the court, its protocols, customs, and corruptions; to another climactic denuding of a king; and to another search for a lost self and an authentic humanness that is concretely rooted in the earth and yearns to be free from the others. The space of the "insignificant" residue, of all that remains when man casts off the frames and varnishings of his social and political experience and identity, might appear narrow at this point, but in the masterly cultivation of one of Lope's contemporaries, it would become a source of immense riches and the full realization of human life in its variety and freedom. It would expand to the unbounded dimensions of a new literary universe that has very little to do with the frames, idealities, and centerings of utopian construction. I am of course referring to Cervantes, unlike the supremely worldly Guevara and Lope de Vega, a reconciled outsider and writer of the open road; to the abdication, disrobing, and departure from the court of his most interesting king, Sancho Panza; and to the new decentered, unframed literary universe of the novel to which he returns.[150]

KING AND WARRIOR: *EL REY DON PEDRO EN MADRID O EL INFANZÓN DE ILLESCAS*

AN EXORCISM OF CRUELTY OR A BEJEWELING OF BLOOD?

The most striking of the numerous oddities presented by the strange play *El Rey Don Pedro en Madrid o El Infanzón de Illescas* is its seemingly contradictory determination to break apart the fundamental reconciliation of two persons in the monarch and present them in an opposition of what appear to be irreconcilable extremes. From the doubleness insinuated in the title itself — king/infanzón, rey/don — to the tragic undertones that remain audible in the spectacular comic triumph of its conclusion — falling crowns and daggers; the king's threatening madness and senseless movements, which seem to coil about the momentarily statuesque, fixed image of his triumphant official body — the play never manages to escape a radical division. A conflict remains, refusing resolution on any rational or anticipated grounds; clinging to a conjunction of doubles that are grotesquely opposed, if not mutually exclusive; failing to declare them definitively either separable or reconcilable. One can say that the play is crafted in a monarchist design, and yet to go on to categorize it as monarchist propaganda, as Maravall has done in his influential studies of the Golden Age theater, is to miss the point that its royal triumph exacts a considerable price and that in fact that price lingers as an alluring alternative beyond the fall of the final curtain. At the heart of the tensions that can never subside are the confused epithets that propel the violent, irregular movements of the dramatic plot, the epithets that crown with an ambiguous halo the sinister figure who himself looms enigmatically over the darkest period in Spain's bloody history: Peter I of Castile (Pedro de Castilla). Is he Peter the Cruel or Peter the Just? Perhaps Peter the Cruel *and* Peter the Just? Certainly the most powerful effect of this grotesque, violent, and disturbing play is its strange vision of the inseparability of justice and cruelty, order and brutality, law and violence—an inseparability that goes deeper than the mere acknowledgment of their historical necessity and that survives all efforts at "reinstatement" of a notorious monarch. The traditional doubleness of the king crystallizes as a hybridity that is truly monstrous. The cycle of cruelty and justice, for its Spanish audience, will continue beyond the historical limit of the play and will climax and finally conclude in the bloody regicide of Montiel, in the brutal assassination of Pedro by his brother, Enrique of Trastamara. However, the implications of the drama's violent themes and characters go well beyond any easy resolutions provided by its background of historical events.

Asserting itself in numerous variations, the resistant doubleness of *El Rey Don Pedro en Madrid* continually raises far-reaching questions concerning the nature of political power; law and governance; the rise of the nation-state; the institutionalization of violence; the suppression of aristocratic individualism; and the glories, obligations, restraints, and attendant miseries of the ascendant monarch. To emphasize such political, ethical, and historical implications of its central conflict is not to say that the play fails to exploit the most primitive kind of tragic and melodramatic effects that the historical and legendary material associated with the violent and bloodthirsty rule of Peter I of Castile—murderer, fratricide, torturer, traitor, blasphemer, conspirator, avenger, rapist—continued to furnish poets, dramatists, and chroniclers throughout the Golden Age. But if it is an aesthetically impoverishing exercise to read the play simply as a work of political thesis, it is equally unrewarding to assume that its political reach and complexities can be accounted for in the narrowness of an *apologia* for a controversial and notoriously maligned monarch.[1] One should avoid the temptation to explain this play simply as a culminating moment in a political project, originating in the period of the Catholic Monarchs and the consolidation of the national state, to rehabilitate the medieval king in the face of a deep and persistent tradition emphasizing his cruelty, undue rigor, vengefulness, lust, and avarice. As is well known, the tradition reaches back to the Trastamarist propaganda of López de Ayala's *Coronica del rey don Pedro* and was continually enlivened in Spain's historical memory by the popular ballads chronicling the most sensational deeds of the infamous king.

For our purposes it is useful to bear in mind that despite all efforts at royalist apologetics, the negative image of Pedro de Castilla survived in the sober writings of the political theorists of absolutism. Even as Philip II could contemplate the portrait of King Pedro in the Alcázar of Segovia, make inquiries concerning the origins of the disturbing epithet in a bearer of the Spanish crown, and officially order that *"el cruel"* be replaced by *"el justo,"*[2] a leading political essayist of absolutism, Diego Saavedra Fajardo, could intelligently analyze the disadvantages of a prince's use of fear and hatred as means of unifying a state and bonding its society and with no hesitation point to Pedro as the exemplary model of the hated monarch: "Todo el reino de Castilla se puso al lado del infante don Enrique contra el rey don Pedro el Cruel, porque aquél era amado y éste aborrecido" (The entire kingdom of Castile sided with the prince [the *infante*] Don Enrique against the king Don Pedro the Cruel, because the former was beloved, and the latter, abhorred).[3] Pedro is the king who loses life and state because "por su crueldad" and his excessively rigorous application of the law, he is incapable of understanding that "el poder absoluto es tiranía." He fails to realize that justice, "la mente de Dios, la armonía de la república, el presidio de la majestad," is achieved through tempering of the severity of the law with mercy.[4]

More relevant in its imaginative power is the portrait of Pedro el Cruel that emerged in the most influential chronicle of Spanish history of the period, Juan de Mariana's *Historia de España* (Latin version, 1592; Spanish version, 1601). For Mariana, whose theoretical treatise on monarchy eloquently stressed the subordination of the royal will to a sovereignty residing in the popular will and in the customary laws of the state and allowed for the justifiability of regicide in certain circumstances, Pedro el Cruel was the prototype of the tyrant in his barbarity, irrationality, bestiality (*fiereza*), reprehensible violence, spectacular cruelty, vengefulness, inhumanity, and madness. Under his rule Spain passed through a nightmarish era of bloodshed, tragic violence, and triumphant evils, which the historian can render intelligible only by falling back on the models of Christian salvationist history, by invoking the mysteries of God's providential plans for the movement of Spanish history toward a deliverance from unspeakable suffering and an eventual stabilization in the ascendance of the Trastamara dynasty.

Mariana's account is frequently punctuated by pessimistic lamentations on the brutality and disorder of Pedro's rule, a spectacle of "bravos torbellinos, furiosas tempestades, varios acaecimientos crueles y sangrientas guerras, engaños, traiciones, muertes sin número y sin cuento, ningún cuidado de las cosas sagradas ni profanas" (wild whirlwinds, furious tempests, numerous cruel events and bloody wars, deceptions, betrayals, countless murders, no concern for things either sacred or profane). So bleak is his picture that at times the historian finds that he cannot go on, his hand paralyzed by the "pointless flow of blood" he beholds; by the fury and excesses of the Castilian king and his Aragonese enemy; by the greed, the betrayals, and the conspiracies of nobles and courtiers; and by the plunder and rapine of soldiers on all sides. Over and over again the *rey jus-ticiero* is associated with animal ferocity (*fiereza*): "Ningún afecto blando podía mellar aquel acerado pecho. Asombró esta crueldad á todo el reino; hízose el Rey mas aborrecible que antes; refrescóse la memoria de tantas muertes de grandes y señores principales como sin utilidad ninguna pública, ni particular injuria suya, ejecutó en pocos años un solo hombre, ó por mejor decir, una carnicera, cruel y fiera bestia, tan bárbara y desatinada, que no tuvo miedo de en un solo hecho quebrantar todas las leyes de humanidad, piedad, religion y naturaleza" (No gentle feeling could make an impression on that steely heart. This cruelty terrified the entire kingdom; the King became more abhorrent than ever before; fresh in the public memory were so many murders of grandees and high-ranking lords for no reason of public utility or for any particular offense on their part; in a period of a few years a single man, or to put it better, a bloodthirsty, cruel, and fierce beast, carried out a slaughter so barbarous and wild that he was not afraid to violate, in one single deed, all the laws of humanity, piety, religion, and nature). Recoiling before the savagery of Pedro's spectacular murder of the Rey Bermejo of Granada, Mariana generalizes: "Desta manera con la sangre de innocentes los campos y las ciudades villas y castillos y los rios y el mar estaban llenos y manchados; por donde quiera que se fuese se hallaban rastros y seña-les de fiereza y crueldad. Qué tan grande fue el temor de los del reino, no hay necesidad decirlo" (In this way the fields and the cities, villages, and castles, and the rivers and the sea, were filled and stained with the blood of innocents; wherever he would go, trails and signs of ferocity and cruelty were to be found. Just how great was the terror of the inhabitants of the kingdom, there is no need to say). As for Pedro's indefatigable and undiscriminating lust, Mariana laments that "A la verdad no había mujer alguna tan casta ni tan fortalecida con defensas de honestidad y limpieza y todo género de virtudes, que tuviese seguridad de no caer en las manos de un rey mozo, loco, deshonesto, y atrevido. No podían estar tan en vela los maridos, padres y parientes, que bastasen á poderle escapar la que él de veras una vez codiciaba; todo lo sobrepujaba y vencía su temeridad y des-vergüenza grande" (In truth there was no woman so chaste and so fortified with defenses of modesty and purity, as well as all the other virtues, that she could avoid falling into the hands of this youthful, wild, unrestrained, and insolent king. Husbands, fathers, and relatives could not be sufficiently vigilant for the woman whom he truly coveted to be able to escape from him; he would outdo them all, and his great temerity and shamelessness would triumph).[5]

Bestiality, inhumanity, senselessness, frenzied motion, mayhem, blood—the motifs saturate Mariana's chronicle just as obsessively and as powerfully as they dominate the imaginative atmosphere of the play *El Rey Don Pedro en Madrid*. However, something very different occurs in their articulation and embodiment in the drama. It is as if the protagonist of the historical calamities of Spain had split into two figures. His monstrosity and violence are shared with and repeated in a double, an unforgettable product of the historical fantasy of the dramatist. The repetition is marked by a crucial asymmetry and disassociation, suggestive of a dialectical process aiming at cleansing, purgation, or exorcism. Nevertheless—and herein lies the fascination of the play—the identification is never broken entirely. The peculiarity of the unfolding metamorphosis is revealed most strikingly perhaps in an elliptical, baffling scene toward the end of the second act, when the impatient king hurls away all official writings on the crafts, ethics, and exemplars of kingship; calls for weapons; steps impulsively into an impenetrable darkness whose challenge he finds irresistible; and, in an aristocratic rite of swordsmanship, draws blood in a duel with one of his obliging retainers. The latter's peculiar response to the king's offer of indemnification can be taken as an emblem of the mystery enacted in the play's imaginative exorcism of the bloodiest period in Spanish history. At the same time it stands as a lurid crystallization of its sublime and disturbing exchange of majesty and monstrosity—a synthesis nowhere to be found in the reassuring "mirrors of princes."

La sangre has hecho rubís.
(You have made of blood rubies.)[6]

THE TRIUMPH OF JUSTICE:
A BAROQUE LESSON IN OBEDIENCE?

> El Rey es de Dios objeto
> En premiar y en castigar,
> Y el que lo llega a culpar,
> Casi pone en Dios defeto.

(The King is God's object in meting out rewards and punishments. And he who would impeach his judgment is in reality nearly attributing a defect to God.)

—Enrique of Trastamara

In the entire Spanish *comedia* it would be difficult to find a more resplendent and triumphant epiphany of the majesty than that which occurs at the climax of *El Rey Don Pedro en Madrid*. All victims of brutal "seignorial" violence converge on the court. Simultaneously the great rebel and regicide of Spanish history, Enrique of Trastamara, arrives amid the shadows and portents of a dark night that has witnessed the king's descent into raw violence. The king himself stumbles about aimlessly beneath an apparent threat of madness before mysteriously departing from the stage and leaving all in suspense as they contemplate the recovered dagger that looms so fatefully in Spain's historical memory and in its various epiphanies in the ballads of the *romancero*—the dagger that links in a meaningful concatenation youthful assassin and blasphemer of the distant past, fratricidal murderer of the present, and royal sacrificial victim of the future. Are we confronting a true crisis, a collapse into chaos and enigma, or are we simply witnessing the climactic contrivance of a manipulative king-dramaturge? It is an occasion for helpless commentary and desperate speculation. "Yo no lo alcanzo;/que en sí mismo el Rey se entiende" (I cannot fathom what's happening; the King must have reasons of his own). The *arcana imperii* are always effectively at work in this drama, and at this moment the curtain opens for their most overwhelming display. The numerous mutations of the erratic monarch— roles, disguises, theatrical machinations—finally achieve what appears to be their monumental fixation. While clarions sound, the king is revealed as majesty, seated on his throne, "crowned, mantled in a scarlet robe, a naked sword and a scepter in his hand, a shield at his feet bearing the motto *Deposuit potentes.*" It is a triumph of justice, an image of imperial power and force guaranteeing just rule and protection of the weak: "Quiero que celebre mi justicia el mundo, donde/En alabastro ha de verme" (I wish the world to celebrate my justice, where it is to look upon me in alabaster). Pedro el Cruel's icons and their motto associate his triumph simultaneously with both the Virgilian prophecy of Rome's imperial destiny to use its immense power to bring justice to the weak (*Aeneid*, VI, 851–853) and the New Testament's proclamation—the *Magnificat*—of Christ's mission to "scatter the proud" and "put down the mighty from their thrones" (Luke, 1, 51–52).[7] The royal lawgiver's advent is envisaged as marking a decisive turning point in universal history.

In a scandalously violent reinvention of Spanish history, the future regicide and usurper, one of the *potentes*, is put firmly in place in the divinely just order and finds himself, despite his fleeting participation up to this point in the play as a figure tenuously paralleled with the king's principal antagonist, the ferocious rebel Tello, called upon to offer the definitive gloss on the theatrical emblem— the charismatic official body of the monarch.[8] As in the climactic unveiling of its counterpart, the body of Christ, in the contemporary allegorical *autos sacramentales*, we might assume that the solemnity of the moment and its invocation of the cult of the king was to leave the audience awestruck:

> De la suerte que lo ves,
> Son divinidad los reyes.

(In the way that you see him, Kings are divinity.)

Clearly the drama moves decisively toward an affirmation of the traditional conception of the majesty and its sharp differentiation from all forms of power that reside in the arbitrary will of an individual (the insane despot, the capricious tyrant, the willful seigneur) and express themselves in acts of cruelty and a politics of terror. It is at this point that the specific questions raised in Act I concerning the alleged cruelty of the sovereign ("¿Cruel es tu Rey, Castilla?/Falso atributo le das" [479]) are finally answered directly, and we can see most clearly the play's political project as a rite of historical purgation — dramatically dissociating Pedro el Cruel from all that is suggested by his legendary epithet, *el Cruel*, even as it reminds its audience, in a moment of emblematic intensity, that the true foundation of monarchy lies in the divine will.

The people of Madrid tumultuously gather before the quasi-divine figure who "comes to offer them his justice."

> Madrid, Madrid, vuestro Rey
> A haceros justicia viene
> De sinrazones y agravios:
> Quejaos de los que os ofenden.
> Llegad, que haceros justicia
> Hoy de sí mismo os promete.
> Justiciero es, no cruel,
> Aunque esta opinión os debe.

(Madrid, Madrid, your King comes to bring you justice for the outrages and grievances that you have suffered. Voice your complaints against those who offend you. Come forth and approach the King, for today the King promises to give you justice himself. He is Peter the Just, not Peter the Cruel, although you hold him to be the latter.) (p.517)

The startling movement toward the "fin alegre con prodigios y sin muertes" (519), an abrupt reversal of direction in which "miracles displace deaths" and which, in the peculiar elliptical superimposition of Pedro's struggle with an accusing shadow onto his foregrounded conflict with the rebellious noble, seems to be modeled on the great miracle narratives of the Counter-Reformation and their pattern of sin, sacrilege, rebellion, self-abasement, and divine intervention, is punctuated by a most concise proclamation of the traditional divine right theory of monarchy — a proclamation all the more startling, if not in fact miraculous, as it is made by Pedro's future assassin, Enrique of Trastamara.[9] Here too the "cruelty" of Pedro is "exorcised":

> El Rey es de Dios objeto
> En premiar y en castigar,
> Y el que lo llega a culpar,
> Casi pone en Dios defeto.
> Dios obra en la majestad
> Que siempre tiene consigo,
> Y es tal vez justo castigo
> Lo que parece crueldad.
> Premio y castigo en la ley
> Del Rey a un reino se da,
> Y en su ejecución será
> Sólo el instrumento el Rey:
> Y ansí, culpar no es razón
> Al príncipe soberano
> Porque le toca la mano
> Con que obra la ejecución.
> ¡Bien al mundo pareciera
> Que, escondido en Trastamara,
> Yo al Rey le huyera la cara!
> Ya en parte delito fuera.
> Deja al Rey en el altar
> Que por serlo le señalo;
> Que es deidad el Rey más malo,
> En que Dios se ha de adorar.

(The King is God's object in meting out rewards and punishments, and he who would impeach his judgment is in reality nearly attributing a defect to God. God disposes through the majesty, which he always has at his side; and what looks like cruelty is perhaps a just punishment. Reward and punishment are given a kingdom in the King's law, and the instrument of its proper execution will be the King alone: And so, there can be no reason for censoring the sovereign prince because it is his lot to be the hand that carries out the execution of justice. What would I be in the world's eyes, if hidden in Trastamara, I were to flee the face of the King! It would already be in some places a crime. Leave the King at the altar. For, as he is the King, I distinguish him from all others. For the most evil king is a deity in whom God is to be worshipped.) (509–510)

As a statement of monarchist theory, Enrique's words invoke the traditional theocentric conceptions underlying the most conservative and anti-humanistic political theories of absolutism concerning the origins and foundations of state power and the authority of its laws. Power descends from above in the fearsome hand of the prince, the creature chosen by God and invested with His sanctity at the altar. He is the descendant of David, God's anointed, whose arbitrary, at times seemingly tyrannical, acts, in ways that human understanding cannot fathom, are manifestations of divine purposes. The law may well be beyond man's comprehension in its specific determinations, but the king's decisions as *judex* are always to be deemed just. Their apparent severity can in no case be construed as cruelty. From this perspective the phrase "King Pedro el Cruel" becomes more than a paradox; it designates in fact a contradiction in terms or a non-existent entity. The king as judge stands at the altar, and his subjects are obligated to gaze on his face and hail him in a ritual of obedience and adoration. Failure to do so is in fact a *delito*, a breach of duty, if not of law. All questions concerning comprehensibility and rational justification are of secondary importance.

"Non est potentia nisi a Deo" (For there is no power but of God) (Romans, 13). The most uncompromising of the principles dominating medieval approaches to the rulers of Augustine's City of Man are resoundingly resurrected and re-asserted with absolute priority. The foundations of law would appear to lie in the secrets of the omnipotent divine will, and its dictates and apparent paradoxes are not to be approached through rational understanding and human calculations of equity. One should emphasize here the fundamental differences between this conception and the more progressive theories of absolutism, which, as I pointed out in chapter 1, are compatible with and perhaps underlie the dialectical inter-action of sage and monarch in *El villano en su rincón*. In such astonishing pro-nouncements as Enrique's dismissal of the conceivability of regal cruelty, it is as if centuries of increasing enlightenment in the understanding of man's possibili-ties as a citizen in a political order subject to his own understanding and control have been forgotten. No mention is made of the rationality, the naturalness, the historicity, and the universal comprehensibility of a law that coerces king and subject alike in a process of self-limitation.[10]

As I pointed out in chapter 1, for contemporary legalists and theorists of sov-ereignty, the issue of the king's subjection to preexisting foundational laws was of vital concern for the successful functioning of a state and the avoidance of its disintegration into tyranny. In his illuminating discussion of laws as the "reins" of a prince's state, Saavedra Fajardo, recalling Tacitus, insists that "no obliga al príncipe la fuerza de ser ley, sino la de la razón en que se funda, cuando es ésta natural y común a todos" (it is not the force in simply being the law that compels the prince to obey the law, but rather the force of the reason in which the law is founded, when this reason is natural and common to all human beings).[11] Perhaps the most instructive rejoinder to the drama's political violence and its archaic aggrandizement of the royal majesty in its divine connection is be found in Mariana's *Del Rey y de la institución real.* As the influential apologist of regicide puts it, if the king

> se confiesa sujeto a las leyes, no solo gobernará mas fácilmente el reino, le hará mas feliz y refrenará sobre todo la insolencia de los grandes, que no se atreverán a creer propio de su alta dignidad ni el desprecio de las costumbres nacionales ni el respeto de las leyes. *Menguará así la majestad del príncipe; mas lo que menguará será el desorden,* inevitable cuando se concede la facultad de quebrantar las leyes nacionales. Respetar la ley, se añadirá, es de almas flojas y cobardes; mas no es sino de hombres depravados y rebeldes despreciarlas. . . . Quede pues sentado que la moderación del príncipe que se cree sujeto a las leyes, prefiriendo a su gusto lo verdadero y lo útil, . . . asegura con mayores y mas firmes fuerzas la salud de todo el reino.

(confesses himself subject to laws, not only will he govern the kingdom more easily, but he will make it happier, and, above all, he will hold in check the violence of the grandees [the powerful], who will not dare to believe it proper of their high dignity to treat with contempt national customs and respect for laws. *Thus the majesty of the prince will be diminished, but what will truly be diminished will be disorder,* which is inevitable when permission to break the national laws is conceded. One might object that respect for the law is for weak and cowardly souls, but the truth is that scorn for the law is only for depraved and rebellious men. . . . May it then be clearly understood that moderation in the prince who believes himself subject to the law, preferring truth and utility to his pleasure, . . . guarantees the health of the entire kingdom with the forces that are most powerful and firm).[12]

Enrique's absolutism would appear to reject all such qualifications. God gives power to kings, not to communities, and it is not for communities to claim insight into a rationally intelligible natural order manifesting and circumscribing the foundations of their powers or insinuating a state's "responsibilities" or "essential" purposes in facilitating its subjects' development as citizens, mature moral beings, and happy individuals. There is no mention of such concepts as natural law, popular will, delegation of sovereignty, or contractualism. In an age obsessed with power, law, anarchy, and obedience, *El Rey Don Pedro en Madrid*'s hieratic display of the king's official body—and promise of its permanent "alabaster" representation, presumably at the altar of the church of his expiation—as a manifestation of the law is striking in its denial of all that the optimistic *El villano en su rincón* affirms regarding the essential attachment of that body to a moral order legible and imitable for all men as inhabitants of a rationally designed universe. Traces of the utopian vision can in fact be discerned fleetingly in *El Rey Don Pedro en Madrid*—in the required classical readings of kings and, arguably, in the world concert invoked by the victim of seignorial brutality and juxtaposed to her tormentor's chaotic natural order—but their most conspicuous significance lies in their failure to develop. Pedro quickly and contemptuously dismisses his exemplary texts when possessed by an inexplicable urge for violence ("swords, not Latin books!"),[13] and Elvira's poetic vision of world harmony, universal love, rationality, hierarchy, and gradation is forgotten entirely in the dramatic restoration of justice and refoundation of law in the royal will.[14]

In this degraded political world of battling egos and epic antagonists, there is no place for such model communities as Juan Labrador's *rincón* or Lope's Fuenteovejuna. The fundamental principle of the jurists, from Azo to Suárez, that "potestas [imperatoris] legis condendae . . . in eum transtulit populus" (the power of the emperor of founding law . . . was transferred to him by the people) and their assumptions that the acts of consent and delegation are involved in the transfer of legitimate authority from populace to king find no resonance in the primitive world of this dramatic celebration of the victory of an ironclad law over naked baronial force.[15] The harmonious alignment of the royal will with a cosmic and natural system of law reflecting universal rationality, love, and morality that has marked the rich tradition of the *specula principum*—from the Aristotelian scholastic Aegidius Romanus (1277–1279), to the Renaissance evangelical humanist Erasmus, to the seventeenth-century Tacitist and minister of the modern state Saavedra Fajardo—is conspicuously cast out of the imaginative world depicting Pedro el Justiciero's education and triumph as a legislator.[16] In its violence and archaic character the play might suggest the most pessimistic political visions of the Baroque period—Calderón's conservative and repressive statist dramas; Quevedo's retrogressive rearticulation of the *speculum principis* tradition, *Política de Dios*; or Milton's account of man's organization of his political life following the loss of Paradise. In the latter politics is a degraded realm, the roots of which, according to biblical tradition, lie not in Adam's perfect garden community of Eden and its "natural law," but rather in the post-lapsarian power state, founded near the mouth of hell by the great hunter and rebel Nimrod, the first human being to savor the pleasures of dominion over his fellow creatures and the construction of towers to rival the heavens and the powers of God.

For Quevedo the presiding spirit of the political world is "Lucifer Angel," the "amotinado inventor" of "la materia de estado," and the master of the cynical practices that formed its philosophy—"statecraft"—is Pilate, who, convinced that his "policy decision" would keep him in Caesar's favor, handed Christ over to his executioners. Amid the corruption, greed, lying, dissimulation, and inevitable betrayal, the only hope for king and citizen lies in the political lessons one can extrapolate from Christ's words in the New Testament and in the "obras de caridad" that alone constitute majesty. As for the "all too human" reality of a king's body, Quevedo reminds his reader that the shudder of the delivering mother, the shrieks of the royal infant, and the shout of the welcoming midwife have nothing to do with the making and coronation of an "immortal" king. If the human creature is to be a king, he must be educated as king. But the overriding tone of Quevedo's prophetic and satirical discourse is one of helplessness and resignation in a world where obedience to established authority is the only course for the political human being.[17] As the "human model" for moral and political perfectioning in this world, Christ becomes in fact the representative of a desperately anti-humanistic and dualistic conception of man's reduced possibilities as a political being. "Muy enfermizo es para la fragilidad humana el sumo poder." A "diet of divine precept" is the only viable cure for the great human sickness of "disobedience."[18] As is the case in so many seventeenth-century pleadings for order, the comforts and simplifications of theological absolutism proved to be occasionally irresistible. The human Christ of individual fulfillment and social perfectioning of Erasmus—the model for the good citizen and the pedagogical practices of the philosopher-king—retreats before the reassertion of the self-denying sacrifice of the pessimistic, authoritarian world of St. Augustine, with its notable indifference to the very possibility of excellences in states and empires.[19] In Quevedo's satirical mirror of the prince Christ becomes the only possible king, and his characteristic appearance is that of a harsh, uncompromising moralist.

In conclusion, *El Rey Don Pedro en Madrid* would appear to dramatize the origin, pacification, and centralization of the nation-state as processes of juridification and the consequent limitation and containment of political power by law. In Pedro's struggles and victories it would appear to celebrate the ascendance of monarchy as an institution founded in a universal demand for justice. This political agenda is most evident in the centripetal movement of its plot, from frontier wilderness to courtly Madrid, and in the spectacular scenes of ritual and iconographic display punctuating that trajectory. It is nevertheless important to recognize that its theoretical resolution of the interrelationship of force and law and its formal definitive separation of justice and cruelty leave sovereignty perilously close to the altar and an exalted but enigmatic divine will that can easily become an ideological mask for tyranny and cruelty, which are officially declared to be merely, to use Enrique's words, "that which appears"—"lo que parece."[20]

It is certainly possible to account for the proliferating oppositions of the fascinating play, from its title to its concluding articulation of the *justicia/crueldad* antithesis, as variants on Saavedra Fajardo's fundamental opposition of force and reason in the dynamics of effective rule. However, to do so would be to fail to see the complexity and irreducibility of the negative side of the opposition—that is, cruelty, violence, fear, power—in a word, Tello, the Infanzón de Illescas, the ambiguous frontier figure who displaces Enrique as the principal representative of the force that historically has challenged the royal protagonist for the right to the title of the work and whose opposition to the work's triumph of law, justice, honor, bureaucratization, and etiquette survives its apparent defeat. By comparison Enrique's role as royal apologist is curiously limited. In addition to his didactic pronouncement on divine right kingship, he offers two highly charged symbolic gestures amid the climactic festivities. He ceremoniously restores the portentous dagger to the royal scabbard—a symbol of the king's laws (519)—and the fallen crown—a symbol of the kingdom—to the monarch as deity. Undeniably such minimally integrated gestures and speeches constitute a hasty doctrinal gloss on the action and would isolate and intensify its essential meaning, closing off a disturbing dialectic springing from Pedro's uneasy position at some midpoint between the extremes of rebel and apologist.

Maravall is perhaps justified in relying on Enrique's speech, lifted out of the context to which it is flimsily attached, as evidence for his view of the celebratory and propagandistic approach toward the contemporary monarchy in the Golden Age theater in general.[21] Seen from this perspective, the play would present a highly contrived image of Spanish history supporting and explicating the ideology of Baroque absolutism: the monarch is accountable only to God; his authority and acts of "justice" are unquestionable, even when apparently arbitrary and cruel; loyalty and service to king and superior in the social hierarchy are the supreme values (thus the significance of the strange shift from complaint to adoration in the abused vassals of the monstrous *infanzón*); the patriarchal family is the nucleus and the model of the social and political order (thus the bizarre transformation of Enrique, the historical usurper and fratricide, who is dissociated from the principal rebel figure and given the role of spokesman, throughout the play, for the supremacy of the majesty, the legitimacy of the king, and the reassuring "naturalness" and reliability of familial bonds).

Extending Maravall's insights into the ways in which the culture of absolut-

ism imposed its transcendentally based models and symbols on the social and
political order of the time, Angel Sánchez has studied the exploitation of the historical material centering on Pedro el Cruel in the literary culture of the Golden
Age. He notes the general silence in the theater concerning the brutal murder of
Pedro at Montiel and expands Maravall's fragmentary comments on the striking
royalist sentiments in works such as *El Rey Don Pedro en Madrid*. "Lope rewrites
the relations of Pedro and Enrique, not according to the past, but according to
the needs of Spanish society at the beginning of the seventeenth century. . . . The
message is directed at everybody in the public that comes to the production and
witnesses the display of monarchic authority, and, specifically at those powerful
nobles, close to the king, who are reminded that they have more than one reason
for obeying their ruler. The reaffirmation of the absolute power of the monarch
is a constant, both in the *comedias* in which Don Pedro's principal role is that
of *galán*, and in the other plays, in which he comes forth onto the stage characterized solely as king."[22] The reinstatement of a frightening king is at once a
reassuring spectacle of exemplary obedience and loyalty.

THE MISERY OF A KING

> Poco hombre debo de ser
> ¡Qué desdichado nací
> En nacer rey, pues no puedo
> Por mis acciones lucir!

(I must not be much of a man. How unlucky I was to be born king, for I cannot
shine by my actions as a man!)

— *Pedro el Cruel*

The problem with the interpretation of *El Rey Don Pedro en Madrid* as a triumph of justice and an *apologia*—a "rebaptism"—of Peter the Cruel is not
that it is wrong in its general outlines. However, the forcefulness of Enrique's
concluding acts of homage and the clarity of his brief concentrated speeches as
"doctrinal commentary" should not be allowed to override the most interesting
aspect of this remote and puzzling play—namely, the fact that the prevailing
conceptions regarding the monarch are presented through much of the action
as an inhibition, as a demeaning limit, and as a concealment of something more
fundamental in a king. As a literary character, as well as a king, Pedro acts as if
he were uncomfortable with his prescribed role, straining against his ideological
bindings, seeking release from laws, *letras*, rituals, books, bureaucratic robes;

from the state itself and its consecrating altar. All the hallmarks of one of civilization's major advances—from the brute violence and terror of the unjuridified landscape wilderness of feudalism to the security and protections provided by the laws and rational regulation of power within the developing environments of city and state—seem to be sources of unforeseen anxieties. As in *El villano en su rincón*, the king yearns for the recovery of a lost humanity.

King Pedro is literally suffering. He finds that he is "miserable" in his official body and would appear to take little consolation in the personified institutional entities of majesty and their elevating, metaphorically conceived designations of his authentic identity—whether as *lex animata, caput* of the corporate body politic, "animating soul" of the social body, or vicar of God. It is useful to recall that the originary anecdote inspiring the creation of *El villano en su rincón* could be viewed either as an expansive, humanizing lesson in courtesy and regal etiquette (Torquemada) or as a lesson in royal misery and human isolation (Botero). As in *El villano*, the urge to descend to the human—*humanarse*—asserts itself. But in this case the quest undertaken moves in the very opposite direction. Fulfillment in the "real body" and transformation of the official body according to the experience of that fulfillment appear to be connected with something primitive lurking in the primordial shadows at the borders of civilization and are achieved not in self-conquest and humane self-transformation but rather in the expression of destructive impulses that bring one perilously close to infernal powers and their transgressive allure.

From its very first scene, the work seems obsessed with a king as an outsider, a warrior, a hunter, an explorer of the wilderness and other shadowy and dangerous terrains—nocturnal city streets, confining chambers of the palace, dark prisons. The king is described as a man of "strange excesses." He is preoccupied with the fear he can arouse in others, and in his estrangement from self and other, he can be taken as the antithesis of the king of France in *El villano en su rincón*, who seeks out the philosophical "soul therapy" provided by a model of self-integration, inner tranquility, the *aurea mediocritas*, and the freedom from fear that characterizes the kingdom of the sage. The strangeness that marks Pedro's nostalgia for a lost humanness is most intriguingly developed in his relationship with an anarchic double, who appears on the stage "vestido de extraño" and incites him into a transformative encounter with madness, chaos, and the monstrous. The primary dramatic movement of the play is focused not, as we might expect, on the relations or opposition of Pedro and his surprisingly bland and benign half-brother, Enrique de Trastamara, the future regicide astonishingly recreated as the rational apologist for the majesty, but rather on the king's complex interaction with a fellow in estrangement—a dark double and a parody "mirror"—the *infanzón,* an invented figure who enabled the dramatist to explore imaginatively some of the most interesting aspects of monarchy and its relation to violence.

El Rey Don Pedro en Madrid appears at the outset to adopt a dramatic formula that we associate with Lope de Vega's most famous "historical" plays and romantic comedies—the abuse of a representative of the *pueblo* or the *campo* by a member of the lawless aristocratic oligarchy and the victim's successful appeal to an idealized monarch for justice. The characteristic alliance of monarch and peasant is immediately established, and it is maintained up to the concluding restoration of order. However, one discovers that the drama quickly turns away from any poetic or philosophical elevation of the world of the *labrador* as a utopian model for governance. In this respect *El Rey Don Pedro en Madrid* is very different from such works as *Fuenteovejuna, Peribáñez y el comendador de Ocaña, El villano en su rincón, Los Tellos de Meneses,* and *La quinta de Florencia.* Certainly the opening speech of the heroine appears to be laying the philosophical foundation for the kind of doctrinal resolution that we find in such romantic comedies. In celebrating the perfection of her love for her intended bridegroom, the victim of rape offers a powerful vision of the universe as a vast community, a harmonious concert linking celestial bodies, elements, plants, animals, and human beings in a metaphysical order founded in love.

> Cuanto ves es ensayo
> del puro amor, y a ser viene
> Delito el amor incasto.
> Mira en discorde armonía
> Esos elementos cuatro,
> Y el sol en tálamos de oro
> Espíritu de los astros. . . .
>
> Pompa es la yedra del muro;
> Alma es la parra del árbol.
> Las palomas, ya zafiros,
> Ya copos de espuma blancos,
> En arrullos por los picos
> Se están las almas brindando.
> Fragancias le dan al día
> Las flores en holocausto,
> Porque en su quietud las deja
> Para besos fingir labios.
> Todos en su especie, al fin,

Se gozan y aman, que amando
Disformemente no hiciera
Naturaleza milagros.
Pues si es ansí, deja que ame
La igualdad, sin ser contrario
Al concierto de las cosas
Que están el mundo aumentando.

(Everything that you see is a demonstration of pure love, and unchaste love becomes a crime. Look at those warring elements in their harmonious resolution of discordant components, and look at the sun, the spirit of the heavenly bodies, shining in his golden bridal chambers. . . . Ivy is the pomp of the wall it clings to. The vine is the soul of the tree it embraces. The doves, now glowing sapphires, now white tufts of foam, are offering their souls in their soft billings and cooings. The flowers offer the day their fragrances in a sacred flame, that it might leave them in peace to feign lips for kisses. In fine, all, in their distinctive species, feel joy and love, for in loving disproportionately, nature would not bring about its miracles. Thus, if this is so, let equals love one another, without making themselves enemies of the concert of the things that are bringing increase to the world.) (482)

As an image of world harmony and plenitude—the *discordia concors*—visible everywhere in nature and realized in the wedded love of equals, the passage forms a striking contrast to the violent natural order and marvelous chaos associated with the vast frontier estates of the predatory aristocrat described shortly thereafter. However, as an alternative to the latter's ambiguous world, it is of little interest to the dramatist. It lingers oddly as an unexploited philosophical possibility, and it can be seen as analogous in its ineffectuality and ironic thrust within the whole play to the innocent vision of the pure majesty that the dramatist would project, in defiance of history's undeniable truths, in his final comedic epiphany and festive celebration of multiple marriages. In this dark and disturbing play, the energies for restoration are not ultimately to be located within a utopian model of Neo-Platonic philosophical or pastoral literary derivation. They reside rather in the ambiguous perfections of the new Baroque machine state, with its concentrated and disenchanted "scientific" political power, its judicial rigor, and its executive severity. The literary world of their fulfillment remains far closer, in its somber, threatening, and potentially tragic tones, to Baroque melodrama and miracle play than to the reassuring visions of pastoral and romantic comedy.[23]

Following the initial scenes, the direction of the play turns abruptly from the

power of love to the power of law, from romance to politics. The country landscape is abandoned entirely, and the action unfolds in the darkening and narrowing spaces of city, court, cloister, prison, and gallows. Statist pacification and
centralization begin to resemble a movement into hell, an effect heightened by
riddles, blasphemies, ghosts, and allusions to tombs and petrifying metamorphoses. At the same time the drama becomes intensely focused on the figures
of the monarch and his dark antagonist-double, a claustrophobic relationship,
tightening like that of two coiling serpents locked obsessively in a death struggle.
It goes without saying that the relationship is far more ambiguous and suggestive
than the conventional oppositions of deliverer and villain marking such romantic and politically optimistic works as *Fuenteovejuna* and *Peribáñez y el comendador de Ocaña.*

Similarly we find that the playwright's efforts to intensify and expand the
dramatic conflict of protagonist and antagonist by coordinating it with a background historical conflict—in this case the civil wars between Pedro el Cruel,
the legitimate king, and his half-brothers of the house of Trastamara—are fragmentary and minimally coherent. The failure to account satisfactorily for the
monarch's frenzied journey in the opening scene, as well as the awkward assembly of background information—in the manner of an afterthought to his
riveting soliloquy at the opening of Act III on the frightening encounter with
the corpse—might suggest that the author is not seriously interested in historical accuracy and logic. One has the impression that history seems to get in his
way, to interfere with effects of concentration and intensity more appropriate
to a work in which the primary stakes and issues are psychological, theatrical,
archetypal, and hence timeless. Curiously Moreto's *refundición* is much tidier
in integrating and motivating historical material. More easily reducible to the
ideological program—the untroubled triumph and harmonious conjunction of
valor and justice—the play moves us far less than its primitive ancestor, with its
haunted, elusive protagonist; his titanic struggles with an avenging shadow; and
the hallucinatory atmosphere of his associations with pure evil.[24]

This play about the rise of the Spanish state in a moment of great historical
crisis is in fact everything that the genuine history play, in its expansiveness and
"panoramic" effect, is not. Its fictional world has the concentrated, intense, and
claustrophobic effects of the nightmare. Its tortured figures seem to move about
nervously in foreshortened, barely marked, hallucinatory spaces, and its two
isolated, very different panoramic visions of the natural world provide no more
than a momentary escape from a world that seems constantly to be closing in on
its inhabitants.

Release from the nightmare would appear to be provided unexpectedly by

Enrique in his role as *deus ex machina*, but in its elliptical character and blindness to the real nature of the king's *miseria*, his conventional pronouncement on the divine authority of monarchs ultimately remains little more than a tantalizing but illogical gesture toward a historical foundation. Even more ineffectual is the future usurper's function as providential agent in the climactic moment of deliverance of Pedro from the powers of hell and the prophecy of his assassination (516). At this point the play abandons history entirely even as it reverses its apparent movement toward tragedy. The fateful dagger linking Pedro's "youthful" sacrilege and his future murderer is fortuitously discovered by the historical assassin and benignly turned over to its owner. The literary self-consciousness of this "Baroque" drama reaches a high point as the "avenging agent" of a developing *Schicksalstragödie* becomes a portent; "an angel fallen from heaven"; a paradoxical "fratricidal slayer of Cain"; and a voluntary, beneficial sacrificial offering in a miracle drama that suddenly, in the astonishing display of a metaphysical backdrop (516), envisages God as the supreme dramatist manipulating Pedro and all mere theaters of state and human beings according to the demands of His ultimately comedic plots. The play momentarily glances at the kind of political resolution that will find its fullest expression in a play such as Calderón's *El principe constante*. What is the true value of the earthly theater and all of its laws? "En los decretos del cielo/Nada es el hombre, y el suelo/Ley de sus prodigios es" (In the decrees of heaven, man is nothing, and the earth subject to the law of its miracles). At this point Pedro approaches the exemplary humility of the miracle protagonist and yields to the theological absolutism the literary form always implies.[25] The cruel man of pure will acknowledges, "Manda en mi voluntad/Voluntad más soberana" (My will is commanded by a more sovereign will), and admits that in its ineffable decrees the Divine Will is an "immense abyss of secrets" (515). As an ascetic foundation for the climactic submissive, "institutional" image of the *justiciero* that immediately follows, the exchange is an interesting indication of the archaic nature of the play's political vision. The institutional image of monarchy in this play is based not so much on law and rationality as it is on *arcana*, pure power, domination, rigorous justice, protection of the weak, and the overthrow of tyrants. As Enrique's words suggest, the majesty that ultimately invests the triumphant king is founded directly in the incomprehensible will of God.

In summary, the arbitrary movements of the conclusion of *El Rey Don Pedro en Madrid*—the swift and decisive enactments of justice; the reconciliation of aggrieved parties by a magnanimous king; the restoration of political and civil order; the arrangement of several "healing" marriages; and the concentrated, emblematic declaration of conservative monarchist theories—might encourage a reading of the work in accordance with the most familiar models of Lope de Vega's "conformist" theater. However, there are striking divergences from the customary design: the introduction and abandonment of the idealistic metaphysics and divine rationality that found and support the optimistic vision of the romantic comedies, the failure to maintain a clear opposition in the relationship of protagonist and antagonist—a relationship dominated by complex mirroring and ironic effects—and the radical rejection of the customary neat and mutually sustaining parallelisms of history and fiction. The drama appears to turn against its sustaining formulas, most strikingly in its obsession with the monarch; his contradictions; his peculiar dissatisfaction with his majesty; his attraction to violence, disorder, impulsiveness, darkness, and irrationality; and, most important, his ambivalent relations with his dark, disorderly double, the invented figure of pure power and civil disorder, the rebel Tello.

At first glance the insistent dissociation of the great historical figure of rebellion, Enrique, and Tello is puzzling. On reflection we recognize that Pedro's assimilation of values embodied by Tello would have been impossible to portray in a relationship between himself and the future regicide and founder of the illustrious Trastamara dynasty. Tello's "truest" home is not the wonderful "Gothic" estate of limitless fertility at the expanding borders of the Spanish conquest that he boastfully describes. Associated with such fabulous monsters as the cyclops and the hydra, his real habitation is in the worlds of myth, psyche, and imagination and in their visions of the chaotic forces of pure energy founding, underlying, and constantly menacing with mutability and disintegration the created forms of civilization. Literally "of the earth [*tellus*]," Tello is the telluric spirit, the unbounded antagonist of Pedro the civilizer; the lawgiver; the founder; the Herculean slayer of monsters; and the delineator of orderly spaces, boundaries, and gradations—hence the rock (*piedra*) at the center of Madrid in his riddle, and hence his concluding act of founding. But the most profound insight of the play—mysteriously insinuated in the subtle mirroring effects in the relationship of Pedro and Tello—lies in its implication that Tello also dwells in Pedro, that in fact he is a facet of the monarch himself and of the political order he represents, just as he dwells also in the psyche and psychology of the self-destructive sinner. As such, he is nothing less than the embodiment of pure force, pure will, pure cruelty—all that in degenerate form can menace the ideal monarchy, and civilization itself, with a collapse into destructive tyranny and the plague of pure selfness and rampant irrationality.

To understand Tello's role in conventional psychological and educational terms as a double who embodies the youthful errors of a prince, the *mocedades* that require expiation and purgation (see below), is but to scratch the surface of

El Rey Don Pedro en Madrid. At the deepest stratum of the play's political and historical significance, Tello should be seen as an archaic, residual impulse in absolutism that aspires to emancipate state power from the restraining dictates of universal reason and its embodiment in law, not to speak of the other advances in its "civilizing" mission—ritual, ceremony, etiquette, documentation, written record, and bureaucracy. Costumed as "un extraño" and confronting a king described as a man of "extraños excesos," he is, in his rhetoric of self-aggrandizement, the strangest figure in a fundamentally strange play. Yet there is a splendor, a charisma, in his monstrous egotism. He is adored by his subjects. He too is described as a slayer of giants. He is honored at the tables of the great. His friendship and admiration are coveted by Pedro. Who is he? Why does Pedro, the celebrated lawgiver, feel drawn to him in his rebelliousness and violent self-expression? We might note that Tello, the Infanzón de Illescas, disappears from the title of Moreto's comfortable *refundición*. The disappearance signals a programmatic occlusion to follow in the play. But the fact remains that the fictional Tello enables the dramatist who created him to explore areas of far greater consequence than the relatively narrow confines of seventeenth-century history, politics, and ideology.

THE VIOLENT HORSEMAN

Perdido va el rey don Pedro
Por los campos de Madrid,
Donde mató a su caballo.

(The king Don Pedro has lost his way in the countryside of Madrid, where he killed his horse.)

The terms of the dramatic development of Pedro el Cruel's relationship with Tello are anticipated in the initial appearance of the monarch. It is a shocking image of violence and cruelty that parodies the climactic epiphany of the *rey justiciero* and its iconic assembly of crown, scepter, sword, and shield. In its vividness and imaginative resonances, it lingers unforgettably and establishes, in conjunction with the concluding *descubrimiento*, a striking emblematic frame for the entire play.

A discussion of love and its sufferings by a group of peasants—victims of Tello's capricious lust, as it turns out—is rudely interrupted by the violent killing of a powerful horse ("fogoso, espumoso, fiero"— fiery, foaming at the bridle, ferocious) under the spurs of an "infuriated" rider. The latter, a dashing ("bizarro") knight, strides onto the stage with his sword drawn, perhaps dripping blood from the act of dispatching the beast, which, he explains, rebellious beneath his command, refused to hurl himself obediently down a precipice and sought instead to unseat his master as if he were "another Phaeton." In what one might characterize as a grotesque articulation of the ubiquitous solar mythology of absolutist depictions of the royal majesty—king as killer of the Apollonian steed[26]—the grisly scene evokes a legendary image of Pedro el Cruel as a restless, impatient, and irascible king who frequently, in his frenzied pursuits and flights about Spain, drove his animals to the limits of their endurance.[27] However, its principal significance lies in the symbolic economy of the play that it introduces and frames. In its functions and effects it is a deeply ambivalent image.

On the one hand, Pedro's slaughter of his steed announces the major conflict that the drama must resolve: the confrontation of the civilizing king and the forces of instinct, irrationality, and chaos that violently oppose his efforts at civilized and lawful rule. As we soon discover, his antagonist is frequently associated with the bestial, the monstrous, and the gigantic—the mythic antagonists of the hero as civilizer.

The image of the hero as animal tamer and slayer was conventional in the national theater's depiction of ideal kings and knights. One need only recall the ritual scenes of heroic jousting in Lope de Vega's popular *El príncipe perfecto*, a work that assimilates the monarch and the activities of his rule to the archetypal epic hero's efforts in clearing away primordial chaos, expanding the boundaries of the human world, and integrating newly explored territories—in this case those of the Portuguese empire—within the cultivated space of civilization. After ritualistically receiving the homage of the inhabitants of the most exotic and remote territories of his new empire ("El remoto Ceylán, el chino, el persa,/Bárbaro y moro sus laureles bajen,/Y la nación más última y diversa"—The remote Ceylon, the Chinaman, the Persian, the barbarian, and the Moor, the nation most distant and diverse, may they all lower their banners to him), Lope's "perfect" king, the youthful Juan II of Portugal, displays himself as a beautiful horseman and proceeds to confront and slay a runaway bull, "bathing the street in blood," to the universal acclaim of his terrified subjects.[28] One might contrast the brutality of the violent horseman of the opening scene of *El Rey Don Pedro en Madrid* with the "Apollonian" splendor of the Portuguese royal figure in his most striking epiphany:

> Leonel: Ninguno como el Rey anda a caballo.
> Caballero: Él es en todo un Príncipe perfeto.
> Leonel: ¡Dichoso el que merece ser vasallo
>   De un Rey en quien jamás se halló defeto!

(Leonel: No one rides horseback like the King. Caballero: He is in every respect a perfect prince. Leonel: Happy is the man who deserves to be the vassal
of a King in whom never a defect was to be found!)

Perhaps nothing demonstrates more aptly the programmatic imposition of
myth onto reality than a ceremony of royal aggrandizement staged in 1631 in the
amphitheater of the royal palace in Madrid. In a resurrection of the tradition of
the Roman emperor cult, Philip IV, dressed in the hero's attire, ceremoniously
stepped forward into the arena, where a defiant bull had scornfully resisted several attempts at domination, and valiantly slew the monster with the "acertado
golpe" of a well-aimed musket shot. The occasion was celebrated by numerous
poets of Madrid, and in their verses they did not hesitate to declare the deed
superior to the triumphs of Hercules, Theseus, and Jason. Saavedra Fajardo's
espinela celebrated the king as Jupiter, whose annihilating lightning bolt transformed his victim into the luminous splendor of a constellation, and Lope de
Vega's sonnet praised the "marcial decoro" of the king, the worthiness of the
adversary, and the dignity and beauty of both victor and vanquished in such an
act of prowess.[29] There is only one note of pathos and perhaps irony to temper
the enthusiasm of the encomiast: the bull, a creature deprived of reason, is incapable of fully appreciating the occasion and realizing "how much he stands
in obligation to his death." The aestheticization of violence, the cultic shedding
of blood, the beautiful kill, the perfection of the single stroke, the worthiness of
the antagonist, the personal superiority of the victor, the utter irrelevance of any
sentiments of compassion—all mark the staging of the event and its description
as a powerful assertion of the aristocratic warrior ethos, its individualistic and
theatrical conception of personal worth and honor, and its cult of fame.[30]

In its contrivances the opening scene of the drama, moreover, hints at the
complex theatricality of King Pedro—as disguiser, dissembler, choreographer,
director, actor, and self-dramatizer—that will distinguish his activity throughout the work (see below). At this point, however, I would simply note that in
his initial image the king appears to be animated by the archaic values of the
medieval knight and epic warrior, an impression that is retroactively confirmed
when later in the play an unseen, anonymous popular poet motivates his
earlier, unexplained intrusion into the peasant maidens' world. Incorporating
and freely modifying various fragments of a traditional ballad of King Pedro
("Por los campos de Xerez/a caza va el rey don Pedro"—In the fields of Xerez
King Don Pedro goes hunting), the singer situates the protagonist of the first
scene in the utopian world of aristocratic military aspiration and erotic pursuit—the hunt.

Perdido va el rey don Pedro
Por los campos de Madrid,
Donde mató a su caballo
Y se le voló el neblí.
Encontrara dos serranas
Retratos de un serafín,
Que lo llevan a su aldea,
Que estaba cerca de allí.

(King Don Pedro has lost his way in the countryside of Madrid, where he killed
his horse and his falcon flew away. He came upon two highland lasses, the
images of a seraphim, who take him to their village that lay close by.) (502)[31]

On the other hand, the opening scene, with its brutal act of bloodshed and
its peculiarly violent encounter of knight and rustic lady—the *caballero* and
serrana of aristocratic fantasy—becomes much more ambiguous if we recognize the imaginative power of equestrian symbolism in the political culture of
the new modern states. In this context the grisly scene of the splendid animal's
destruction by a monarch would have radically different implications, and they
certainly would run counter to any chivalresque exaltation of the heroic deeds
of civilizer-lawgiver-knight-lover. To understand them and the complexities they
bring to the drama's portrait of a king, we should recall that the horse was a central symbol in the literature and visual representation of the absolutist political
order. As H. R. Trevor-Roper has noted in his study of the Baroque courts, all
over Europe the new kings turned to the equestrian portrait as the emblem of
correct rule, an image that suggested the civilized control of raw power; the
rational and skillful direction of energy; the commanding, guiding, and yet restraining force of the rider's hand; and, in a beautiful, "centauric" image, the
reconciliation of man and animal, art and nature, rationality and instinct, force
and beauty.[32]

Political theorists readily seized on the equestrian image in their discussions of
the skills required for successful rule. Particularly relevant for an understanding
of the dissonances in the play's introduction of Pedro is Saavedra Fajardo's essay,
"Con halago y con rigor" (With blandishments and with rigor), which he includes in his *Empresas políticas*. It is a commentary on an emblem depicting an
unsaddled, stately horse standing tranquilly in a pleasant field, his head gently
and respectfully inclined toward a hand holding a staff before him (see figure 4).
The instrument of discipline is held at an angle that produces a single, continuing straight line uniting animal and master in an image suggesting ease, politeness, and regularity. Saavedra Fajardo writes that the emblem depicts the bonds

Fig. 4. "Con halago i con rigor" (from Diego
Saavedra Fajardo, *Idea de vn principe christiano.*
[Monaco: Nicolao Enrico, 1640], Empresa 38).
(Photograph courtesy Hilaire Kallendorf.)

of benevolence and love uniting the natural order of the creation ("la monarquía
de lo criado") and teaches kings to "preserve their persons and their states with
the love of their subjects." Love is in fact the greatest fortress of a government.
History is full of calamities brought on by rulers who sought to assure the success
and survival of their political power through the arousal of fear in their subjects.
Here Saavedra Fajardo turns to Pedro el Cruel, the murdered tyrant, for his most
revealing example. Fear produces hatred, the precarious political bond of the
tyrant state and the society of barbarians and beasts. There is, however, another
kind of fear, based in respect and admiration, achieved by the good king through
disciplining and strengthening the character of his citizens, just as the skilled and
benevolent rider tames and strengthens the horse. "Y así, estudie el príncipe en
hacerse amar y temer juntamente. Procure que le amen como a conservador de
todos, que le teman como a alma de la ley, de quien pende la vida y hacienda

de todos" (And so the prince should study the art of making himself loved and feared at the same time. He should bring about that his subjects love him as the protector of everybody, and that they fear him as the soul of the law, on whom their lives and property depend).[33] The benevolent monarch is the embodiment of law and justice (the *lex animata*), civic discipline, rationality, and the security of life and property. All the principal concerns and the hallmarks of the rising state easily found their objective correlative in the endlessly invoked vision of horse and rider, the readaptation of a central image of feudalism and chivalric Europe to the expressive needs of a new age and a new political and civil vision of man, society, and government.

As I shall point out below, the equestrian image of the monarch had a particular kind of significance in Spain that we must bear in mind when considering its prominence and ambivalence in this dramatic depiction of the great *justiciero* of Spanish history. Here I would emphasize merely that the destruction of the horse, the fury of the rider, and the naked, presumably bloody sword might suggest that King Pedro of Spain, in this unorthodox royalist play, cannot be understood simply as the charismatic figure who, with his scepter and shining sword of justice and his sheathed dagger of peace restored, is revealed in the *descubrimiento* of its final scene and who is to be perpetuated, we are told, in the alabaster statue of the shrine he will construct. The image is far different from the luminous figures of the official portrait of the king shining forth reassuringly at the conclusion of plays such as Lope's *El Brasil restituido*. His role cannot be reduced to that of spokesman for official doctrines of monarchy. In fact, the slaughtering sword and the animal carcass look very much like a parody of the equestrian images of command so prominent in Spain's history, from the medieval seals of Castile to the great portraits of the triumphant Habsburgs by Titian and Velázquez. As a work celebrating the ascendance of the Castilian monarchy, the drama appears from the outset caught in a self-destructive contradiction. It is not surprising that in Moreto's rational, statist *refundición*, the scene is radically altered. Any possible tones of political blasphemy are silenced. Now a valorous, responsible king is furiously pursuing his outlaw brother and his troops. His horse collapses of exhaustion, and fortune allows the rebels once again to escape. There is no bloodshed; there is no disturbing, self-destructive violence or ruthlessness in the protagonist; and there is no avenging shadow to associate his mission as *valiente justiciero* and state builder ambiguously with infernal powers and primal sins.[34]

As the action continues to unfold, it becomes clear that the initial image of Pedro as animal slayer has more to do with his relation to the implacable enemy of the state—the anarchic, violent feudal lord of Illescas, the mirror of his "strangeness"—than with his identity as corporeal manifestation of the royal dignity. As I pointed out above, the whole play develops its dramatic power from the king's dissatisfaction with the restraints of his majesty and chronicles his struggles to escape the confines of his official body and the frames of its royal portrait. Killing the royal horse is the first and certainly the most blasphemous of his wrathful fits at the expense of the restraints in the early nation's "transcendentalizing" project for its monarch.

To recall the dynamics of doubling in *El villano en su rincón*, the French king's dissatisfaction with his identity as majesty is intimately connected with a mysterious attraction he feels for a double, in his case a figure conceived according to the legendary philosophical encounter of Alexander and Diogenes. Yearning for the power and the "majesty" that only moral consciousness and perfection can bestow, he admits, "If I were not Alexander, I would like to be Diogenes." A parallel impulse appears to be driving Pedro el Cruel mysteriously toward an opposite who holds the secret of a fullness of being that appears to be withheld from the consecrated individual who wears the crown. The exhilaration that Tello can provide is far different from the tranquility of mind that the king of France seeks in Juan Labrador's pastoral world. At this point we should ask: who is Tello and why is his agonistic involvement with the monarch, forming the heart of the play and culminating in the climactic scene of disrobing and dueling, developed in such an ambivalent way? Why is Tello in fact a mirror of the king's "strangeness," an ill-understood "strangeness" that is coveted and ferociously defended as something truly human, a humanness that is denied the holder of the royal identity?

VIOLENCE OR VALOR?
A LOOK AT SPAIN'S MEDIEVAL HISTORY

"La dimensión imperativa de la persona."

To address the questions raised by the puzzling encounter of the king and warrior in *El Rey Don Pedro en Madrid*, it is useful to recall historians' recent interpretations of Spain's medieval history, the specific circumstances of its origins as the first modern nation-state of Europe, and the features distinguishing it in its conception of monarchy from the other principal kingdoms of Europe. As Américo Castro has emphasized in his numerous historical studies, Spain came into existence as a nation in the course of several centuries of warfare against a common enemy, a frontier situation in which bonds of unity and a communal identity were forged by the necessities of military operations and objectives, and standards of value took root in the capacities of human beings for waging warfare successfully. Such capacities included not only the warrior virtues of valor, strength, decisiveness, the will to act, and the "heroic fury" aroused in battle, but also the skills of leadership and the pragmatic intelligence of the commander and the politician. In other words the Spanish nation came into existence understanding, defining, and representing itself as a society of warriors, bonded by the priorities of an inescapable public project and subject to approval or disapproval—honor or shame—according to a public performance of duty. A primitive cult of honor and a theatrical sense of one's identity appeared to leave little time for cultivating the private or engaging sympathetically with the alien. The sense that one's individual worth, that the fulfillment of one's proper identity, lay in personal feats of *grandía* and *grandeza*—words invented by the Spaniards of the period and passed on to the vocabularies of the rest of Europe—developed in the concrete situations of daily life with an intensity and immediacy beyond anything that the fantasies of heroic individualism of chivalresque literature could bring to the consciousness of other Western nations. "The consciousness of nobility [*hidalguía*], of lordliness [*señoría*], increased simultaneously with the eagerness to seize land from the Moor or from one's Christian neighbor. As far as the Spaniard was concerned, the law was connected with personal and concrete decisions, rather than with generic and depersonalized juridical principles." For Castro the manly image of the Cid, "sometiendo y reduciendo" (subjecting and bringing under control) the lion with his powerful hand, commanding and compelling obedience, is paradigmatic for a culture that, for historical reasons it certainly could not anticipate, founded its hierarchy of values in the priority of the "dimensión imperativa de la persona," the capacity to "dominar personalmente a otros." Within the general medieval culture of Europe with its aristocratic, warrior values, Spain stood out in the intensity of its emphasis on the humanness and individuality, understood as manliness, that one achieves through heroic self-assertion on the battlefield, the site of Pedro's final exchange with his rival.[35]

The historical situation described by Castro perhaps accounts for a distinguishing feature of Castilian conceptions of monarchy, which continued to be maintained even as, to recall Kantorowicz's formulations, the official body of the king expanded enormously in the royal cults of absolutism. Henry Kamen has recently pointed out that Philip II, unlike his European contemporaries, showed little interest in mystifying or transcendentalizing royal power; Kamen has suggested that the king's attitude was consistent with the distinctive historical traditions of Spain:

Previous rulers of Castile and Spain had consciously rejected many of the symbols of power used by monarchies outside the peninsula. They did not consider their office sacred, did not claim (like the rulers of France and England) any power to heal the sick, and enjoyed no special rituals at the time of their birth or crowning or death. The imagery of magical power, common in other monarchies, was notably absent in Spain. Philip followed this tradition perfectly. He encouraged no cult of his person, as Elizabeth of England did in subsequent years and as Louis XIV was to do on a grand scale later. Like his predecessors, he firmly asserted his authority to rule, and the trust he received from God, but he did not inflate these claims into a mystique of royal power. A pragmatic attitude to kingship accorded perfectly with the businesslike approach he preferred. He never encouraged royalist imagery.[36]

In several studies Teofilo Ruiz has discussed the effects of Spain's distinctive historical situation on its developing political institutions and specifically on its conception of a monarchy that, compared with those of the rest of Europe, can best be characterized as "unsacred." Ruiz speculates on the benefits Spain might have derived had its history followed European patterns. An ideology of sacred kingship that would have founded constituted authority in divine selection and consecration, in the sanctity of the royal body, in the legitimacy of the royal blood—verified by genealogical studies, documentation, and occasional forgery—and assured stability and continuity through established rights of succession, uncontestably defined and repeatedly confirmed through punctiliously codified and enacted ceremonies of anointment, coronation, and enshrinement, might well have enabled Castile to be spared the continuing disorder that plagued its history from the reign of Alfonso VIII, in the twelfth century, to the period of unification under the Catholic Monarchs. However, such an ideology failed to come into being. Standing in a warrior tradition with its respect for force and martial prowess and its willingness to bestow the rights of command on the strongest man of the moment; faced with the inescapable emergencies of a frontier situation and its continuing opportunities for territorial conquest and sudden, unforeseen expansions of power; confronting in the institutions of their Islamic adversaries an image of a kind of rule centering on personal resource, political calculation, and a capacity to survive in a world of intrigue, assassination, violence, and continuous conspiracy, the *ricoshombres* and the magnates of Castile—the *reyecillos* that oppose King Pedro's indefatigable efforts at pacification in the drama—as well as the princes of royal blood and the royal bastards, developed a "deep belief in their own individual worth." They "could and did assert their right to be king."

Ruiz points out that Visigothic law opened kingship to anyone of Gothic blood and good character and that in the continuous struggles of Castilian kings for three centuries prior to the unification, their adversaries, whether rival kings or rebellious nobles, always claimed the crown. Such was not the case in the rebellions of magnates and princes in France and England during the period: "Unlike France or England, the institutional traditions that, through several centuries, had slowly subordinated the king's human personality to the needs of the realm and the strengthening of royal institutions were not as developed in Castile." While France and England were elaborating the official body of the king in a variety of ways—for example, the *lex animata*, the head of the secularized *corpus mysticum* of the state, the crown that contains the polity—that would reduce the scope of personal and individual self-assertiveness within the institutional space and keep in check the arbitrary desires and activities of a private individual with his potential for capricious, irrational, savage, and tyrannical conduct, in Spain "those who ruled and those who wanted to rule had, more often than not, one body instead of two. They often placed their own political ambitions, their pursuits of pleasure and revenge, over the welfare of the realm and the survival of royal institutions."[37] As I shall attempt to show in the following pages, the most puzzling features of *El Rey Don Pedro en Madrid*—for example, the slaughter of the horse, the king's strange alienation from his royal body, the various discomforts he feels with his statist tasks, the scene of his disrobing and descent into solitary violence, his attraction to the pure power represented by Tello, and the unresolved tensions in the articulation of the justice-cruelty antithesis—become intelligible only when we recognize the historical conditions of medieval Spain that Ruiz and Castro have illuminated so suggestively.

While one might find in the "unsacred" conception of monarchy in Spain a tradition that ultimately facilitated the development of a modern, "demystified" political science (visible in the practices of a man such as Philip II) and nourished the pragmatic approach to the institutions of governance that distinguished Spanish Tacitism and the policies of a statesman such as Olivares in the following century, its destructive historical roots and its disturbing moral implications were obviously well understood in the political culture of absolutist Spain.[38] Mariana concludes a long discussion of the legal advantages of hereditary over elective kingship by conceding that theory and legal argument are "worth little, for it was the custom of men to carry the title of kingship in the point of their lances and in their weapons. The strongest is the one who captures the jewel [crown]. And he wins it from his opponent without regard for the laws, which are silent in the face of the clamor of arms, trumpets, and drums. And there is no one who, being able to become king by the strength of his hands, will venture his business to the opinion and judgement of jurists."[39]

Ruiz points out that Spanish rulers from 1135 on consciously rejected the traditional emblems of power and authority in use elsewhere in the medieval West and refused to consider their office subject to the obligations imposed by its alleged "sanctity." He suggests that Alfonso XI's anointment and self-coronation at the altar of the monastery of Las Huelgas in Burgos in 1332 is a unique event in Spanish political and institutional history, and he draws the following conclusion: "With far greater consistency, the rulers of Castile, in spite of the law and the tokens of royalty, expressed their power in the evident and ultimate manifestation of individual power: in personal acts of violence." Chroniclers described these kings as creatures of "extreme ferocity" who marked their assumption of power not by the rituals of legitimacy and obligation, self-reduction within a transcendent body, and communion, but rather by acts of bloodshed—the brutal killing of family members, pretenders, and rebellious nobles.[40] The most famous of such murders was committed at Montiel by Enrique de Trastamara, who, oddly enough in the historicist illusionism of the play under consideration, becomes the most prominent spokesman for a sacred and conservative conception of the monarch's authority. However, as we are discovering, the play is much more revealing in the starkness of its unwitting historical disclosures than in its efforts at historical illusionism and apologia.

In conclusion, *El Rey Don Pedro en Madrid* bears witness to the distinctive realities of kingship in Spanish medieval history that Ruiz has clarified. It furnishes insight into the violence underlying the absolutist state even as it attempts to cope with its disturbing consequences through aesthetic form and resolution. The brutality in its initial image of the king—the violent horseman—in itself might suggest as much.[41] The suggestion becomes even more compelling if we consider the paradoxical image both in its antithetical relationship to the resplendent image of the "reclothed" Pedro, no longer *el Cruel* in the epiphany of royal justice at the climax of the play, and in its bizarre configuration of the rich equestrian symbolism of monarchy. Here Ruiz's companion studies of the royal seals of medieval Spain cast considerable light on the least accessible aspects of the play. He points out that unlike those of English and French monarchs, the Castilian seals varied remarkably to suit and reflect different political aims and situations; that their configurations of symbols and images were not dominated by abstract signifying procedures or the need to express divine and universal truths; and that the most consistently appearing image—"le seul motif vraiment permanent de la royauté en Castile"—was the equestrian figure of the monarch-knight brandishing the unsheathed sword menacingly: "le roi comme guerrier."[42] For Ruiz, the implication is inescapable: the authority of the king rests on his warrior skills; the essence of the developing nation-state lies in his personal and physical power; it is most appropriately represented not in the iconic abstractions of crown, scepter, and sword preferred by "sacred" and legalistic monarchies, but rather in a hand of force that imposes the will of a dynamic ruler, the hand of the *fiero hombre* (fierce man) or the *hombres de hierro* (men of iron), who, to recall Américo Castro, brought Spain historically into existence. Certainly one of the most famous hands of this sort was that of Pedro el Cruel, whose dreaded grip is featured in numerous dramatic and poetic orchestrations of his legend. In one of the most conflicted of the various "institutional" moments of the play under discussion, we observe this hand intruding literally and violently into the king's *audiencia*, repossessing the statist army, and, as it were, displacing the bureaucratic machinery on which a modern state's military operation is based.

EL REY DON PEDRO EN MADRID: HISTORICAL ALLEGORY OR THE EDUCATION OF A KING?

> Rey: Alejandro
> Vive en pórfido y marfil,
> Despreciando eternidades:
> ¿Qué más glorioso vivir?
> Los Comentarios de César
> Me traed también. Si ansí
> Sus espíritus al mío
> Quiso el cielo reducir,
> ¿Quién se estrellará con ellos?
> Fortún: Voy por los libros.
> Rey: ¡Latín
> Y libros agora! Aguarda.

(King: Alexander lives in porphyry and marble, holding eternities in scorn. Can anyone live more gloriously? Bring me also Caesar's *Commentaries.* If heaven wished to accommodate their spirits to mine, who would quarrel with them? Fortún: I will get the books. King: Latin and books now! Hold.)

At this point it might become tempting to interpret *El Rey Don Pedro en Madrid* as a historical allegory, framed and dominated conceptually by two powerful iconic moments, demonstrating the troubled passage of Spanish political institutions from the chaotic, personalistic governance of the long period of clashes within the aristocratic oligarchy of willful feudal magnates and *ricoshombres*, to the legalistically ordered rule of state absolutism. The symbols of the reclothed king are perfectly intelligible in relation to contemporary theories of monarchy—the "imperial purple" of central authority, the scepter of unifying law, the sword of justice, and the Virgilian-biblical motto declaring the promise of protection for the weak. The reinvention of medieval history is arbitrary, and the transformation of the celebrated regicide might strike us as scandalous. But in neither case is the dramatist going beyond well-established conventions of the theater of absolutism in exercising his freedom "to manipulate" history for political purposes.[43] Following this mode of interpretation, one can easily situate Tello, the outlaw noble, within the historical allegory as a spectacularly virulent representative of the social class that opposed the rise of European monarchy. There is nothing wrong with this reading other than that, like the interpretation of the work as a lesson in obedience, it fails to account for the most fascinating aspects of the character. One quickly finds that Tello's boundless disorder escapes any efforts at such limiting conceptual confinement. His relation to the protagonist and his central role in the carefully developed agon holding the disorderly play together are far more complex and elusive, and they raise questions with profound historical, political, social, ethical, and psychological implications.

One of the principal functions of Tello as antagonist is to "exorcise" imaginatively Pedro's legendary cruelty and capriciousness by providing a dark double of the king—a projection of the anarchic, personalistic, individualistic, and aristocratic elements in a body that the redeemed king can literally overthrow, purge, symbolically kill, or, as it ultimately turns out, integrate in a reconciled form. Between the opening ritual of gratuitous violence and the closing *descubrimiento* of auratic monarchy and justice, there is in fact a third, more important, ritual moment—a torchlit illumination in the claustrophobic darkness of the night of the king's self-conquest. Resolving the fundamental dramatic agon of king and baron, the dreamlike scene of man-to-man struggle, submission, renunciation, disengagement, and purification is the true climax of the play. In view of the power and ambiguity of this epiphany "in the middle," the turn toward the concluding epiphany of the *rex judex* as a fulfillment of an elegantly articulated, "dialectical" intention seems mechanical and unconvincing. As I shall point out below in the final section, Tello is not to be disposed of as facilely as the overt doctrinal scenes of the work might suggest. Despite the neat separation of the characters in the dramatic action and the methodical movement from one epiphany to its transcendence in another, an imaginative bonding of the two violent warriors survives uneasily at the closure of the play.

In this schema the presentation of King Pedro and the striking exorcism of his cruelty and personalism as he metamorphoses into the majesty at the conclusion might be considered as a version of the drama of the king's education, a passage from youthful *mocedades*, egotism, and errantry, across the threshold of adulthood, toward "morality," self-control, and political wisdom. The play certainly makes several gestures in the direction of the thematics and dramatic formulas of the conventional "education of the prince." The most striking are concentrated in the shadow plot enfolding the foregrounded political plot. The accusing ghost of the murdered cleric confronts Pedro with his brother's dagger and prophesies: "De tus juventudes locas/Dará a Castilla escarmiento" (It will give Castile an exemplary lesson regarding the madness of your youthful escapades) (514). In vowing to found a convent in Madrid, the remorseful king will atone for the worst of the misdeeds caused by the madness of youth.

> . . . . Intento
> Consagralle en Madrid a Dios un convento
> De santas religiosas,
> Ofreciéndole en él vírgenes rosas,
> En recompensa, ¡oh juvenil locura!
> De una que le corté de su clausura.

(In Madrid I intend to consecrate to God a convent of holy nuns, in it offering Him virgin roses, in compensation, oh youthful madness! for one that I cut away from His cloister.) (516)

It is consistent with the educational paradigm that the play refashions one of Pedro's cruelest and most horrific deeds, recorded in legends, ballads, and chronicles—the burning to death of a Dominican friar who angered him by prophesying that he would die at his brother's hand if he failed to reform—as the accidental slaying of a young Dominican who tried to prevent him from breaking into a convent and kidnapping a nun. The event is configured as "youthful" and "erotic"—as belonging to the more conventional escapades of young, unruly princes. One might compare what has been considered Lope de Vega's most popular *speculum principis* play, *El príncipe perfecto*. Don Juan II of Portugal is described by Fernando el Católico as "el ejemplo, en efecto,/De la mayor perfección." In attempting to "correr/la cortina a su retrato" (draw aside the curtain of his portrait), the ambassador Juan de Sosa invokes one of the most influential classical models for the Renaissance "portraits" and "educations" of rulers, Xenophon's *Cyropedia*: "Pero vanamente emprendo,/No siendo yo Ienofonte,/Pintaros con rudo ingenio/Tan nuevo cristiano Ciro" (But as I am not Xenophon, in vain do I attempt, with my rude genius, to paint for you such a new Christian Cyrus). At the opening of this play the young prince, dressed as a *galán*, accompanies a friend who has an assignation; stands guard at the woman's door; laments, in an impressive sonnet, the absence of the sun and the night's obliteration of all distinctions ("[las piezas de ajedrez] son en ti [la noche] confusamente iguales,/Y del peón al rey no hay diferencia"/[chess pieces] are in you [the night] confusingly equal, and from pawn to king there is no difference); and, descending into the universal confusion, challenges and kills a rival. In an encounter with the ghost of the dead man years later, the perfect king, now a mature man, asserts that he is "no longer a *galán*," that his "*mocedades* are forgotten," and that he will pray for the soul of his victim. Pedro's persecution by the shadow in *El Rey Don Pedro en Madrid* and his atonement to some extent reflect this phase of the education of the prince paradigm. One might compare the function of the nocturnal Eastcheap society and escapades of the young Prince Hal in the most famous version of the theme in the English theater, Shakespeare's *Henry IV*.[44]

In the middle of Act II, after a series of exemplary acts of governing, solving dilemmas with "Solomonic" insight, and administering justice in the familiar *audiencia del rey*, Pedro asks for some reading—Quintus Curtius and Caesar, two canonic texts in the tradition of political writings regarding the prince.[45] But what is most interesting about this scene is its immediate disintegration in the king's sudden fit of impatience with books, *letras*, laws, exempla, and presumably with a whole "humanist" tradition of rationality, restraint, morality, literacy, and socialization lying therein. As the "educational" moment collapses, Pedro cries out for his sword: "¡Latín/Y libros agora! Aguarda. . . ./Traedme aquí/Espadas negras" (Latin! And books now! Hold. . . . Bring me black swords) (503). The startling words by which he expresses his needs suggest a refusal to be bound by the educational paradigm in which his dramatist appears to be containing him and in fact a determination to reverse its direction—to metamorphose not from man to king but rather from king to man.

> Si hasta aquí respeto ha sido
> Apuntarme sin herir,
> ¡Vive Dios, que al que esta noche
> Con esfuerzo varonil
> No me tirase a matar,
> Le he de matar, pues decís
> Que me veneráis por rey,
> Y no me teméis por mí!
> Poco hombre debo de ser.
> ¡Qué desdichado nací
> En nacer rey, pues no puedo
> Por mis acciones lucir!

(If up to this point it has been a sign of respect to aim at me without wounding, by God, tonight I shall kill anyone who does not attack me to kill with manly effort, for you say that you venerate me as king, but you do not fear me for myself! I must not be much of a man. How unlucky I was to be born a king, for I cannot shine by my actions as a man!) (503)

The king's "declaration of independence," his determination to recover his humanity, leads him to immerse himself in the "shadows, silence, and horror" of the most tenebrous and threatening of nights. He is drawn by temperament to this chaotic order, where "no se acreditan lisonjas" (flattery is given no credit), where the true condition of the kingdom is revealed, and where *true* "aphorisms of kings" are born. (We are reminded at this point of Juan Labrador's forest kingdom and its dark crossover zone for a frustrated king seeking a human condition denied him by his institutional self and associating his transgressive "descent" with the creation of a true and unvarnished literature of kings.) The dramatic pace suddenly accelerates, and we are carried rapidly from the anecdotal portrait of Act II and its static ritual scenes in the tradition and technique of the *speculum principis* violently toward the play's strangest moment and its true climax. In its imaginative and dramatic power, it thoroughly overshadows the brief and arbitrary display of the official royal body at the end. The latter, in dramatic terms, becomes just as insubstantial as the great classical texts of Quintus Curtius and Julius Caesar invoked by Pedro immediately before his descent into the night.

Casting away such traditional "scripts," Pedro at this moment can be said to take full control over his own play and bring his numerous acts of royal dramaturgy to fruition. It is in Pedro's mastery of theatricality and in the ambiguities of its rich metatheatrical constructs that *El Rey Don Pedro en Madrid* achieves its most unusual effects. And it is in the triumphs of a personal theatricality, rather than law, bureaucracy, and etiquette, that the play arguably carries out most effectively its agenda of overcoming Pedro's legendary cruelty and violence. Here I would emphasize historical dimensions and specifically the role of theatricality in the absolutist state and the king as master dramaturge. Using illusion to uncover illusion, for the benefit of both internal and external audience, and to display and thematize the illusionary aspects of power, persona, state, and society, the play's theatrical imaging of a theatrical king, while proceeding from a very different direction, touches on the most profound insights that we have discovered in Lope's treatment of Juan Labrador in *El villano en su rincón*. In his five major moments of disguise and theatrical self-presentation, the monarch discloses paradoxically both the substantiality and the insubstantiality of the necessary theatricalization of life.[46]

THE KING'S PLAY

At this point it is useful to return to the moment of the king's decision to put aside his royal identity and engage with his rival, man to man—*cuerpo a cuerpo*.[47] The moment of the disrobing and disguising of the monarch is certainly the most puzzling moment of the play, but as it quickly leads to what is the work's true climax, it illuminates retrospectively the various enigmas marking the king's behavior in his relationship with his double. At the same time it provides a key to deciphering all the mysteries of monarchy that are condensed into this seemingly inaccessible work. In its imaginative power and centrality within the play, it is comparable to the disguised French king's secret visit to the *rincón* and his nocturnal meal with his double in *El villano en su rincón*. Standing above his defeated adversary, Pedro offers a systematic clarification of the three principal events of the drama that he decided to stage following his encounter with the victims of the aristocrat's violence in Act I. Instead of responding with crude violence or the harshest forms of justice, he formulates a complex political plan involving the machinery of state institutions, the legal system, deception, secrecy, and theatrical instruction. At the climactic moment, having laid aside the regalia of his own illusory persona, he explains his complex use of illusion. The three principal phases of the struggle of protagonist and antagonist are cogently analyzed as the agon of a play created by the king and celebrating three different victories by three different identities in three different spaces:

> Que has visto que reñir puedo
> Contigo en *campaña*, y sabes
> Que por *mí mismo* te venzo
> Y no por la majestad
> Ni el soberano respeto,
> Y sabes que te vencí
> En tu *casa* por *modesto*,
> Y en mi *palacio* por *rey*;

(You have seen that I can battle you in *the field*, and you know that I defeat you by *my own efforts* and not by the power of the majesty, nor by the respect owed the sovereign; and you know that, as *a person of modesty*, I defeated you in your *house* and in my *palace as king*.) (512; emphasis added)

MODESTY, MANNERS, AND COURTESY:
VICTORY IN THE SUBJECT'S HOME

The first two phases of the king's victories are decisive affirmations of the institutionalized power of the monarchist state in the civilized spaces of house and palace, spaces established by morality, law, rationality, and etiquette. In each case the emphasis of the conflict is on self-restraint and the diffused power that regulates the interactions of people in a rationally ordered social formation.[48] In the first scene the legendary cruel and irascible King Pedro, having chosen the disguise of the ordinary *hidalgo* Acevedo, must conquer what would be justifiable anger in the face of his host's impoliteness, as revealed in such rituals of etiquette as seating arrangements based on distinctions between chairs and footstools; the wearing of hats in the presence of superiors in the social hierarchy; the depth of one's bow to the superior; and disrespectful conversation concerning honorable people not present—in this case, the king and his notorious mistress, María de Padilla. As the barbarity of the monstrous aristocrat ("grosero," [492]) brings the act to an end in chaos, King Pedro's self-mastery in the suppression of violent and justifiable impulses and his careful calculation in secrecy of a strategy for remedying an intolerable situation are all the more striking. His victory through "modesty" lies in this refusal to let the civilizing frames of politeness collapse and reveal their fundamental arbitrariness, a refusal on which the survival of human society would appear to depend. The king's self-conquest suggests that the system of courtesy is founded by and respected by the monarch himself, who willingly submits his absolute power to its containing "laws." The king, the paradigmatic socialized human being—masking all affects and spontaneous impulses according to the inviolable standards of appropriateness represented by his persona—bears the burden of sustaining society, courtesy, etiquette, and law in the face of pure power, will, and egotism.

The dramatic impact of the scene in the nobleman's house is, of course, heightened by the ironies that the audience perceives in the obtuse host's impolite conduct toward an ordinary *hidalgo* who happens to be the king of Spain. There is certainly a farcical note in the king's mechanically repeated asides expressing exasperation at having to conceal his identity and conquer such impulses as the desire to send the braggart "flying down to hell with a good kick." Moreover, there is for the modern reader an undeniable quaintness in the aristocratic social system underlying the scene, with its anxieties regarding reciprocal recognition and inclusion; its elaborate ritual and laborious rhetoric of courtesy and obligation; and its required exchanges of symbolic and concrete gifts in public gestures and performances that often strike one as stiffly, if not awkwardly, choreographed.[49] However, the more significant aspect of this confrontation in the larger context of the drama's articulation of its historical and political themes is its extended development of a revealing conflict between monarchy and aristocracy, both in Pedro's explanation of his willingness to endure his opponent's abuse and in his struggle to suppress the powerful desire to avenge himself and assert his physical superiority over the individual who dishonors him. Tello claims that he would not rise from his chair to receive the king himself, that he has no interest in traveling to the court to gaze on his majesty, that the king's authority in his province requires his consent, and that the observation of the laws and civil procedures of the state is in general a waste of time. His words of contempt regarding petitions to the central government anticipate the sharpening of the conflict in the following two acts.

In the face of such provocative claims and attitudes, Pedro manages to maintain his self-control, "modestly" adopts an accommodating attitude toward the questionable codes of courtesy regarding seating arrangements prevailing in his host's home ("la ley alterar no quiero"), and continually expresses his respect for the law and for the king as minister of justice. He will not forget that his obligation is institutional rather than personal and continues to adhere to his politically calculated plan to make of his antagonist not an object of a personally satisfying revenge and display of heroic anger, but rather an enlightening "example" of justice and wisdom for the benefit of his kingdom (486). His shrewd analysis of the differing consequences of his action as dishonored noble or as responsible statesman and judge offers a concise revelation of the profound conflict the drama is struggling to resolve:

> ¿Hay tal desvergüenza? Dalle (Aparte)
> Cuatro torniscones quiero,
> Descubriéndome. . . . Mas no,
> Que en otra ocasión pretendo
> Ilustrar con este loco
> El blasón de justiciero;
> Y si aquí á coces le mato,
> Mi misma justicia ofendo,
> Y me infamo.

(Could anything be more shameful? [Aside] I would like to give him four slaps in the face, revealing who I am. . . . But no, on another occasion I shall seek, with this madman, to embellish my blazon as bringer of justice; moreover, if I kick him to death here, I offend against my own justice, and I dishonor myself.) (487)

The conflict within the king that has been building up throughout the scene reaches its climax in a moment of heightened dramatic lucidity and intensity. Despite his subsequent characterization of this episode as a "victory" through modesty, the price of self-effacement, subjugation of the body, submission to law, and the commitment to effective rational methods of rule—involving of necessity the "base" behavior of adaptation, accommodation, secrecy, and dissimulation—at this moment appears to be humiliation and shame. The king's predicament is clear: if he responds to personal affront with the justifiable violence of the dishonored, he falls into the greater infamy of breaking the law—his own law. There is no room for maneuver: as man, he dishonors the majesty; as majesty, he dishonors the man. The irresolvability of the paradox reflects the general violence of the tensions that the play—in this respect, the opposite of the *Villano*—generates in articulating the doubleness of the monarch. The reach and seriousness of its historical implications become clearer if we recall Montaigne's bemused formulation of the same contradiction in his analysis of the opposing mentalities and systems of values of the *noblesse d'épée* and the *noblesse de robe*, the latter the ally of the king as minister of the modern state and its laws. "There are two sets of laws, those of honor and those of justice, in many matters quite opposed. The former condemn as rigorously a man's enduring being given the lie as the latter condemn his avenging it. What could be more barbarous than that by the code of arms the man who endures an insult should be degraded from honor and nobility, and by the civil code he who avenges an insult should incur capital punishment? He who appeals to the laws to get satisfaction for an offense to his honor dishonors himself; and he who does not appeal to them is therefore punished and chastised by the laws."[50]

The dilemma of the king's doubleness—as humiliated man and as steadfast institution—intensifies as the act climaxes in disorder. The dishonored victims of Tello's lust suddenly appear on the scene and assert their determination to appeal to the king for redress. The disguised monarch is compelled to listen helplessly while Tello derides his lack of manliness beneath the protective body of his majesty. "Siempre en los reyes se teme/Más el poder que el esfuerzo" (In kings one always fears their power more than their courage) (489). As in the case of the *Villano en su rincón*, the opening act ends with an implicit challenge to the king to find his humanity, to be both man and king. As in the former case, the second act compels the monarch to face the familiar problems of the "miseria del Rey" and to contrive a plan to slip out of the confinements of his royal robes.

POLITICS, ETIQUETTE, AND COURTLINESS: VICTORY IN THE PALACE

Act II concentrates on Pedro in his official role as majesty, performing cere-moniously before his subjects' gaze in the traditional public and community spaces of sovereign activity and self-display—the tribunal and the palace. The opening scene marks an abrupt shift from the pervasive disorder of the first act with its absent monarch and victims of feudal abuse. In a theatrical epiphany of royal power, Pedro el Justiciero comes forth to conduct his legendary tribunal and give audiences in the streets of Madrid. He responds laconically, enigmati-cally, and incisively to all petitions, and he resolves judicial dilemmas with a per-sonal flair, uncanny intuitiveness, and a gift for the aphoristic and memorable pronouncement that characterizes the sage king.

The charismatic image of the ruler in the act of declaring law, making diffi-cult judicial decisions, or establishing proper measurements and limits, as well as the dramatization of his arousal of awe and fear in his beholders through such activity, was commonly featured in absolutism's theater of kings.[51] How-ever, if we compare this elaboration of the royal ritual with more conventional versions—for example, the idealized portrait of the same king in Lope de Vega's *Audiencias del rey don Pedro*—it is impossible to overlook some "extraneous" features that bring certain ambiguities to the customary celebratory displays of royal justice, severity, mercy, and intelligence.[52] We note immediately that the king in our play reveals a curious contempt for literacy, legalism, bureaucratic documentation, and the rational machinery of state institutions. For example, he dismisses a written certificate verifying a soldier's years of loyal service, re-fusing to waste time by processing it through the appropriate ministry and pre-ferring rather to base his promotion on the personal encounter of the present moment and its ritual act of his homage. "El memorial excusad/Si presente me tenéis" (Dispense with the memorial, since you have me present) (490). He goes on to tear up a written petition from a civil servant, impatiently remark-ing: "Estos excusados son; Decid vuestra pretensión/Vocalmente" (These are excused; speak your claim vocally). Once again he prefers voice to writing and the direct command (the personal *fiat*) to the measured actions of a governing bureaucracy.

Pedro's impatience with writing and his commitment to orality are revealing indications of how deeply he belongs to the world that he is historically destined to challenge.[53] As has often been pointed out, the aristocrat inhabits a world of personal encounter and public gesture, where the spoken language, as rheto-ric—for example, the oath; the ritualistic assertions of honor, precedence, and obligation; the claims to title; the act of witnessing; the curse—is embraced as an instrument of self-assertion and physical interaction, and utterances are viewed as transient events in the present and unmediated experiences of the life-world. Words are not to be disjoined from a physical body who has command over them and asserts its will and energy through them. In its primary concern for what I have described in its intensified Spanish manifestation as "la dimensión imperativa de la persona," aristocratic culture was not particularly inclined to understand or to cultivate with enthusiasm the possibilities and benefits of literacy and the expansion of print culture. It is not surprising that it would in fact find in those very benefits a direct threat to its basic ways of seeing, understanding, and ordering the world. From the perspective of the aristocrat, the spread of printed language brings lifelessness to the word. Establishing an immense and prestigious verbal order of reality disconnected from the physical presence of a commanding individual voice or a charismatic personal beauty, print culture deprives the word of its substantive and theatrical powers while reducing the confrontational, dramatic quality of life. Language becomes the cold instrument of objectification, distancing, separation, reflection, and regularization through recollection and abstraction. At the same time it makes available to the individual an enormous range of experience lying beyond the boundaries of the immediate, bringing substance to solitude and enhancing the quality of private life.[54]

As the king's *audiencia* proceeds, it becomes evident that Pedro's insistence on the decisive force of his spoken word and his scorn for written documents are more than simply the transgressive lapses of a strong personality or momentary reversions to an aristocratic ethos. The ritual scene of royal spectacle in fact becomes most notable for the king's systematic derogation of statist institutions and his displacement of them by the prerogatives of his own personality. Dismissing the request of the clerk, he would appear to be willing in fact to abolish the accounting office, and he goes so far as to suggest that the entire class of "letrados" is a hindrance to the fruitful exercise of executive power by a king: "Rey que recibe y paga,/No ha menester Contadores. . . ./Que se embotan las espadas/Después que las premian plumas" (The king who receives and pays has no need for accountants. . . . For swords are blunted after receiving their remuneration from the pens of clerks) (491). The personal bonds that must unite warrior-king and loyal soldiers can only be weakened by the interposition of the institutional machinery of the modern state army. The money that the soldier earns is in reality a gift from his lord, to be reciprocated by repayment in the bodies of slain foes ("Pagarlas [cien doblas], señor, espero/En moros"—My Lord, I hope to repay them [one hundred doubloons] in Moors).[55] The king goes so far as to suggest an abolition of all intrusive bureaucracies of war. The pen will inevitably blunt the sword. The concrete, personal nature of the exchange is underscored by the physical pain of the ritual handclasp, a symbolic transplantation of the master's hand into the servant's body ("Alférez: Pero sin mano voy. Rey: Es porque en facción o en puesto/Veáis la mano que os dí"—Alférez: But I leave without a hand. King: It is so that you might find present the hand that I gave you, whether in battle or at your post), where it becomes metaphorically a bolt of lightning destroying the enemy, animating the former's law, and bonding king and soldier in love. In a pronouncement characteristic of the thematics of the play, the king concludes the ritual aphoristically: "Porque es desdichado el rey/A quien no aman sus soldados" (Because unfortunate is the king whom his soldiers do not love). Once again, we hear of the "misery of kings"!

Regardless of the extent to which the dramatist is modeling this peculiar scene on the historical reforms of Pedro el Cruel and the legendary eccentricities of his character, it is impossible to deny that his attitudes toward governance are distinctly anachronistic and seigniorial and that in his treatment of soldier and bureaucrat—a variation on the old theme of *armas y letras*—he is repeating sentiments expressed in Act I by his destructive rival, shifting his position, as it were, in the debate that designs the work.[56] Tello, the furious antagonist of royal authority, the modern state, and the nobility of the "letrados," is beginning to take shape as an alter ego of the king of Castile.

> Rey: Al Rey me hacen seguir pleitos.
> Don Tello: Necedad. ¡Habiendo espadas,
> Gastar la hacienda en procesos!
> Rey: La ley se ha de obedecer.

(King: They require me to pursue lawsuits to the king. Don Tello: Nonsense. That's silly. When swords are available, to waste one's holdings in legal proceedings! King: The law is to obeyed.)

As contradictory as all of this seems, the fact is that it is perfectly consistent with the play's "dialectical" elaboration and attempted resolution of the central opposition of the king's two identities (*rey-don*) and its imaginative negotiation of a wide-ranging set of cultural contradictions marking the threshold of modernity and the period of the birth of the modern state—contradictions between medieval and modern, personal and institutional, individual and social, warrior and *letrado*, hero and citizen, chivalresque and statist, and orality and print.[57]

The ambiguity of Pedro in his role as majesty in this seemingly conventional scene of royal ritual increases notably in his farewell to the soldier and in the climactic episode of his *audiencia*, his response to the petition of the dishonored noble Rodrigo. Publicly honored by the extended hand of a ruler who expresses his contempt for *plumas* and associates the law and its effective implementation with his powerful grip and with his personal bonds with his warriors, the loyal soldier nevertheless cries out in pain and fury and, while in his king's grasp, struggles with a violent impulse to answer force with force. The ruler's personal law appears to have its own cruelty, as well as its power to humiliate and to provoke defiance. The ritual of the royal handclasp fails to conceal a violence underlying its bonding process and only with difficulty resists disintegrating into a personal confrontation of brutal and potentially equal rivals. The order established by a personal imposition of force, always open to the strongest, is at best precarious, and within it the impulse to contest, challenge, and rebel can never be fully dormant. At this point we might begin to suspect that Pedro's relationship to his villainous double is going to be deeply paradoxical. Whatever resolution is to occur, its key will lie in the resemblance as much as in the opposition of the antagonists. It is now clear that the formulas of plays such as *Fuenteovejuna* and *Peribáñez*, suggested by the initial oppositions and scenes of violence of Act I, will not contain the complexities of this play.

While the king's conceptions of governance, law, and loyalty in the ritual of majesty echo the "archaic" elements that mark Tello's opinions in Act I and receive their most powerful orchestration in his self-definition and description of the world he inhabits (see below), the final episode of the *audiencia* anticipates the nocturnal climax of Act III and its collapse into lawlessness. Astonishingly, the king openly asserts his existence as two identities, acknowledges their potential for opposition, and even suggests the priority of the one that resembles most closely his anarchic, archaic adversary. In response to the appeal of Don Rodrigo, whose betrothed has been kidnapped by Tello, Pedro advises the *hidalgo* to take matters of personal honor into his own hands, insinuating an endorsement of an act of revenge that as king he can only find "unspeakable":

> Rey: Mi ley
> Temed, y haced lo que os digo,
> Que uno es consejo de *amigo*,
> Y otro advertencia de *rey*.
> Don Rodrigo: ¿Qué haré?
> Rey: Lo que hiciera *yo*.
> Don Rodrigo: Pues ¿atreveréme aquí?
> Rey: *Don* Pedro dice que sí,
> Y el *rey* don Pedro que no.

(King: Fear my law, and do as I tell you, for one thing is the advice of a *friend*, another the warning of a *king*. Don Rodrigo: What shall I do? King: What *I* would do. Don Rodrigo: But shall I dare to do so here? King: *Don* Pedro says yes, and *King* Don Pedro says no.) (492; emphasis added)[58]

As in the final scene of Act I, the king finds himself once again in a dilemma rooted in his inescapable doubleness. Again he seems suspended between honor and law, violence and justice, blood and rationality, self and institution. However, his dilemma intensifies as he suddenly envisions himself in fact as two distinct beings. The doubleness latent in the title becomes the central enigma in an enigmatic work. The process leading to his climactic disrobing and descent into lawlessness takes a decisive turn. The actual splitting apart of the king and the articulation of different aspects of his person and destiny in the projection of doubled characters—Tello and the avenging shadow—begin at this point.

KING PEDRO'S PALACE PLAY: DRAMATURGIC KING, PERFORMATIVE THEATER, *COMEDIA DE ENREDO*, AND ROYAL FARCE

As the action shifts from the street tribunal to the palace chancery, where the monarch's second confrontation with his rival occurs, King Pedro must once again struggle to keep Don Pedro in check, clinging to his identity as majesty and *homo politicus* in the face of insufferable provocation. His victory occurs in a long scene in the palace that continues the depiction of the king in his official role, wearing the robe of the *letrado*, dealing with a continuing flow of papers, and energetically managing the affairs of state. This is probably the most remote episode of the play, and an appreciation of its meaning, as well as its dramatic effectiveness, presupposes a knowledge of the dynamics of court etiquette and ceremony in the age.

The characters circulate mechanically and silently about the stage. They offer and withhold glances in what is clearly a signifying system of facial expressions and bodily movements and positionings. Their gestures, locations, and costuming are carefully choreographed by a silent, immobile king who stands ceremoniously amid his secretaries as they monotonously present him with documents for his consideration. His withholding of attention, the coveted "animating glance" that invests the political subject with identity and existence—the "confining" investiture that Juan Labrador abhors—can be devastating. If Pedro appears as *justiciero* in the preceding scene, here his role is that of master of court ceremony, or, in more general terms, that of dramaturgic king, the master of the resources for theatrical effects and manipulated appearances available in the absolutist states. This aspect of rule was obsessively discussed in the flourishing new politi-

cal science of the period.[59] From Machiavelli's endorsement of the art of feign-
ing and his enthusiastic analyses of the gruesome theatrical politics of a despot
such as Borgia to Saavedra Fajardo's precepts concerning the all-important political art of maintaining reputation, theorists assisted kings in developing an art
of staging their rule; "costuming their policies"; concealing their secret purposes
in the artful manner of the backstage director; inspiring awe and "salutary" fear
in their audience of subjects; and framing their policies, victories, and exemplary punishments within theatrically designed and rhetorically inflated public
rituals.[60]

One of the most remarkable features of *El Rey Don Pedro en Madrid* is the
degree to which the play associates its protagonist and legendary state-builder
with the mastery of the "modern" political skills of theatrics and the controlled
projection of appearances. As the opening scenes make clear, such skills in fact
include the arts of acting, disguising, and dissembling and differentiate the
calculating monarch sharply from his guileless double, whose aristocratic incapacity to understand such questionable behavior and the indirections in its
assertions of power can be occasionally quite comical.

All of Pedro's disguises and "robings," from the opening scene, in which he
takes on the identity of the humble *hidalgo* Acevedo, to the climactic epiphany
of the imperial regalia of the *rex judex*, are connected with a reduction of self
and a developing antithesis between his identity as "statist" being and that of the
self-expansive *ingénu* Tello, a charismatic creature of impulse, will, and force,
the unsocialized, "unstated" human being who lives to gratify any desire of the
present moment (see below). It is this continuously developed opposition rather
than the play's repeated cultivation of striking tableaus and emblematic effects —
for example, the equestrian king; the ruler's powerful hand; the epiphany of the
judicial majesty and its symbols; the sudden, "clandestine" illumination of the
momentarily "unkinged" and "lawless" monarch standing above and treading
down the defeated antagonist — that reveals its most intimate engagement with
the political culture of its time. It is this elusive interchange that distinguishes
the play from the conventional court masque and the simplicities of its spectacular victories of civilizing hero-king over monstrous chaos (for example, Hercules
and the Hydra, Odysseus and Polyphemus, Zeus and the Titans). The juxtaposition of Tello and Pedro dramatizes (among other things) the historical rise of
a new political vision and style but at the same time hints at all that is lost in its
ascendance. As I shall point out below, a nostalgia for the beauties of a heroic,
agrarian, and Gothic past is discernible in the ravings of Tello. The nostalgia
itself reveals traces of the yearnings of Spain's greatest literary character, Don
Quixote.

From the beginning to the end we note not only that the triumphant king is a dissimulator and a disguiser, but also that his disguises are characteristically connected with moral self-restraint; affect control; and, in terms of his "twinned" reality as king and man, ultimately with self-effacement—the subordination of the demands of a personal or "pure" self to the obligations of an institutionally "refashioned" displacement, a pure *rex politicus*. In Act I, following his violent outburst at his rebellious horse, he conceals his identity from the victims of injustice and graciously accepts their gift of a donkey, one of the various comic moments in the play's articulation and distortion of the rites, symbols, and gestures of seignorial culture and absolutist rule.[61] Disguised as *hidalgo*, he enters the house of Tello, where, despite infuriating mistreatment amid comically disfigured rites of precedence, he maintains his distance and rational control and conceives of a plan both to teach the errant *infanzón* a lesson and to make his case an instructive example for public edification. When in Act III he is no longer able to suppress the urge to display his personal strength in the primordial ritual of self-assertion of aristocratic culture, the duel, he carries out his transgressive feat in secrecy, cloaking himself in the shadows of the night; stripping off his royal robes; donning the armor of the "pure, non-regal" person; concealing his identity from his opponent; and committing his act of violence in the *campaña*, beyond the walls of his palace and its civilized prohibitions. In effect, he breaches the state's so-called "monopoly of violence," which he so rigorously asserted earlier in his imprisonment of the outraged noble Rodrigo, who drew his sword in the palace.

It is in the central scene of Act II, however, that King Pedro's mastery of the public and courtly theaters of absolutism is most evident. The scene is crucial in the monarchist design of the work, as it dramatizes the creation of the state as a historical process centering on the sublimation of violence. Here King Pedro achieves, as a *sovereign*, in a complex theatrical duel, a second victory over his adversary. One might say that we observe in the strange interactions of king and aristocrat a dramatic representation of what Norbert Elias has called the "civilizing process." In "taming the wild boar Infanzón of his ferocity," the king becomes a dramatist, a *virtuoso* of political stagecraft, preparing costumes for the *villanos*, using a "paper" to trick his antagonist into making an appearance in the palace "theater," and providing his courtiers with a script (491). The king is highly pleased with his strategy, and the play repeatedly draws attention to the word *papel*, which figuratively suggests both written document as "weapon" and the theatrical "role" to which the *infanzón* must submit in the agon of the entrapping drama. Pedro himself acts out the part of the ceremonial king, creating a play-within-the-play, which, after holding all participants—and its audience—in increasing suspense, abruptly culminates in the humiliation of the "antagonist," caught helplessly in a "mouse trap" (*ratonera*) and manipulated in a "chess game" by the "moves" of an inaccessible, unfathomable master and in the comedic restoration of the damaged honor of his victims (497).

The king's play is designed as a *comedia de enredo.* Nearly all participants find themselves swept helplessly into a situation of confusion in which they misinterpret the actions, motives, words, dress, and spaces of those around them. Only the king, the motivator of the action, fully understands its coherence, and like a *duende* (mischievous phantasm) in his mysterious, invisible power, he leads his principal victim on a labyrinthian course as doors mysteriously slam shut and the ominous sound of keys turning in locks punctuates the collapse of space and the latter's increasing immobilization. As the mastermind of the meaningful confusion continues to vanish, like a spider, into the unseen depths of his palace and the sources of his power, the *arcana imperii* and the devices of the *comedia de enredo* fuse in a remarkable scene of theatrical statecraft.[62]

If Pedro, in his disguises, scriptings, emplotments, and rhetorical strategies of manipulation and influence, should be seen as the "dramaturgic" master of the new political order of the absolutist state, the resulting scenario of his palace drama in Act II offers a concentrated image of the new social formation of the court society, in which the civilized system of etiquette and ceremony established rules, boundaries, and channels for the non-violent expression of ambitions, competitive urges, differentiations, gradations of value (for example, honor, prestige, rank, relational positions, and prescribed activities) and decisively directed the individual's need for self-esteem toward the recognition that the society he inhabited could provide as an audience. In his studies of the fundamental changes in human self-consciousness brought about in the reconfiguration of society in the early modern period, Norbert Elias describes the courtly world as a field dominated by rationality, the evolution of civilizing constraints enforcing a "control of affects," and the "extensive transformation of external into internal compulsions."[63] Within this world etiquette and ceremony "operate as a ghostly *perpetuum mobile* of interacting and competing forces" in a complexly differentiated system of locations and levels of prestige and visibility. The stability of the system is founded in the authority of the monarch, who, like the traditional Christian God—currently resurrected and celebrated in the great hexameral poems published throughout Europe—creates, situates, and differentiates and sets all in motion through the *primum mobile.*

The scene of King Pedro's second triumph, distinguished from the other two as the triumph of a *sovereign* as opposed to the triumphs of a *man* or a *moral exemplar,* can be viewed as a dramatic representation of the ascendance of the courtly system and its displacement of the primitive social construction, founded on brute force and individual deeds of prowess, characterizing the archaic aristocratic-feudal mode of political and social organization. Speaking as sovereign and "political theorist," the king derides his opponent's "absolute majesty" in Illescas, where he is "el ánimo de la gente;/Tan preciado de valiente/y tan dueño en las espadas" (the spirit of the people, so esteemed for bravery and so masterful in his swordsmanship) (499)—in other words, personal valor, military prowess, and dominion, the three great qualities of the feudal master and the pillars of his system.[64] In the play's complex political dialogue of doubles, Tello's function is not only to inflict violence, to pursue impulse, to overstep boundaries, to grab, to plunder, to rape, to rage, to mock authority, and to desecrate its emblems, but also *to misunderstand*, to be *an alien* in a social formation and discourse that he absolutely fails to comprehend.[65] His arbitrary integration in the restored society at the end—necessitated by the comic design—strikes one as so awkward precisely because of his power as a figure who simply does not belong. He is characterized in the dialogue and described in the stage directions as an *extraño*. As Covarrubias put it in his dictionary, the "stranger" is "singular" and "extraordinary"; he is defined by his otherness to the spaces of our world, specifically as a creature that is non-locatable or definable within the boundaries of "our house, our family, or our place."[66] The play seems to acknowledge as much in the strange moment when the king steps out of his official world and his own royal identity and, bonding with his adversary in competitive violence, counsels him to escape to Aragon, beyond all boundaries of state, social etiquette, and courtly protocol.[67]

It is significant that when Tello's unseen opponent—state power in its incomprehensible invisibility and universal coerciveness—finally appears in the figure of the king, the latter is dressed in the sober garb of the royal minister of state, the sovereign *letrado*, perusing the papers and documents of government and noticeably investing them with a priority that infuriates the unacknowledged— the marginalized—"great warrior." The "papers of state" in fact become powerful dramatic agents in the strange confrontation, silently exerting a force that stops in his tracks, *dehumanizes*, and obliterates the intruder from another world.

To understand the dynamics and the historical resonances of the peculiar scene, one should recall the wide recognition of Philip II as a "paper king," a monarch who valued skilled secretarial activity and stressed the paramount importance of written information, document, certification, and report in the efficient management of a state government.[68] Impatient with public audiences and spoken pronouncements, petitions, and interchanges, he preferred to spend hours every day in his study, perusing the papers that his secretaries and ministers continually brought him. To complaints that administration "through notes and paper" distanced him from his subjects, he responded that oral presentation needlessly consumes time and prevents accomplishment. In his second confrontation with Tello, who, as we have seen, has nothing but scorn for the *letrados*, Pedro is the silent embodiment of the modern state, its invisible power, its "print machinery," and its new bureaucracy. In the complex vacillations that mark the monarch's development throughout the work, he is, at this point, reversing his position as revealed in the *audiencia*, in which he rips up the printed documents of state ministries, and in the night of his descent to his face-to-face encounter with his human double, when in disgust he hurls away the printed books on statecraft. In the extended scene of non-encounters and anti-climaxes of Act II, the distanced confrontation of protagonist and antagonist suggests nothing less than a triumph of the written word over the sword and the great civilizing movement of sublimation of raw power that the modern state historically came into existence to bring about.[69]

Pedro's palace comedy is, in its own terms, a masterpiece of performative theater. From the moment he finds himself compelled to enter the palace through the postern gate, Tello rants helplessly and brandishes his imposing sword futilely against the irresistible, unseen power of an ubiquitous king, who intends, as Alfonso puts it, to curb the raw strength — *fuerza* — of the bestial aristocrat and calmly and methodically moves him and the other players of his drama from room to room as if on the spaces of a chessboard. Frustrated in his expectations of confrontation with a concrete adversary, Tello rages defiantly as a "member of the Castilian nobility" against a king who apparently is determined to "irritarle" with papers and compulsory "roles" and discovers that he has been lured into an incomprehensible, "enchanted" field of forces where "Todos lisonjean/y ha puesto la pretensión/Hasta en las pinturas lengua" (Everybody flatters, and ambitious pretension has placed tongues even in the paintings). Momentarily the space of the triumphant new order reveals a trace of an ambivalence that will develop as the scene unfolds and that will ultimately drive Pedro toward an astonishing embrace of his manly double.

For all its rationality and civility and despite its historical necessity, the modern world turns out to be marked by a frightening quality, the dehumanizing inauthenticity so powerfully presented in Juan Labrador's spectral vision of the court. Tello's terrified companion asks: "¿Qué intenta este Rey? . . . ¿Si es duende el Rey?" (What is this king doing? . . . Could the king be a ghost?) (496). In perhaps the most shocking of his various metamorphoses and disguises, the protean king of Spain conjures forth the powers of state mysteries in the comical, unnerving antics of the poltergeist. In its engagement with new conceptions of power and governing institutions, the play at this point goes a step beyond Machiavelli's folkloric trickster, the dissembling fox, for its model of artful state-craft. The success of the modern state depends on the actions of a supernatural trickster and his ghostly manipulations of his subjects through an unseen, omni-present, and unconfrontable power.[70] In the eeriness of its alienating effects, the sinister palace into which the traditional knight falls looks more like the future world of Kafka's castle than the recently envisioned power state of Machiavelli's prince.

To recall Elias's studies of the new court society, we might say that the genius of the play *El Rey Don Pedro en Madrid* lies in its capture and dramatization of the perspective of an estranged visitor in a new world, where the arts of penetrat-ing observation, of "spying," and of secretly calculating have gained ascendance over traditional modes of personal interaction and where a new arena for indi-vidual achievement and competition for reward has rendered the sword obso-lete; heroic "rage" and intensity of emotion (hatred or eros), counterproductive if not laughable; and the field of combat, the *campaña* of heroic individualism, irrelevant. As the coldly rational political observer and satirist Gracián put it, the protective armor for heroes of the new age is secrecy, distance, dissimulation, and the verbal obliquities of wit. As its utopian counter-image, he could sardon-ically envision the creation of the human being with a window installed on his breast.

In the palace triumph, which the monarch, in the curious metaphor of the opponents, achieves not as "swordsman" but rather "as physician," we see how the court setting and its ceremonial can be used by its master as a means of ma-nipulation and absolute control of his subject.[71] The spaces and decorations of this theater are invested with an aura of the sacred, and its inhabitants, players and audience, as it were, are constantly seized by terror. When Juan advises the ladies to enter the royal chambers with *decoro* and *aviso*, they prepare to kiss their *indios tapetes* (Indian rugs) and suspect that they are being handed over to a sacrificial rite. All express bewilderment and fear as they are moved about by an inscrutable royal will. As Tello moves through a series of narrowing chambers and reaches the third, he discovers that the wall cloths have been removed from the bare stones and that the frigid walls are closing in on him. An entombment of the grandiose self of the "pure person" appears to be taking place. At this point Tello admits that he fears the king's majesty, "que estos doseles conservan" (con-served by these canopies), and as yet another door opens to reveal the numenous figure in a *sanctum sanctorum*, in holy dread he announces that he has "turned to stone" and attempts to prostrate himself at the feet of the awesome figure. Pedro, dressed as a *letrado* and clutching state papers in his hand, responds to

the gesture of submission with astonishing and devastating indifference. It falls
to Tello to formulate the doctrines and lessons lying in his humiliation and his
unendurable invisibility. The majesty of kings endows the ordinary man with
divine powers.

> Esta majestad que ves,
> Es la que los hombres tiemblan;
> Que por sí solos son hombres
> Los reyes, mas la grandeza
> Los pasa a divinidades.
>
> Ya temo al Rey,
> No por lo que dél me cuentan,
> Sino por la majestad
> Que estos doseles conservan.

(This majesty that you see is what strikes fear into men. For by themselves
alone kings are but men. But the grandeur of majesty transforms them into
divinities. . . . I already fear the King, not for what they tell me about him, but
rather for the majesty that these canopies conserve.) (497)

If the play, then, in its complex engagement with the institution of monarchy, dramatizes, metatheatrically as it were, the manufacture of the king's suprahuman body by an intelligent, intensely passionate, and political individual and
its effective use in the domination of a kind of subject whose resistance to the
institutionalization of power in the modern state was widespread throughout
Europe of the early modern period, its dramatic image of that process appears
to reflect quite accurately the primary features of the Habsburg court ritual as it
had been developed from its Burgundian antecedents by Philip II. In contrast
to the style of spectacular self-display adopted by the court of France, the Spanish ceremonial chose to emphasize the withdrawn, invisible, immobile, silent,
and frightening character of the royal figure. "How different were the spatial
relationships between king and court in France and Spain. In Spain the king
was approached through a succession of rooms, each one more exclusive of access than the one before. Even in the eighteenth century after the advent of the
Bourbons, Saint-Simon noticed how bare these rooms in the Alcázar looked—
primarily because they contained no chairs." The monarch displayed himself to
those privileged to pass through the mysterious doors leading toward the "holiest
of holies" in a pose of impassivity, a statue-like figure who would raise his hat mechanically as the visitor would enter and then stand motionless, as if "arrimado

a un bufete" throughout the audience. The distinctive character of the Spanish ceremonial was widely recognized in the period, and if there were those who expressed admiration for it—for example, Marshal Gramont wrote that "there was an air of grandeur and majesty which I have seen nowhere else"—others glimpsed something burdensome in its "gravity." "No prince lives like the King of Spain; all his actions and all his occupations are always the same, and move with such regularity that, day by day, he knows exactly what he will do for the whole of his life. . . . So the weeks, the months, the years, and the divisions of the day bring no change in his pattern of life, and never allow him to see anything new."[72]

I would like to suggest that Gramont's observations cast a revealing light on the most remote aspect of the play under consideration. The dramatic movement and power of the crucial scene in Act II, the king's palace victory, depend on the unquestionable authority of an extraordinarily punctilious ceremonial and etiquette. As the episode moves from Tello's anger at being forced to enter through the postern gate; to his exasperation at the impersonal, infuriating responses of indifference to his various demands—the mechanically repeated "No hay orden"; to his complaints concerning the confiscation of the weapons of his guard and the nature of "preeminencias" in the palace; to his bewilderment by the formalized, mechanical movements of the inhabitants, who appear as if stiffened by "two thousand spits" ("dos mil asadores llevan") (496); to his involuntary transfer from one appropriate room to another in a system of gradations that he cannot comprehend; to his confused discussion of the majesty, it builds up an increasingly violent conflict between the individual will of the aristocrat and an unseen but inviolable protocol.

To construe the scene as merely a satirical humiliation of a comic humor— a social anachronism—would be to overlook its most complex and interesting dimensions. Its association of correct protocol with immobilization, repression, and deathliness is impossible to deny. A frozen rigidity, a menacing petrification, surrounds all who enter the palace world, including its king. The association implies the extreme violence of the play's numerous elaborations of the foundational antagonisms on which it is built: state and individual, literacy and orality, order and chaos, law and license, reason and will, form and energy, self-control and desire, justice and valor, monarchy and aristocracy, norm and alien (*extraño*), man and animal, civilization and barbarism. As I shall attempt to argue below, the play's fascination with Tello cannot avoid disclosing an anxiety of loss that survives the ascent of the rational state and a sense that the state's triumphant rigors are in fact touched by traces of a *rigor mortis*. At the center of its icy labyrinth Tello must confront the unfamiliar language of the dead, the Egyptian hieroglyph of the omnipresent king with one thousand ears, who knows all secrets and compels fear, submission, and silence in his subjects.

Following Tello's frigid entrapment in the third room, the king's mousetrap has been sprung, the wild animal has been tamed, and the black king has been defeated. Tello yields before the overwhelming gravity of his repressive adversary. Admitting his fear, he confesses defeat and appears finally to understand and respect the king in his official identity as sovereign majesty. He kneels before the legendary *justiciero,* who brings his play-within-the-play to its climax with a solemn entry through a slowly opening door ("¡Qué majestad! . . . . Al fin Rey").

The climactic epiphany of the king-dramatist's performance parallels the epiphany by which the playwright will conclude the entire play, replacing the papers of the statesman with the scepter and sword of justice. But here too the resolution is immediately disturbed by a violence that the king cannot control, an apparent incapacity to confine his own "manly" impulses within his "royal body." As in the case of the slaughtered horse, the momentary mistreatment of the soldier in the king's audience, the rejected classics on kingship, and the clandestine recommendations of revenge to the dishonored noble, the king once again betrays his impatience with his own majesty and its discourse. As if in defiance of any vindicating design inspiring his creator, he once again falls victim to his penchant for violent self-expression. Noting the "strangeness" of a man who in his house has seated a visiting king on a footstool, Pedro proceeds to denounce the kind of "monarchy" (*reyecillos*) that his aristocratic rule in Illescas represents—an absolutism that subordinates reason to the *gusto,* will, pleasure, and caprice of the strong.

The climactic dramatic confrontation would initially appear to pit the institutional monarchy, limited by law and reason, committed to the pen as its principal executive instrument, against the personal, barbarous rule of the tyrant. However, as if responding to an alien force in the only language—and literary genre—it can understand, Pedro impulsively butts his adversary as if he were a disobedient animal and contemptuously throws him out of the room. The king's drama concludes in the degrading conventions of the *entremés.* The corporeal humiliation of his opponent, which can be viewed as a grotesque parody of the finely graded system of ritual challenges governing the aristocratic codes of honor, expresses a denial of all respect for the physical person of the *infanzón* and constitutes the deepest of insults in the seigniorial system that he obtusely inhabits. It is followed by a barrage of verbal abuse in the three accusing tirades by the female victims of Tello's monstrous sexual crimes. The theatrical climax concludes in the black humor of the stylized criminal world of *germanía* with its grotesque intensifications of violence and torture, its religious travesties, and its ritual cursing.

> Parezcas colgado
> Mono de Tolú,
> Los ojos opuestos
> Al Norte y al Sur.

(May you, when you are a hanging corpse, look like a monkey of Tolú, your bulging eyes staring in opposite directions, northward and southward.) (502)

The king's drama is certainly dominated at its conclusion by farcical effects in action, caricature, invective, and degrading humor, and the *gracioso*'s reference to an unfolding *entremés* is a mark of its self-awareness as theater. In view of the emphasis on royal solemnity that one finds in seventeenth-century political theory, public ritual, and courtly etiquette, the often repeated reminder by Lope that kings and *entremeses* do not go well together, and the popularity of recent critical approaches to the *comedia* in its ideological contexts and "propagandistic" and satirical functions (see chapter 1 above), it is at this point perhaps well to note that dramatists and the public of the period were capable of enjoying a comedic exploitation of the whole system of the cult of the majesty and presumably adopting a kind of critical and flexible approach to the make-believe nature of kings, queens, princes, pretenders, royal prerogatives, stuffy retainers, quaint ceremonies, and dynastic wars that looks forward to the "post-monarchist" sophisticated worlds of Gilbert and Sullivan operetta and bourgeois romance.[73]

However, precisely at this point the most suggestive ambiguities of the containing play are beginning to assert themselves. They can no longer be dismissed as personal idiosyncrasies of a notoriously strange ruler or integrated smoothly in an interpretation of the play as, to use Stephen Gilman's phrase, a "royal romp." The obedience of the king's subject and the triumph of the royal will are associated with suffocation, petrification, and freezing. The play's "celebration" of monarchy, its political agenda, is starting to reveal fissures, insinuate ambiguities, hint at irresolution and ideological conflict. The rigorous fulfillment of the protocol of the state and the frozen rituals of its majesty in reality bring lifelessness to its monumental spaces. As we discover in the third act, the king himself will find that he is incapable of submitting to the repressive order of his own majesty. A shocking, potentially tragic, change of direction in this dramatic "portrait of a king" is already anticipated following the climax of Pedro's palace victory. Having thoroughly humiliated the rebellious aristocrat in his chambers, he suddenly laments that since he was born a king, his personal response to his adversary can go no further than his "symbolic head-buttings," and he proceeds to invoke the theme of the "misery of kings" in order to scold his courtiers for not attempting to kill him in their fencing exercises.

Trapped in the rationalized predeterminations of such restraints and rites of precedence, Pedro yearns for the opportunity to enjoy a triumph of his own "manly effort" (*esfuerzo varonil*); to experience the exhilaration of a total dominance, involving personal risk and resting on primitive fear rather than ritualistically formalized respect; and to be invested with a radiance drawing its energy and authority from his own actions—here he invokes the Cid in his single combats with the Moors—rather than from the "majestad de sus doseles" (his canopied majesty) or the divine connections of the royal institution. In the play's central paradox, Pedro, the mythic lawgiver and state builder, remains the anxious captive of his belief in the primacy of the "dimensión imperativa de la persona."[74] Lamenting that in his royal misery he "cannot be much of a man," he plunges into the shadows to do battle as a man with the demonic specter that has been haunting him since the opening scene. His words anticipate the full separation of the king's two bodies that enables his third and proudest victory, over his accusing double, in Act III. At this point we must turn to the major enigma of the play—the indestructibility of Tello.

TELLO AND THE SUBLIMITY OF VIOLENCE: A VICTORY IN THE *CAMPAÑA*?

> Infanzón de Illescas,
> Pimpollo de oro,
> Pues que mueres sin culpa,
> Llórente todos.

(Knight of Illescas, golden bud of the earth, since you die without guilt, may all weep for you.)

In order to understand the third victory that Pedro triumphantly claims, as well as its "stage management," it is necessary to look at his double, Tello, more closely and to consider the ambiguities that destabilize what initially appears to be a neat, formulaic, and familiar opposition of protagonist and antagonist. Is Tello simply the stereotypical rebel aristocrat of the more conventional monarchist dramas of Spain's national theater, the kind of figure required by the balanced economy of Moreto's tepid reconstruction of the work as a reassuring celebration of the triumph of king, state, law, and justice and a comforting disarmament of the outsider, who disappears from its title? "¿Qué intenta ese Rey?/Intenta irritarme e irritar/La castellana nobleza" (What is this king doing? He is trying to irritate me and irritate the nobility of Castile). Tello's words certainly suggest the availability of a reliable historical allegory for the resourceful adaptor, Moreto. Once again it is revealing to consider the significance of the unusual stage direction describing his garb—*extraño*. To recall Covarrubias's definition of the word *extranjero*, Pedro's double is "one who does not belong" to our familiar spaces of family, city, or country—one who is alien. The question at this point becomes where in fact does he belong?

In introducing Tello, the play gives considerable attention to the world that he inhabits and a language that is appropriate to it. Tello's home is in an agrarian order of lawlessness, vitality, bestial impulse, and brute force, with its own kind of "sovereignty" and its own form of "majesty." It is in this sense a "counter-kingdom," just as Juan Labrador's philosophical *rincón* is a counter-kingdom to the offical kingdom of France in *El villano en su rincón*.

> Un Tello, un infanzón,
> Que en Illescas soberano,
> Deidad se hace de los montes
> Y majestad de los campos;
> Dueño en las vidas y haciendas,
> Poderoso, despreciando
> Con atrevimiento loco
> Los soberanos mandatos,
> No haciendo caso del Rey,
> Ni haciendo del cielo caso,
> Soberbio a lo poderoso,
> Y sacrílego a lo sacro,
> Al fin tirano.

(A Tello, a knight, who as a sovereign in Illescas, makes himself a deity of the mountains and a majesty of the fields, a powerful master over lives and properties, scorning with insane insolence the commands of his sovereign, paying attention neither to the King, nor to heaven, arrogant before the powerful, sacrilegious before the sacred, in short, a tyrant. (481)

While he certainly represents, as literary historians have pointed out, the anarchic, violent culture of the feudal aristocracy, it is important to note that Tello is simultaneously connected with areas of human experience that are far more fundamental and universal than anything that can be accounted for by reference to a specific social class or historical moment.[75] In various allusions to his gigantic aspects; his mythic associations with the forces of chaos, untamed nature, and savage animals; and the titanic nature of his final struggle—a "battle of mountains"[76]—with Pedro, the drama reaches back toward the roots of Western epic literature, and its effort, as Thomas Greene puts it, to respond to "man's need to clear away an area he can apprehend, if not dominate," an area that commonly "expands to fill the epic universe, to cover the known world and reach heaven and hell."[77] Tello, like his mythical forebears, the giants and the titans, draws his strength "from below" and turns the mountains into weapons in his assault on true power, which, as St. Paul's famous text (and his spokesman in the play, Prince Enrique) puts it, descends "from above." With his characteristic fine intuition, Karl Vossler expressed his admiration for this strange play by noting that the most powerful "forces of heaven and earth are mingled" in its characters more violently than in all other mortals.[78] Here the narrow boundaries—historical, political, and social—that circumscribed Lope's vast literary production and that Vossler understood so well are left far behind. In this perspective the historical cruelty of the Spaniard who managed to impose law on his particular nation can be seen in fact as the burden of the archetypal hero's quest, his engagement with mysterious forces in an alien, dark underworld that holds secrets, powers, and riches that are indispensable for the civilizer's success. "A hero ventures forth from the world of common day into a region of supernatural wonder; fabulous forces are there encountered and a decisive victory is won; the hero comes back from this mysterious adventure with the power to bestow boons on his fellow man."[79] Amid the beautiful chaos of his estate in Illescas, Tello in reality dwells in another world, far beyond the confining circle centered by the royal palace of Act II and ultimately by the foundational stone that Pedro lays in Madrid in the final moment of the drama.

The secret of Tello's appeal can in fact be glimpsed early in the play in a detailed description of his natural world. It follows closely on a parallel description of nature by the victim of his "aristocratic" violence. The images counter one another and establish, at the very beginning of the drama, a powerful opposition that will be reiterated in action, character, and theme throughout the work. Initially unrecognized as king, Pedro finds himself challenged to restore the harmony of the disrupted pastoral existence of Tello's victims, Elvira and Ginesa. The order of being that the former eloquently describes appears initially to be comfortably aligned with Pedro's civilizing quest. It is a metaphysical vision that is familiar and generally unambiguous in its function in several of Lope's most famous romantic comedies.

In her account to Pedro of her rape by Tello and his devastation of her village, Elvira recalls the speech by which she attempted to persuade the monstrous aristocrat—a "poderoso"—to seek a woman who is his equal and to respect her own "hermosura que es de pueblo" (beauty which is that of the common people). She finds that her aspiration to a harmonious and fruitful love with a partner belonging to her own class is mirrored and validated in the universal "concierto de las cosas," in the "discorde armonía" of "esos elementos cuatro," and she exhorts her violent suitor, who "loves *disformemente*," to gaze on the symbols of a world that eloquently reveals both the loftiness of the conjunction brought about by chaste love—the sun and the stars, the tree and the vine, the wall and its ivy, the springs and the mountain peaks they embrace—and the fruitfulness and pleasure that reward a love shared by equals—the flowers whose kisses regale the benevolent day with fragrances "en holocausto" and the doves, "gems of white foam," whose sweet murmurings express the bliss of their united souls. In contrast to Tello's universe of violent conflict, transgression of limits, polymorphous abundance, monstrous mutation, destructive self-assertion, and defiant individuation, Elvira describes a universe of loving correspondences, orderly plenitude, enduring bonds, and the hierarchic beauty of *discordia concors*. Rooted in the Neo-Platonic metaphysics of eros, beauty, rationality, and universal concert, it is a world order founded on a highly spiritual conception of love, and her argument reaches its climax as she beseeches her persecutor, who frankly admits that his attraction to her is a caprice fired by instinct, to allow her to marry her beloved.

> Deja que ame
> La igualdad, sin ser contrario
> Al concierto de las cosas
> Que están el mundo aumentando.
> Dueño tengo, esposo tengo,
> Mañana con él me caso,
> Mañana al tálamo viene;
> Que de Toledo le aguardo.
> Amor en desigualdades
> Escarmienta desengaños,
> Porque es la humildad pechera,
> Y el poder es soberano.

(Let equals join in love, do not oppose the harmonious order of things that are giving increase to the world. I have a lord, I have a husband. Tomorrow I will marry him, tomorrow he comes to the bridal chamber. I await his arrival from Toledo. Love between those who are not equals teaches harsh lessons and disillusionments, because the commoner pays the tribute, and the powerful is the sovereign.) [482][80]

According to the patterns of Lope's most familiar works dealing with the conflicts articulated in Act I of *El Rey Don Pedro en Madrid*, we might expect that this traditional vision would be smoothly assimilated to the triumphant assertion of the institution of monarchy, the suppression of aristocratic individualism, and the ascendence of statism.[81] However, as I noted at the outset, the play turns sharply away from its anticipated utopian directions. Elvira's speech is all but forgotten, remaining perhaps audible as a faint and undeveloped echo in the hastily contrived comedic denouement. The glimpse of a universal, harmonious order of things is fleeting. An essentialized, utopian world of the peasantry never quite comes into existence. The kind of alignment of monarchy, cosmos, nature, and idealized pastoral community celebrated in a work such as *Fuenteovejuna* is out of the question. The play turns away from the countryside, and the events of its final two acts unfold in dim and oppressive spaces of city street, palace, and prison. Rather than the victimization of the weak and innocent, it instead focuses on the irresoluteness of the king, his complex fascination with the villain, and the ambiguities in their relationship of doubles. However, a hint of the subsequent direction is already visible in the countryside of Act I, where we find that Elvira's eloquent speech is answered by Tello's powerful declamation celebrating the natural order that he inhabits and offering it as temptation to the woman he would seduce. In effect the antithetical speeches are of central importance in providing a metaphysical foundation on which all the other thematic oppositions that structure this intricate play of doubles — political, social, geographical, moral, religious, and aesthetic — can fall into place.[82] Here, in the doubleness of the natural order, we find the root analogy, a point of convergence where the seemingly fragmentary and centrifugal contexts of the dense play disclose their identity as parallels.

The oppositions could not be more carefully drawn. In Tello's panoramic enumeration of his possessions, nature is displayed as an order of continuing metamorphoses, unlimited fecundity, expanding vistas, and a continual overflowing of boundaries. The mountain range of his lands "extends its reach" and "dares to compete" with the Guadarrama, the "living silver" of its treetops (*copos*) "mocking" the "snow tunics" of the latter. His herds of cattle are armies that, as it were, erase the boundary separating water and earth, turning the riverbanks of their grazing into "seas of precious stones" (485). Clearly the violence of the passage lies not merely in its themes and specific references but also in the imaginative boundary breaking and crossovers that the magic of metaphorical and perifrastic language brings about. The exuberant enumeration yields extravagantly expansive visions commingling what is normally separated in the traditional world concert invoked earlier by the aristocrat's victim — the elemental orders, the gradations of the cosmic hierarchy, the stable assignments of place fixed by the divine fiat.

Through Tello's entire declamation nature and language become the image of inconstancy and excess, metaphysical and aesthetic qualities that correlate perfectly with the restless voluntarism that lies beneath the "dimensión imperativa de la persona" that founds its political and psychological dynamic. However, there is a countervailing movement in this passage, and its implications are in fact more interesting than the striking verbal correlates of political and metaphysical violence and inadmissible disorder. It lies in its *aestheticization* of violence[83] and in its assertion of an individuality, a freedom, and a creative power that refuse to be buried amid the statist themes and their reassuring recollections of the order of the "great chain of being."[84]

In boasting of the armies of his herds of cattle, Tello claims that they are so beautiful that they are suspected by a personified April of being in fact daughters of the sun, who fathered them disguised as a bull and emblazoned them with the "stains" of divine markings:

> Unas pórfidas son, otras de estrellas
> Manchan la piel en hemisferios de oro;
> Y es tal la multitud, que cuando pacen
> Golfos de jaspes las riberas hacen.

(Some are porphyries; the fur of others is spotted by stars in hemispheres of gold. And their multitude is so great, that when they graze, they make of the banks of rivers gulfs of jasper.)

At this point it should become obvious to any reader of Golden Age literature that Tello's world and all the disintegrating forces that it juxtaposes to the "universal concert" of Elvira's description of order, balance, and number is the world of Góngora. It is a site where an imaginative alchemy can wrest an undeniable beauty from the feudal lord's most violent acts of conquest, subjugation, rape, and pillage. The magical realm that stands in defiance of the heroic lawgiver becomes at this level the world of the sublime. It is impossible to overlook the evocation of the famous opening of *Las soledades* in the expansive and intricate mythic-astronomical conceit of Tello's description of his luminous herds. At this moment one must also recognize in the play's complex assimilation of doubles another text that is simultaneously rearticulated in Tello's resounding octaves— Góngora's *El Polifemo*. Its presence is far more important in the dramatist's development of the aesthetic implications of his encounter of doubles. The sweeping landscape of Tello's description is not merely the centrifugal feudal estate of medieval Spain. It is simultaneously the fabulously beautiful and fecund natural world of Sicily and its gigantic earth spirit, the cyclops ("Sicilia mía son . . . esas viñas"). His speech is the pained lament of the self-obsessed, rejected lover who proudly introduces himself to the object of his desire, offering gifts to the beautiful beloved, enumerating the riches of his natural kingdom, asserting his exalted ancestry, extolling his beauty and strength, voicing his disbelief that anyone could resist his attractions, and threatening with violence those who stand between him and the fulfillment of his romantic desires.

As odd as this convergence of literary modernism and political traditionalism might appear, it would be wrong to dismiss the interlude's "literary" prominence as a gratuitous digression on a major contemporary literary controversy or as an entertaining display of the fashionable peculiarities of Gongoresque discourse. It should be noted that Tello's opening stanza in fact heightens the emphatic display of egotism of his model:

> Yo, don Fernando, *soy* Tello García
> De Fuenmayor, *yo* el Infanzón de Illescas:
> Cuanta campiña veis, se nombra *mía*,
> Que *mías* son sus cazas y sus pescas.

(*I* don Fernando, *am* Tello García de Fuenmayor, *I*, the knight of Illescas: *Mine* is the countryside, as far as your eye can see, *mine* is the bounty of the forests and streams.) (485; emphasis added)[85]

However, his bravado should not be accounted for merely as one more example of the inexhaustible riches of Baroque parody and mock-heroic literature. If, as Elias has argued, the historical moment of the play's appearance witnessed a decisive alteration in Western man's consciousness in his increasingly complex relations with the rising environment of modern society and if that alteration centered on the internalization of restraint and the broad recognition of the imperative of the control of affect and instinct, it is not surprising that the culture of the period would be fascinated with the Ovidian tale of the gigantic embodiment of the torment of uncontrollable and unrequited desire and the disastrous effects of self-indulgence.[86] Such individual and societal development of the mechanisms of repression—the so-called "civilizing process"—is perfectly compatible with the ascendance of statism and the rule of law as the repression of the aristocratic ethos with its emphasis on self-assertion, personalism, action, will, and the domination of the weak by the strong. The colossal image of lawlessness is simultaneously the image of discourtesy and the pathos of unacceptability according to prevailing codes of the social environment. Grotesquely impetuous and sentimental, wildly "romantic" and self-centered, Polyphemus is everything that the coldly cerebral, calculating, and controlled courtiers of the king's society must suppress in themselves.

At the same time one should note the aesthetic implications that the play draws out of its political conflicts and the perfections of their parallels. The Ovidian-Gongoresque moment is, like the nocturnal duel and blood-letting that I discussed above, an instance of sublimity that supports the drama's fundamental aim of aestheticizing violence and preserving it within a majesty that is in reality rigidly circumscribed by the rationality of law, justice, courtly etiquette, and various other forms of social and military ritual. The blood shed by the "cruel" king in his primitive rituals and games turns into the illustrious emblazonment of the beautiful ruby. From the shattered corpse of the youthful Acis, lying beneath Polyphemus's gigantic boulder, crimson blood slowly and irregularly trickles forth and begins a thrilling metamorphosis into the leaping waters of a beautiful river and the rising body of a young god. Tello's "Sicilian" estate is not only the "unjuridified" landscape of the unruly, restless nobility, the ricoshombres of Spain's Reconquest and its cult of the pure person; it is not only the domain of the ferocious Gothic warrior of its mythic past (see below); it is not only the sinister realm of the tyrant, the fascinating figure that seemed to haunt the imagination of all contemporary political theorists. It is simultaneously the territory of the sublime, and to understand its effects and its importance in the design of the play, one must recognize its contrasts with the vision of nature marking Elvira's lengthy declamation on Tello's violence. It is a response that, as we might expect, was all but silenced in Moreto's comfortable *refundición* of the drama and, in its evident Baroque "bad taste," found no sympathy in Menéndez y Pelayo's modern critical response to the play.

Lingering at the threshold of the sacred—whether located at the altar, at the throne, or in nature—the sublime finds its imaginative power by gesturing toward regions that cannot be reached, that "lie ever beyond," and by violating the bonds that secure the world from which there can in reality be no escape— reason, law, order, government, natural system, balance, coherence, the regular movement of time, repetition, and routine. Unlike the *sosiego* achieved by mystics, quietists, and "negative theologians," the thrill of the feeling here pursued lies in the intuition that there is in fact "more," a fertile emptiness beyond, but that it can be experienced only through the "un-ordering" or severing of such bonds, the abandonment of the detached stance that they presuppose, and the destruction or humiliation of reason and all conventional patterns of coherence. It is an experience of radical reorientation, a rapture in sweeping momentarily beyond all limits.[87]

Tello's declamation is a striking concentration of the techniques of verbal disorientation that Góngora developed in his controversial Baroque style, with its characteristic thematic, conceptual, syntactical, and rhetorical violence. Extended periphrases; trans-elemental metaphors; paradoxical conceits; and illusionistic, purely formal antitheses—all the Gongoresque figures are exploited for an extravagantly expansive vision, commingling what is normally separated—the elemental orders, the gradations of the cosmic hierarchy—in the traditional order of things, the great static "chain of being." The overwhelming beauties of the landscape are founded in conflict and the violation of boundaries. As the examples above demonstrate, the panoramic description is marked by bizarre and imaginative "military transfigurations" of natural processes. Towering mountain peaks rival one another in splendor, the flocks of one competing with the snow—metaphorically transfigured as brilliant white tunics—of the other. The stylization of the opposition is far more suggestive than its simple "allegorical" replica and imaginative expansion of the opposition of the protagonists ("Esa sierra que en cumbres se dilata,/Con Guadarrama a competir se atreve"—That mountain range that spreads out in its pinnacles dares to compete with Guadarrama). Tello's bees, unruly "squadrons of winged raiding parties" (*alada soldadesca*), "plunder the flowers in order to flood and destroy republics of corkwood," which they "inundate with honey." Everywhere boundaries between elemental orders break down. The flocks on the mountains—"treetops of living silver"—"unwind" in a brilliant skein that instantly becomes an unleashed torrent, offering "crystalline pennants to the wind" as it plunges down the mountainside and, in its violent descent, drowns the thirsty fields in "abysses of wool." The armies of cattle, shining brilliantly as the "decoro del sol," erasing the boundary separating water and earth, transform the shores of the river, where they pasture into "gulfs of jasper." All mingles at the horizon beyond the fixing reach of vision. The fields metamorphose into an ocean, a "green deluge," that in turn becomes a sweeping expanse of emerald. The cascading metaphors incorporate the seasonal cycle in their continuing mutations. The abundant grains of the fields, tinted in the gold of the harvest, will offer their owner "empires of hyacinths." Innumerable clusters of grapes become the "pomp of August," the "vanity of October," and finally ruby droplets that vanish when sampled in crystal goblets.

As in the most marvelous visions of the natural world in Góngora's poetry, Tello's declamation records the agitated reaction of the observer, who expresses wonder (*admiratio*) before an unfolding and restlessly expanding spectacle. At the same time he surveys the natural world from a commanding perspective, taking possession of it, disassembling it, and recreating it according to the imperatives of his own autonomous imagination.[88] As in the case of Góngora's cyclops, Tello's association with the Baroque poet and his radical reconstructions of the cosmos disclose with a disquieting literalness that the root of the sublime and the most extravagant forms of Baroque poetry lies to a great extent in the fascination of violence.[89] In the case of the poet, it is an aesthetics of spectacular appropriation and power rather than of reflection and repose, and its intended effect on its audience is one of possession and subjugation rather than individuation and detachment.[90] The two monsters—Tello and Polyphemus—flourish in an order of exuberance, extravagance, and eccentricity where there is no center to be reached; where containing totalities and balancing perspectives are unknown; and where the distanced and rationalistic approach toward human affectivity that founds the strength and appeal of classicism—in its aesthetics of unity and beauty, its morality of integrity and constancy, and its politics of lawful community—is unthinkable. Lured into the center of the new world, Tello flails about futilely with his useless sword in the presence of the invisible and reticent powers of the palace and the state. But in an astonishing single moment of vindication, he compels his victorious rival fleetingly to lose control, to regress metaphorically to the telluric world of the cyclops, where in a nocturnal battle he must "hurl mountains" about in the shadows that envelop a mutual descent into an alluring chaos.[91]

TEMPERING THE GOTHIC LEGACY

Nunca vi poder tan necio.

(Never did I see power that was so foolish.)

—*El Rey Don Pedro en Madrid*

Pues bien se puede hacer un rey de un godo.

(For one can make a king even out of a Goth.)

—*La comedia de Bamba*

Tello's spectacular vision of the vitality, plenitude, and multiformity of his feudal estate, as well as the rhetorical, stylistic, metaphorical, syntactic, and thematic violence informing his declamation, points indirectly to the most profound philosophical issues raised by the play's doubling of Pedro el Cruel and the Infanzón de Illescas. However, it is equally important in the foregrounded political and historical contexts of the work. If the fierce warrior's estate is the sublime landscape of pagan mythology, it is simultaneously the heroic setting of Spain's national history and the backdrop of its major historical myth.

The second half of Tello's speech situates the Infanzón clearly in the epic world of the *Reconquista*. As I have pointed out above, Tello's declamation begins with a resounding display of self-aggrandizement ("*I*, Don Fernando, *am* Tello García. . . . *Mine* is the countryside as far as your eye can see"). The vast panorama of the "Sicily" of this Cyclopian figure is a possession earned through the individual deeds of warriors in the heroic struggle against the Moors. May Oviedo and Covadonga bear witness to "Quién son los infanzones y en qué partes/Contra la eternidad bronces fatigan" (who the knights are and where their bronze statues outlast eternity)! He and the other *infanzones* are the "descendents of the Cides," and his bloodlines reach back into the dark era preceding the restoration of the lost Visigothic crown by the redeemer Pelayo. He asserts that his ancestral blood flowed in the veins of the kings of Castile ("Mía es su Majestad, mía es su Alteza"); insists that the proper veneration of a ruler must be based on deeds and bloody conquests; claims, by the "right of the sword," to possess a majesty and an absolute authority over his province; insists that there can be no constraints on his will (*gusto*); and, disdaining any commercial activity, relishes the tribute guaranteed by the fears of his subjects. His riches appear to be unlimited and might recall the legendary wealth won by the heroic "Goths" of Spain's medieval conflicts, memorialized most unforgettably in Jorge Manrique's elegiac recollections—"Las dádivas desmedidas,/los hedificios reales/llenos de oro,/las baxillas tan febridas,/los enriques y reales/del thesoro,/los jaezes, y cavallos/de su gente, y atavíos/tan sobrados" (Gifts unmeasured, the royal buildings full of gold, dishes so burnished, the golden coins of the treasury, the caparisons, the horses of her people and finery in such excess).[92] For Tello the implementation of power and the language of power are very simple: "Hablen tantos castillos conquistados/en sangre y no en vergüenza colorados. . . . Por mi y por esta espada/soy la primera casa desta tierra" (Let the many castles speak that were vanquished in the blood of conquest and not colored in the blush of shame. . . . By myself and by this sword I am the principal house of this land) (485).

If Pedro is, however ambiguously, identified with the rise of the institutional order of law, internalized restraints, documents, *letras*, and states, Tello is the idolatrized personal power, the ego, of the individual hero.[93] His body, like that of a god, is metaphorically transformed into a cosmos, and his pronouncements ring with the omnipotence and paradoxes of an unapproachable deity: "Mi voz es como el cielo venerada;/Dueño soy de la paz, y de la guerra,/Tanto, que es en la cárcel de mi labio/como amable el favor, dulce el agravio" (My voice is venerated like heaven. I am the owner [the lord] of peace and war. So much so that in the prison of my lip, just as the favor is lovable, the rebuke is sweet) (485).[94] Scandalously appropriating the place of divinity, nature, and monarch in conventional legal thought and making a mockery of all contemporary political doctrine asserting the ubiquity of the royal presence in its icons, documents, and laws, he suggests to the disguised and infuriated king that it is only through his personal consent that the laws of Spain are recognized in his province. "Por acá, hidalgo, conocen/Por su firma y por su sello/Sólo al Rey, y algunas veces/Es con mi consentimiento" (Here, hidalgo, they know the King only by his signature and royal seal, and some times it is with my consent) (487).

It is tempting to read Tello's speech as burlesque, an extended exercise in stylized braggadocio in the tradition of the stock caricatures of mock-epic, popular melodrama, puppet theater, and *entremés*, the latter a genre that the play self-consciously evokes to describe the king's palace play, and, as such, a crude satirical degradation of the antagonist of the heroic king. It is undeniable that many of the grotesque (*esperpénticos*) effects that Stephen Gilman noted in the play spring from the deeds and posturings of this blustery and irascible villain.[95] And yet, as the play takes its unusual turns, we discover that Tello is loved by his subjects and praised as "padre de la patria"; that the king seems to yearn for contact with the sources of his mysterious powers; that he is abruptly incorporated in the comic society of the conclusion; and that, most hauntingly, in anonymous ballads overheard in the darkness of Madrid on the eve of his execution, children sing of his innocence, mourn his unjust imprisonment, and extol his physical beauty—the "golden bud of the earth, for whom all weep."

Who then is this Tello? Is he the monstrous earth spirit, the Cyclopian embodiment of destructive energy, anarchy, and violence whom the king-civilizer at one point describes as a "giant that he must prostrate at his feet" in a battle of mountains (506)?[96] Or is he, like the most famous representation of perfect knighthood in Lope's theater, the "archaic" knight of old Castilian descent, the Caballero de Olmedo, the archetypal figure of the youthful hero, the beautiful flower cut down before reaching its full blossom? Is he in fact Adonis or Polyphemus? Both myths seem to hover in his imaginative background, and, astonishingly, we discover, as in the case of the more famous play, that the *romancero* already appears to have laid claim to the "gallant knight" (*bizarro caballero*) for its pantheon of Spanish heroes.

The paradoxical nature of this fantasy figure and his complex relationship to the historical kings of the play—a group that includes not only Pedro el Cruel, but also Enrique II of Trastamara and Alfonso XI, who, apparently, has honored his table—become clearer if we recognize, in the play's complex engagement with the political and social culture of its period, the incorporation of the Gothic myth. Originating in the Middle Ages, a nostalgic recollection of an Edenic period of Christian unity founded, preserved, and tragically lost by an empire of heroic warriors from the north was sustained in chronicles such as those of El Tudense and El Toledano; became a unifying myth in a period of subjugation to a colonizing foreign power; and flowered as a championed model of religious, racial, and national purity following the rise of Castile and the completion of the Reconquest in 1492.

An integral component of the Gothic myth was an idealized vision of the natural patrimony of Spain, a bountiful land of overwhelming beauty and un-matched fecundity. Only such a fabulous paradise offered the attractions that could persuade the itinerant armies of the noble Goths, who had moved through-out the known world, conquering all armies standing in their paths—Romans, Huns, Medes, Vandals, and Franks—to found a permanent kingdom. "Espanna era el meior de todos, et muchol preciaron mas que a ninguno de los otros, ca entre todas las tierras del mundo Espanna a una estremanca de abondamiento et de bondad mas que otra tierra ninguna" (Spain was the best of all, and they esteemed it more highly than any of the others, for among all the lands of the world, Spain enjoys an extreme of abundance and goodness beyond all others).

With their "healing medicine" the Goths "cured the wounds" left on the peninsula by previous invaders and restored a paradise, enclosed and protected by natural fortifications, "esta Espanna que dezimos tal es como el parayso de Dios, ca riega se con cinco rios cabdales que son Ebro, Duero, Taio, Guadal-quiuil, Guadiana" (this Spain that we are describing is like God's paradise, for it is watered by five large rivers, which are the Ebro, the Duero, the Tagus, the Gadalquivil, and the Guadiana). In an excited display of rhetorical *amplificatio*, the medieval chronicler of the Gothic experience presents an exhaustive, over-flowing catalogue detailing the bounty, the plenitude, and the fecundity of the peninsula. Spain is rich in its soaring mountains and cascading rivers; it is a cor-nucopia of fruits, grains, milk, cheeses, honey, grapes, and wines; it teems with herds of cattle and horses, wild game, fish, and bees; it offers its inhabitants iron, gold, silver, and other metals, as well as precious stones and valuable minerals. The crowded enumerations of the patriotic declamation come to a climax in the assertion that there is no other land in the world so blessed by God; none that equals it in its abundance, its goodness, and its grandeur: "Espanna sobre todas es adelantada en grandez et mas que todas preciada por lealdad! ¡Ay Espanna! non a lengua nin engenno que pueda contar tu bien" (Spain surpasses all in grandeur and is respected more highly than all others for its loyalty! Oh, Spain! No tongue or genius can tell of your goodness).[97]

To return to Tello's striking evocation of the Gothic heritage, one finds that practically all the descriptive elements in his rhetorical declamation on his fabulous "frontier" estate can be accounted for in the traditional "loor de España." Its excesses might suggest parody, but one should note that such excesses were characteristic of the serious nationalist myth it is incorporating; that its enthusiasm for the energy, vitality, and beauty of the countryside persists amid the undeniable bravado in its self-assertiveness; and that its poetic articulations in the Gongoresque mode effectively convey the beauty of a perception of nature that has a particular vividness in its opposition to the parallel description of the natural order in universalist, abstract, and Neo-Platonic terms by Elvira, the victim of his cruelty, in the same act. Tello belongs to the fabled landscape of Spanish history and the collective memories that, however benighted and bloody, lie deep and ineradicable in its soil. As far as the play is concerned, such immortality must be denied the cerebral Pedro, who, situated in the natural order of Elvira's world concert, finds himself obligated to carry his nation into the modern age of monarchy, law, reason, hierarchy, historicity, and statecraft. Despite his excesses, the rebel, the *reyecillo*, is surrounded by the aura of a myth that will not vanish even as he is committed by Pedro to the night of historical oblivion.

As the Spanish nation rose from the ashes of its past, Diego de Valera celebrated the "Visigothic blood" of Fernando el Católico and exhorted him to restore the "imperial throne of the Goths."[98] A century later, as an overextended Habsburg Empire found itself once again compelled to defend the borders of Christendom and maintain firm control over potential internal enemies, the Gothic myth was resurrected and orchestrated with renewed intensity in the social and political orders, its appeal heightened by contemporary racial anxieties concerning purity of blood that followed the edicts of expulsion. In Spain's triumphalist vision of its past, the national history was conceived as a religious crusade in which the Spanish leaders distinguished themselves primarily as warriors heroically committed to battling the infidels at the frontiers and maintaining order in a population menaced by internal divisions of race, "blood," and religion.

In the period of crisis that followed the confrontation of the Turkish enemies in the East, the rebellion of the Moriscos in the Alpujarras, the secession of the Protestant states of the Low Countries, and the ill-fated mission of the Spanish Armada, it is not surprising that the Gothic heritage would take possession of the collective imagination and assert itself with the obsessive grip of a dominant ideology. In 1541 Florián de Ocampo published his updated edition of the *Primera crónica general*, emphasizing the invincibility of the Gothic tribes and offering the reading public the inspiring nationalist vision of its famous "loor de España."

In this period, as Augustín Redondo has noted, Spaniards began to lavish extraordinary energy on genealogical studies establishing links with Gothic ancestors: "It is not surprising that at this point—and especially from the middle of the sixteenth century on—legendary genealogies multiply that establish roots of aristocratic families in Visigothic Spain, or at least in the primitive Christian kingdoms to which it gave birth, notably in the Castile of the national origins, the Castile of the first judges, of Count Fernán González, of the Cid, or of the celebrated and entirely invented Bernardo del Carpio."[99] In 1582 Julián del Castillo wrote the *Historia de los reyes godos* and traced the line of their descendants directly to Philip II, exploiting the imaginative power of the myth to exalt the contemporary monarchy and to identify its institutions with the primal perfections of the Gothic paradise.[100]

By the late sixteenth century, Spaniards appeared to agree that the word "Gothic" implied above all else bravery, goodness, strength, nobility, honor, wealth, and beauty.[101] It was at this moment that the national theater came into existence, and Lope de Vega, perhaps following a recommendation by the Sevillian dramatist Juan de la Cueva (transcribed in his *Ejemplar poético* of 1606) concerning the riches available for poetic treatment in the "ingeniosa fábula de España," quickly turned to the Gothic material for some of his memorable early works. As has often been pointed out, Lope's most characteristic response to the complex historical pressures of the time was to support the resurgent Gothic myth and exploit its potential for powerful and reassuring dramatic effects, and his most compelling heroes—monarchs, nobles, and even *villanos*—are frequently exalted through an unproblematic identification with the Gothic heritage. It is in fact the "racially pure," "old Christian" heritage of the early northern heroes that Lope claimed for the family of his father, an embroiderer from Asturias, throughout his career as an aspiring and frequently frustrated courtier, court poet, official chronicler, and panegyricist of the Spanish nobility.

The Gothic ideal was easily assimilable to chivalric images and values, and we find that Lope's perfect knight, Juan Ramírez de Arellano—warrior, lover, independent counsellor, and exemplar for kings—is celebrated as a "fénix de los godos" to whom the "patria" is indebted, a Navarese incarnation of Pelayo, the Gothic chieftain who founded Spain and inaugurated the Reconquest at the legendary Battle of Covadonga. The identification is common in numerous plays in which the monarch is presented in unambiguous heroic roles. For example, in *Las paces de los reyes y judía de Toledo*, the heroine exhorts her king, Juan II, to imitate the celestial example of Pelayo, the illustrious Gothic prince; in the celebrative depiction of Pedro the Cruel as *justiciero* in *Las audiencias del Rey don Pedro*, the plaintiff Laurencia seeks redress at the tribunal of the "Sucesor monarca digno/Del godo rey Recaredo" (the monarch, the worthy successor of the Gothic king Recaredo).[102] In such doctrinaire, "untroubled," incorporations of Spain's monarchic institution and its historical traditions, kings "incarnate" and "validate" their Gothic exemplars perfectly. In a striking *audiencia* of perhaps the most popular of Lope's royal portraits, Columbus reminds King Juan II of Portugal that had he listened to his petitions, he, rather than Fernando of Spain, would be the beneficiary of "cosas raras:/Oro, indios, aves, plata, y sobre todo,/De imperios grandes esperanzas claras" (rare things: Gold, Indians, birds, silver, and above all, the clear hopes of great empires). The "perfect prince" responds graciously: "Dios lo guardaba al castellano godo:/El lo goce, Colón" (God was keeping it for the Castilian Goth: May he enjoy it, Columbus).[103]

As we have seen, it is precisely in the ritual scene of the *audiencia* in *El Rey Don Pedro en Madrid* that the monarch's underlying dissatisfactions with his statist "reduction" as hero and the depersonalized institutions of modern state government are most dramatically expressed. The most interesting aspect of the "double portrait" announced in its modern title, "king *or infanzón*," is its uncoupling of the monarch and Goth, a feature that sharply distinguishes it from such straightforward dramatic exploitation and reinforcement of contemporary ideology. It in fact calls into question the system of values underlying the myth of Gothic Spain, and in the note of comic bluster in Tello's declamation, it would appear to be easily explained as a dramatic version of a theme more common in contemporary satire: the condemnation of *goticismo* in its association with pride, vainglory, social climbing, and class prejudice. Covarrubias notes in his dictionary that "para encarecer la presunción de algún vano, le preguntaron si desciende de la casta de los godos" (in order to emphasize the pretentiousness of a vain person, they asked him if he was the descendant of the caste of the Goths).[104] The perverse effects of the Gothic fashion are abundantly illustrated in the popular satirical writing of the Golden Age, from Mateo Alemán to Baltasar Gracián, and expressions such as *salir de los godos*, *ser de los godos*, and above all, *hacerse de los godos* became clichés of ridicule from the second half of the sixteenth century. As that unsparing critic of human folly, the notorious female *pícara* and *conversa* of López de Úbeda's fantasy, put it, "Yo confieso que éste es un tiempo en que el zapatero, porque tiene calidad, se llama Zapata, y el pastelero gordo, Godo" (I confess that this is an age in which the shoemaker, in his delusions as a man of quality, names himself Zapata, and the fat [*gordo*] pastrymaker, "Godo").[105]

However, the play under examination is not primarily concerned with social satire or with the comic effects of a conventional *comedia de figurón* (comedy of the inflated fool). The reach of its bizarre fantasies goes far deeper. *El Rey Don*

Pedro en Madrid is in reality a complex, densely thematic work that presents an analytical reconstruction of the history of Spain; examines its political traditions—above all the institution of its monarchy; and at its deepest stratum of significance illuminates a fundamental crisis marking the origin of the modern state, literalizing with eerie precision its incorporation and monopolization of raw violence and imaginatively disclosing the precarious embrace of violence and codified law that continues to underlie and preserve its existence.[106] One might say that its ultimate position on these matters, insofar as it is related to the prominence and power of the Gothic myth and legacy, is to reveal the ascendence of the modern state as an overcoming and simultaneously a preservation of the Gothic heritage—a reconciliation of it with the necessary primacy of law, bureaucracy, and the organizational machinery of written record, ceremony, and etiquette that provides the concrete foundation of the institution of the new political order.

Beneath the comic bluster of Tello, the playwright is pointing to something of far greater consequence: the pure individuality that, if uncurbed by the institutionalized restraints of a civilized community founded in reason and law, will naturally degenerate into the pure willfulness of the human self that politically realizes its fullest development in the figure of the tyrant and in the forcefully, but precariously controlled, anarchy that is the tyrant's state. At one point Tello is denounced as a tyrant, and it is oddly appropriate that the Gothic hero who, in his most violent moment of self-expression, turns the icon of law and the state— the staff/scepter of the village judge—into a lethal weapon should commit in the graphically described rape of Elvira the archetypal act of the tyrant, the violent appropriation for his own capricious purposes of the body of another human being, contrary to the most fundamental and universal principal of natural law. To recall Kriegel's theory on the civilized advances underlying the emergence of statist order, we can see in Tello's nocturnal deeds the marks of a stark regression, a return to the shadows of feudalism and its rule of the strong.[107]

As a young dramatist Lope was immediately attracted to the Gothic material, and some of his early plays reveal his sensitivity to the ambiguities of its heroic traditions and a recognition of the incompatibility of their individualistic ethos and the maintenance of the ordered collectivity of the state. One finds germs of the oppositions that twenty years later will found a complex dialectic in the interactions of Pedro and Tello already in his plays on the most famous of the legendary Gothic kings. Amid the rapid actions of a grand cast of characters, the sensationalist scenes and melodramatic declamations, and the bloody tableaus of the spectacular history play *El último godo*, Lope develops a simple contrast between the willful destroyer of Spain, King Rodrigo, who tyrannically follows his impulses in his on-stage rape of Florinda, the mythical La Cava, and the disciplined Pelayo, the sturdy, anti-courtly primitive of the northern mountains who stoically endures the national trauma and initiates the liberation struggle against the Moorish invaders.

Much more interesting, however, is Lope's imaginative reworking of the Gothic material in *Comedia de Bamba*, for here he directly develops an opposition between an ideal king and his warriors that suggests a necessity of tempering and channeling the latent violence in the pure individualism sanctioned by the Gothic tradition. The play is directly concerned with examining and redefining the Gothic legacy and conceives of the problem in terms of state institutions. Its opening scene suggests the prominence of the political theme. We witness a dramatic conflict based on a commonly discussed question in contemporary statecraft, the relative merits of hereditary and elective monarchy—the latter frequently represented by the Gothic kingdom—and the precarious approximations to chaos in the brief interregna of systems based on election. The ensuing argument presents the Goths as a squabbling group of warriors, all of whom assert their claims to an empty throne, ritualistically raising their swords and repeating the word *yo*, as if in a choral declamation of a comic operetta, and challenging one another to duels to determine who is the "top Goth" (*el primer godo*). One could hardly find a more resounding proclamation of the "dimensión imperativa de la persona." The quintessential Gothic qualities are exposed as leading to competition, divisiveness, violence, anarchy, and an obsession with precedence.[108]

Lope juxtaposes to this concentrated celebration of sword, self, blood, and deed the modesty and tranquility of the self-effacing farmer Bamba, a figure in the biblical tradition of Saul, who, when miraculously called from his fields and his plow, gives up the satisfactions of contented solitude together with his simple wife, free from the terror of "seeing the king's face," and reluctantly accepts the crown with exemplary humility, charity, wisdom, strength, and saintliness. He is associated not with the sword but rather with a miraculous flowering branch and crown, the cape of St. Martin, the chasuble of St. Ildefonso, the image of the Virgin, and a marvelous infant prophet who appears in a vision. It is noteworthy that in this legendary "counter-figure" of the Gothic monarch, Lope separated himself from the official historiography of the crown, which rejected as apocryphal the traditions of a farmer-king and chose to present Bamba as an ideal Gothic noble whose heroic conquest of Narbonne preserved his empire against the disintegrating effects of Paulo's treachery and perverse political machinations.[109] It is also important to recognize that Lope's ideal king is frequently the victim of the scorn of the Gothic warriors, rooted in their pride in rank and lineage, and that his evil opponent Paulo, the "Greek Goth," is master of the arts of politics and the "political" virtue of prudence.

The fact is that in Lope's early play we already discover a rift in the Gothic image and glimpse the profile of his future mythification of the ideal Spaniard as the humble, peaceful *villano* who insists on subordinating the heroic manly virtues of Spain's aristocratic tradition within a scheme of values rooted primarily in Christian and humanistic ethical principles and metaphysical foundations: the reinvented Goths of Tello de Meneses' family; the saintly Isidro, el Labrador de Madrid; the humble, patriotic farmer Peribáñez; and the independent classical sage Juan Labrador.[110] The early *Bamba* seems determined from the very outset to examine analytically, to deflate satirically, and to redefine and reincorporate the official Gothic identity in its picture of a perfect peasant king. In his first appearance Bamba concludes his celebrative depiction of the pleasures and personal fulfillments of the simple life spent far from the court and its political intrigue with the declaration: "Para godo y español,/Bástame eso y sóbrame eso" (For a Goth and a Spaniard, this is enough for me, and in reality it is more than enough for me) (44). In a scene rich in comic contrasts of the type familiar in Cervantes's *Don Quixote*, Bamba's simple wife reacts to the arrival of the embassy of elegant Gothic nobles with endearing naïveté.

> Sancha: ¡Oh, que galanos vestidos!
> 　　　　　Decid, Bamba, ¿son danzantes?
> Bamba: No, sino godos.
> Sancha: ¿Quien?
> Bamba: Godos.
> Sancha: Decid, ¿qué son godos?
> Bamba: Son
> 　　　　Gente de sangre y blasón:
> 　　　　¿No lo echáis de ver en todos?

(Sancha: Oh! What elegant dresses! Tell me, Bamba, are they dancers? Bamba: No, they are Goths. Sancha: Who? Bamba: Goths. Sancha: Tell us, what are Goths? Bamba: They are people of good blood and a coat of arms: Can't you see it in all of them?) (53)

In his climactic triumphs Bamba's emergence as a redefined Gothic hero is emphasized, his political science marked by honesty and his ferocity tempered by compassion: "Español soy de nación;/Godo soy, que no soy griego" (I am a Spaniard by nation; I am a Goth, and not a Greek). He reproves Paulo in his worship of power and empire: "Que es ser vasallo del cielo/Más que ser rey del infierno" (For it is better to be a vassal in heaven than a king in hell) (67). Unlike the rigorous Bamba of the chronicles, who humiliates and blinds his enemies, he weeps on being told of the necessary castigation of the rebels and finds himself reproved for a weakness that is unusual in kings.

In one of the most telling moments of the climax of Lope's suggestive early engagement with the ambiguities of the Gothic myth, we hear the menacing figure of Ervigio, Bamba's successor, point out that just as one observes the metamorphoses of a "small snake into a serpent" and the soul of a sinner into the soul of a saint, one can "make a king out of a Goth" (68). It is undeniable that *La comedia de Bamba*'s representation of the Gothic myth, its association of particular aspects of the myth with questions of political theory, and its disclosure of archaic and disturbing features of the fashionable myth and ideology illuminate several of the most remote aspects of the later and much more complex work, *El Rey Don Pedro en Madrid*. And yet the early *comedia* is not really concerned with the issues of statist institutions, the power of law, the complexities of the king's double identity and "misery," and the incorporation of violence in a new political order. In effect it turns from the Gothic ethos to an alternative that has little to do with politics and the ruinous world of statism. Here the necessary tempering of Gothicism points not to law, rationalization, and modernity but rather to the kingdom that is not of this earth. While clarifying much in the striking investment of the Gothic tradition in Pedro el Justiciero's gigantic opponent, its resolution suggests a theocentric approach to the political problems of the time that looks forward to Calderón's dramatic world, where there can in reality be no true kingdoms of this earth and where man realizes the ultimate goal of the earthly existence in statelessness and in a condition of awareness far more expansive than the confines of citizenship could ever contain.

CONCLUSION: THE REGICIDE OF MONTIEL AND THE RETURN OF TELLO

It is tempting to simplify *El Rey Don Pedro en Madrid* and interpret its central conflict of monarch and aristocrat according to the most conventional patterns of the drama of European absolutism, with its characteristic interest in the theme of the king's two identities and the problems that his peculiar double existence — simultaneously man and institution — can present. As I have pointed out above, the play can easily be rendered intelligible as an unusual version of the education of the prince. In this case the monarch exhibits the traditional excesses of youth — anger, violence, blasphemy, lust, and inconstancy[111] — is offered instruction in the familiar textbooks for princes in need of moral improvement; and ultimately reaches maturity in self-control, respect for law, the equitable

administration of justice, defense of the honor of the weak against those of superior social rank, heroic military victory over enemies of the state, and a public
act of expiation for his sins. In defeating an opponent whose vices image his own
in exaggerated forms, he rises above his ordinary humanity, so to speak, and he
becomes worthy of wearing the robes and regalia of the royal body; these he
dons at two climactic moments in the drama: his triumph as *letrado* over his
opponent in his palace rituals and his display of the king's body with the sword
and scepter of law and justice in the final scene. His concluding words are those
of the builder of a state: "Let us go, for the construction of the royal edifice is
now to begin."

Pedro becomes the model king and is associated, as "piedra de Madrid," with
the literal act of laying the foundation for a monastery in the city that was to
become the center of the Spanish Empire and creating an alabaster effigy to
perpetuate the quasi-divine aura of his royal body. These are the fulfillments of
the specific commands of yet another accusing alter ego in this complex play
of doubles: the specter haunting him as a bad conscience in his nightmares of
sin, fearlessly besting him in combat, and calling for an act of expiation of his
youthful violence. In more general terms, Pedro, as winner in an ongoing inner
struggle for self-control, is associated with the moral virtue of constancy—parodied grotesquely in the erotic adventures of his dark double—and with the stabilizing foundation of the state in a code of law. The punning riddle-prophecy,
an admonition by one of the many victims of his murderous rage, ambiguously
associates his foundational act with the most holy of holies: "Thou art Peter,
and upon this rock I will build my church, and the gates of hell shall not prevail
against it."[112]

At the same time one should not overlook the conventionality of the drama's
central conflict in terms of a more general pattern in the historical vision of the
theater of European absolutism: the chronicling of the triumphant struggle of
the monarchy to establish its control against the anarchy and violence of the
deeply entrenched aristocracy, its feudal heritage of independence, and its centrifugal political energies. Certainly the denouement of the play might at first
glance suggest an effort at "exorcising" the legendary cruelty of King Pedro, a
cleansing of the historical image in accordance with the alleged remarks by
Philip II as he contemplated Pedro's portrait in the palace of Segovia. Celebrating the precedence of law over force, the pen over the sword, the document over
the voice, and the palace over the *campaña*, the play can be seen not only as an
effective apologia for a specific maligned king, but also as a comprehensive piece
of monarchist propaganda.

While such neat paradigms might usefully serve the purposes of generalized

historical clarification, they fail to explain the paradoxes and respond to the undeniable dramatic power of this play. The interactions of the doubles, around
which the familiar conceptual oppositions and dramatic conflicts try in vain to
crystallize and find resolution, become more and more elusive; opposition becomes attraction; conflict becomes embrace. The result is the rarest of hybrids,
in reality a reconfiguration of the official body of the king that refuses to cast
off the monstrous. In its strangeness it invites psychological interpretation—the
dark ambivalences of a deeply conflicted identity: Pedro el Justiciero is Pedro
el Cruel. Might the enigma in fact point beyond mere political and historical
forces to schemas of coherence lying in the more hidden depths of human nature? Insisting that the play is one of the major achievements of the Spanish
national theater, Menéndez y Pelayo emphasized the "strange and somber profundity of the character of Don Pedro . . . a sinister and terrible, but grand, Don
Pedro," a figure whose complexity, like that of Hamlet, imposes an unfathomable, sublime mystery on the entire drama.[113]

All the "positive" forces unfolding triumphantly in history and overtly endorsed
by the drama—as if in accord with Philip II's directive concerning Pedro's unacceptable appellative—begin to appear ambiguous; the price that they exact refuses to be denied. The "educated" king impatiently throws away his manuals on
monarchy and complains that burdened by the regalia and his official body, he
cannot be a man, with a man's "honorable" prerogative to violent self-expression
when circumstances so demand. There are no hints of a consoling heroism in
regal responsibility of the type that the vigilant, uneasy, and humanized Henry V
finds amid his simple slumbering soldiers on the fields of Agincourt. There are
no hints of a greater sacrifice of a self-abasing Fernando of Portugal, a *príncipe
constante* who similarly tears up the documents of state but is rewarded in the
burst of light that emblazons his martyrdom. The written language—the idiom
of law, political science, diplomacy, accommodation, and the machinery of
state—suppresses the power and the authenticity of the human voice. The state,
in the form of the labyrinthine palace that diffuses and elegantly veils an ever-
present coercive power, becomes a tomb of cold marble walls, stifling tapestries,
frightening Egyptian hieroglyphs, and spectral figures moving about mechanically in the rituals of a regulating and distancing etiquette. Here is where Tello
is truly most alien, most incapable of "serving"; where his "strangeness" is most
evident; and where his own feeling of estrangement becomes most unbearable.
In the palace the sword is banned, reduced to serving as an abstract and subordinate signifier in the monarch's emblem of justice. The sublimity of its deeds
that the living voice of the populace celebrates through the night in its ballads
of the warrior Tello will be denied the king. The latter will from now on be left

with only the "medicine" of the new, rational political science, the ingeniously controlled "games" of the palace world, to assert whatever manly heroic impulses he feels.[114] As we have seen, the "negative" forces overcome in the *justiciero's* triumph voice their resistance in a resounding orchestration of a natural and metaphysical order, countering the traditional classical world picture that frames, confines, and dignifies the ascent of the rational modern state and its "loving" collectivity. The careful separation of monarch and tyrant, the program determining numerous political dramas of the Baroque, begins to blur, and the play seems to turn on itself and express a nostalgia for tyranny and its institutionalization of a sublime individualism.[115] Pedro the "rock" in effect cannot hide his discomfort with his destiny to be the foundation of the new state.

The play then attempts in vain to stifle a yearning for the sublime. Its resistance to its own avowed monarchist purposes and structures is unmistakable. As discussed above, Pedro's third triumph is that of *don* Pedro the man. Standing above the body of his antagonist, prostrated at his feet in the darkness that has stripped him of his identity as king, he admits that this clandestine act—forbidden to rulers according to the contemporary political manuals—was necessary because he "wished to know that he is a man" (511). He informs his antagonist that he can "hacer hombre con la espada/Lo que rey con el respeto" (as a man I can accomplish with the sword what the king can with respect) and adds, "que por mí mismo te vengo,/Y no por la majestad" (for by myself I take vengeance on you, and not by the majesty). In Pedro el Justiciero's decision to violate his own laws, secretly opening his prison, releasing the traitor, and engaging in the forbidden duel—the supreme ritual of the heightened individualism of a historically superseded way of life[116]—the play achieves its most intense moment of paradox, briefly opening up the numerous enclosures that it programmatically constructs in its sequence of civilization's triumphs. Demonstrating the magnanimity of the primitive chivalric warrior cult, Pedro allows his rival and "friend" to vanish into the night, counseling him to take refuge in the *campaña* and flee to Aragon, the kingdom historically most hospitable to the lawless aristocracy of the Trastamaran civil wars and the most resistant of the peninsular kingdoms to the consolidation and empowerment of the Castilian state.

The play quickly turns from its brief crossover and retreat into the world of chivalry and its individual heroes. Tello returns to be incorporated into the world of law and order and to accept a subordinate role within the king's theater of power. Pedro triumphantly displays his majesty—the full regalia of the *rex judex* and the emblems of the juridified modern state. In terms of both the historical forces it chronicles and the political theory it articulates, we might think that in its metamorphosis of sword from weapon to allegory, a more appropriate title for the play would be that which Calderón was to use several years later, when addressing archaic aspects of Spain's aristocratic traditions: *El postrer duelo de España.*[117] However, the realities of history remained to mock the perfections of the play's efforts at neat resolution of its conflicts, and the dramatist could not fail to attend to them. Amid the celebrative display of the official body of the state, the crown falls from the head of the helpless monarch, and the legendary dagger slips from the hand of the future assassin as he attempts to sheath it. King Pedro's final triumph in his use of regal theatrics, a calculated peripeteia of salutary fear, suspense, and unexpected clemency, is marred by omens that he could not control nor his audiences fail to miss.[118] In the concluding words of the play it falls to the astonishingly transformed Tello to celebrate comedy's triumph over history.

> Y aquí tenga fin alegre
> De Illescas el Infanzón,
> Con prodigios y sin muertes.

(And here, with wonders and with no deaths, *the Knight of Illescas* shall have its happy ending.)

But for the Spanish public it was perfectly clear that there would be many more deaths and that in fact a very real duel would occur in the years following the fantasy of Pedro's momentary conquest of violence. Rather than a carefully regulated confrontation according to codes of honor, artistry, and beauty, it would be a brutal collapse into a condition of barbaric violence, a regression into chaos matching the most shocking that the drama could offer. Lured into Enrique's tent in an effort to escape from the fortress of Montiel, where he had been pinned down by an unexpected attack of the French mercenaries serving his half-brother, Pedro finds himself betrayed by the "chivalric" French knight Bertran du Guesclin, who cynically promises to provide him with a means of escape, only to turn him over to Enrique, whose monetary offer he finds more attractive. The decades of rivalry, hatred, anger, and violence climax in a desperate hand-to-hand struggle to the death by the half-brothers. For a moment Pedro appears to have the advantage, only to find himself betrayed once again by one of the French knights, who intervenes to pull him off his adversary. Enrique immediately seizes the moment and plunges his dagger into Pedro's heart. The unseemliness of the whole episode is perhaps registered in a comment by the French chronicler Froissart: "Those who killed him left him lying on the ground for three days, which in my opinion was an inhumane thing to do. And the Spaniards came and mocked him."[119]

One might say that the reality of history was not yet ready for the "integration" of Tello and his chaos. The Furies would remain implacable in their demands for blood. The civil violence of aristocratic Spain was to continue for more than a century beyond the illusory epiphany of law and the state that this play situates in Pedro's confrontation of his dark double. Perhaps the greater irony in the relation of subsequent real history and the irrepressible contradictions in its dramatic reinvention is an insight into the continuing attractiveness of Tello and his sublime violence for human beings and their societies in all ages. Nowhere is the resurrection of Tello—the unappeasable, indestructible spirit that will always rise renewed from an earth (*tellus*) soaked with blood—more sublime than in the ballads of Pedro el Cruel that sprang up almost immediately following his murder.

Los fieros cuerpos rebueltos
entre los robustos braços
esta el cruel Rey don Pedro,
y don Enrique su hermano.
No son abraços de amor
los que los dos se estan dando,
que el vno tiene vna daga,
y otro un puñal azerado.
El Rey tiene Enrique estrecho
y Enrique al Rey apretado,
vno en colera encendido,
y otro de rabia abrasado. . . .

Yo derrame de mi hermano
la sangre que clama y llora,
y es justicia que la mia
otro bierta con inopia. . . .

Y la mano executora
baxa el probocado Henrique,
y la cabeça destronca
con duros, pessados golpes
de aquella ceruiz briosa,
que en tierra quedo saltando
con mil muestras espantosas.

(Henry and King Pedro clasping/Hold in straining arms each other,/Tugging hard, and closely grasping/Brother proves his strength with brother./Harmless pastime, sport fraternal/Blends not thus their limbs in strife;/Either aims with rage infernal,/Naked dagger, sharpened knife./Close Don Henry grapples Pedro./Pedro holds Don Henry strait,/Breathing, this, triumphant fury/That, despair and mortal hate. . . ./I shed my brother's blood,/It weeps and screams for justice,/And it is only right/that another brother should spill my own. . . ./And the enraged Enrique/brings down the executioner's hand/and with hard and heavy blows/he severs from that spirited neck/his brother's head,/and it continues to leap about/on the ground with a thousand frightful grimaces.)[120]

The fascinating imaginative alchemy that human beings have always brought to their most horrific deeds of bloodshed could hardly be more spectacularly in evidence. To use the language of the play, we might say that the "deluges of blood" of Pedro's reign shine with the charismatic beauty of the ruby.

Fig. 5. Giovanni Lorenzo Bernini, *Equestrian Statue of Louis XIV*
(Palace of Versailles). (Réunion des Musées Nationaux/Art Resource, NY.)

EPILOGUE: REFRACTIONS AND DISINTEGRATIONS OF THE MAJESTY: THE KING AS STATESMAN AND MARTYR

In 1685 Bernini's equestrian statue honoring Louis XIV was presented at Versailles. It had been commissioned by the king's minister of finance, Jean-Baptiste Colbert, who wanted it to resemble the sculptor's recent statue of Constantine's vision of the Cross—a moment of interruption and rapture in which the rider spiritually rises above a frightened and agitated creature that he will presumably subdue and command with aid from on high. The king was displeased with the work, refused to let it be displayed at Versailles, and suggested that it be destroyed. A ruler, it would seem, must be displayed only in a pose of complete domination, as a stabilizing power amid the powerful political and social energies of the new state. Louis subsequently commissioned numerous equestrian statues that would bring his commanding presence to public spaces throughout his kingdom; the statues adhered to the reassuring conventions of royal depiction that had been developed in the Italian Renaissance from imperial Roman models and were to be perfected in the resplendent figures of Velázquez's equestrian portraits: iconic figures of animal and man, harmoniously connected, executing the perfect *levade* of artistic horsemanship; displaying clearly signifying regalia of royal dress, armor, and ornamentation; and fixing the motionless, untroubled gaze of the quasi-divine rider on an unspecifiable, transcendental point in the distance. Individuality, restlessness, temporality, and *inconstantia* were to have no place in the world of monumental containment displayed within the frames of the official portrait of the king.

But what light might Bernini's sculpture and the controversies surrounding its questionable appropriateness throw on the depictions of kings that I have studied in a different artistic medium, in a different country, and in specific works of art that, at first glance, appear to have very little in common with each other? All three works are concerned with elevating monarchy and the monarch, and all three are fully conversant with the idiom and system of representation that had developed in the so-called cult of the king. All were undoubtedly created to fulfill the celebratory purposes of that cult, and yet all required correction. In the case of Bernini the problems ultimately allowed for no fixing up, no exemplary rearticulation or satisfactory expurgation. As far as the king was concerned, the only remedy was the complete censorship of demolition. One might say that in all cases the key problem was the image of the king's loss of control and the anxieties that such an image might stir up in a viewer. In each case the loss of control is concentrated in a disturbing vision of horse and rider. Juan de Matos Fragoso's rewriting of *El villano en su rincón* eliminated entirely the crucial moment of the king's sexual pursuit of the village women and its imaginative association with a hunter's loss of control of his horse in a chaotic mountainous wilderness. Moreover, Matos Fragoso ensured the cultic elevation of his king by displacing the play's unhistorical French monarch with the venerable Spanish philosopher-king Alfonso el Sabio and transforming the *villano*'s critique of certain aspects of monarchy into the inconsequential grumblings and *caprichos* of an amusing comedic stereotype. From the beginning of the play the king is the sage, and the most interesting dynamic of the paradoxical model, the challenge presented by the charismatic philosophical alien, is disregarded entirely. With the drastic reduction of the philosophical and political main plot, the author foregrounds and expands the fragmentary and seemingly superfluous secondary plot and in effect transforms the play into an honor drama in which a scornful, class-conscious aristocrat emerges as an antagonist and the king assumes his conventional exalted role, representing divinity, restoring a just order, and protecting the abused lower class. The king is, as it were, resituated in his suprahuman frame.[1] More striking is the rewriting of *El Rey Don Pedro en Madrid* by Moreto, who eliminates entirely the king's initial fall from the horse and his immediate slaughter of the rebellious animal—certainly the most powerful image of disorder within the state that one finds in these works. It is worth pointing out that Bernini is thought to have been drawn to the myth of Pegasus in conceiving his royal statue and that the quintessential artist of the conventional royal portrait, Le Brun, perhaps inspired by such unorthodox fantasies, sketched the plan of an equestrian monument in which King Louis rides an agitated horse on top of a rock.[2] The plan was never carried out. In *El Rey Don Pedro en Madrid* such Baroque images of sublimity and risk surround the violent king, who describes his deed at the beginning of the play as the wild pursuit over a mountainous rocky terrain and a "fall of Phaeton" from his rebellious mount. The opening to such intensity and such a superhuman display of energy by both rider and horse—the latter is mysteriously resurrected and rushes off, seeking nourishment in supernatural fire—is immediately closed off by Moreto, who motivates Pedro's furious flight rationally and historically as the pursuit of his rebellious brother, the future regicide Enrique de Trastamara, and the death of the horse as the result of the king's historically documented tendency to overstress his mounts. Moreto goes on to attenuate all such rifts in the standard mirror-of-prince paradigm to which he adheres. Tello's violence, like that of Pedro, is drastically reduced. Rape is replaced by seduction; the raw sexual violence in the lord's abuse of peasants disappears. The grotesque aspects of the prison world and its grim stylizations of torture, execution, and erotic bonding, the gallows humor reminiscent of the literary world of *germanía* or the picaresque are all but eliminated. The Gongoresque expansion of Tello's alien world and the challenging sublimity of his alternative kingdom are sharply muted; the emphasis shifts decisively away from the supernatural and the deep theological contexts of Pedro's murder and expiation to a straightforward and banal development of the juridical and rational triumphs of Pedro and the assertion of the primary importance of law, equity, forensic rhetoric, and judicial power in the consolidation of the state. Horrific portents of impending tragedy are removed from notable locations at beginning and end of the original play, and, in effect, the free flowing blood of the model is wiped clean. The paradox of Tello-Pedro, the fascinating and ultimately unstable symbiosis of violence and law, is tepidly developed in a reposeful and satisfying composite, the *valiente-justiciero* ideal that emerges at the end. A worthy *caballero* has yielded to a just king, and, in an atmosphere of mutual admiration, chivalry figuratively departs from Castile and gracefully yields to the new order of the state, founded in an impersonal and hence a more humane order of justice.

> la justicia que es más sacra
> con freno que con azote;
> la corona que avasalla
> más al perdón que al castigo;
> la ley que es más soberana
> por la hojas de la oliva
> que los filos de la espada.

(the justice that is more sacred with bridle than with whip; the crown that subjugates through pardon rather than punishment; the law that is more sovereign through the leaves of the olive tree than the blades of the sword.)[3]

The king's disturbing attraction to his violent enemy and to the values his enemy represents, in its dilution within traditional conceptions of friendship and chivalry, all but disappears. To recall Leo Spitzer's most influential studies of Baroque literature, one might say that the whole play produces a tidy, precise, and unified exercise in *klassische Dämpfung*, a "classical muting" that can succeed only by eliminating the boundless realm of expansive energy and multitudinous forms that distinguishes the primitive order of the Infanzón of Illescas, the most memorable figure in its "Baroque" model.[4]

It is needless to remind ourselves that the three works of art that looked so deeply and provocatively into the ascendant regal power of the early state and took their spectators toward limits beyond which contemporary orthodoxy refused to pass in its understanding of the consequences of such historical developments continue to be remembered, whereas their "corrections" and "reframings" have been long since forgotten or relegated to secondary status as works of art and as revelations in the history of human consciousness. The most famous survivor is of course Bernini's soaring king, an exiled victim of absolutism's insecurities who, standing triumphantly at the gate of the Louvre Palace and Museum, currently occupies the most honorable location in post-regal and post-modernist France and has achieved a visibility, if not a stabilizing centrality, beyond anything the ubiquitous Sun King could have hoped for in his carefully choreographed staged appearances. In the case of the two Spanish plays that I have examined, there are no comparable stories of disappearance and spectacular deliverance of a lost king. If they quietly survived their immediate trivializations, their success was probably due not only to their powerful theatrical effects, their depictions of unforgettable characters, and their archetypal settings and actions, but also to their complex and audacious relations to traditional celebrative representations of the monarch and to serious political, social, and moral issues connected with the rise of monarchy, city, court, and state.

Both plays are concerned with disrobing a king and emphatically remind the audience that the ascendant regal identity—institutional, legal, executive, political—requires analysis and critical inspection. Bearing unmistakable marks of the *speculum principis* tradition, their procedures can be more properly described as refracting rather than mirroring, anatomizing rather than constructing. Even when reasserting traditional philosophical and moral claims and evoking blandly the reassuring patterns of princely education, they go far beyond the superficial critical revelations of the prince-pleasing paradigms of such literature. Alexander Parker and numerous other historians of the Spanish theater are probably right in arguing that in the Golden Age drama the monarch generally represented the standard to be appealed to in the adjudication of moral and philosophical dilemmas and in the resolution of difficult dramatic conflicts.[5] He was, undeniably, the exemplary representative of authority, law, and order. It is interesting that Maravall could find in the lapidary royalist pronouncements of the two plays I have analyzed powerful evidence in support of his theories regarding the unassailability of the monarchy in the Golden Age theater and its dramatists' commitment to an agenda of absolutist propaganda. However, the fascinating aspect of these two plays lies in all that distinguishes their royal figures from the doctrinaire "fascinations" of monarchs and their awe-inspiring, curious ornamentation and "robing"; their ritualized existence; their hieratic *descubrimientos*; and their symbolic institutional roles in the new states. The fact is that in their disrobing of the monarch, in their imposition on him of a quest beyond the frame of his official existence, in their critical exploration of the implications of the injunction that he descend to his humanity, and in their fascination with the complexities rising from the inescapable doubleness and the attendant burdens of self-integration and self-knowledge that intensify his existence, these plays refuse to stop short of confronting the fundamental historical issues, problems, advances, and sacrifices involved in one of the major transitions in the historical life of Western man—the rise of the state; its monopolization of violence; the accompanying realization of the social determination of the human being; the origin of the consciousness we associate with self-division, privacy, and individuality; and the so-called "civilizing process" and rationalized sociability associated with the ascendance of courtly and bourgeois environments, values, and perspectives. If the king is the *exemplary* human being, the ideal pattern for ethical self-fashioning, he is simultaneously the *paradigmatic* human being, divided from this moment on into a puzzling doubleness in his awareness of self and other, role and reality, illusion and authenticity.[6] The misery of the king, the issue at the heart of both of the plays I have studied, will eventually become the condition of every man and woman. In dramatizing the trials of strikingly unorthodox rulers, in exposing their confusions of identity, in highlighting their uneasiness and their nostalgia for humanness, and in emphasizing the discomforts produced by the royal robes and the burdensome crown, these plays succeed in laying bare the foundations of state power and point to all that is gained and lost in the necessary political organization of human life. Their construction and display of the royal body are simply the point of departure for visions that are far larger. To find comparable dramatic methods and philosophical insights rising from inquiries into the peculiarities of the double royal identity, one must turn to the plays of the greatest dramatist of kings, William Shakespeare.

I would like to conclude my argument with some observations on two of the most famous plays by Calderón, each of which carries on the process of the disrobing of rulers that I have explored above and develops it in different directions—*La vida es sueño* and *El príncipe constante*. Both plays reflect the pessimistic political philosophy characteristic of the Counter-Reformation period of the seventeenth century. In doing so, they leave the optimistic, classical vision of *El villano en su rincón* and its philosopher-king far behind and find little to salvage in the archaic heroic individualism that *El Rey Don Pedro en Madrid* would resurrect in its peculiarly conflicted utopian metamorphosis of cruelty into judicial rigor; its celebration of the alliance of manly heroism, beauty, and judicial brilliance; and its uneasy statist conciliation of the independent self and the rational demands of the new polis and its secular institutions and machinery. Each of Calderón's plays in its own way emphasizes the ineffectuality of human efforts in the ordering of man's political life. The humanness of the king, rather than an immense resource and a true foundation for all that the state must achieve, survives, and is valorized, solely in its stringent disciplinary confinement or its total renunciation. Whether the severed foundation of governance is to be sought in the transcendental order, as in the past, or in some secular abstraction such as the sovereignty of the machine state, the general will, or the nation, it will never again be sought in the perfected humanness of the monarch. While each work views the limitation of the political possibilities of humanness in its own unique way, each clearly looks forward to the end of the great age of kings in the political development of the Western world.

As I have noted above, *El Rey Don Pedro en Madrid*, in its numerous contexts and contradictions, is intermittently marked by traces of theological absolutism. In its overdetermined central agon, one quickly notes that King Pedro has in fact multiple adversaries to confront and that all of them appear to hover about or crystallize into the one fascinating, elliptical figure who has frequently usurped the title of the play, the Infanzón de Illescas. They include the rivalrous medieval knight and epic warrior—a powerful figure to contend with in the *campaña* of personal heroism and honor; the tyrannical political counterfigure of the feudal lord, the *reyecillo* who persecutes and despoils his subjects in defiance of the centralizing power of the rising monarch; the specific dynastic rival of the historical Castilian king—the half-brother Enrique, who is destined to assassinate him; and the telluric monster of pre-civilized life who terrorized the planet before the existence of kings, laws, societies, and states. But Pedro's most dreaded antagonist is in fact his most fleeting and most powerful—the specter serving a mysterious Divine Providence that has enfolded the hero in a plan that necessitates his fall, humiliation, prostration, expiation, and atonement before an incomprehensible and invincible higher power. In a remarkable scene that could not survive without drastic curtailment in the rationalizing scheme of Moreto's rewriting, the legendary handclasp of Pedro el Cruel, which produced unendurable pain in his hardest and most admired soldiers, melts in the fiery exchange with the accusing spirit of the victim of his youthful rage and lust who demands an oath of expiation. The most heroic of kings, the giver of law, the founder of states, the builder of rational bureaucracy, the choreographer and lead actor of palace etiquette, and the *piedra en Madrid* must confess that he is helpless before the Divine Will: "pues manda en mi voluntad/voluntad más soberana" (for a will more sovereign than mine commands my will). Obedience and atonement are his only hope.

> Que en los decretos del cielo
> Nada es el hombre, y el suelo
> Ley de sus prodigios es.

(For in the decrees of heaven man is nothing, and the earth, governed by the law of its miracles.)

It is as if centuries of slow and costly progress moving the political order out from under the shadows of Divine Omnipotence, willfulness, and rule by miracle are to be brought to a halt. The rationalizing and secularizing arguments of scholastic and humanistic theorists; the practical efforts of coping with concrete administrative problems rising with economic, technological, and demographic change; the imaginative attempts to reconceive, if not to remythify, the "official body of the king" in legalistic, political, and ethical terms—all would appear to be forgotten in a pessimistic return to St. Paul and St. Augustine, to the fallen Adam, and ultimately to the conveniently incomprehensible powers that descend from above and animate the dominating arm of any consecrated ruler. "I am who I am"—"soy el que soy,/y sin mí nadie ay que sea." Jahwe's willful declaration is the king's sternest rebuke to the independent *villano* in Valdivielso's somber response to Lope's humanistic comedy.

THE OBEDIENT PRINCE:
HUMANNESS CONFINED AND DISCIPLINED

> Sueña el rey que es rey, y vive
> con este engaño mandando,
> disponiendo y gobernando;
> y este aplauso, que recibe
> prestado, en el viento escribe
> y en cenizas le convierte
> la muerte (¡desdicha fuerte!)
> ¡que hay quien intente reinar
> viendo que ha de despertar
> en el sueño de la muerte!

(The King dreams he's a king, and so he lives with this illusion, making rules, putting things in order, governing, while all the praise he is showered with is only lent him. Written on the wind, and by death, his everlasting sorrow, transformed to dust and ashes, who would ever dare to reign, knowing he must wake into the dream of death?)

— *La vida es sueño*

Among the distinguishing features of the seventeenth century, historians have frequently noted the brutality of the European wars; the fascination with politics as a field of study, not only in courts and chanceries, but in universities as well; and the obsession with the new concentrations of power in the modern monarchic state — the leviathan.[7] In his influential study of the prominence of Machiavellianism in the age, Friedrich Meinecke wrote that the desire for power became an obsession, and the understanding of its necessity and uses, cynical and ruthless. Man is understood as *homo politicus*, a creature driven by an insatiable lust for power. The tyrant becomes an inexhaustible source of fascination. It is as if he were to become the exemplary figure. Meinecke points to the writings of one of the most brilliant Machiavellians of the age, Traiano Boccalini, and specifically to a passage in his commentary on the works of the favored classical historian of the instrumental "aulic humanism" of the period, Tacitus. Obsessed by the maxim that above all else he must "maintain and conserve himself in the state," the political man — *l'uomo politico* — is, as Boccalini puts it, ready to "set his foot on the neck of every other value in heaven and earth." For the "desire to rule [*dominare*] is a demon which even holy water will not drive out."[8] The passage has an imaginative appropriateness for plays such as those I am examining.

Such sentiments reach their fullest realization in the great political theater of Calderón. In his most famous play, *La vida es sueño*, a celebrated philosopher-king, Basilio, confident in his scientific knowledge and control of the new arts of statecraft, devises an experiment to determine whether his imprisoned son can find in his own resources the powers to overcome a prophesied destiny to dethrone his father, plant his foot on the ruler's neck, and establish a tyranny.[9] The latest scientific knowledge and political calculation both backfire disastrously in their presumptuous misuse. The newly robed prince and legitimate heir to the throne fails in all his tests as king, and, immediately stripped of all his regalia, he is reconfined in his bestial nudity in a tower dungeon. Shortly thereafter the king's "fallback" political solution through diplomacy and dynastic marriage fails, as the kingdom, faced with the divisive presence of a foreign ruler, collapses into revolution, chaos, and the uncontrollable barbarity of an angered mob of citizens. The victorious heir, raging for the benefits and freedoms of the tyrant and proclaiming that justice is founded in his pleasure, fulfills the prophecy and is exhorted to place his foot on the neck of his defeated and humiliated father, who recognizes his error: "Pisa mi cerviz y huella/mi corona . . . cumpla el hado su homenaje,/cumpla el cielo su palabra" (Here's my neck—stamp on it! Here's my crown—trample on it! . . . Let fate receive its due, and the word of heaven be fulfilled at last) (202). One is tempted to read Boccalini's analysis of the political world as a gloss on the scene. Providence is, in this case, benign and ultimately works things out to nearly everybody's satisfaction, but this darkest of divine comedies and dramas of princely education exacts a severe price in human— and statist—limitation. Both prince and father learn that human beings can never read God's starry language correctly, although it is written in the natural creation of which it is part and although it is never fallacious or deceptive.[10] In their human incapacities and their vulnerability to pride and passion, they must deal with problems—familial and political—only by humbly and subserviently "relying on the eternal" and repressing the "all too human" in themselves—the *fiera condición* that is the legacy of Adam. As for the uncontrollable vicissitudes of fortune and a providence that works at times in the most oblique ways imaginable, the prince learns the difficult Stoic lesson that freedom lies not in exercising control but rather in reacting correctly after the fact to whatever the future brings.

> Quien vencer aguarda
> a su fortuna, ha de ser
> con prudencia y con templanza.
> No antes de venir el daño
> se reserva ni se guarda
> quien le previene; que aunque
> puede humilde (cosa es clara)
> reservarse dél, no es
> sino después que se halla
> en la ocasión, porque aquésta
> no hay camino de estorbarla.

(And so, the man who wishes to control his fate must use judgment and be temperate. He cannot keep an injury from happening, even though he sees it coming, though, of course, he can mitigate the shock by resignation. This cannot be done till after the worst has happened, since there's no way to ward it off.) (203–204)

For rulers, the proper attitude lies in caution, readiness, humility, self-reduction, self-control, and even fear. The final words of the play bring a somber note to the restoration of the prince and the celebrated deliverance of the kingdom: the "educated" young ruler reminds his audience that he must henceforth live in anxiety ("estoy temiendo en mis ansias/que he de despertar y hallarme/otra vez en mi cerrada prisión"—I still tremble at the thought that I may waken and find myself again locked in a cell). In a world of such disorder, prevention becomes one of the most fundamental of strategies, and prevention attaches special importance to fortifications, prisons, convents, casuistical accommodation, exclusion or containment of any disordering forces, and any effective means of internal reassurance for individuals and fearful citizens.[11] Since the earthly kingdom, the regalia of the official body of the king, as well as the human body itself, are mere phantasms in the "dream of life" that the omnipotent, and at times mysterious, God has designed for man, the state must be conceived as little more than a means of staving off chaos and maintaining order. At crucial moments of this play we find once again the horse symbolism and its imaginative expansion of the enormous forces of disorder that the successful monarch must confront and control. Described in the Baroque dramatist's most spectacular trans-elemental and trans-special metaphorics and associated with the outbreak of chaos in the cosmos, war in the kingdom, betrayal in society, violence in the family, and madness in the individual, Calderón's horses might bring to mind the uncontrollable, soaring horse that Louis XIV refused to accept in his kingdom of rationality, law, and light. The most memorable is the "horse-hippogryph" that appears at the beginning of *La vida es sueño*. The spirited creature leaps above the rocky landscape of Poland's wilderness and sends its rider tumbling before plunging into the circumambient chaos and disappearing in the threatening darkness, from which it will imaginatively reemerge subsequently as one of the various motifs of futile repetition that mark the play's climactic vision of political disorder. The scene can be understood as a reversal of the opening of *El Rey Don Pedro en Madrid,* where the heroic monarch slaughters a furious horse, which has rebelled beneath his spurs and hurled him into a ravine. But the dream world of Tello's kingdom and the archaic vision of manly power and heroic individualism, beauty, and triumph—the "dimension imperativa de la persona"—seem no longer reconcilable with Calderón's chastened and stately portrait of a prince. It survives in his most famous dramatic depiction of Pedro el Cruel, but it is transformed into the lurid splendor of the future usurper and fratricide, Enrique de Trastamara, whose spectacular fall from a beautiful horse in the opening scene seems to unleash a chaotic sequence of disasters that will eventually engulf the entire kingdom in bloodshed and whose aristocratic warrior ethos is successfully countered by the artful "political science" of the sinister king and his prudent protégé, the "médico de su honra," uneasy masters of strategic machination, dissimulation, manipulative choreography, and the obliquities of language. Such are the arts of the new politics and the king as statesman.

THE PRINCE AND THE MAIDEN: HUMANNESS SANCTIFIED AND TRANSCENDED

> Don Fernando: ¿Quién soy yo?
> ¿Soy más que un hombre?
>
> . . . .
>
> Cautivo: Dame, señor, tus pies.
> Don Fernando: . . . Alzad, amigo,
> no hagais tal ceremonia ya conmigo.
> Don Juan: Vuestra Alteza. . . .
> Don Fernando: . . . ¿Qué Alteza
> ha de tener quien vive en tal bajeza?

(Don Fernando: Who am I? Am I more than a man? Cautivo: My lord, give me your feet. Don Fernando: Rise, my friend, do not perform such a ceremony with me. Juan: Your Highness. . . . Don Fernando: What Highness can one have who lives in such lowliness?)

—El príncipe constante

At the midpoint of Calderón's *El príncipe constante* the young prince renounces the world of politics and in a revealing theatrical gesture rips up the written document of state ("estos vanos poderes,/hoy divididos en piezas"—these vain powers, today divided in pieces) in which the king of Portugal offers his captor, the cold and calculating king of Fez, the Spanish colony of Ceuta in exchange for his royal prisoner. The speech is the longest and most thunderous of the various rhetorical pronouncements of the hero, who insists repeatedly that he has no special value as a royal human being over ordinary Christians, for whom such an exchange would be a betrayal. "¿Quién soy yo? ¿Soy más que un hombre? . . . Cristianos, Fernando es muerto;/moros, un esclavo os queda,/cautivos, un compañero/hoy se añade a vuestras penas" (Who am I? Am I more than a man? . . . Christians, Fernando is dead; Moors, a slave remains with you; captives, a companion is today added to your sufferings). He renounces his identity ("Perdí el ser, luego morí"—I lost my being, and then I died); disrobes himself; and embraces slavery, pain, and martyrdom as an act of love.[12] His stripping down will become, in a paradoxical but genuine sense, a coronation in a kingdom of sufferers. The dung heap on which his wracked body is discarded will become his loftiest throne. In a series of figurative disrobings, he metamorphoses from national hero—member of the order of Avis—and crusading Christian warrior; to independent chivalric knight, ideal friend, and heroic horseman; to honored captive; to Stoic hero and consoler; to diseased slave and malodorous beggar; and to a prophet speaking with the voice of Job. At the end of his descent through multiple forms toward nothingness and the paradoxical constancy of his reward, he remains a skeletal cadaver, accepted joyously by the triumphant Christian army in exchange for its Moorish captive, one of the most beautiful princesses of the earth. The locations of his journey downward shift from the ocean and battlefield of epic, to the outlying paths of adventure of the heroic knights errant, to the Moorish palaces and hunting parks of his honorable captivity, to the pleasure gardens of his degrading slave labor, to the pestiferous dung heap concealing beyond the city limits of Fez the scandal of his suffering, and finally to the coffin and the sepulcher. The range of movement steadily narrows; the immobilization becomes more and more suffocating. The divestment of a king could not be more radical. The injunction that we have found in Philip IV and Gracián—¡*humanarse*!—is pursued toward unimaginable limits. Beyond the animal ferocity of Segismundo and its moral challenge to king and commoner—¡*reprimamos*!—we continue downward to the putrescent flesh of the dying prince and its challenge to our belief in the very existence of a viable political order and the possibility of an earthly kingdom. The "unstating" of the human being and his political world could not be more devastating. A true society becomes imaginable only as a shrinking community, a remnant of sufferers bound by the shared experience of pain and by the immense and spontaneous tasks of charity and brotherhood in a world of selfishness, war, cruelty, hatred, and confusion. If the supra-personal identity of the monarch remains, it does so only by separating from its stately developments in law, rationality, polity, and ethical exemplarity through the centuries of the rising secular political sphere and returning to its medieval Christological foundations, its position at the altar, and its destiny to enter a world of filth, abjection, and impurity and to redeem it by propitiatory suffering and sacrificial atonement (see figure 6).

Stephen Rupp is certainly correct in insisting that Calderón will not abandon his orthodox commitment to a rational and ethicist anti-Machiavellian political tradition, "stressing that the true reason of state commands those who govern to respect the order of providence and the limits of temporal authority." But he is also correct in conceding that Calderón's engagement with political problems in his secular *comedias*—for example, *La vida es sueño*—is most eloquent in

Fig. 6. "Non Magna Relinqvam" (from Sebastián
de Covarrubias Horozco, *Emblemas morales*
[Luis Sanchez, 1610], Centuria III, Emblema 7).
(Photograph courtesy Hilaire Kallendorf.)

displaying the near helplessness of human rulers, particularly those who, like Basilio, confidently adopt the "realist," pragmatic, and "interventionist" approach to governance only to come up against the repetitious cycles of tyranny, usurpation, intrigue, betrayal, and violence that continuously afflict the realm of earthly politics. In general the secular political dramas reveal a "pronounced skepticism concerning the realist attempt to separate technical issues in statecraft from ethical questions and to reconcile political flexibility with Christian principles. Calderón is clearly aware of the discomforts of this enterprise, and one of the somber lessons of his *comedias* is that any form of political manipulation will induce a cycle of Machiavellian expedience," which inevitably brings violence, discontinuity, and disorder. As Rupp points out, the efficacity of the traditionalist views of monarchy, morality, and natural law appears to find its demonstration and confirmation only in the utopian "divine comedies" of the *autos sacramentales*, where earthly, "manipulative" politics is repeatedly demonstrated to be hopelessly vulnerable to demonic disruption; where the earthly king is displaced by the body of Christ in the revealed host; and where a "true" reason of state — in one of the most striking "political" *autos, A Dios, por la razón de estado* — is resituated in the divine will. Here the triumphant movement of human reason — allegorically expressed in the doublet of *Ingenio* and the historical figure of Dionysius the Aereopagite in his dialogue with St. Paul concerning the partial revelations of the divine logos in the historical religions preceding the full revelation of the law of divine grace — leads man smoothly, along the time-honored scholastic and humanistic paths, to the recognition that the whole natural order of the creation is bound by the benign and rational laws of a providential God of power and suffering.[13] In a witty paradox "state reason," the frequently maligned "diabolical" faculty, as well as its science, allegedly created by Lucifer, is transvaluated into the spark of reason that man shares with his creator.

In a startling reversion to the standard rhetoric of the mirror of princes and its underlying optimistic metaphysics, Calderón's dying hero, the Constant Prince, turns to these paths and invokes the natural order and its hierarchies to assert that the king of every species of the animal, vegetable, and elemental worlds — the lion, the eagle, the dolphin, the diamond, the pomegranate — is distinguished by a natural impulse to charity. True majesty is rooted in a rejection of cruelty — a humanitarianism that ironically the beasts appear to understand better than human beings.

> Pues si entre fieras y peces,
> plantas, piedras y aves, usa
> esta majestad de rey
> de piedad, no será injusta
> entre los hombres, señor;
> porque el ser no te disculpa
> de otra ley, que la crueldad
> en cualquiera ley es una.

(If then among the beasts and fishes, plants, stones and birds, this majesty of a king expresses itself in compassion, it were not unjust, my lord, that men do the same; because being of a different faith does not excuse you, for cruelty is the same for every faith.) (112)

The tone is angry and desperate. The prince's declamation rises to the intensity of prophecy. But the Moorish king, an embodiment of cold political calculation, remains indifferent, if not scornful, in the face of such philosophical imaginings and political naïveté. Sacrifice, martyrdom, and punishing divine intervention provide the only relief in the bleak City of Man.[14] Recrowned in the celestial light of the saint, Fernando rises above the invading Christian army and effectively directs God's descending power to victory over the infidel and the recovery of the human remains of a martyr. Meanwhile the political enterprise of the crusade—diplomacy, strategy, exchanges, accommodations, rituals of honoring, formal displays of mutual respect—degenerates into the bellicose bluster of the respective representatives of earthly kingdoms—Muslims and Christians—as they pursue their selfish ends. Disturbing ironies darken the celebratory rituals of the conclusion and its restoration of the pitiful bones of a king.[15] The painful price of purity's victory over pragmatics is plain for all to see.

Around the central character of the suffering prince revolve a number of refractive figures that Calderón juxtaposes to the hero as momentary companions, or doubles, in the different phases and identities of his descending quest.[16] By far the most important is the beautiful Moorish princess, Fénix, who in her passivity, self-absorption, and deep melancholy seems to be mysteriously drawn, in attraction and perhaps anxiety or envy, to the suffering, selfless prince. An original development of the infidel princesses and pleasure gardens of the crusading epics that Calderón recreates and reexamines in this play, Fénix inhabits an alluring world of natural beauty and boundless variety, sensuous delights, dazzling metamorphoses, and flowing creative energy.[17] A counter-figure to the prince in his Stoic *constantia* and *gravitas*, she has something of the imaginative appeal of Tello in *El Rey Don Pedro en Madrid* amid the abundance, mutability, and sublime vistas of his inexhaustible natural world. And as in the case of Tello, we clearly gaze on the poetic world of Góngora in her depiction.[18] Amid the multiple literary "disrobings" that the play parallels to the regal disrobing that it enacts in the foreground, it is clear that Fénix, anxiously gazing into her mirror as she first appears on stage, represents the *blason*, the imaginatively created beautiful woman of the European lyric—a creature self-dispossessed within the imaginative metamorphoses of her highly figured representation.[19] However, unlike the case of the exuberant warrior in his Gothic paradise, Fénix appears to be alienated from the spectacle around her. In her first appearance she strangely attempts to find pleasure in the mournful songs of the Christian prisoners in their confinement and endless labors. In dissatisfaction she turns to visual experiences for diversion, contemplating the dazzling "artwork" that nature provides at the shore of her garden. Here sea and land mingle and compete in a marvelous painting producing the distinctive beauty that each possesses. She seems a creature of preternatural lightness, fleeing the "jasmine temple" and "rose statues" of her garden and flashing like sunlight from a gilded boat that aimlessly floats ("errando") amid the waves of the sea. Pausing to sleep on the mountainside beneath its crown of carnations, she fashions in her "scarlet cot" a "grave of emerald."[20] Slipping sensuously into its embrace, she finds herself suddenly terrified by a nightmare visitation of a hideous female cadaver who prophesies her destined exchange for and identification with a dead man and whose paralyzing touch freezes her into the form of a solidly rooted, sinister tree trunk. Such beauty is spectacular, and its power has been registered eloquently by readers such as Goethe, who claimed that if poetry were to disappear from the world, mankind could recover it and restore it by reading Calderón's play.[21] At the same time the Baroque dramatist makes it evident that Fénix's garden is insubstantial and fleeting and in fact represents most powerfully the worldly order that one must reject if one would enjoy authentic beauty, which is to be found in spirituality, love, and constancy of character. The agon—the dialectic—of the king and his double, unlike the philosophical and martial contests of the plays I have examined, is far more decisively and somberly resolved. There is a tantalizing moment of expectant rapprochement as the enslaved prince offers the suffering princess a bouquet of flowers—the "gift of lovers" in the worlds of traditional lyric and pastoral erotic poetry. The maiden feels genuine pity for a fellow sufferer ("dos desdichados"), but her feeling turns to horror as she immediately interprets the fading flowers as hieroglyphics of mortality and mutability and attempts to destroy them. As she enigmatically puts it, the colorful marigolds remind her of the stars. Psychology, literature, eros, and metaphysics converge decisively at this most intense moment of the dreamlike play, which crystallizes in two sonnets that concentrate the dominant motifs that sound obsessively, over and over again from beginning to end—Stars or flowers? Eternity or time? Constancy or mutability? Spirituality or worldliness? Selflessness or selfness? Depth or surface? Love or egotism? *Vanitas* or *veritas*? West or East? The delicacy of this relationship of fellow sufferers and its most fleeting traces of intimacy are not overwhelmed by the clearly discernible presence in the background of the grandest dualities of Augustine's vision of *saeculum* and eternity.[22] For the melancholy Moorish princess the stars are sinister ciphers of a blind fatality and, in their nightly passing, emblems of continual extinction rather than, as the Christian prince attempts to explain, the permanent traces of a divinely founded, trustworthy order in which human beings can find metaphysical re-

assurance.[23] The intensity of the moment is unendurable for her, and casting
the flowers down, she flees before an insight that she seems incapable of understanding.[24] On the other hand, the prince, in his imperturbable constancy, is
baffled by the identification — "What on earth can stars have to do with flowers?"
Once again she is fleetingly drawn to her alien sharer of human suffering at the
climax of his trials. She pleads with the king of Fez to alleviate his torment, but
almost immediately she finds herself incapable of countering her own feelings
of disgust at the smell of his decaying flesh. As the dead prince, following the
liberation by the Portuguese army, which he guides as a resurrected saint, is
exchanged for the Moorish beauty, the latter, incapable of understanding the
inner restlessness that the encounter with the prince has brought to her life,
clings desperately to her self-absorbed, worldly existence, and the play proclaims
its most powerful and stringent endorsement of the ascetic, sacrificial Christian
body of the king. The stasis of the hardened figure might suggest a return to the
earliest medieval conceptions of the royal body, now bereft of all monumental regalia and splendors. The *constantia* of the state is closely allied with the
somber rigor and the grim stability of death. And yet the final articulation of the
antithetical motifs founding the imaginative world of the entire drama suddenly,
unexpectedly, reaches beyond the neat symmetry of its customary boundaries,
as the syntax, parallels, and logically positioned epithets, in a brief and miraculous suspension of the laws of geometry, bring momentary conceptual disruption and the revealing dissonance of an ecstatic summation. The royal body is
offered forth as the snow of winter and the chill of January in exchange for the
"mayos" — the budding delights of spring — of the radiantly fresh and beautiful
maiden. But suddenly, astonishingly, as the Baroque accumulation of parallels
continues to develop, the decaying body becomes the fragrant, fleeting rose, and
the opposing living beauty hardens into the cold, petrified, and self-contained
beauty of the diamond. In the strangest of all the elaborations of the elliptically
insinuated, thought-provoking "courtship" of prince and princess — a "love affair" that is surely disappointing for all sensitive spectators and readers — Calderón has redeemed the floral world of the lost princess and touched the cold
marble of *constantia*, renunciation, and hope with an ineffable but undeniable
earthly and poetic beauty.

> Rey de Fez, . . .
> Envía, pues
> la nieve por los cristales,
> el enero por los mayos,

> las rosas por los diamantes,
> y al fin, un muerto infelice
> por una divina imagen.

(King of Fez, . . . Send then snow in exchange for white crystals, January for May, roses for diamonds, and finally, an unhappy corpse for a divine image.)[25]

The prophesied exchange is complete. Once again the king and his double have bonded in a mutual enrichment.

SYNOPSIS OF *EL VILLANO EN SU RINCÓN*

ACT I

The play begins on the streets of Paris. Lisarda, the ambitious, restless, and highly intelligent daughter of the wealthy farmer Juan Labrador, has come to the court in disguise and won the attention of one of its highest ranking nobles, Otón. Smitten by her beauty, he has bestowed several gems on her as pledges of his devotion. He follows her as she and her cousin Belisa leave the palace. Fearful that he may discover that she is not a lady of high quality, she offers him a diamond ring, which he accepts, promising that from that moment on, he will follow her only in his soul. Otón's cynical companion Finardo suspects that the gift may be counterfeit and warns him that the court is full of predatory ladies who, like fisherwomen, have a variety of ways to hook amorous and unsuspecting young gentlemen. At this moment Otón's lackey, Marín, who has continued to follow Lisarda, reports that on separating from them, she entered an inn at the outer edge of the city; emerged shortly thereafter transformed into a beautiful country girl—a "humanized seraphim"; and set forth in a cart for Belflor, a village on the road to the king's hunting forest.

In the second scene the action shifts to Juan Labrador's estate near Belflor. The farmer speaks with great eloquence of the activities and rewards of his rustic life. He gives thanks to God for his bountiful gifts; supervises the activities of plowing, planting, and harvesting; and prepares a gift of freshly picked grapes for an ailing neighbor. He expresses scorn for the idle life of courtiers and refers to himself as God's steward ("mayordomo de Dios"). His greatest satisfaction lies not in the overflowing abundance of his fields, pastures, and gardens, but rather in the peace of mind that is the reward of honorable labor. An advocate of Stoic independence and Horatian enjoyment of the simple pleasures of nature, he boasts that he has lived in the village since birth and that he has not seen the court in sixty years. Juan's lyrical expression of harmony and tranquility in the natural world is rudely interrupted, and the principal action of the drama begins: the conflict of king and peasant. Juan's son, Feliciano, who shares his sister's ambitions to enjoy the excitement and glamour of court life, informs him that the king, his sister, the *infanta*, and the beautiful ladies of the court are coming to his woods to hunt. He urges him to attend the royal spectacle, to cheer up his old age with its colorful pageantry, and to "kneel to the king," who bears the awesome burden of providing his privileged life with peace. Admitting that he adores the king and recognizes that a king is "a perfect being," Juan Labrador nevertheless points out that he is himself king in his little nook—his *rincón*—and that while he is prepared to serve the French king, in no circumstances will he look upon the "sun of his face." On hearing the approach of the latter's procession, he determines to hide.

Lisarda joins her brother Feliciano, and they speak with enthusiasm of their clandestine visits to the court, their desire to see and be seen by nobles and princes, their enjoyment in attending games and jousts, and their excitement in the presence of grandeur. The ambitious young woman confesses that she finds farmers "laughable by nature" and that she has determined to marry a gentleman of the court. Lisarda dreams of leaving the village and Juan Labrador's farm, his beloved *rincón*, far behind and speaks of the family wealth as a means of buying her way into the nobility.

The action shifts to the village and the front of its church. The peasants have gathered to witness their ruler as he comes to hear Mass. The latter is amused by an epitaph that he reads on a tombstone describing a man who is to be remembered as a person "who never saw the court or the king." The king's curiosity is aroused by the inscription, and he interrogates the villagers about the strange wealthy farmer who dwells so contentedly in his home, takes no interest in seeing the king, and lives with his grave already prepared. They present Lisarda to him, and, responding to his questions, she displays her wit to everybody's delight. The marshall Otón reveals his presence to her and assures her that although he is a member of the king's chamber, he respects her as his equal. She tells him to meet her secretly in the evening at the village elm tree, where they will be able to communicate their feelings safely.

ACT II

The king has returned to the palace and finds himself upset by his experience in Belflor and his discovery of Juan Labrador's indifference to the royal figure. Admitting that he envies the peace of mind and body that the farmer appears to enjoy, he decides that he must return to the village and look upon the subject who refuses to look upon him.

The following scene is set in the rustic world of Belflor, where the peasants have assembled at the foot of the elm tree to participate in their customary festivities. These center on discussions of love, courtship, virtue, harmony, and equality and include dances, songs, riddles, and jests. Maintaining that love overcomes differences of class, Otón woos Lisarda and gives her his word that he will honor her in marriage. She invites him to come secretly to Juan's house later in the evening. The highlight of the depiction of the idealized forest world of Juan Labrador's village is a beautiful ballad (a *serranilla*) narrating the erotic encounter of a hunting knight and a mountain lass, lovely as a seraphim, who is lost in the wilderness.

At this point the play returns to the main plot. Disguised as a hunter, the king arrives on horseback in a nearby wood. He goes to Juan's house, where he presents himself as the

Alcaide of Paris and claims to have lost his way in the darkness. Juan receives him with notable courtesy and hospitality, insisting on seating him, as his guest, at the head of the table. He proceeds to offer him, in the central scene of the drama, a detailed description of his way of life and his values. The king is overcome with admiration, hailing his host as a *villano filosófico* and confessing that "his envy of such a lofty life" is greater than before. The "royal banquet" concludes with a chorus of peasants singing a gloss on Horace's *Beatus Ille*.

The king retires to his bedroom, where he makes some inappropriate advances to the three village maidens, including Lisarda, who are attending to his needs as guest. He is harshly rebuffed by each one of them, and in a state of great confusion, he discovers Otón, who has come to meet with Lisarda, hidden behind a curtain.

ACT III

The final act begins with a peasant festival of songs and dances marking the harvesting of the olive, celebrating the beneficence of the natural world, affirming the value of community labor, and condemning the idleness and corruption of the world of the courtier. A messenger from the court arrives with a letter from the king requesting money of Juan Labrador, who responds as a loyal vassal willing in fact to sacrifice everything for his lord. He makes the point mysteriously by sending his money with an accompanying enigma that puzzles the king—the gift of a sheep with a knife hanging at its throat.

The following scene is set in the royal palace. The king has decided to favor the marriage of Lisarda and Otón. He speaks philosophically about the nature of man, stressing his divine rationality, his individuality, and his fundamental equality. Recalling Alexander's admiration for Diogenes, he notes that his encounter with Juan Labrador has had a transformative effect on him. His philosophical discourse climaxes in a sonnet that, borrowing from Epictetus, emphasizes that human happiness depends on inner peace and detachment from the life of ambition and toil.

In Belflor Juan Labrador discusses the importance of a good marriage for his children. At this moment a second messenger arrives from the king, who now demands the service of the children at the court. Juan is heartbroken, admits that he was presumptuous in his satisfaction with his happy life, and resignedly sends his children to the palace. They, on the other hand, are exultant, as it seems that their wildest dreams of social ascent are to come true.

The villagers arrive at the palace, where they are ceremoniously dressed in courtly attire and warned concerning the traditional dangers in the calculating, hypocritical society of their new environment. As the final move in his theatrical machinations that thoroughly dominate the play's last act, the king summons Juan Labrador to the court. Juan fears the authority of his master and the possibility of punishment for his independence. Otón assumes that the king has designs on Lisarda and falls into a fit of anxiety. With so much hanging in suspense, the king arranges a banquet, stages an allegorical masque displaying the iconology of the monarchy—the sword of justice, the scepter of unity, the sun of royal ubiquity, the mirror of virtuous emulation—and offers, through a commentary on the symbols, a lesson in the proper exercise of power to his needlessly frightened subjects. The spectacle concludes with the bestowal of the honored position of the king's steward on Juan Labrador, the granting of the title of Alcaide of Paris to his son, Feliciano, and the announcement of a marriage, to be sponsored by king and princess as godparents, of his daughter, Lisarda, to Otón, the Marshal of France.

SYNOPSIS OF *EL REY DON PEDRO EN MADRID O EL INFANZÓN DE ILLESCAS*

ACT I

The play opens with the lament of two young rustic women, Elvira and Ginesa, who have been brutally raped by an infamous feudal lord, Tello García, the Infanzón of Illescas, and his villainous page, Cordero. As they clamor for justice, they witness a frightening scene in the distance. A wildly charging horse hurls its rider to the earth. The latter strides onto the stage holding an unsheathed sword and announces that he has slaughtered his disobedient steed in a satisfying act of revenge. When he informs the women that he belongs to the king's entourage and is on his way to Madrid, they remark that it would be futile for them to appeal to a king so widely known for his cruelty. The violent rider is in fact the king, Pedro of Castile, and, while not disclosing his identity, he urges them to trust in their ruler to redress their grievances. He assures them that for the fearsome monarch justice rather than cruelty should be recognized as the highest attribute. Sparing few details, Elvira gives an account of the awful crime, vividly depicting how her childhood of pastoral innocence and her chaste love of her companion, Bustos, were rudely crushed on the day before her marriage by the tyrannical aristocrat, Tello, who has exalted himself as a "divinity of the mountains" and "the majesty of the fields." The disguised king is outraged by the Infanzón's violence and lack of respect for royal authority, and he laments that Castile is full of such "miniature kings." He assures Elvira that he will restore her honor.

At this point a ghost appears, a *sombra*, who will haunt the king throughout the play. He resurrects the dead horse and mysteriously dares the king to follow him and meet him in Madrid. As he speeds away, as if "yearning for flames," King Pedro's retainers arrive and note that the king is pale and visibly shaken by his encounter with the supernatural.

The action shifts to Tello's house in Illescas. He has imprisoned another of his victims, the lady Leonor, whom he has kidnapped on the eve of her wedding to Don Rodrigo, a petty aristocrat whose modest rank has aroused the Infanzón's contempt. She deplores the absence of justice in Castile and appeals to God for help. Tello responds in a long speech in which he boasts of his glorious ancestry of warriors and heroes; his vast, seemingly unbounded land holdings; his enormous agricultural wealth; and the veneration in which he is held throughout the land. The calculating king, now disguised as the ordinary knight, the *hidalgo* Acevedo, pays him a courtesy visit. Tello receives his guest with indifference and rudely boasts that he would not rise from his seat to receive the king himself. On learning that his visitor is pursuing his interests through legal means and state agencies, he derides the unheroic act of submitting oneself to the world of legality and bureaucracy when swords are available. As he listens, Pedro must struggle to repress angry impulses to violent self-assertion and the infringement of the very laws that he represents as king. The confusion of the scene increases as the victims of Tello's rape arrive to demand justice from the feudal lord and threaten to present their case to the king. Tello belittles the latter, claiming that he draws his power from the royal office and the majesty rather than from his strength and heroism as a man. He announces that he would be glad to meet him in hand-to-hand combat. Frustrated in their demand for justice, all the victims determine to take their cases to God and King Pedro.

ACT II

The king has formulated a complex plan to humiliate the lawless Infanzón and to teach the anarchic nobles of Castile a lesson in obedience. He summons the offender and the abused villagers to the palace in Madrid. Meanwhile, he impressively fulfills his duties as king, holding an audience and responding justly and prudently, although with his characteristic harshness, to the appeals of soldiers, ministers, poets, and political advisers. In advising Don Rodrigo, who seeks revenge for Tello's kidnapping of his bride, Pedro offers an enigmatic double counsel: as the man Don Pedro and as friend, he endorses the restoration of honor through revenge; as King Pedro and as head of state, he condemns such an act as a violation of law. On arriving at the palace, Tello is infuriated to discover that he has fallen into a trap. He is compelled to enter by the back door; is transferred helplessly from chamber to chamber in increasing confinement; is unacknowledged by members of the palace; and is treated with indifference by his peasant victims, whom the king has instructed in the roles they are to play in a dramatic performance he is staging to punish their persecutor. An invisible power that the befuddled aristocrat feels helpless to resist is attributed to a "king-poltergeist," who, when finally taking shape in the nobleman's presence, busies himself, as bureaucratic king and *letrado*, holding in his hand the numerous papers representing the affairs of state. He initially pays no attention to the furious creature caught in his "mouse-trap."

Tello is mortified when the king finally turns to him and recounts the insults that he had to endure in his house while disguised as Acevedo. Pedro points out that it is not permitted for the king to fight a duel as a man, but losing his temper before the "wild boar" that he has determined to tame, he, crudely and insultingly, butts him with his head. At this moment of humiliation, Tello's two victims appear and denounce him as a travesty of the virtues of nobility and as a tyrant who has usurped the absolute power of God and his representative on earth, the king. Their indictment in this bizarre royal trial climaxes in a diabolical diatribe by Ginesa, the victim of Cordero's violence, in a ballad in the *jacaresque*-picaresque mode, envisioning her tormentor's approaching execution as that of a lowlife thug, dancing at the end of a rope.

Still acting as a dutiful monarch, King Pedro prepares for his nightly inspection of the city (the king's *ronda*), but responding to a momentary impulse, he demands that his retainers fence with him with manly courage, apparently suspending the rules and safeguards of the exercise. Threatening them with death if they do not attempt to kill him, he quickly draws blood in the first opponent, and when the others are too frightened to face him, the ghost that has haunted him reappears and accepts his challenge. Boldly proclaiming that he has no fear of spirits from hell, Pedro immediately attacks him. The shadow eludes his wild sword thrusts, announces cryptically that the king is to be "a rock in Madrid," and disappears into the darkness.

ACT III

In a surprising turnabout, Tello's victims request that King Pedro pardon their persecutor in order to appease his many admirers among the common people and to preserve peace in the state. The rigorous Pedro refuses the appeal and reminds them that the scepter demands justice as well as mercy. The king continues to be disturbed by the mystery of the ghost's prophecy, and, in a troubled soliloquy, speaks anxiously of his brother's rebellion and the civil strife that is menacing his state with disintegration. Once again he is attracted to the impenetrable darkness of a frightening night and exits the palace to inspect the city. Always a schemer, King Pedro now conceives a secret plan to trick his antagonist into combating him as a man, and concealing two swords, he goes in disguise to the tower where Tello is awaiting execution on the following morning. Associated with Satan in the grotesque humor of Tello's squire, Cordero, the disguised king frees his villainous antagonist, who fails to recognize him in the total darkness of the prison. At this moment of suspense the action shifts to the arrival in the city of Prince Enrique, the half-brother and future assassin of King Pedro. In one of the most important of the various doctrinal and emblematic scenes of the drama, the prince announces that he comes to Madrid to gaze upon his royal lord, and he offers an eloquent speech on the divine foundations of monarchy.

The scene shifts to the encounter of Tello and King Pedro, who battle as "giants" in the darkness. The Infanzón is defeated, and, chivalrously requesting the name of the unknown warrior who has vanquished him, learns that the victor is a man rather than a king, a friend rather than a sovereign. King Pedro claims a triumph of the sword and personal skill rather than a victory of institutionally generated awe and respect. The central conflict of king and aristocrat ends in mutual admiration and respect. As the independent noble departs from Castile toward the aristocratic haven of Aragon, the avenging shadow returns for his final challenge to the king. He reveals himself as the spirit of a cleric whom Pedro, in his impetuous youthful escapades, had stabbed to death many years before while violating the sanctity of a convent. He gives the king the dagger of the crime and warns him that he too will die by it if he does not reform his life and build a shrine in Madrid as an act of penance. Claiming that he can now be released from his purgatorial suffering, he squeezes Pedro's hand in a fiery grip that strikes fear into the heart of the legendary king, who earlier in the play boasted that he feared nothing.

In its concluding scene the play turns abruptly toward a comedic climax. In a striking ceremonial scene King Pedro is displayed on his throne and seat of justice in full regalia.

He announces the marriages of the three victims of the untamed Infanzón's ferocity and the reconciliation of Tello, who has been captured and returned to Madrid. Although some ominous notes sound and remind the audience of the tragic historical events that will follow, the play ends with the celebration of Pedro's ascent as lawgiver and founder of his kingdom.

NOTES

INTRODUCTION

1. In a recent study, "Imágenes de poder y evocaciones de la memoria: Usos y funciones del retrato en la corte de Felipe II," in *Felipe II, un monarca y su época: Un príncipe del Renacimiento* (Madrid, 1999), 203–227 (esp. 208–209), M. Falomir Faus describes a more conventional type of painting involving the exhibition of one person's image by another—e.g., El Greco's painting of the sculptor Pompei Leoni as he works on Philip II's bust and the (lost) self-portrait of Titian holding the image of Philip II. He argues that in such works the principle of hierarchy is clearly maintained and that a substantial "secondary" (or contained) image holds the key to the value and significance of a "primary" image (i.e., the artist's). I would suggest that in the case of Velázquez's contained phantasmagoric figures the effect is the opposite.

2. For the extraordinary efforts of Philip IV and his favorite, the Count-Duke of Olivares, to create such an image and the spectator that it in turn creates, see J. H. Elliott, "The Court of the Spanish Habsburgs: A Peculiar Institution?," *Spain and Its World: 1500–1700* (New Haven, 1989), 142–161. Elliott points out that "according to a recent estimate, 223 writers held positions in the personal service of the king. . . . In their books and plays these men would sing the praises of the Planet King, and project to the world the brilliant image of Spanish kingship which the regime of Olivares was seeking to promote. The same theme was developed in the visual arts, especially in the celebrated Hall of the Realms in the palace of the Buen Retiro, for which Velázquez and his fellow artists executed a series of paintings designed to glorify the dynasty and commemorate the victories of a triumphant Philip IV" (159). Much of my study will be devoted to the deconstruction and the reconstruction of this image in the drama of the period. See chapter 1 for my treatment of the "cult of the king" in connection with Lope's *Villano en su rincón* as a dramatic portrait of a king. For Philip II's collection and placing of pictures of all the kings of Spanish history in palace galleries for viewing—e.g., Madrid, Segovia, Seville, the Pardo, El Escorial—see Faus, "Imágenes de poder," 220–221. See chapter 2 below for Philip's reaction to the portrait of Pedro el Cruel.

3. Leo Steinberg, "Velázquez' *Las Meninas*," *October* 19 (1981): 45–54.

4. See my "Sancho Panza and Cervantes' Embodiment of Pastoral," *Literature, Culture, and So-*

ciety in the Modern Age: In Honor of Joseph Frank, Stanford Slavic Studies 4, no. 1 (1991): 57–75. Several analysts of Velázquez's puzzling masterpiece have approached it as thematically and pictorially related to the symbolic discourse, the allegorical methods, and the moral didacticism of the tradition of the *speculum principis*. In the most detailed of these studies, "Les Ménines de Velázquez: Miroir des Princes pour Philippe IV" (*Nederlands Kunsthistorisch Jaarboek* 12 [1961]: 50–79), J. A. Emmens points out a remarkable number of elements evoking the specific paintings and emblems of this tradition—e.g., the mirror of prudence; the three Graces; the allegorical figure of education; the three aspects of prudence (past, present, and future); the cup of *amicitia*; the dog of faithfulness and simplicity; the providential fool; the wise counsellor; and the princess's gesture of refusal as a counsel of patience for the observing monarchs. Emmens concludes that the work should be viewed as a straight, if complex and original, articulation of the mirror-of-the-prince painting: the light falling on the king in the tiny mirror brings the powerful solar myth to the representation of the royal figure, who stands as educational exemplar before his daughter, who herself, in the complex reciprocality of the work's mirroring strategies, symbolically teaches the attentive king such virtues as *amicitia* and patience; and the unusual presence of the queen in the mirror of princes invests the exemplarity of the picture with the Roman, Ciceronian ideal of the family as the origin and the essence of community, society, and republic. In my opinion, Velázquez's painting is most striking as it invests its depicted figures with a humanity and presence that rise from their negation of ideals and symbolic paradigms visible in the background. The procedure, familiar also in such works as *Los Borrachos* and *Las Hilanderas*, is of course analogous to the novelistic methods of Cervantes. In his thorough search for the iconology of the *specula*, Emmens notes, on the basis of an inventory in 1689 of the chamber depicted by the painting, that the great elevating myth of Spanish and French kings, Hercules, is depicted in the actual paintings on the right hand wall between the windows. They have disappeared in the shadows.

5. For a detailed reconstruction of the perspective, see Joel Snyder, "*Las Meninas* and the Mirror of the Prince," *Critical Inquiry* 11 (1984–85): 539–572. Jonathan Brown suggests that the gestures of the figures imply a focal point outside the frame and that "it is now clear that Velázquez tempered geometry with intuition when he composed the picture." See *Velázquez: Painter and Courtier* (New Haven, 1986), 259. One suspects that the spectators of *Las Meninas* will always look momentarily for the phantasmic monarchs, seemingly standing beside them in their "real" world.

6. See Snyder's speculations, "*Las Meninas*," 571.

7. See Fernando Marías Franco, *Las Meninas* (Madrid, 1999), 30–31.

8. Such interpreters have attempted to account for the multiple paradoxes of the painting by arguing that it was in fact a *repainting* of an original version that presented the heiress to the throne in 1656 in the appropriately elevating and hieratic imaging procedures of royal portraiture but that almost immediately had to be "reprocessed" or "disassembled" following the birth of Philip IV's male heir. Of the massive alterations necessitated by such changing political circumstances, one of the most suggestive is the transformation of the attendant's act of homage, a genuflection focusing the royal cynosure, into a ministration, the offer of a drink of water. The princess is strikingly indifferent and maintains her "original" imperious posture. X-rays revealing *pentimenti* would appear to support the argument. See J. Nash's summary of Manuela Mena's presentation of this theory in "How the Birth of a Son Altered 'Las Meninas,'" *Times Literary Supplement*, April 4, 1997, 8–9. For a review of the possibilities and problems raised by this political approach

to the genesis of the painting and by the recent discoveries of the numerous *pentimenti*, see Franco, *Las Meninas*, 33–35. Whether this theory is true or not, the nature and effects of Velázquez's alterations in any case go well beyond the aims of "erasure of charisma" or "domestication." If the mirrored monarchs and their projected space are present in an alleged first version, their function nevertheless is limited to that of sovereigns, parents, and spectators in an act of ceremonial admiration. The radical innovation of the "reprocessed" painting, the placing of the easel and an artist at work, imposes a compelling enigma on what would otherwise be a relatively conventional scene: what is in fact on the unseen side of the huge canvas? As in Manet's famous reaction, we might momentarily wonder where exactly the picture we are viewing is. Are the kings now the *objects of portraiture*? Do they, as it were, exist on two planes? Is the outside, "original," world now *mere* reality when juxtaposed to a higher reality of all that the artist places on that enigmatic far side of a flimsy canvas but is itself barely visible in the mirror that reflects it? Is the picture in effect not about a domestic scene or a ceremony of unveiling or an exalted royal family but rather primarily about the construction of the royal identity by an artist, a figure standing reflectively and confidently amid the flow of illusions around him, holding a palette dotted with the colors from which the majestic portrait of the king will arise, his brush poised to invest that portrait with a life that can exist only in the imagination?

9. For *Las Meninas* as Velázquez's proclamation of the nobility of painting and its endorsement by the king, see Snyder, "*Las Meninas*," 570. Also see J. Brown, *Images and Ideas in Seventeenth-Century Spanish Painting* (Princeton, 1978), 101.

10. See Brown, *Velázquez*, 257.

11. One is tempted at this point to find in Velázquez's declaration of "artistic sovereignty" an appropriation or displacement, not only of royal sovereignty, but of divine sovereignty as well. In the widely disseminated contemporary hexameral vision of Fray Luis de Granada, *Introducción al símbolo de la fe* (Salamanca, 1582), God is likened in his creative activity to a painter whose manner demands absolute clarity, determinate outline, rational disposition of space, fixed symbol, and decipherable scripture. As a hypothetical counterstyle to that of God, Granada describes a "borrón de tinta, que asertó a caer sobre una tabla" (a blob of ink that happened to fall on a board), which he associates with the randomness and ambiguities of the godless Epicurean world picture. See Biblioteca de Autores Españoles (hereafter BAE), ed. (Madrid, 1944), 6:192a. The most celebrated visual effects of Velázquez's paintings rise in fact from his development and mastery of the style of the *borrón*, a style ideally suited for a vision of the world subject to the free movement, ambiguities, and indeterminacies of subjectivity, mind, visual perception, and individual consciousness, as well as to the mutability characteristic of temporality. See Kenneth Clark's description of the "blobs, streaks, and veils of paint" by which Velázquez "achieved the magic" of *Las Meninas*; cited in Nash, "How the Birth of a Son Altered 'Las Meninas,'" 9. If Velázquez's painting paradoxically recovers a "non-artistic" order of reality, his success resulted in the transvaluation of a term that traditionally connoted something "non-artistic"—a "blot" or a "blemish"—into a term of praise. Nash notes that the painting is a "mirage rather than a mirror: from afar, inviting our absorption by it, but on our approach, metamorphosing to a bespattered surface."

12. For the relative scarcity of kings in Cervantes's theater, as well as their unorthodox functions within it, some of which are consistent with the iconoclasm of the sonnet (e.g., the buffoonery of comic stereotypes of raging tyrants and sultans or the metamorphosis of Pedro de Urdemalas

and his fairy tale world of benign trickery into king and court), see J. Canavaggio, "La figura del rey en el teatro de Cervantes," *Crítica Hispánica* 16 (1994): 31–42. One might include in such independent literary conceptions Elizabeth I of England in the exemplary novel *La española inglesa*, where the charismatic figure—a kind of fairy queen in her radiant regalia—is surprisingly "unveiled" in the second part of the tale as a master of the practices of international finance.

13. The references here and in the following several paragraphs are from F. Gerónimo Collado, *Descripcion del túmulo y relacion de las exequias que hizo la ciudad de Sevilla en la muerte del rey Don Felipe Segundo* (1611), ed. Sociedad de Bibliófilos Andaluces (Seville, 1869), 86, 116, 130–133, 136, 160, 166–167, 172, 190. For the pictorial celebrations of monarchs in such allegories and myths, see Faus, "Imagenes de poder," 212.

14. Collado's translation: "Esto usaste siempre Philipe, rey suntuosísimo, perdonar a los sujetos y desbaratar a los soberbios" (*Descripcion del túmulo*, 170–171).

15. Collado, *Descripcion del túmulo*, 210–211.

16. Miguel de Cervantes Saavedra, *Obras completas*, ed. A. Valbuena Prat (Madrid, 1956), 50–51; the translation is from Melveena McKendrick's *Cervantes* (Boston and Toronto, 1980), 185.

17. In her fine reading of the sonnet, Adrienne Laskier Martín points out that the description of the clothing, the bravado, and the aggressive gestures of the thug who intrudes to assert his dominance in an absurd challenge to anyone who would question the soldier's comically inflated praise of the splendor of the setting resembles closely Quevedo's description of a type that he calls "valientes de mentira." See *Cervantes and the Burlesque Sonnet* (Berkeley, 1991), 107–108. The scandalous, and ingenious, effect of Cervantes's satirical use of the type familiar in the discourse of *germanía* is the identification of king and thug.

18. Cervantes, *Obras completas*, 51; translation from McKendrick, *Cervantes*, 185. One should note that precisely at this point, the reader's perspective on the unfolding sonnet is suddenly complicated by a confusing dispersion of voices. The voice of the opening eleven verses (seemingly the poet himself) unexpectedly yields to the voice of a mysteriously lurking interlocutor. But at the same moment another voice, that of a third-person observer, takes over what suddenly becomes a narrative and distances the directly apprehensible utterances of the two braggarts. For the "vaporous" effects of such shifts and the resulting confusions, see the fine analysis of the sonnet by Mary Malcolm Gaylord, "'Yo el soneto': Cervantes's Poetics of the Cenotaph," in *Self-Conscious Art: A Tribute to John W. Kronik* (Lewisburg, 1996), 128–150. Cervantes's imaginative transformation of the solemn ritual of honoring and mourning into a nonsensical competition in linguistic violence of two comedic stereotypes, the "soldado fanfarrón" and the "valentón," is plausibly the reflection of the actual circumstances surrounding the construction of the monument and the performance of the memorial ceremony. The occasion was troubled by continuing rivalries among the various agencies involved—the city administration, the royal tribunal, the Holy Inquisition, and the local clergy. The obsessions with protocol, precedence, and the importance of maintaining proper distinctions and the anxieties raised by the violation of sacred boundaries led to the most undignified altercations one can imagine—concerning such questions as whether one sits on a French chair or on a bench, which group marches first in the funeral procession, which agency has the honor of supplying the sermonist, and whether even the poor peasants should be forced to wear the black garments of mourning. Such conflicts led to outbursts of rage, angry confrontations, invectives, arrests and imprisonment, excommunications, and paralyzing stand-offs—all taking place in the exalted spaces of the Sevillian cathedral and beneath the monumental altars,

facades, and paintings of the carefully framed and spectacularly projected royal majesty of the greatest of the kings of the earth. For the documentary testimony of this degrading spectacle of non-literary human vanity, see S. B. Vranich, *Ensayos sevillanos del siglo de oro* (Valencia, 1981), 94–104.

19. For the eeriness of the satirical fadeout—the shrinkage of the braggart as he metamorphoses into a "strange twin" and finally "disappears behind the scenes of an illusory stage," see Francisco Ayala, *Cervantes y Quevedo* (Barcelona, 1974), 201.

20. Cited by M. Herrero García, "La Monarquía teorética de Lope de Vega," *Fénix* 2 (1935): 177–224; see 203.

21. For the king's "unreality" and "hiddenness" as paradigmatic for the condition of modern consciousness, see my discussion of the split of King Pedro and his persona, Acevedo, in chapter 2 below. For the shift in world orders reflected in it, see my "At the Threshold of Modernity: Gracián's *El criticón*," in *Rhetoric and Politics: Baltasar Gracián and the New World Order*, ed. N. Spadaccini and J. Talens (Minneapolis, 1997), 3–70. For the social determinants of the emergence of this distant, divided subject and the "three dimensionality" of human experience in a world torn by tensions between private and public spheres of experience, the fundamental study is N. Elias, *The Court Society*, tr. E. Jephcott (New York, 1983). See also Kristen B. Neuschel's observations concerning the publicness and personal directness that traditionally marked aristocratic life and continued to influence behavior and literary expression in the early period of printing, urbanization, and state formation (*Word of Honor: Interpreting Noble Culture in Sixteenth-Century France* [Ithaca, NY, 1989]). As has often been pointed out, the Spanish theater was deeply aristocratic in the values it endorsed and the types of heroic behavior it celebrated. The split consciousness that marks the exceptional world of *Las Meninas* finds its proper literary form in Cervantes's novelistic world and its depiction of human beings mythologizing their lives.

22. Félix Lope de Vega Carpio, *El príncipe perfecto, Obras de Lope de Vega*, ed. Real Academia Española (hereafter RAE) (Nueva edición), vol. 10 (Madrid, 1930), 460–464. The self-consciousness of this celebrative drama becomes more complex in its second part, where one discovers intimations of the process of looking behind the surface of the mirror of majesty that I am examining in this study. In the dedication, Lope introduces his subject as "truly a mirror of every perfection" and a guide for the young prince Philip. Yet two of the play's seemingly most conventional royal episodes surprisingly draw attention to ambiguities in the imaging of kings and to the lack of substance in the official displays of the majesty. In the most startling a painter appears before the judicial tribunal, charged with making and selling bad portraits of the king to the ignorant populace. Such portraits have no artistic quality and "hang in the streets." The king surprises everybody by acquitting him of all charges and reminding everyone of the primacy of spirit over letter and icon in the royal cult: "Que ya que pinta mi rostro/Con mano torpe y grosera,/No a lo menos mis costumbres" (524) (Although he paints my face with a crude and vulgar hand, at least he does not do the same with my qualities of character). In a more intricate interrogation of the "cult of the king," Juan, while offering ingenious and profound aphorisms at his *audiencia*, rejects the offer of a book containing the "dichos y hechos de claros varones." The genre belongs to the literature of the cult of the king. He considers the collection, in its limitation to his own pronouncements, a *lisonja*, a calculated act of flattery. He goes on to criticize the pride of a peculiar craftsman of royal portraits who claims to have "cut out of paper" the Kings of Portugal. Juan refuses to look at paper images and notes that kings are made by God and laws (513). In a bizarre meta-critical

moment the episode mirrors and ambiguates the conventional process that is being articulated at this moment by the dramatist in his own celebrative representation of the king. For the wide diffusion of such visual representations of the monarch in prints and engravings and their importance in royal rhetoric and propaganda, see Fernando Bouza, *Imagen y propaganda: Capítulos de historia cultural del reinado de Felipe II* (Madrid, 1998), 140–144.

23. "The Uniqueness of the *comedia*," *Hispanic Review* 27 (1959): 303–316.

24. Munich, 1947, 235–237. "In a country where the highest power of the state, the absolute king, stood beyond good and evil and above common standards of decent conduct, how could the natural feeling and conscience of the individual human being in the given case [of conflict with the entrenched political powers and institutions] affirm its own rights?"

25. See "Lo español y lo universal en la obra de Galdós," *Materia y forma en poesía* (Madrid, 1960), 187–205, esp. 191. See also Alonso's "Karl Vossler y Lope de Vega," ibid., 137–143, and "Lope de Vega y sus fuentes," *Thesaurus* [Bogotá] 8 (1952): 1–24, esp. 3.

26. A concise formulation of this view can be found in José María Díez Borque's influential *Sociología de la comedia española del siglo XVII* (Madrid, 1976). Lope de Vega's theater, "without the slightest trace of criticism," supported a program of "sacralización real," envisioning the monarch as a "charismatic figure, beyond rationality and contingency and consequently beyond human limits" (131–132). See also Alfredo Hermenegildo: "Placing his art at the service of the dominant ideology, Lope de Vega created a public. And at this moment the state took control of the theatrical apparatus and carried out an authentic nationalization of such an effective propaganda medium for support of the prevailing power structure" ("Virués y los signos teatrales del horror," *Horror y tragedia en el teatro del siglo de oro: Actas del IV Coloquio GESTE*, Toulouse, 1983, *Criticón* 23 [1983], 93).

27. See *Estudios de historia del pensamiento español* (Madrid, 1984), 3:255–321.

28. See P. K. Monod's refinement on Maravall's argument in his discussion of the theatricalization of royal power and the necessary transformation of the king into an actor. The resultant figure was in fact a more human and complex entity than his medieval and Renaissance "sacral" predecessors because he had to represent a plausible, imitable human moral exemplar (rather than a hieratic image) in a cultural exchange with an increasingly rational and pre-bourgeois audience. See *The Power of Kings: Monarchy and Religion in Europe, 1589–1715* (New Haven, 1999), 84–86. The recovery of the king's humanity in the plays I am examining, as a critical counter-force to the "sacral" figure, is fundamentally different.

29. See José Antonio Maravall, Alberto Blecua, and Noël Salomon, "Del rey al villano: Ideología, sociedad y doctrina literaria," in Bruce W. Wardropper, *Siglos de oro: Barroco, Historia y crítica de la literatura española*, ed. F. Rico III (Barcelona, 1983), 265–271.

30. *Bulletin of the Comediantes* 34 (1982): 1–36.

31. Melveena McKendrick, "La comedia y los límites del conformismo: La dignidad real en Lope de Vega," *Crítica Hispánica* 16 (1994): 43–58; see 46. McKendrick is referring to the extremism of a recent reassertion of the view that Lope's exploitation of establishment values, attitudes, and anxieties in his "myth-making" drama was superficial and cynical; see Francisco Márquez Villanueva's *Lope: Vida y valores* (Río Piedras, 1987). See also McKendrick's "Values and Motives in the *Comedia*: A Revisionist View of the Maravallian Orthodoxy," *Journal of Hispanic Research* 1 (1993): 263–269.

32. *Playing the King: Lope de Vega and the Limits of Conformity* (London, 2000), 103, 112, 185. Mc-

Kendrick cites Melchor de Cabrera y Guzmán's *Defensa por el uso de las comedias y suplica al Rey nuestro señor para que se continuen* [1646].

33. *La creación del "Fénix": Recepción crítica y formación canónica del teatro de Lope de Vega* (Madrid, 2000), esp. ch. 5. For the impoverishment in our experience of the *comedia* by the dominant ideological approaches and the elimination from the canon of hundreds of works that do not overtly concern themselves with political issues and paradigms, see Joan Oleaza, "El nacimiento de la Comedia: Estado de la cuestión," in *La Comedia*, ed. Jean Canavaggio (Madrid, 1995), 181–226, esp. 209: "my principal interest is the recovery of the plurality of a dramaturgy that was neither aesthetically nor ideologically uniform, that passed through different stages, and that responded with different genres to different necessities, to different functions, and to different tastes and expectations." See also Ignacio Arellano, *Historia del teatro español del siglo XVII* (Madrid, 1995), 116–118.

34. See Stephen Rupp's fine study of the conflicts and ambiguities in Calderón's political theater and its engagement with Machiavellian and "Christian" state reason: *Allegories of Kingship: Calderón and the Anti-Machiavellian Tradition* (University Park, Pa., 1996). See also the epilogue below.

35. See Stern, "Lope de Vega, Propagandist?"

36. In my opinion the theological absolutism that distinguishes the dramatic world of Calderón marks an end to the development to which I am pointing in this study—the recovery and celebration of the human resources (e.g., morality, civilizing powers, military abilities, judicial capacities) of a king amid the rising political institutions of the modern prince-state. The diminished humanness of Prince Segismundo of *La vida es sueño* is recovered through discipline, confinement, fear, and renunciation. The humanness of the Constant Prince is valorized paradoxically in its mortification and ultimate annihilation. Once again the political world, returning to Paul and Augustine, looks upward for its guidance.

37. See Ernst H. Kantorowicz, *The King's Two Bodies: A Study in Medieval Political Theology* (Princeton, 1957), ch. 8. Also Georg Jellinek, *Adam in der Staatslehre* (Heidelberg, 1893).

CHAPTER 1. KING AND PHILOSOPHER

1. Marcel Bataillon, "*El villano en su rincón,*" *Varia lección de clásicos españoles* (Madrid, 1964), 329–372, esp. 372.

2. Félix Lope de Vega Carpio, *El villano en su rincón*, ed. Juan María Marín (Madrid, 1987), 125. All page numbers cited in the text are taken from this edition.

3. Noël Salomon concludes that the king's monarchist pronouncements in the final scene resolve all problems raised by Juan Labrador's contestations and "close off," as if "by decree," the play's suggestive openings to the moral and philosophical concerns of humanism. See *Recherches sur le thème paysan dans la "comedia" au temps de Lope de Vega* (Bordeaux, 1965), 911. See also Bruce Wardropper's comments on the "cruelty" of the king's behavior in this scene ("La venganza de Maquiavelo: *El villano en su rincón*," in *Homenaje a William L. Fichter : Estudios sobre el teatro antiguo hispánico y otros ensayos*, ed. A. D. Kossoff and J. Amor y Vázquez (Madrid, 1971), 765–772. For Valdivielso's resolution of the play's conflicts, see his rewritten version, *El villano en su rincón; Teatro completo*, ed. R. Arias and R. Piluso (Madrid, 1975), 1:58–59. The ritualistic character of Lope's dramatic action and its dense traditional symbolism have inspired modern readings not unlike those of its first interpreter, Valdivielso. The most ambitious is surely that

of B. Brancaforte, who argues that the play is an intricately sustained religious allegory dramatizing the passage from the Old Dispensation to the New. The fearful Juan Labrador resists the
liberating movement of love, and before being incorporated into the court, which symbolizes
"the mystical body of Christ," he is subjected to a series of trials by the king, who is both the Old
Testament God of authority and Christ the loving hunter. See "Lope's *El villano en su rincón:*
A Vision of Universal Harmony," in *Perspectivas de la comedia,* ed. A. V. Ebersole (Chapel Hill,
1978), 49–66. As I shall point out below, I find the religious connection most interesting for its
intermittent character and its support of a sustained secular—political and ethical—range of
significance and symbolization. The play should in fact be seen as a critical disengagement from
the theological schemes in which traditional conceptions of sacral monarchy were rooted. For
the divinization of secular drama according to the models of the *auto sacramental* as epitomizing
a distinguishing feature of the entire culture of the Baroque—a *Diskurs-Renovatio* that would
counter and redirect the powerful centrifugal energies of "Renaissance discourse" (e.g., irony,
paradox, fragmentation, and mimesis) through the reassertion of a theologically based, ideologically predetermined, characteristically allegorical literary discursive system—see Joachim Küpper's *Diskurs-Renovatio bei Lope de Vega und Calderón* (Tübingen, 1990). The following analysis
of the paradoxical structures and the humanist political-moral implications of Lope's play and
all that distinguishes it from its subsequent divinization, while perhaps confirming the validity of
Küpper's general claim regarding the reactionary directions of much seventeenth-century literature, would at the same time call into question its unqualified applicability to Lope's theater.

4. Rather than a paradoxical "other world" for the dialectical provocation and enlightenment of
a "challenged" viewer or reader, Valdivielso's *rincón* is thoroughly stabilized by the dominating
Augustinian-Christian motifs of its conception—e.g., the condition of forgetfulness; the slumber
of sin; the proliferating, disorderly delights of the pleasure garden; and the displacement of reason by laughter (see esp. 1:49).

5. In *Playing the King: Lope de Vega and the Limits of Conformity* (London, 2000), Melveena
McKendrick presents a subtle reinterpretation of the play that emphasizes its indeterminacy. "It
is something of a conundrum, curious most of all for its reluctance to display its hand and take
sides. . . . The lack of resolution is central to the fashioning of the work itself. . . . It is possible,
just about, to read the play in diametrically opposed ways" (188, 196, 194). McKendrick's reading
offers fine insights into the drama's political and social themes, their historical context, and the
tensions rising from the interaction of its two worlds and two protagonists.

6. *Coloquios satíricos,* ed. NBAE (Madrid, 1907), 7:485ff.

7. *El político Don Fernando el Católico, Obras completas,* ed. A. de Hoyo (Madrid, 1960), 67.

8. *El criticón,* ed. E. Correa Calderón (Madrid, 1971), 2:258–259; emphasis added. While Gracián's
articulation of the anecdote, in his characteristic laconic abstraction and condensation of ideas
in sharpened paradoxes, endows it with an extraordinary range of suggestiveness, its fundamental
emphasis is on the discovery of a hidden truth and the experience of *desengaño.* This emphasis
is anticipated in G. Botero's version, appearing in *Detti memorabili de personaggi,* a collection of
worthy pronouncements that he allegedly collected while serving as ambassador at the Spanish
court. The king's encounter with the peasant is presented in a section titled "Miseria de prencipi" and emphasizes the latter's candor regarding his royal guest's reliance on worthless, flatter-
ing advisers in his "molti negotij di gran consequenza." On awakening, the king, *desengañado,*
announces to his courtiers: "Io non haveva inteso una sola parola veritevole della persona mia,

sino a hieri sera" (I have not heard a single truthful word about myself until yesterday evening) (Turin, 1608). Perhaps the germ of Lope's incorporation of Juan Labrador into the palace world as ethical model and critical counsellor lies in Botero's version of the confrontation.

9. *Don Quijote de la Mancha*, part II, ch. 53. Perhaps the most familiar serious depiction of the experience is Segismundo's sleep and awakening to the awareness of the "fiera condición" of his humanness and the consequent obligations of kingship, despite the disclosure of the fundamental insubstantiality of the majesty, in Calderón's *La vida es sueño*.

10. "Autosemblanza de Felipe IV," *Epistolario español*, ed. BAE (Madrid, 1958), 109:231. For the legal and theological traditions behind the distinction to which Philip IV alludes (e.g., Baldus: "magis dignum trahit ad se minus dignum"; Plowden: "His [the king's] body politic, which is annexed to his Body natural, takes away the Imbecility of his Body natural"), see Ernst H. Kantorowicz, *The King's Two Bodies: A Study in Medieval Political Theology* (Princeton, 1957), 8–10. Relevant also is Kantorowicz's discussion of the belief, traceable at least to the period of Frederick II of Sicily, in "certain royal qualities and potencies dwelling in the blood of kings," mysterious qualities infused by nature and grace, and "creating, so to speak, a royal species of man," whose acquisition of knowledge is more perfect than that of private persons (see 331–332). It is precisely such deeply entrenched dualisms and hierarchies of value that are called into question by the paradoxical reexamination of kingship and politics in such works as Lope's comedic *Villano en su rincón* and Shakespeare's tragic *King Lear*.

11. With his characteristic respect for the "sens littéral," Marcel Bataillon has written of Lope's carelessness in *El villano en su rincón*, a drama "marred" by "extravagant" anachronisms, geographical confusions, and inaccurate historical references, and he has looked to a marginal and fragmentary scene in Act III as holding a key to an underlying, determining political agenda (see "El villano en su rincón," 329–330; also Marcel Bataillon, *Défense et illustration du sens littéral* [Leeds, 1967], and G. Díaz-Plaja, "'Beatus ille,' fuente de 'El villano en su rincón,'" in *Soliloquio y coloquio* [Madrid, 1968], 111–143). Apart from its tendency toward philosophical abstraction, a quality distinguishing the *Villano* among Lope's numerous "historical" plays of kings and peasants, its spectacular "literariness"—in its conventions, structural design, characterizations, poetic language, and dramatic effects—might suggest that an approach aimed at its presumed "facticity"—either in its "represented" events or in its alleged biographical, social, or political conditioning or functioning—will yield results that are secondary to, if not in fact quite remote from, the central and certainly the most interesting elements in its imaginatively expansive language system. A relevant discussion of such problems of interpretation, with specific reference to the so-called American "new historicism" and its limiting perspectives on the rich and comprehensive dramatic world of Shakespeare's drama, can be found in Alvin Kernan's *Shakespeare, The King's Playwright: Theater in the Stuart Court, 1603–1613* (New Haven, 1996); see esp. 183–187.

12. Rodríguez notes that the only two dramas that exceed the *Villano* in song are *El nacimiento de Cristo* and *San Isidro labrador de Madrid*, and he argues that the carefully designed blend of popular and elite poetic forms achieves a lyrical reconciliation that is not matched by the dramatic affirmation of monarchy at the play's conclusion. See "Los cantables de *El villano en su rincón*," in Kossoff and Amor y Vázquez, *Homenaje a William L. Fichter*, 639–645. As the following makes clear, I would like to suggest the opposite conclusion: that the blend of poetic forms supports a reconciliation of opposites that occurs at all levels of the work—e.g., king and peasant, law and love, power and reason, *corte* and *aldea*, and artifice and nature.

13. For the imaginative incorporation in the *Villano* of the *romance La infantina encantada*, with its unusual metamorphosis of woman into tree, see Salomon, *Recherches sur le thème paysan*, 568–571, 593–599. For the bejeweled tree, see G. Umpierre, *Songs in the Plays of Lope de Vega* (London, 1975), 84–85. Casalduero correctly emphasizes the function of the songs in charging the imaginative atmosphere of the work with erotic energy and dismisses as idle the efforts of critics to approach them in relation to the questionable verisimilitude of the plot and setting ("Sentido y forma de 'El villano en su rincón,'" in *Estudios sobre el teatro español* [Madrid, 1972], 45–63, esp. 56–59). For the popularity of Belflor as a fictional place of withdrawal, refuge, tranquility, and pleasure—marked primarily by its short distance from an urban, political, or courtly center (e.g., Paris, Cracow, Bologna)—in the dramatic worlds of Lope and his followers, see Warren T. McCready, "The Toponym Belflor in Golden Age Literature," *Revista Canadiense de Estudios Hispánicos* 6 (1982): 379–387.

14. In my opinion the *rincón* has been forsaken by Lope criticism, which, inspired by the valuable historical insights of Castro and Maravall, has for the most part preferred to approach this mythical space through sociological, economic, political, and ideological explanations that tend to be general and frequently reductive. Of the various simplifications resulting from these approaches, perhaps the most misleading is the dismissive conception of Lope as "a royal propagandist." See following note.

15. See Luis Cortés Echánove, *Nacimiento y crianza de personas reales en la corte de España: 1566–1886* (Madrid, 1958), 38–40. In *Teatro y literatura en la sociedad barroca* (Madrid, 1972) José Antonio Maravall cites numerous plays that vindicate the incontestability of the royal will and do so precisely through contrived dramatic cases in which its intentions are marked by the brutality and injustice of the tyrant. If in such cases the dramatic presentation of the monarch contradicted the arguments on the sources and limits of sovereign power by the political theorists of the period (e.g., Mariana, Molina, Bellarmino, and Suárez), it was because the drama came into existence to carry out an "extensive and insistent ideological propaganda campaign"—to legitimize and consolidate a reactionary neo-seignorial society with its traditional hierarchy of classes (or estates), its denial of social and political mobility to members of its lower ranks, and its self-affirming exclusion of outsiders. At the pinnacle of this structure was the mediating figure of its divine ordination, the charismatic, consecrated body of the monarch—"el vicario de Dios"—whose "quasi-numinous" powers, assumed to descend from above rather than to rise, through delegation, from the people below, were put on display in countless restorations of order and suppressions of a threatening individuality in the plays of the age. Maravall finds a definitive statement of this view of monarchy in the shocking words of the great usurper and regicide of Spanish history, Enrique de Trastamara: "Que es deidad el rey más malo,/en que a Dios se ha de adorar" (The most evil king is a deity in whom God is to be worshipped) (Lope de Vega, *El Rey Don Pedro en Madrid*). Maravall would appear to find little variation in the purposes of this vast outburst of cultural productivity. "None other is the aim of the thousands of works written in our seventeenth century, essentially unanimous in that requisite ideological content" (No otra es la finalidad de los miles de obras que se escriben en nuestro siglo xvii, unánimes esencialmente en ese preciso contenido ideológico [see ch. 11, esp. 134–135]). *El villano en su rincón* has an important place in Maravall's considerations. The neo-seignorial sociopolitical system was founded in a revitalized agrarian economy in which a small group of wealthy peasants played an important role. It fell to the *comedia* to dignify this powerful class, investing its representatives with the at-

tributes of the socially privileged groups (e.g., honor and the capacity for love as conceived in traditionally aristocratic codes of erotic self-fulfillment) and glorifying cases of their support for the
monarchs. In Lope's play the king's forced integration of the peasant outsider and his bestowal of
an honorable position at the court upon him should be viewed as social propaganda of this sort
(see chs. 8, 11). Maravall follows Bataillon in failing to find any problematization in the "exaltation of royal power" in the *Villano*. For a subsequent consideration of Lope's monarchism and
his treatment of the peasant, see E. Forastieri, *Aproximación estructural al teatro de Lope de Vega*
(Madrid, 1977), ch. 2. For the concrete economic conditions of Lope's Spain reflected in the
Villano and his other "agricultural" plays and his occasional allusions to contemporary physio-
cratic approaches to national problems, see Salomon, *Recherches sur le thème paysan*, esp. parts
2 and 4. Also see R. O. Jones, "Poets and Peasants," in Kossoff and Amor y Vázquez, *Homenaje a
William L. Fichter*, 341–355. Also relevant are H.-J. Neuschäfer's analysis of *Fuenteovejuna's* complexity in its perspective on the *pueblo* ("Lope de Vega und der Vulgo," in *Spanische Literatur
im goldenen Zeitalter: Fritz Schalk zum 70. Geburtstag*, ed. H. Baader and E. Loos [Frankfurt
am Main, 1973], 338–356), and R. A. Young's reminder of Lope's dramatic endorsement of traditional restraints on the tyrannical will articulated in contemporary political theory (*La figura del
rey y la institución real en la comedia lopesca* [Madrid, 1979]).

16. On the drudgeries and discomforts see, for example, Jorge de Montemayor's epistle, "The
Ordeals of Kings," which describes the depressing nature of court life and its endless and thoroughly unglamorous pile-up of routine bureaucratic demands on the royal executive (F. J. Sánchez Cantón, ed., "Los trabajos de los reyes por Jorge de Montemayor," *Revista de Filología Española* 12 [1925], 43–55). For the well-documented awareness of this "all too human" aspect of
the life and job of a king, as well as his subjects' readiness to refer to his failures with insulting
epithets, see C. Lisón Tolosana, *La imagen del rey: Monarquía, realeza y poder ritual en la Casa
de los Austrias* (Madrid, 1992), 59–74.

17. See Kantorowicz, *The King's Two Bodies*; also see Ernst H. Kantorowicz, "Mysteries of State:
An Absolutist Concept and Its Late Mediaeval Origins," *Harvard Theological Review* 48 (1955):
65–91.

18. A revealing indication of the unquestionability of the commonplace view among historians, following Maravall, of Lope as a simple apologist and ideologue of the monarchy can be observed
in their various appropriations of the verses cited above. In his *Philip IV and the Government of
Spain: 1621–1665* (Cambridge, 1988), R. A. Stradling compresses them into an effective, rhyming
couplet: "That princes are human, no one can doubt,/But poetry must make their divinity shine
out" (4). The condensation suggests that Lope believed that the royal figure was divine. The appeal of the couplet and, presumably, the acceptability of its political implications, led to its translation and incorporation into the Spanish version of Stradling's study (1989); the repetition of
the latter by Lisón Tolosana in *La imagen del rey* in 1992; and finally, in P. K. Monod's *The Power
of Kings: Monarchy and Religion in Europe 1589–1715* (New Haven, 1999), its retranslation, from
Lisón Tolosana's version, back into English (43). All of this perpetuates the conception, apparently acceptable as a historical commonplace, that Lope believed literally in the divinity of the
king and his duty to venerate it poetically. At the conclusion of *Playing the King*, McKendrick
points out Stradling's misrepresentation of Lope's words. I would add that the subsequent for-
tunes of the translation and its resistance to any correction would certainly bear out her conclusion that the "myth of Lope's royal idolatry dies hard" (206).

19. See Maurizio Viroli, *From Politics to Reason of State* (Cambridge, 1992); J. G. A. Pocock, *The Machiavellian Moment: Florentine Political Thought and the Atlantic Republican Tradition* (Princeton, 1975); Wilhelm Berges, *Die Fürstenspiegel des hohen und späten Mittelalters* (Leipzig, 1938).

20. For the features of the hexameral deity and its relations to Baroque monarchy and cartography, see my "At the Threshold of Modernity: Gracián's *El Criticón*," in *Rhetoric and Politics: Baltasar Gracián and the New World Order*, ed. N. Spadaccini and J. Talens (Minneapolis, 1997), 3–70.

21. Lope de Vega (attributed), *El palacio confuso*, ed. Charles H. Stevens (New York, 1939), 49.

22. *Empresas políticas: Idea de un príncipe político-cristiano*, ed. Q. Aldea Vaquero (Madrid, 1976), 242.

23. Ibid., 612–614.

24. Ibid., 313–314.

25. Ibid., 374.

26. London, 1606, 33–34.

27. The scene in *El Brasil restituido*, in which Philip IV's portrait nods solemnly to his victorious commander, can be compared with Juan Bautista Maino's famous pictorial celebration of the victory—a depiction of historical events in the foreground while a formal portrait of the king receiving a crown of laurel is dramatically unveiled in the background. *El arauco domado* climaxes with the confession of error by the Indian chieftain Caupolicán, who failed to see that the light of the sun, which he idolatrously worshipped, flowed from the "autor del sol," whose true "rayo" he now adores. At this point the portraited figure of Philip II, "as if he were a statue," is revealed. The conquerors "kiss the hand" of the monarch, and the "famoso retrato" confirms "en ausencia suya" (in his absence) the rewards that they receive in the distribution of the spoils. See Félix Lope de Vega Carpio, *Comedias*, ed. J. Gómez and P. Cuenca (Madrid, 1993), 9:846–848.

28. See K. Emery Jr.'s discussion of the mystical tradition in connection with Benet of Canfield and his predecessors ("Mysticism and the Coincidence of Opposites in Sixteenth- and Seventeenth-Century France," *Journal of the History of Ideas* 45 [1984]: 3–23). For the classical and Christian traditions lying behind the elaborate solar mythology and imagery in the court ceremonial of seventeenth-century absolutist monarchy, see Ernst H. Kantorowicz, "Oriens Augusti–Lever du Roi," *Dumbarton Oaks Papers* 17 (1963): 111–177. The degree to which Lope's play problematizes such absolutist conceptions and ceremonies can be measured by a comparison with the "stabilization" of his work in Valdivielso's "divinized" version, where theological absolutism thoroughly absorbs the imagined political order and the most immense distance conceivable separating "creator-state" and created being is affirmed. In a rhetorical *tour de force* consisting of ten stanzas beginning with *ver*, Reason enumerates the allegorized features of the king and their benefits and concludes with the supreme gift: "Y ver quanto bien desseo/en el Rey que me da el ser;/pues sin él nada ay que ver/y en él quanto quiero veo" (And to see as much goodness as I desire in the King who gives me my very being; for without him there is nothing to see and in him I see all that I desire to see) (*El villano en su rincón*, 1:36–37). Shortly afterward the king appears in a frightening epiphany of omnipotence, and, in the words of the Old Testament Jahwe, declares his anger with the *villano* and the disorder of his unintegrated *rincón*. "Yo que soy Rey de los reyes y onze esferas;/yo que tengo plaça de armas/con mil reforçadas pieças/de truenos, piedras y rayos/de que las montañas tiemblan . . . yo, pues, que soy el que soy,/y sin mí nadie ay que sea,/del Villano-en-su-rincón/tengo de formar querellas" (I who am King of kings . . . I who have parade

grounds with a thousand pieces of artillery, reinforced by thunderbolts, stones, and lightning flashes that cause mountains to tremble . . . I, then, who am who I am and without whom there is nobody, I have occasion to bring charges against the Villano-en-su-rincón) (1:40–41). In Valdi-vielso's rewriting there is certainly no challenge to this imperious being in a rationally designed other world governed by an ideal "mayordomo." While Brancaforte's allegorical reading trans-forms Lope's work into something resembling Valdivielso's, he is certainly correct in suggesting that R. Otto's insights into the holy are relevant for an understanding of the play (see Brancaforte, "Lope's *El villano en su rincón*," 51–53). Noting that in Philip IV's palace the ultimate privilege for the courtier was to see the king, J. H. Elliott describes how the fortunate receiver of an audi-ence would approach the royal study through a succession of rooms, each one more exclusive of access than the one before. The ritual passage would climax with his entry into the dreaded "holy of holies," as it were, where the king, impassive as a statue, would reveal himself, *arrimado a un bufete* ("The Court of the Spanish Habsburgs: A Peculiar Institution?" *Spain and Its World: 1500–1700* [New Haven, 1989], 142–161; see esp. 148–150). The most interesting aspect of Lope's romantic comedy, from a political point of view, is its humanistic reaccentuation of the cult of the king and its dramatic disengagement of that cult from the rigors lurking in its theological affinities and its continuing practices of awe-inspiring ritual and the distancing procedures of taboo. In my opinion, the play in fact lifts both of its protagonists out of the most primitive areas of experience exploited in the sacralization of authority characteristic of the Age of Absolutism and the Counter-Reformation. Juan Labrador's obstinacy about his children's ambitions and his hysterical behavior as the king approaches his space point not only to the laws of comedy and the psychology of the generations, but also to a proverbial fear of kings: As Petrus Alfonsus put it in the twelfth century, "Rex est similis igni; cui si nimis admotus fueris, cremaberis" (The king is like fire; if you approach too closely, you will be burned). The play concludes with a sharing of space and food by the rivals and with an emphatic declaration of the "end of fear." On the question of taboo in the cult of royalty, see Lisón Tolosana, *La imagen del rey*, 147–151. For the official, institutional, and cultural exploitation of fear in the period, see section below on "The King's Theater."

29. Jean de La Bruyère, *The Characters of Jean de la Bruyère*, tr. H. van Laun (London, 1929), 213. Fascinating examples of the cult of the king are provided by J. E. Varey's study of court spectacles of the period. For example, on one occasion the chair of state faced the proscenium of the the-ater and was separated from it by a long empty space. In effect, it constituted a parallel stage and provided an alternate spectacle for the courtiers grouped at the edges of the empty space. As they watch the fictions of the staged performance, the royal spectators become the primary play for the assembled courtiers. In describing the complex theatrical effects that resulted, a foreign ob-server noted that at a court play she could see "como en idea en los Reyes la representacion, y por accesorio lo representado de la comedia" (in the actual monarchs present the represented drama as in an idea, and that what was concretely put on in the staging of the *comedia* was accessory). "For the courtier, then, the King is the true spectacle, the play being merely of secondary im-portance." Varey also describes the *loa* (the introductory playlet) in a performance of Calderón's *Hado y divisa de Leonido y de Marfisa* (1680). The curtain rises and reveals a splendid throne and a canopy above a display of two portraits, which as perfect mirrors reflect the features of the king and the queen, seated before them in the auditorium. "Pareció ser un espejo en que trasladaban sus peregrinas perfecciones; y el ansia que desea verlos en todas partes, quisiera hallar más repe-

tidas sus copias" (It seemed to be a mirror in which were copied their extraordinary perfections; and the yearning that desires to see them everywhere would wish to find their copies more often repeated). The description of the performance also points out that the gentlemen in the audience "estaban realzando su grandeza con el primor de su rendimiento, asistiendo como luces a la vista del sol de quien la recibían" (were highlighting their grandeur through the elegance of their obeisance, attending, as beams of light, to the sight of the sun, from which they received their radiance). See "The Audience and the Play at Court Spectacles: The Role of the King," *Bulletin of Hispanic Studies* 61 (1984): 398–406, esp. 402–403, 405; also M. Greer's suggestive observations in *The Play of Power: Mythological Court Drama of Calderón de la Barca* (Princeton, 1991), ch. 7. Juan Labrador's "remote" obsession with seeing and being seen can be correctly understood only if one bears in mind such extravagant manifestations of the centrality of royal cynosure in the political culture of the period.

30. See Kantorowicz, *The King's Two Bodies*, ch. 3.

31. Lisón Tolosana, *La imagen del rey*, 163.

32. Ibid., 164–165.

33. See the descriptions and illustrations provided by S. N. Orso, *Art and Death at the Spanish Habsburg Court: The Royal Exequies for Philip IV* (Columbia, Mo., 1989). For such displays for the deceased Philip II, see introduction above.

34. *Tratado de República y Policía christiana. Para Reyes y Príncipes. . . .* (1619); cited by Lisón Tolosana, *La imagen del rey*, 168.

35. Ibid., 169–170. See Pierre Civil's study of the "remarkable investment in the king's body as a visible and permanent sign of power," its representation of that body in an imaginative visual rhetoric that completely obscures his human reality, and the effectiveness of its rhetoric in "a regime accustomed to conjugating the divine and the royal cults." He cites Philip II's words of advice to his son: "from the instant . . . that you arrive at the majesty, you must divest yourself of yourself [debes despojarte de ti mismo] . . . and put on the dress of the majesty [y vestirte de la magestad]." ("Le corps du roi et son image: Une symbolique de l'état dans quelques representations de Philippe II," in *Le corps comme métaphore dans l'Espagne des XVe et XVe siècles*, ed. A. Redondo [Paris, 1992], 11–29). Also see Fernando Bouza, *Imagen y propaganda: Capítulos de historia cultural del reinado de Felipe II* (Madrid, 1998), 67–68. For the spectacular "robing" of the royal creature in the period, see L. Marin, *Portrait of the King*, tr. M. M. Houle (Minneapolis, 1988); J.-M. Apostolides, *Le roi-machine* (Paris, 1981); Monod, *The Power of Kings*, esp. ch. 5; and A. M. Schmitter, "Representation and the Body of Power in French Academic Painting," *Journal of the History of Ideas* 63 (2002): 399–424.

36. Erasmus and Pontano cited in Quentin Skinner: *The Foundations of Modern Political Thought* (Cambridge, 1978), 1:231–233, and *Machiavelli* (New York, 1981), 34–35. For the medieval background and the immense influence of Aegidius in establishing the tradition, see Berges, *Die Fürstenspiegel des hohen und späten Mittelalters*. J. A. Fernández-Santamaría notes that works of this type reached epidemic proportions in the early seventeenth century as their political moralism—originally rooted in medieval theological culture and its priorities, subsequently intensified in the climate of Italian civic humanism, and frequently embodied in idealizing mirrors of specific princes—was compelled to come to grips with unprecedented complexities created by the practical operative needs of the new nation-states. See *The State, War and Peace: Spanish Political Thought in the Renaissance: 1516–1559* (Cambridge, 1977), 247–252. The response to

such complexities by the Spanish writers in this tradition is lucidly and informatively presented in Ronald W. Truman's *Spanish Treatises on Government, Society and Religion in the Time of Philip II: The "de regimine principum" and Associated Traditions* (Leiden, 1999). A new kind of approach to the quintessential political virtue of prudence was inescapable, and the resultant conflicts and anxieties are frequently registered in Baroque political literature. As I shall point out below, the *Villano en su rincón* can be (and has been) read as a dramatic version of the *speculum principis* tradition, but what is most interesting in it as such is its adaptation to the distinctive features of absolutist political life as it reasserts traditional moral values.

37. The Ribadeneira citations are taken from the abridged translation of the treatise by G. A. Moore, *Religion and the Virtues of the Christian Prince against Machiavelli* (Washington, D.C., 1949), 316.

38. See Saavedra Fajarado, *Empresas políticas*, 171–173; also 227–237, 332, 611.

39. *El villano en su rincón*, 200.

40. For the altered focus of recent historical study of absolutism, see Elliott: "It has been less impressed by the effectiveness of monarchical power in Early Modern Europe than by its limitations. It has paid more attention to participation than coercion, more attention to resistance than to the exercise of power, more attention to survival than to innovation. In so doing, it has tended to cast doubt on what was previously taken for granted: the *transforming* power of the state" ("Power and Propaganda in the Spain of Philip IV," *Spain and Its World*, 162). On the "fragmented," "centrifugal," "supranational," and "disobedient" character of the Spanish Empire; the necessity of an intensely developed royal cult for its unification; and the frustrations plaguing Olivares's tireless efforts at developing centralizing institutions, see 170–188. Lisón Tolosana has stressed the awesome disintegrative energies that beset all efforts at national unification and imperial centralization in Spain's medieval and Golden Age history and made its "monarquía la más heterogénea y plural de Europa" (*La imagen del rey*, 17–55). On Louis XIV's state, see Monod: "'Absolute' power, in short, was to a large degree a consoling myth. The king's practical authority was obtained only through accommodating a bewildering array of interest groups" (*The Power of Kings*, 224). See also F. Dumont, "French Kingship and Absolute Monarchy in the Seventeenth Century," in *Louis XIV and Absolutism*, ed. R. Hatton (London, 1976), 55–84; and F. Hartung and R. Mousnier, "Quelques problèmes concernant la monarchie absolue," *Relazioni del X Congresso Internazionale di Scienze Storiche*, vol. 4 (Florence, 1955), 1–55. Bodin argued that the state will threatened "to degenerate into arbitrary action, and thus into a dissolution of all real law" unless held within bounds set universally by divine and natural law. The ruler must act with a "natural moderation" and must reject the useful if it is by nature disgraceful. Cited in Friedrich Meinecke, *Machiavellism: The Doctrine of Raison d'Etat and Its Place in Modern History*, tr. D. Scott (London, 1957), 61–64. Maravall points out that theories of sovereignty originating in Spain responded to a political situation in which the central authority was not threatened by the divisive forces of a powerful feudal nobility and reformist religious groups that brought so much disorder to Bodin's France. Hence their even greater tendency toward restraint. Their conception of the king as carrying out Christian responsibilities and fulfilling the rational purposes of civil law—despite his formal release from its authority, his incontestable superiority over all subjects and institutions, and the "divine" nature of his majesty—marks them, among the European expressions of absolutism (e.g., Bodin, Hobbes), as particularly moderated and traditionalist in their Thomistic emphases. See J. A. Maravall, *La teoría española del estado en el siglo XVII*

(Madrid, 1944), ch. 5; also see his "Sobre el pensamiento social y político de Quevedo," *Estudios de historia del pensamiento español* (Madrid, 1984), 3:257–321, esp. 290–295.

41. For the medieval tradition binding king to natural and rational law (e.g., Frederick II of Sicily: "For although our imperial majesty is free from all laws, it is nevertheless not altogether exalted above the judgement of Reason, herself the Mother of all law"), see Kantorowicz, *The King's Two Bodies*, 105–110. For the prominence of rationality in the traditions of Roman and scholastic jurisprudence from Azo and Aquinas to Suárez, see my discussion below of *El Rey Don Pedro en Madrid*. Also see Skinner's account of Thomist and legalist medieval political traditions in *The Foundations of Modern Political Thought*, esp. 2, part 2, "Constitutionalism and the Counter Reformation," 113–184.

42. For the ruler's subordination to reason and morality, see Santa María: "Entonces le conviene el título de Rey cuando lo fuere de sí mismo y poniendo rienda a sus apetitos, se hiciere vasallo de la razón y justicia" (the title of King is well suited to him whenever he is king over himself and whenever, reining in his passions, he becomes a vassal of reason and justice) *(Tratado de la Republica*; cited by Maravall, *La teoría española del estado*, 219). In an emblem that precisely concentrates the humanistic perspective on the king's responsibilities, his necessary education, and the exemplary content of his visibility—i.e., as an educator himself—Saavedra Fajardo presents at the beginning of his treatise for the young prince, Baltasar Carlos, an empty canvas on an easel facing a hand holding a bundle of brushes and a palette loaded with paints. The hand of art will fill the receptive and benign blank of nature, dressing man's nakedness with "images of arts and sciences" and "documents" of the proper education, ultimately bringing about a "mysterious" process that unites society in gratitude, love, and mutual dependence (see *Empresas políticas*, 81–87).

43. *Política de Dios: Govierno de Christo*, ed. J. O. Crosby (Madrid, 1966), 165. "Insensatos Electores de Imperios son los nueve meses. Quien debe la Magestad a las anticipaciones del parto, y a la primera impaciencia del vientre; mucho haze, si se acuerda para vivir como Rey, de que nació como hombre" (The nine months are senseless Imperial Electors. The man who owes the Majesty to the first stirrings of the birth process and the first impatience of the womb would do well to remember, in order to live as King, that he was born as man).

44. Saavedra Fajardo, *Empresas políticas*, 654. Manifestations of this agricultural model for good government are frequently visible in Lope's plays. See, for example, *Fuenteovejuna*, *La quinta de Florencia*, and *La comedia de Bamba*, as well as his specific conception of the *villano*. Probably the most famous of its invocations in the theater of absolutism is in Shakespeare's play about a king who appeared to understand himself only as idol, Richard II. As he moves blindly toward destruction, the gardeners lament that he has let the weeds choke up the flowers, the unpruned trees deny the fruit, and the garden beds of the "sea-walled garden" of England fall into disorder (III, iv).

45. See *Empresas políticas*, 285–291.

46. Cited in Moore, *Religion and the Virtues of the Christian Prince against Machiavelli*, 299–300.

47. Ibid., 316–317. It is interesting that in Matos Fragoso's recast, thoroughly monarchist, version of *El villano en su rincón*, the crisis scene in the dark bedroom climaxes in the king's escape from temptation, described as a triumphant act of self-conquest and magnanimity. Curiously the model for the king's "regal heroism" is a member of the high nobility, Otón, who, subsequently and somewhat clumsily when considered in the perspective of dramaturgic consistency,

becomes the villain of the work and, in his seduction of Juan Labrador's daughter, the innocent Beatriz, a "tyrant." The classical model for moral exemplarity shifts from Alexander's humbling confrontation of Diogenes to Alexander's liberality and self-conquest in the bestowal of his beloved mistress Campaspe on her artist Apelles. As I shall point out below (see the epilogue), the most revealing feature of the recast version (the *refundición*) is the reduction of Juan Labrador and the transformative paradoxes in his relationship with the king. The peasant's humanistic challenge to absolutism's orthodox political and social conceptions is contained and trivialized through comedic stereotype. The only truly wise man in this conservative drama is the Spanish monarch, who displaces the troubled French king—no less a figure than medieval Spain's great philosopher-king Alfonso el Sabio. See Juan de Matos Fragoso, *El sabio en su retiro y villano en su rincón*, ed. BAE, vol. 47 (Madrid, 1858), 211.

48. *De republica libri sex* (Lyon, 1609); specific references here and in the next several paragraphs are from 6:ch.3, 137ff.; emphasis added. See Kantorowicz's discussion in *The King's Two Bodies*, 418–419.

49. Lope de Vega, *El villano en su rincón*, 116. The paradoxes continue as the king learns that the "ricos tesoros" of David and Solomon are contained in the dust of their funeral urns. At this point he describes the provocative words on Juan Labrador's tomb as an "octava maravilla" that deserves to be written in "letras de diamante."

50. See the epilogue below.

51. For suggestive psychoanalytical observations, from a Lacanian perspective, on this obsession, see W. R. Blue, "The Imprisoning Look: *El villano en su rincón*," *Gestos: Teoría y Práctica del Teatro Hispánico* 7 (1992): 37–49.

52. For the celebratory depiction of exemplary models in the *Fürstenspiegel* tradition, see Skinner, *The Foundations of Modern Political Thought*, 1:118.

53. *Empresas políticas*, 313–314; emphasis added. One should note Saavedra Fajardo's sensitivity to the antithesis *ojos-entendimiento*. Lope's utopian play dramatizes the overcoming of an opposition that the pragmatic theorist takes to be an inescapable fact of political life.

54. For the widespread elevation of rulers through metaphorical identification with cosmic and natural powers, see Roy Strong's *Art and Power: Renaissance Festivals, 1450–1650* (Suffolk, 1984). Strong points out that the ceremonial entry of Henry IV in Avignon "includes an arch dedicated to Henry as Apollo Economico, the god who '*gouverne tout l'Universe par ses rayons et occultes influences,*'" and in which the king appeared bearing up the celestial sphere. For Olivares's project to "deify" Philip IV as the "rey planeta," see Elliott, "Power and Propaganda," 162–188.

55. See J. Le Goff, "La structure et le contenu idéologique de la cérémonie du sacre," in J. Le Goff et al., *Le sacre royal à l'époque de Saint Louis* (Paris, 2001), 19–35. For the Porte St. Denis as the traditional entry gate of kings and the spectacular celebratory passage in 1549 of the new king, Henry II, identified with Typhis, the inventor of navigation, and Hercules, the latter likened to Francis I in features, see R. E. Giesey, "Models of Rulership in French Royal Ceremonial," in *Rites of Power*, ed. S. Wilentz (Philadelphia, 1985), 41–64.

56. It should be noted, however, that the comic counterpoint in the play's analytical examination of the awesome character of the royal figure, which is to be so prominent at thé climactic moments of Act II (in the ludicrous and ineffectual seductive powers of the king) and Act III (in the scatological notes in the peasants' chorus of terror before the royal icons and their impending castigation), actually begins in Act I. In the scene of the king's initial appearance in the play (115),

a group of peasants fail to recognize him at the church where they await his entry (the dialogue is reproduced at the beginning of the preceding section, "The Human King and His Limitations"). Their reaction humorously points up the difference between the human body and the official images of rulers. To recall Gracián, the humorous reaction of the spectators emphasizes "lo humano," and it is here quite literally dissociated from the official imaging or representation of the king, the "discursive" composition of the official monarch that Louis Marin has studied as the "portrait of the king." In its peculiarities the little scene demonstrates the pervasiveness of the play's concern with analyzing the charisma of the royal body and exposing the humanity of the real body that it conceals.

57. "Item, Rex Franciae duos habet bonos angelos custodes: unum ratione suae privatae personae, alterum ratione dignitatis regalis" (The king of France has two good angels as his guards: one for his private person, the other for the sake of his royal dignity) (Grassaille, *Regalium Franciae libri duo*, I ius xx [Paris, 1545], 210; cited by Kantorowicz, "Mysteries of State," 88). In emphasizing the fundamental difference that distinguishes king and court favorite (*privado*) even in the most perfect friendship that they can enjoy—described as the composition of a "double creature," conjoined in "being and will"—the Marqués de Valisero reminds Philip IV that the minister, a "mere atom," can never possess the light that the sun has given the king and reminds him: "Si dos ángeles ha dado/Dios al Rey, su parecer/más acertado ha de ser/que el parecer del Privado" (If God has given the King two angels, his opinion must be more on the mark than that of his royal Favorite [the chief minister]) (Quevedo, *Cómo ha de ser el privado*, in *Teatro inédito* [Madrid, 1927], 10–11).

58. In "The Imprisoning Look," Blue notes that the verb *ver* appears more than one hundred and fifty times in the play.

59. Cited in Marin, *Portrait of the King*, 32.

60. One can understand the king's agitation in traditional ethical and psychological terms as a condition of envy. The king and his interlocutor describe it as such: "¿Cómo envidias a un villano,/tú con el cetro en la mano;/y él con el arado allí?" (How is it that you envy a *villano*, you with the royal scepter in your hand; and he with his plow out there?) But the grounds of such envy appear to be unfathomable. A parallel with the second canto of the hagiographic epic *Isidro de Madrid*, Lope's greatest attempt to elevate the plow over the scepter, is difficult to overlook. In the earlier work it is the allegorical figure Envy who experiences and expresses the king's sentiments, exhorting the devil to attack the pious farmer Isidro with slander and disturb the contented, saintly idyll of his world, where the simple peasant is honored more highly than the most gallant courtier, pride is trampled by oxen and asses, and the irresistibly attractive powers of monarchy and its consecrated insignias are unknown. "¿Mirad de qué gran Monarcha/envidió el rico dosel?/¿o qué armas cuelgan dél,/sino allí un trillo, una abarca/y una antipara de piel?" (Look, who was the great king whose richly adorned canopy he ever envied? Or what arms hang from the curtain of his dwelling other than a threshing fork, a rustic sandal, and a leather screen?) (Lope de Vega, *Obras sueltas* [Madrid, 1777], 11:52–55). However, in transposing or "rewriting" his hagiographic scene, Lope is not concerned with demonizing the king or looking on his motivation in theological terms. The king's agitation should be seen as rooted in his troubled awakening to a voice within, a voice of a secret sharer as it were, which, calling his attention to the other self that exists beneath his royal persona, arouses anxieties about the substantiality of that persona, demands recognition, and imposes moral obligations. While absolutist thinking, as Kantorowicz has pointed

out, tended to deemphasize the traditional distance between the royal body of the monarch and an underlying real body, Lope's unusual play calls attention to the importance of that distance and suggests the kind of profound insights into the dynamics of monarchist absolutism that we associate with the critical *desengaño* of Pascal or the laments of some of Shakespeare's kings (e.g., Henry V on the eve of the Battle of Agincourt, envying those whose identities are not burdened with the responsibilities and ceremonies of the royal figure). Is the king's anxiety and confusion simple envy or merely stoic perturbation, or does it conceal a piercing intuition into the fictional and even phantasmic character of the king's consecrated royal body—an awareness that in such a theatrically constituted political world order, the king, as spectacle, is just as dependent on the gaze of the spectators as the latter are dependent on his animating gaze? See Marin, *Portrait of the King*, 32. At this point Lope's king can recognize that his tormenting desires are far deeper and far more complex than those generated by sexual instinct (suggested by his initial admiration of Lisarda's wit and suspected by Finardo when he observes the king's perturbation at the beginning of Act II), but he has yet to discover that their object is integrity of being and authenticity—the true crown—within a society dominated by political and social ritual (see below).

61. The intimate connection of Lope's play with moral philosophy, a connection that monarchist interpretations tend to overlook, is clearly revealed by Victor Dixon's fine study of the sources of the play. Drawing on popular Renaissance encyclopedias, miscellanies, and other reference works—compendia of anecdotes, aphorisms, and apothegms; anthologies of classical philosophers' speculations; and emblem books visualizing their insights—Lope succeeds in populating his work with a striking number of classical philosophical voices (e.g., Seneca, Epictetus, Diogenes, Aristotle, Solon, Isocrates, Philemon, and Plutarch) and associating the issues of morality, politics, and power raised in the encounter of king and peasant with their insights. "*Beatus . . . Nemo: El villano en su rincón*, las 'Polianteas' y la literatura de emblemas," *Cuadernos de Filología* 3 (1981): 279–300. For the prominence of emblems in the total conception of the work, see my discussion of the king's theater below.

62. See C. L. Barber, *Shakespeare's Festive Comedy: A Study of Dramatic Form and Its Relation to Social Custom* (Princeton, 1959), 136. See also P. Demetz, "The Elm and the Vine: Notes toward the History of a Marriage Topos," *PMLA* 73 (1958): 521–532.

63. See Louis Delatte, ed., *Traités de la royauté d'Ecphante, Diotogène et Sthénidas* (Liège, 1942); esp. Diotogène, 52–56.

64. *Empresas políticas*, 609. In view of the paradoxical overcoming and integration of "Machiavellianism" in the dominant political utopianism of Act III (see below), it is useful to recall Machiavelli's advocacy of the fruitful cultivation and balancing of divisiveness, discord, and conflict in the politics of states.

65. In the numerous exchanges that are enacted in the relations of Juan and the king, the most important are their parallel "metatheaters."

66. One might note that *desengaño* in this context suggests nothing less than that the royal majesty is *engaño*. Nevertheless, Lope's traditional conciliatory approach to the split between office and humanity should be distinguished from the severity of the dark perspective that was to become customary in Baroque art—e.g., Valdés Real's scenes from the crypt, Saavedra Fajardo's concluding emblem depicting the skull of the prince, Calderón's Segismundo's discovery of the phantasmic nature of the royal body (see epilogue below). See L. Spitzer's study of Saint-Simon's descriptions of the court of Louis XIV ("Saint-Simons Porträt Ludwig XIV," in his *Romanische Stil- und*

Literaturstudien [Marburg, 1931], 1–47), and W. Benjamin's discussion of the representation of kings and tyrants in the German *Trauerspiel* of the epoch (*Ursprung des deutschen Trauerspiels* [Berlin, 1928]). Focusing as it does on a philosophical exploration of the nature of man in the context of the realities of royal power, Lope's play can be viewed as the antithesis of Shakespeare's *King Lear*, where the king's journey into the natural world culminates in a destructive vision of the cruelties of the most debased kind of political activity and of political power as completely disconnected from any substantial model, whether in a metaphysically founded cosmic order or in an ideal human being exemplifying universal reason.

67. In his late *Egloga a Claudio* Lope asks his patron to retire from the "center" of the palace to the "margin," where, as "Democritus and Heraclitus," they can quietly review his life. As he stoically "intenta desatarse de sí mismo" (attempts to detach himself from himself), prepares to say farewell to hope, and readies himself for his "fatal destino" and the "senda del morir mas clara," he offers an account of his literary achievements and the numerous specific works that he leaves to posterity. The review climaxes in a description of his *villano*, a description that might recall the fascinating vision that awaited the king of France. "Describir el villano al fuego atento,/quando con puntas de cristal las tejas/detienen las ovejas,/o quando mira exento/como de trigo y de maduras uvas/se colman trojes, y rebosan cubas,/¿A quién se debe, Claudio?" (To describe the *villano* tending to his fire while, with their barbs of ice, the lime trees restrain the sheep, and he, freed from toil, contemplates his barns filled to the brim with wheat and his casks overflowing with the wine of ripened grapes, To whom, Claudio, is all this owed?) (*Rimas humanas y otros versos*, ed. Antonio Carreño [Barcelona, 1998], 696–697; 715–716).

68. See Y. Malkiel, "Las vicisitudes etimológicas de rincón," *Revista de Filología Española* 70 (1990): 5–44.

69. See *Epistolario de Lope de Vega Carpio*, ed. A. G. de Amezúa (Madrid, 1935–1943), 3:193. See also: "Bien aya vn rincón sin obligaciones ni capillas, donde son los gustos gustos, y los daños no son daños. Los frenos se hizieron para los caballos. Quien se dexa gobernar de otro, con el herrador se calza. . . . Al fin al fin se cansan todos, y el tiempo passa, que va siempre quitando la vida" (Blessed is a corner free of obligations, free of chapels, where pleasures are truly pleasures, and injuries are not really injuries. Bridles were made for horses. Whoever lets himself be governed by another wears shoes put on by the blacksmith. . . . At the end of it all everybody becomes weary, and time continues to pass, continually snatching away their lives) (4:54–55).

70. See *Paradoxas racionales*, ed. E. Buceta (Madrid, 1935), xl.

71. The particular tensions that mark Lope's adaptation of the event are illuminated by the contemporary version in the political writings of Botero. To sharpen the contrast of emperor and philosopher, he precedes the encounter with a lengthy, detailed description of the tireless movements of the conquering Alexander and the immensity of his empire ("Hor l'imperio, da lui conquistato, dalla Gange alle Are de' Fileni, dalle bocche del Danubio all' Oceano Indico"; the empire, conquered by him from the Ganges to the Altars di Fileni [Libya], from the mouth of the Danube to the Indian Ocean). Despite such achievements and such splendor, the stationary Diogenes "does not deign" to leave his sufficient space and visit the conqueror. Botero goes on to interpret Alexander's desire "to be Diogenes" as indicative of his awareness that the philosopher has achieved the very goal to which he, the ruler, aspired. He has paradoxically gained eminence above other men through not esteeming the greatest prince of his time. See *I Prencipi* (Torino, 1600), 7–8. In

El villano one can compare the parallel descriptions of the vast expanses of the sprawling French kingdom and the firmly integrated estate of Juan Labrador, centered behind a containing grove of chestnut trees with which he identifies.

72. *Obras de Lope de Vega,* ed. BAE (Madrid, 1972), 250:179–183. C. Bruerton points out that this play, based on a novella by Bandello, was first published in 1609 in *Parte II* of Lope's works but was mentioned in the catalogue of the *Peregrino* in 1603, titled, fittingly in view of its elements of royal panegyric, *El primer Médicis.* In my opinion, Bruerton's argument for its remarkable aspects in anticipating the *comendador*-peasant honor masterpieces is reinforced by its early articulation of the philosophical and political concerns of Lope's later works. See "*La Quinta de Florencia,* Fuente de *Peribáñez*," *Nueva Revista de Filología Hispánica* 4 (1950): 27–39.

73. While the king's insight into human heterogeneity is focused primarily on differences in moral behavior, conceived hierarchically in terms of bad–good, it points to an aspect of Juan Labrador's determined "apartness" and "resistance"—incomprehensible initially to the doctrinaire monarch—that in fact rises above all conventional wisdom of the age (and its literature) and touches on the most profound implications of the paradoxy of the play (see my final section below).

74. See *The Moral Discourses of Epictetus,* tr. E. Carter (New York, n.d.), 275. The sonnet's antithetical development of the fundamental images of the muddy torrent and the clear fountain incorporates recurrent Stoic motifs associated with tranquility, clarity, proportion, and spiritual freedom. Compare, for example, Seneca's *On Anger* (III, vi): "There is no surer proof of greatness than to be in a state where nothing can possibly happen to disturb you. The higher region of the universe, being better ordered and near to the stars, is condensed into no cloud, is lashed into no tempest, is churned into no whirlwind; it is free from all turmoil; it is in the lower regions that the lightnings flash. In the same way the lofty mind is always calm at rest in a quiet haven" (*Moral Essays,* tr. J. W. Basore, Loeb Classical Library [London, 1928], 269). Dixon has suggested that Epictetus's text, as well as the argument distinguishing man from the animals, attributed to Philemon, was available to Lope in Stobaeus's *Sententiae, ex thesauris Graecorum delectae* (Geneva, 1609) (see "*Beatus . . . Nemo,*" 279–300). He notes that Lope's mistaken attribution of Epictetus's insights to Socrates can be accounted for in the anthology's presentation of a series of passages from Isocrates immediately preceding the cited material. For an attempt to dissociate Lope's literary elevation of the *labrador* from any substantial engagement with classical and humanist values, see F. Márquez Villanueva, *Lope: Vida y valores* (Río Piedras, 1988). According to Márquez's argument, Lope's creation of the "myth" has nothing to do with either an ethical ideal or an accurate reflection of economic conditions and agricultural realities. It is rather a centerpiece of an obscurantist ideological project designed to conceal the true conditions of misery and ignorance of the peasantry and, more important, to counter, with an archaic utopian fantasy, the various progressive historical forces menacing Spain's traditional social order and value system—humanism, cosmopolitanism, technology, *arbitrismo,* and specifically the caste most receptive to modernist critical thinking, the *conversos.* See 68, 77, 87–88, 92–93, 103.

75. See Nussbaum, *The Therapy of Desire: Theory and Practice in Hellenistic Ethics* (Princeton, 1994), esp. ch. 9; on Seneca's image of the sage (*Epistle* 41), see 339–341. One should note that Lope's bonding of king and Stoic sage extends a tradition that goes back to the late medieval jurists. Sage and prince possess everything—the former, philosophically; the latter, juridically. Possession is in neither case literal or *de facto.* The "dominion" of both should be understood

as founded in morality. Seneca, the "best jurist," proves this in *De Beneficiis*, 7:3ff. See Kantorowicz, *The King's Two Bodies*, 472–473, who points out the importance of the connection in the historical elaboration of the suprahuman side of the "two-body system."

76. Juan Labrador in the court becomes the missing mirror, sought by the lost king, both as "modeling mirror," holding the image of perfection by which to measure oneself, and the "mirror of truth," in its uncompromising revelations of the candid *privado*. See, for example, Quevedo's offering of his treatise *Marco Bruto* to Philip IV: "Yo hago oficio de espejo, que les [los reyes] hago ver en sí lo que en sí no pueden ver" (I am doing the job of mirror, for I make them [the kings] see in themselves what in themselves they cannot see) (*Obras completas*, ed. Astrana Marín [Madrid, 1932], 1:601). See Ariadna García-Bryce, "On Rulership and Conspiracy in Quevedo's *Marco Bruto*," *Confluencia* 18 (2003): 182–195.

77. See Northrop Frye, "Varieties of Literary Utopias," in *The Stubborn Structure: Essays on Criticism and Society* (Ithaca, NY, 1970), 109–134. In its development of pastoral elements, *El villano en su rincón* can be compared with Lope's most famous "peasant" play, *Fuenteovejuna*. In both dramas, the village, with its bucolic order of philosophical symposia, games, gardening, dances, perfect love, morality, courtesy, and sociability, becomes the model for a perfected Spanish order and is carefully aligned with the aspirations of the monarchs. In their representations of monarch, peasant, and noble, as well as in their explorations of political issues, the plays are, of course, very different.

78. They have, for the most part, preferred to ignore its climactic positioning in the action and to turn a deaf ear to its striking dissonances, particularly when arguing that the play is a celebration of monarchist ideology or a "rectification" of the pastoral ideal for its various shortcomings—its moral egotism, its retreat from civic responsibility, its advocacy of idleness, and its escapism. F. D. Wardlaw argues that Lope is criticizing Juan Labrador in his "self-centered pursuit of happiness" and "selfish spontaneity" and affirming that "a life responsibly lived amid the difficulties of civilization offers greater personal rewards than a complacent vegetation in the peace and security of a country retreat." Finding no paradoxical or contestatory power in the peasant's position, the interpretation regards the plot as clumsy and inept ("*El villano en su rincón*: Lope's Rejection of the Pastoral Dream," *BHS* 58 [1981]: 113–119). Implicitly invoking the familiar arguments based on Lope's alleged sloppiness and lack of concern with inconsistencies, Bataillon briefly describes the fragmentary secondary plot as "el mínimo indispensable de intriga sentimental" and dismisses it as marginal to the central concerns of the play ("*El villano en su rincón*," 351). Dixon argues that any "lasciviousness" on the part of the king would clash with his presentation in the rest of the *comedia* and suggests that his indecorous behavior should be understood as disorientation rather than lust and that it indicates "the extent to which the courtier is a fish out of water in the rural environment" ("*Beatus . . . Nemo*," 294). Dixon appears to be endorsing J. E. Varey's refusal to attribute lascivious desires to the king (Varey, "Towards an Interpretation of Lope de Vega's 'El villano en su rincón,'" *Studies in Spanish Literature of the Golden Age Presented to Edward M. Wilson*, ed. R. O. Jones [London, 1973], 315–337, esp. 325–326). Casalduero provides a more imaginative, if even less convincing, approach by arguing that in his sexual aggressiveness, the king is subjecting the chastity of the house to a test, which, in its perfection, it easily passes ("Sentido y forma de *El villano en su rincón*," 54, 58). Brancaforte goes well beyond Casalduero in transposing the scene into a religious context. The king's pursuit of Lisarda must be looked at as an allegory of "an envious Christ who wants all love directed toward him" ("Lope's *El villano*

en su rincón," 65). While insisting on the importance of love in the play's resolution of the political problems that it confronts, Wardropper says nothing about the king's erotic advances ("La venganza de Maquiavelo"). On the other hand, McKendrick finds in the episode support for her rejection of the fashionable view that Lope's drama should be understood as monarchist propaganda. The king's sexual behavior is an indication of a "lack of royal judgement," as is his retention of Juan Labrador at court at the end. She argues that the former's "astonishing vision of social equality" is unrealistic and cannot be taken seriously. The play, despite its extraordinary suggestive power, remains illogical and caught in unresolved contradictions. See *Playing the King*, 192–193.

79. The transgressive implications of his soliloquy in the forest at the border of Juan Labrador's world become clearer at this point. In an unexpected display of literary self-consciousness, one of the numerous "meta-literary moments" of this complex play, he speaks of his intentions to provide material for an *historia* that preserves the *memoria* and the *fama* of princes. In other words, he appears to have in mind precisely the genre of royal anecdote and historiette with which the collections of Torquemada and Botero furnished Lope as he designed the primary plot. At the same time the king (and the playwright) signal their awareness of a radical alteration of the literary paradigm in its conventional purposes of instruction and glorification and foreshadow the approaching collision of the two systems. "Hubiera pocas historias/si pensamientos no hubiera,/con que la fama tuviera/en su tiempo estas memorias./No todas añaden glorias/a un príncipe" (There would be few histories if there were no such capricious thoughts [such as those I have acted upon] so that fame might conserve these memories through time. Not all of them add glories to a prince) (149).

80. Maravall, *Teatro y literatura en la sociedad barroca*, 130. Quevedo's statement, from his *Política de Dios*, is cited by Maravall in his *La teoría española del estado*, 224. Maravall's own words paraphrase Machiavelli's *Discorsi*: "The majesty of the dignity trailing the presence of a prince . . . can paralyze a would-be assassin even if the intended princely victim were in a prison. . . . How much greater then when he is surrounded by the majesty of the decorations, the pomp, and his entourage" (cited in Sebastian De Grazia, *Machiavelli in Hell* [Princeton, 1989], 331). In its humanistic treatment of politics, monarchy, and morality, Lope's play can be said to reverse an illustrious imperial maxim that originated in ancient Rome and was frequently invoked by the Canonists of the late Middle Ages in reference to the papacy: "Rome is where the emperor is," even were he "secluded in a peasant's hut." Its survival and topicality in the discourse of absolutism is attested to by one of Spanish drama's many flamboyant spokesmen for the cult of the monarch, Don Gutierre, the protagonist of Calderón's most famous honor tragedy, *El médico de su honra*. The doubling of king and protagonist is one of identification; the latter welcomes the *infante*, who unexpectedly arrives in his country house, in the extravagant rhetoric of the cult of the king and its metaphysical conceptions concerning royal ubiquity and beneficence: "Y honrad por tan breve espacio/esta esfera, aunque pequeña;/porque el sol no se desdeña,/después que ilustró un palacio,/de iluminar el topacio/de algún pajizo arrebol./Y pues sois rayo español,/descansad aquí; que es ley/hacer el palacio el rey/también, si hace esfera el sol" (And honor, briefly, this sphere, although small, because the sun is not too proud, after having illuminated a palace, to brighten the topaz of a straw-thatched aurora. And, as you are the sun's rays of Spain, rest here, for it is the law that, just as the sun creates its sphere, the king creates his palace). See D. W. Cruickshank, ed. (Madrid, 1989), 90. *El villano*, with its eccentric *rincón*, points in a different

direction: true majesty has nothing to do with such metaphysical emanations, magical spaces, and confirming rituals (including "honorable" bloodshed). It is rather to be found wherever a truly good man dwells (see Kantorowicz, *The King's Two Bodies,* 203–205). In its momentary collapse of generic boundaries, Lope's scene appears to go beyond the limits of the shocking surprises and intrigues characteristic of the *comedia de capa y espada.* It in fact incorporates the coarse humor and contemptuous ironies at the expense of palace behavior and the hypocrisies lurking behind its elaborate codes of etiquette that are recorded in numerous satirical anecdotes that circulated privately in the court and were frequently transcribed in the personal writings of foreign observers. For example, François Bertaut and Madame d'Aulnoy describe the tart response of a lady who refused to open her bedroom door to the prowling Philip IV: "Vaya, vaya con Dios; no quiero ser monja" (Go, go with God; I have no desire to be a nun), alluding to the fate of numerous palace ladies who dutifully respond to the king's erotic needs and expectations and subsequently found themselves with no alternative to the cloister when they were inevitably discarded by the sated monarch or discovered by the jealous queen. Cited in José Deleito y Piñuela, *El rey se divierte* (Madrid, 1935), 24–25.

81. See Le Goff, "La structure et le contenu idéologique de la cérémonie du sacre," 19–35, 270.

82. J. A. Rodríguez de Lancina, *Comentarios políticos a los Anales de Cayo Vero Cornelio Tácito;* cited by Maravall, *La teoría española del estado,* 224.

83. Of the numerous imaginative links between the dream landscape and the subsequent scenes in Juan Labrador's house, probably the most interesting, aside from the displacement of lost hunter and angelic quarry by the king and Lisarda, are the song's complex articulation of doubles (e.g., two *galanes,* two hunters, two mistresses, and two victims of betrayal) and the confusion occasioned by the shifting occupation of two erotic triangles by the knight-hunter. Such procedures and fluid effects, which are quite conventional in the elliptical, suggestive, and oneiric language of folksong, reinforce the ambiguous mingling of agents (e.g., Otón-king-hunter, Lisarda [*serafín*]-*serrana* [*serafín*], Otón's "labyrinth"-king's "labyrinth") that dominates the imaginative atmosphere of the entire play and climaxes in the gemination of peasant and king in the transfigured *palacio-aldea* at the conclusion.

84. See Maravall, *Teatro y literatura en la sociedad barroca,* 14. Monod emphasizes the importance of the equestrian royal portrait in the early period of the nation state: "Representations of the king on horseback were meant to demonstrate the ability to rule, with the horse standing for the kingdom and the people" (*The Power of Kings,* 319–320).

85. See Hans Flasche, "Die Struktur des Hof-Laudatio in den 'Loas' der 'Autos' Calderóns," *Europäische Hofkultur im 16. und 17. Jahrhundert,* Kongress des Wolfenbüttler Arbeitskreises für Renaissanceforschung und des internationalen Arbeitskreises für Barockliteratur (Hamburg, 1981), 2:277–283.

86. *Empresas políticas,* 224–225; emphasis added.

87. *The State and the Rule of Law,* tr. Marc A. LePain and Jeffrey C. Cohen (Princeton, 1995).

88. Bk. 3, ch. 2. See Francisco Suárez, *Selections,* tr. G. L. Williams et al. (Oxford, 1944), 373–374.

89. In one of Lope's most festive and doctrinaire celebrations of the royal figure and the royal institution, *Carlos V en Francia,* among the emperor's most important triumphs is his exemplary refusal to accept the sexual favors of a respectable woman who, driven to insanity by his charisma, celebrity, heroics, and power, imagines that she is his queen and desires his embraces. Claiming that men "aman quanto/cerca de los ojos ven" (love whatever comes in sight), she insists: "Gózele y

muérame luego" (May I enjoy him and then die). He politely refuses her offer and determines to provide for her proper care as a madwoman. See *Carlos V en Francia*, ed. A. G. Reichenberger (Philadelphia, 1962), esp. 93, 111, 123. One might recall that Spain's most famous dramatic celebration of the education of a king, *La vida es sueño*, reaches its climax in the young prince's temptation to rape the woman he desires.

90. The view of an "emancipated" human agency in this turn toward the conception of the state as "humanly empowered" was characteristically pessimistic, whether the pessimism was rooted in Christian-Augustinian or secular and Machiavellian anthropologies. (The ways in which the scene could validate a Freudian model for the understanding of the disorderly forces and the mechanisms of control in the self, society, and state [i.e., id-hunter-king/superego-shepherd-philosopher] are obvious.) At the beginning of his deeply pessimistic *Política de Dios* Quevedo underscores the fallibility of the human will and the "internal" usurpation that erupts in the destructive behavior of tyrants: "Les conviene [a los Reyes] no solo no dar el primer lugar a la voluntad propia, pero ninguno . . . y no desluzirá su nombre aquella escandalosa sentencia, que insolente y llena de vanidad, haze formidables a los Tiranos: *Sic volo, sic iubeo, sit pro ratione voluntas*" (It is fitting for kings not only not to give the first place to their own will but to give it no place at all . . . and their name will not be tarnished by that scandalous *sententia* which, insolent and full of vanity, makes tyrants formidable: *Thus do I wish, thus do I decree; may my will be reason enough*) (44). As I suggest below, Lope's resolution of political problems raised by the play should be situated in the more optimistic anthropological traditions of Christian humanism and Scholastic philosophy. For a suggestive analysis of *King Lear* as a pre-Hobbesian work that nearly calls into question the very possibility of kingship and state, given such pessimistic insight into darker directions of the human will and the fundamental emptiness of the cosmos (it "drove the foundations of legitimacy to bedrock"), see Kernan, *Shakespeare*, 102–104.

91. *Obras de Lope de Vega*, ed. RAE, vol. 7 (Madrid, 1897), 66.

92. Prudence, as the "master virtue for the prince or político" (see R. Bireley, *The Counter-Reformation Prince: Anti-Machiavellianism or Catholic Statecraft in Early Modern Europe* [Chapel Hill, 1990], 200), was associated with attention to particular situations and circumstances, caution, moderation, and the capacity for timely intervention. As a practical virtue focused on the goals of bringing about the success and assuring the conservation of the state, it could easily be interpreted in such a way as to countenance and dignify such morally questionable political practices as accommodation, equivocation, dissimulation, and outright deception—an area associated with Machiavelli's precepts. Lipsius developed a concept of "mixed prudence" based on a useful distinction that Saavedra Fajardo describes as follows: "Huyendo de los extremos de Maquiavelo y pareciéndole que no podría gobernar el príncipe sin alguna fraude o engaño, persuadió el leve, toleró el medio y condenó el grave. Peligrosos confines para el príncipe" (Fleeing from the extremes of Machiavelli and recognizing that the prince could not govern without a measure of fraud or deception, he counseled the minor, tolerated the medium, and condemned the serious. Dangerous boundaries for the prince) (*Empresas políticas*, 404). Saavedra Fajardo attempts to set the boundaries for such licit equivocation. The prince must not lie and present things that do not exist. However, he must develop the "astuteness" of the dissimulator, who hides things through silence ("el príncipal instrumento de reinar" [406]), and allows others to misinterpret appearances and "things unsaid." Christ himself practices such equivocation for beneficial effects. As I suggest below, the confusing machinations of Lope's king in Act III, which are essential to the

buildup of suspense at the crisis of this romantic comedy, can be interpreted as an exemplification of this kind of attempt to reconcile the new political theories with traditional moral values.
Lope's denouement has, of course, no place for the more disabused qualifications by Saavedra
Fajardo, who concludes his discussion of prudence with a "Calderonian" admission that "las
sombras de la razón de Estado suelen ser mayores que el cuerpo" (the shadows of state reason are
usually larger than the body), with frequent destructive results for those who involve themselves
in the activities of politics (see *Empresas políticas*, 401–408; for Lipsius and "mixed prudence,"
see Bireley, *The Counter-Reformation Prince*, 85–88).

93. *Empresas políticas*, 310.

94. Ibid., 401.

95. See my discussion of *La vida es sueño* in the epilogue below.

96. See *El criticón*, 1:94–114. For Gracián, not only the state, but the individual himself as well is situated theatrically on an "unfounded" stage amid a surrounding emptiness. Hence he formulates
a rhetorical "state reason of the self" and can depict, in one of the climactic epiphanies for his
questing pilgrims, the image of the tightrope walker performing perilously above a gaping crowd
of adorers. See my "Gracián's Theaters of Nothingness," in *Sin fronteras: Ensayos de literatura
comparada en homenaje a Claudio Guillén*, ed. D. Villanueva, A. Monegal, and E. Bou (Madrid,
1999), 215–229.

97. While one might be tempted to speak of the importance of considerations of genre in this
"comedic" overcoming of such "threats" of regal power—true to the spirit of the folkloric version
of Torquemada's fairy tale—one might also argue, following Victoria Kahn's recent reassessment
of Machiavellian rhetoric, that Lope's resubstantiation of a theater and iconology of power in
Act III represents a true understanding of the neutrality in Machiavelli's advocacy of rhetoric for
political purposes and as such goes well beyond the commonplaces of the countless contemporary denunciations of the Italian theorist. On the other hand, it is consistent with interpretations
of several theorists of the age, particularly those of the leading Machiavellian of the Counter-
Reformation, Giovanni Botero, whose *Ragion di Stato* (1589) went through hundreds of editions.
See V. Kahn, *Machiavellian Rhetoric: From the Counter-Reformation to Milton* (Princeton,
1994).

98. Loa, *La segunda esposa y triunfar muriendo, Obras completas*, ed. A. Valbuena Prat (Madrid,
1967), 3:427. The importance of the visualization and theatricalization of dogma and power in
the religious culture of the period has been well studied by art historians, but only relatively
recently have critics looked closely at the importance of visibility in the absolutist state's establishment and maintenance of authority. As Hobbes put it, the state must "rely on a manifest
visible power to keep the subjects in awe" (cited in C. Pye, "The Sovereign, the Theater, and
the Kingdome of Darknesse: Hobbes and the Spectacle of Power," *Representations* 8 [1984]:
85–106). See also C. Geertz, "Centers, Kings, and Charisma: Reflections on the Symbolics of
Power," *Anthropology* (New York, 1983), 121–146. For the psychological dynamics of such rituals
of display and royal "choreographing," see Rudolph zur Lippe, who considers analogies with sha-
manistic practices and the process of self-appropriation that attends them (*Naturbeherschung am
Menschen II: Geometrisierung des Menschen und Repräsentation des Privaten im französischen
Absolutismus* [Frankfurt am Main, 1974]). For the deeper implications of Juan Labrador's strange
anxiety concerning loss of identity, see my final section below. Again Gracián is one of the most
penetrating analysts in such matters, noting that the willful self-prostration of the adoring subject

is achieved by the activation *within him* of a psychic process of investing the object of his attention with power over himself, a supernatural spirit, or numen, the source of which is in himself.
"No hace el numen el que lo dora, sino el que lo adora" (The numen is not created by him who
gilds [*dora*] it but rather by him who adores it). In its analogies with traditional understandings
of idolatry, the remark is characteristic of the fluidity marking the religious, political, and social
interchanges of the period. See *Oráculo manual, Obras completas*, 152, where Gracián claims
that the process is inevitably the consequence of dependence. For his criticism of the abuse of
such powers by the king-tyrant, see *El criticón*, 1:94–114, where he describes a hidden tyrant who
carefully choreographs a brutal drama of religiously sanctioned scapegoating to the delight of a
cruel mob of his subjects-audience.

99. It should be noted that the scene, which Bataillon finds explicable only in connection with the
alleged historical and political circumstances of the play's composition, is part of the system of
imaginative elements identifying philosopher and king. The latter's action parallels Juan Labrador's activity as family man and marriage maker in Act II.

100. Otón's assumption regarding the prerogative of a king in acting on his sexual desires was undoubtedly shared by most members of Lope's society and, if the notorious womanizing of a ruler
such as Philip IV is any indication, by the monarch himself. A play such as *El poder en el discreto*
(*Obras de Lope de Vega*, ed. RAE [Nueva edición], vol. 2 [Madrid, 1892]) suggests that it could
be effectively exploited for the entertaining and generally unproblematic confusions of the light-
hearted *comedia de enredo*. Here an attractive young couple's desires to marry are threatened
because the *galán*, a loyal *privado* of the king of Sicily, realizes that the latter is helplessly enthralled by his beloved Serafina. Celio, the *galán*, determines that it is his duty to let the king
have Serafina, even though he knows that the ruler would give her to him if made aware of their
love. Celio's reaction offers a witty reformulation of conventional doctrines of the king's "divine"
connections and the "pleasure principle" commonly invoked to define the tyrant. "Pero nunca
el Cielo quiera/que le quite al Rey su gusto" (But Heaven never wishes that we deprive the King
of his pleasures). He reasons that if one happily loses one's life for a king, what is the loss of a
woman by comparison? The plot runs its conventional course through numerous concealments;
partial truths; misunderstandings; "asides"; witty equivocations; silly fibbing; hilarious evasions
(for example, the *galán* claims to be melancholy and impotent in order to escape marriage with
the king's former lover); and clever tricks by the *gracioso* (his loyal servant and companion in
intrigue), who is constantly menaced with the cruelest of punishments for his brazen manipulations. The king, who can be quite cynical about women and a more than willing schemer, ultimately proves to be benign and wise, suggesting that the traditional assumptions concerning his
absolute privileges are nothing to be feared and that the *galán* had acted on false premises, failing
to recognize that a discreet king would be reasonable in such a case if only the other party had
directly informed him of his love. In effect, the prerogative of the king is, in this play, primarily
a version of the traditional indispensable "blocking agent" of the Plautine comedic formula, a
role usually taken by parents or other representatives of the older generation. It is not called into
question, and no anxieties surround it. Unlike *El villano en su rincón*, the play is not concerned
with exploring in serious terms the complex question of the relation of power to reason and of
the necessary limitation of absolute power of monarch and state. As for the perspective on "royal
sexuality" so frequently developed in the most advanced political theories of the time, its bizarre
deformation borders on the parodistic. Amid the *Villano's* striking integration of various dramatic

genres, literary modes, and poetic forms, the *comedia de enredo*, perhaps the most commonplace of all in its actions, effects, and themes, assumes, like all others, a highly complex and original function.

101. Critics have noted the striking number of emblems in the play. D. W. Moir suggests that its conception owes something to a depiction of a "villano en su rincón" in Sebastián de Covarrubias's *Emblemas morales* (Madrid, 1610). The shepherd is seated beneath a tree, contentedly playing a rustic fiddle before his flock. When asked why he lives *arrinconado*, he responds: "Este *rincón* . . . es el seguro/Dado por Dios, y otro no procuro" (This *corner* . . . is the safe haven given by God, and I seek no other) ("Lope de Vega's *Fuenteovejuna* and the *Emblemas Morales of Sebastián de Covarrubias Horozco* [with a few remarks on *El villano en su rincón*]," in Kossoff and Amor y Vásquez, *Homenaje a William L. Fichter*, 537–546). The commentary emphasizes a quietistic, religious note. See also P. Halkhoree, "Lope de Vega's *El villano en su rincón*: An Emblematic Play" (*Romance Notes* 14 [1972]: 141–145), and Dixon, "*Beatus . . . Nemo*." Antonio Sánchez Romeralo argues that the "political lesson" of the play is far more subtle than Bataillon realized and that its seriousness can be understood if one recognizes its close relations with the flourishing contemporary genre of the political emblem book. Refining on the traditional view of the play, he offers an illuminating exegesis of the final display of the royal icons and concludes that its "lesson" lies in the "punishment" of Juan Labrador for his excessive concern for his own well-being and his insensitivity to the responsibilities of community life ("'El Villano en su Rincón': Lección política," in *Lope de Vega: El teatro*, ed. A. S. Romeralo [Madrid, 1989], 2:299–319). From his early work, *La teoría española del estado* (1944) to his late studies of Baroque culture, Maravall continued to emphasize the intimate connections between the Spanish theater and the rich emblem literature of the seventeenth century. In his view both are instruments of social and political control directed at a new kind of public in the expanding urban centers ("al que se destina el consumo de la literatura barroca"), and both consciously exploit the power in imagery to "move," "overwhelm," and "persuade" their audience. Both aim not at conceptual demonstration, but rather at rhetorical persuasion through the address of the senses. Maravall finds no contradiction between the enigmatic elements of the emblem, and their inevitable activation of an intellectual response, and the rhetorical purposes and effects he attaches to their fundamental plasticity. See "La literatura de emblemas en el contexto de la sociedad barroca," in *Teatro y literatura en la sociedad barroca*, 149–188, esp. 176ff. Also see "Objetivos sociopolíticos del empleo de medios visuales," in *La cultura del barroco* (Madrid, 1975), 497–520. The thematization of viewing and the ambiguous interplay of incorporated emblems in *El villano en su rincón* would suggest that a "Baroque" dramatist could exploit visibility for much more complicated effects and much more enlightening purposes than Maravall's interpretation would appear to allow. The most unconventional and profound aspect of this play, one that none of its imitators and few of its commentators have appeared to notice, is its problematization of the social, political, and existential aspects of "visibility" and "image-making."

102. See Pablo de León, *Guía del Cielo*, ed. V. Beltrán de Heredia (Barcelona, 1963), 153–154).

103. S. L. Brown has noted the echoes of Job in the scene of Juan Labrador's self-prostration ("Goodness and *El villano en su rincón*," *Romance Notes* 14 [1972–1973]: 551–556).

104. See Kriegel's analysis of the violence of feudalism and its opposition to the development of state sovereignty and its fundamental values. "Feudalism is war, *jus vitae necisque*, conscription of human life; sovereign power is peace, security, and prohibition of the taking of human life. It

substitutes law for force and order for death. It consists of a powerful constraint on the Roman *patriae potestas*, on the right to determine who shall live and who shall die. . . . Henceforth, the sovereign who abstains from taking the life or property of his subjects is no longer acting as master. . . . Feudalism 'governs its subjects as the father of a family does his slaves,' writes Bodin. Likewise Loyseau: 'Feudal monarchy runs directly counter to nature, which has made us all free.' . . . For the early modern writers [jurists and political theorists], the individual is not a slave, a thing, or property in any sense, but rather a subject, a person, a locus of liberty. The monarchy and the state profess to enlarge precisely what feudalism sought to annihilate" (*The State and the Rule of Law*, 24–29). As Saavedra Fajardo put it, "la dominación es gobierno, y no poder absoluto, y los vasallos, súbditos y no esclavos" (see above).

105. See Skinner, *Machiavelli*, 21, 41; De Grazia, *Machiavelli in Hell*, 332. One might recall Machiavelli's admiration for Borgia's successful use of a grisly emblem — a man's split body and a knife at its side.

106. Ribadeneira, *The Christian Prince*; cited in Moore, *Religion and the Virtues of the Christian Prince against Machiavelli*, 352.

107. *Empresas políticas*, 654. See also Botero, *Practical Politics* (English translation of *Ragion di Stato* by G. A. Moore) (Washington, D.C., 1949), 86.

108. Dixon notes a possible connection between this scene and Reusner's collection but fails to attribute any particular significance to its function in "the most emblematic of Lope's plays." In his view the drama should be understood primarily as a severe criticism of the peasant's commitment to *autosuficiencia*. See "*Beatus . . . Nemo*," 297.

109. See *Obras de Lope de Vega*, ed. RAE (Nueva edición), 2:519.

110. For this tradition in Stoic thought, which goes back to the teachings of Hierocles, see M. Nussbaum, *The Therapy of Desire*, 342. On the question of the compatibility of self-concern and other-concern in Stoic morality and specifically in Juan Labrador's model sage, Epictetus, see Julia Annas, *The Morality of Happiness* (Oxford, 1993), 274–276: "Stoic theory about other-concern thus differs radically from Aristotelian. . . . It does so in its view of the scope of other-concern, its insistence on progression to completely impartial concerns for all humans as such instead of stopping with a form of *philia* or commitment to particular other people" (276).

111. Cited in Viroli, *From Politics to Reason of State*, 290.

112. See Valdivielso, *El villano en su rincón*, 57. Seen another way, Valdivielso's authoritarian play reaffirms all the dualisms that Lope's dialectical play has overcome. In his most striking and dramatically effective reconstruction, he transforms Lope's opposition of the king's two bodies — king as sacred/king as human (i.e., as the morally exemplary philosopher Juan Labrador) — into the doubleness of God the *transcendent father* and Christ the *human son*, a doubleness and identity that becomes and remains a traditional theological mystery. The "divested" *villano* falls out of a positive opposition of sharing and exchange and becomes *humanus* in its fallen, unregenerate aspect, as simply a Christian desperately in need of divine help, absolutely uninvolved in any mutually enhancing relationship. This is most clear in the transformation of Lope's forest symposium, where an unrecognized Christ displaces the unrecognized king at the table, and the focus of the table talk shifts from the *villano*-sage's reasonable humanity to the mysterious, incomprehensible humanity of Christ, which at this point has no regal, recognizable charisma but which enables the fundamental Christian mystery to occur, the redemption of a helpless sinner — the *villano* (see esp. 50–53).

113. See, for example, Suárez, *A Treatise on Laws and God the Lawgiver*, bk. 3, chs. 1–4, esp. 371 (on Eden), in Suárez, *Selections*.

114. See Kantorowicz, *The King's Two Bodies*, ch. 8, esp. 493.

115. See also Kriegel's historical reconsideration of the origin of statism, in which she stresses its opposition to medieval feudal and imperialist traditions and its foundation in law and a conception of absolute sovereignty (e.g., Bodin) that limits itself by law. One is tempted to turn around her suggestive observation that "Kant's notion of individual morality as self-legislation by a good will is modeled on the politico-legal notion of sovereign power" (*The State and the Rule of Law*, 32). In Lope's play we might go so far as to say that the self-legislating power of sovereignty is modeled on a conception of individual morality represented by the Stoic sage. For a relevant discussion of the Stoic sage's moral fulfillment and Kant's kingdom of ends, see Nussbaum, *The Therapy of Desire*, 354.

116. *Empresas políticas*, 311.

117. See Botero's interpretation of Ovid's myth of creation and his association of majesty, fear, and reverence with the establishment of a cosmic order of distinctions and gradations and with the overcoming of the original chaos. Fear is what enables reputation to "make [minds] shrink back, to separate and make unequal" ("The Reputation of the Prince," in *Supplements [Aggiunte] to the Practical Politics (Ragion di Stato)*, tr. and ed. G. A. Moore [Washington, D.C., 1949], 235–236). For the recurrent emphasis on the political functions of fear in contemporary theories of state and monarchy, see Bireley, *The Counter-Reformation Prince*. See also Jean Delumeau, *Sin and Fear: The Emergence of Western Guilt Culture, 13th–18th Centuries*, tr. E. Nicholson (New York, 1990).

118. Northrop Frye, *Anatomy of Criticism* (Princeton, 1957), 184.

119. Salomon, *Recherches sur le thème paysan*, 911.

120. See Kantorowicz, *The King's Two Bodies*, 473.

121. *De Beneficiis* 7:1–4; see *Moral Essays*, ed. Loeb Classical Library (London, 1935), 3:455–469.

122. "The mind of the wise man is like the ultra-lunar firmament"; Seneca, *Epistle* 59:16; see *Epistulae Morales* 1, ed. Loeb Classical Library (London, 1917), 420. See also, *De Ira*, 3:6.

123. Seneca, *De Brevitate Vitae*, 7:3; also see *De Ira*, 3:43. See B. Groethuysen, *Philosophische Anthropologie: Mensch und Charakter* (Munich and Berlin, 1931), 63, 69.

124. *Henry IV*, part 2; III, i, 3–31. To understand the subtleties of the philosophical and, implicitly, the psychological and political motivation of the encounter, it is useful to compare it with the theologically grounded scene of Lucifer's assault on Lope's *villano* saint in *El Isidro*. The peasant hero's contentment, humility, innocence, and joy in family, labor, and cultivation of God's creation arouse envy and fury in the antagonist and, of course, the simple desire to destroy. See 33–64.

125. Modern interpreters have tended to disregard the significance of the secondary plot, following Bataillon: the love affair of Lisarda and Otón offers "el mínimo indispensable de intriga sentimental." See *"El Villano en su rincón,"* 351. On the other hand, contemporary readers such as Valdivielso and Matos Fragoso appear to have been much more aware of the unappealing side of Lope's protagonist, transforming him, in the one case, into the obstinate sinner and, in the other, trivializing him as a quaint, amusing rustic whose simplemindedness offers absolutely nothing of a philosophical challenge to the monarch, who, transformed into Alfonso the Wise, is the only

wise man in the play. Both "rewritings" are notable as deambiguations of Lope's open, para-doxical, and transgressive dramatic world. In an English drama inspired by Lope's play, James Shirley's *The Royal Master* (1637), the peasant is similarly transformed into a comic figure, stub-bornly refusing attention and honors, never coming into contact with the royal master, and never standing as a focus of moral value and purity in opposition to a courtly world marked by excessive ambition and the deceitful use of language. See Luciano García, "The Motif of the Reluctance to See the King in Lope de Vega's *El Villano en su rincón* and James Shirley's *The Royal Master*," Review of English Studies 54 (2003): 365–385.

126. The play is attributed to Lope de Vega. See *El palacio confuso*, ed. Charles Henry Stevens (New York, 1939), 7, 79–80.

127. See *Obras de Lope de Vega*, ed. BAE, 247 (Madrid, 1971), 373, 376, 345–346, 382. It should be pointed out that the *comedia*, despite its cynicism and irreverence, ends with an abrupt comedic turn, a reward for all the deserving players, and an arbitrary act of beneficence by the "ungrateful" king following the unlucky hero's failure in the fairy tale ordeal of the choice of chests.

128. The danger of loss of autonomy under the awesome gaze of the king had in fact become prov-erbial by the epoch of Charles V. In his *Diálogo de la lengua* (1536) Juan de Valdés offers the following as his first example of the pure Castilian language contained in proverbs: "Esse es rey, el que no vee rey," a proverb to which the folkloric figure of Juan Labrador became attached by the early seventeenth century. See Bataillon, *El Villano en su rincón*, 347–348. Antonio Sánchez Romeralo points out that the proverb survives in the modern tradition: "Quien no ve al rey, ése es rey" ("'El Villano en su Rincón,'" 300). Already in the twelfth century, the "incinerating effects of the royal figure on those who approach" was acknowledged in Pedro Alfonso's *Disciplina clericalis*: "Rex est similis igni" (see above). Lisón Tolosana notes that the Habsburg court situated the king in "el místico universo del tabu." "Lo sagrado es peligroso, *tremendum*; debe ser respetado, protegido, aureolado de inaccessibilidad, vetado" (*La imagen del rey*, 148–149). The conception is evoked by Juan Labrador's daughter, the self-assertive Cos-tanza, whose "modernist" defiance of class boundaries in her approach to the tabooed royal figure—associated with the transgression and punishment of Icarus—is in fact rewarded by king and playwright. When in the climactic scenes of the play Lope's peasant tells the king, "Me pareció que solamente el verte/pudiera ser la causa de mi muerte" (195), his extremism is less interesting as a mark of personal idiosyncrasy than as a complete reversal of the central myth of absolutism—the king as vivifying force of all individuals in his state. I suggest that the power of its challenge persists despite the king's response, which concisely formulates the traditional doctrine that universal reason and proportion shine through the image of the king, the mirror and the model being for his subjects' harmonious self-formation. "Vasallo que no se mira/en el Rey, esté muy cierto/que sin concierto ha vivido,/y que vive descompuesto" (200). While the *Villano*'s abiding interrogation of the prevailing political order clearly points up the possibilities for tensions between individual and state and is not entirely silenced in the play's abrupt move-ment toward reconciliation, it falls far short of critically uncovering an absolutist "discourse of power," a kind of calculated manipulation of traditional myths and theological-philosophical conceptions as a "narrative of domination" to be exploited by the absolute monarch as "meta-narrator." The implications of its "counter-discourse" are social and anthropological rather than political. See Marin's comments on the dynamics of "seeing the king" in the imposed, totalizing

theatricality of the absolutist state. "As source producing all light, unbearable to the eye and the gaze, the king's portrait is not only the sun in the central place of the narrative but also the light that spreads out everywhere and that lands in bursts on all and on everyone and *makes* them be seen" (*Portrait of the King*, 67).

129. See A. Forcione, "El desposeimiento del ser en la literatura renacentista: Cervantes, Gracián, y los desafíos de *Nemo*," *Nueva Revista de Filología Hispánica* 34 (1985–86): 654–690.

130. *Oráculo manual, Obras completas,* 186. This is not to say that Neo-Stoic and Neo-Platonic models of cosmic rationality do not appear in Gracián's work and that he does not occasionally speak of man's obligation to attune himself to their harmonies. However, the most interesting feature of Gracián's anthropology is a drama of disengagement from those models, a subversive drama that one can frequently discern even in his seemingly conventional discussions of man. See my "At the Threshold of Modernity."

131. In discussing the "immobilizing function" of the topic of the world theater in Spain of the period, Maravall goes so far as to argue that the drama of Spain's Golden Age accepted and celebrated a heteronomous conception of the self, in which the individual's identity and value were determined entirely by his position within the socio-political configuration of the Baroque state. The reiterated "soy quien soy" of heroes is based on a "concepción estamental de la persona" and has nothing to do with traditional (e.g., Stoic or Christian-Augustinian) notions of autonomy or integrity. Personal fulfillment lies in acting according to what is expected of a person of a certain rank in the social structure—i.e., performing correctly according to a prescribed script before an observing audience of others. See *Teatro y literatura en la sociedad barroca,* chs. 9, 10. Perhaps the most grandiose formulation of the conservative reaction to the contemporary obsession with reality as dependent on visibility is in the numerous, widely read hexameral epics, which situated man as confident spectator in a metaphysically reliable, benign, and readable *theatrum mundi.* See Forcione, "Gracián's Theaters of Nothingness."

132. Miguel de Cervantes, *La Galatea,* ed. J. B. Avalle-Arce (Madrid, 1961), II, 38–39; emphasis added. The translation is based, with some modification, on H. Oelsner and A. B. Welford, *Galatea* (Glasgow, 1903), 161–162.

133. For Gracián's "reaccentuation of the traditional Stoic philosophical anthropology" in his hallucinatory satirical visions of the court in the *Criticón*, see my "At the Threshold of Modernity," 43–44. While the ancient Stoics approached man's existence in terms of such a division, it should be pointed out that their focus was, in a fundamental way, the very opposite of Gracián's. Their project was the sharp delineation and "fortification" of an authentic self that through its spiritual power harmoniously integrated itself into a universal metaphysical order of nature and reason while fighting off the intrusive forces of an external world that would possess the individual and deprive him of authentic being, stability, and integrity. Separation, distance, and the preservation of inner autonomy are the conditions of this self, even when it is at home within the community of fellow citizens and works for the common good. While "theatricalization" is recognized as an inescapable aspect of life in an illusion-ridden society, it is viewed primarily as a disordering of the self rather than as a means of accommodation or a strategy for success. For Seneca the "deepest disgrace" of the soul is to "take the stage in role after role" and never to be itself. In *Epistle* 120 he condemns the inconstancy and "multiformity" of the majority of human beings in their adoptions of different roles and masks. "Believe me, it is a great role—to play the role of one man.

But nobody can be one person except the wise man; the rest of us often shift our masks" (see *Epistulae Morales*, 3, ed. Loeb Classical Library [London, 1925], 395). For the Stoics' emphasis on the self as a firmly delineated, stable, and bounded possession menaced by the alien, see Groethuysen, *Philosophische Anthropologie*, 54ff. Lope's utopian play aims at bringing the universal nature and rationality of the Stoic tradition into alignment with the political order and its official representations and overcoming the division between interior and public fulfillment. The "classical" design does not manage, however, to neatly contain the "modern" notes of protest, alienation, and "individualism."

134. *Paradoxas racionales*, 41–43, 73–74; emphasis added.

135. The relocation of *grandeza* within the new world of state and society is a feature of both plays under consideration in this study. See my discussion of *grandeza* and the "dimensión imperativa de la persona" in the following chapter.

136. In transfiguring the ubiquitous myth of disastrous overreaching, that of Icarus, and the traditional solar motifs of royalty to dignify her transgressiveness—as peasant; egalitarian humanist; intelligent, self-assertive daughter and woman; defier of boundaries and forbidden spaces—Lisarda might be compared to the great contemporary literary modernist, Góngora, as celebrated by his admirer Villamediana: the revolutionary poet is a triumphant Phaeton who displaces the sun, his father; defies the king of the gods, Jupiter; and reilluminates the very cosmos he has grasped and consumed. See my "At the Threshold of Modernity," 27, 55, 57; Rachel Schmidt, "Challenging the Order of the Sun in Góngora's *Soledades*," in *Imagining Culture: Essays in Early Modern History and Literature*, ed. Jonathan Hart (New York, 1996), 165–182.

137. See P. M. Smith, *The Anti-Courtier Trend in Sixteenth Century French Literature* (Geneva, 1966). More recently, C. S. Jaeger, *The Origins of Courtliness: Civilizing Trends and the Formation of Courtly Ideals (930–1210)* (Philadelphia, 1985), and F. Márquez Villanueva, *Menosprecio de corte y alabanza de aldea (Valladolid, 1539) y el tema áulico en la obra de fray Antonio de Guevara* (Santander, 1999).

138. See my observation on the claustrophobia and "desubstantializing" effects of the "palacio sin puertas" in the *Criticón* in "At the Threshold of Modernity," 43–44. In his *comedia de enredo El servir con mala estrella*, Lope's satirical anatomy of the palace world can approach such visionary effects and their pessimistic implications concerning man's sociability. Abandoning Spain as a place of monumental injustice, ambition, envy, ceremony, flattery, and hypocrisy, the disillusioned French knight Rugero offers a grotesque denunciation of the court. It is a "gold coffin whose inhabitants are buried in life"; a "labyrinth" where time, in the form of a Minotaur, torments a weeping figure of "pretensión," whose locks of hair quickly turn white as she stands helplessly amid thousands of "papeles," and where the figure of forgetfulness erases all numbers registering services except the cipher zero. Above the throng the ruler, "el poder," in a travesty of a central myth of the cult of the king, monotonously gives identity to men as figures of clay with one hand, while the other hand disintegrates them. In the heavens above the spectacle, hidden by the clouds, a sinister balance—concentrating the central themes of chance, blind fatality, capricious power, and injustice—distributes rewards in ways hidden from all below (see *Obras de Lope de Vega*, ed. BAE, 247:380–381).

139. Antonio de Guevara, *Menosprecio de corte y alabanza de aldea*, ed. M. Martínez de Burgos (Madrid, 1952), 151.

140. "En la corte muchas cosas haze un cortesano más porque las hazen otros, que no porque las que-
rría él hazer. O pobre del cortesano, el qual . . . aun anda enmascarado por no ser singular" (In the
court a courtier does many things more because others do them than because he himself would
like to do them. Oh, the poor courtier, who . . . even wears a mask in order not to be singular)
(107–108). For the constant surveillance that the courtier must endure, an experience evoked
in Juan Labrador's anxieties centering on the powerful gaze of the monarch, see 113–114. "No
ay hombre en la corte que no le miren do entra, no le aguarden de do sale, no le acechen por do
va, no le noten con quién trata, no espíen a quién busca" (There is not a man in the court whom
they don't observe closely—where he enters, where he exits—no one for whom they do not lie in
wait, to spy on him and to register where he goes and with whom he socializes, and whom he is
looking for). Needless to say, Guevara's satirical work is not at all concerned with the monarch as
the stable foundation of the courtly social system.

141. For the Stoics' immense confidence in man's "urge to be healthy" and their therapeutic approach to the sicknesses that can afflict the soul in its exposure to the illusions, blindnesses, mind-
less opinions, and ritual habits marking life in society, see Groethuysen, *Philosophische Anthropologie*, 57–59; also see Nussbaum, *The Therapy of Desire*, ch. 9.

142. Guevara, *Menosprecio de corte*, 127–128.

143. See N. Elias, *The Court Society*, tr. E. Jephcott (New York, 1983), 240–256, esp. 240, 246, 254–
255. At another point, when Elias's rhetoric betrays his sense that there might be something stifling in the "ascent of human consciousness" that he details so lucidly and sympathetically, he
speaks of the court as a "golden cage" closing on the French nobility and leaving its members
with the choice between sharing the glory within its carefully regulated order or living inglori-
ously a nonexistence outside its confines. In Lope's play Juan Labrador's behavior strikes us as
that of a man who fears stifling. For the appeal and challenge of quietist spirituality (e.g., Miguel
de Molinos) as an alternative to the intensification and "mechanization" of man's social life in
the new courts, see my "El desposeimiento del ser en la literatura renacentista." For Lope and the
majority of his compatriots it would seem that there was in fact no alternative. Matías de Novoa's
words on the banishment of a noble from the court offer an interesting commentary on Juan
Labrador's "barbarism"; the scandal of his refusal to leave his *rincón*; and his conflict with his
children, who seek the gilding light of the king. "Salir de la corte es salir de la órbita de nuestro
mayor planeta, marchar . . . lejos del calor y de la luz, vivir solo en un mundo inhabitado, esteril
e inhospito" (To withdraw from the court is to leave the orbit of our major planet, to depart . . .
far from the heat and the light, to live alone in a world that is uninhabited, sterile, and inhospit-
able). Cited in Lisón Tolosana, *La imagen del rey*, 135. Juan Labrador refuses enclosure within
the golden frame of the immense and spectacular work of art that Baroque society has created
of itself. One might compare Molière's misanthrope's retreat to the wilderness from the "golden
cage." In a very real sense the portrait of the king is in fact part of the larger portrait of society.
As Lope's profound work insinuates, the result of that creation is both plenitude and depletion,
enrichment and impoverishment.

144. For the enormous popularity of Guevara's writings, see Márquez Villanueva, *Menosprecio de
corte*, 162: The *Menosprecio* "immediately became required reading (a 'bedside' book) for the
entire profession of men of letters."

145. *Sincerity and Authenticity* (Oxford, 1980), 59.

146. See Ramón Díaz Solís, "A Spanish Book in the Hands of Hamlet? An Apparent Echo of Gue-

vara's 'Familiar Letters' in Hamlet," *Estudios en homenaje a Enrique Ruiz Fornells* (Erie, PA, 1990), 157–161.

147. See Francis Barker's suggestive discussion of *Hamlet's* implications in relation to the historical emergence of a valued space for subjectivity and the comfortable reconcilement to the public-private division of life that distinguished the rise of the bourgeoisie and the transition to modernity. In his sensitivities as an individual Hamlet finds no adequacy in the roles scripted for him in a pervasively visualized, theatrical world, whether as young prince and successor in a conventional comedy of the education of a king or as dutiful avenger in a conventional revenge tragedy. In an unquestionable, encompassing world order identified with universal rationality, cosmos, king, and self, all of which are coterminous and indivisible, boundaries are clear and visible to all, and nothing beyond their limits is allowed to exist. What is not present to the ubiquitous, "illuminating" monarch, what he does not see, does not exist. The throne, metaphorically identifiable with all these orders—cosmos, sun, macrocosmic and microcosmic rationality—is the center containing the universe. For the lonely Hamlet, all of this is fictional artificiality, a "mute and resistant externality" that alienates the subject from the authentic richness of his unique interiority. In his incapacity to exist in the world of seeming in which he is venerated as the supreme appearance, Hamlet utters "a first demand for the modern subject." In simple terms, Hamlet cannot participate in the actions "that a man might play," and his elusive motivation, which has inspired so many theories through centuries of fascination, in reality lies in the fact that in the world that he inhabits, he has no place, that he is in fact nothing. Politically more archaic than Lope's exploration of the travails of a new European consciousness, *Hamlet* envisions no alternate spaces for the estranged individual, whether in a reaccentuated classical privacy of a good citizen or in a humanization of the implacable world order founding the absolutist state. The protagonist can do little more than clumsily stumble toward his "tragic" fate, botching things up considerably along the way. See Barker, *The Tremulous Private Body: Essays on Subjection* (London, 1984), 33–37.

148. The convergences of Act III include a brief scene in which the king arranges the marriage of his sister to the king of Spain. The episode certainly has as much to do with the imaginative identification of the two protagonists and their worlds as with the contemporary royal wedding (1612) of Ana of Spain and Isabel of France. Bataillon argues plausibly that these historical circumstances and allusions provide us with a key to an "occasion" for Lope's play. See *"El villano en su rincón,"* 332–339. In the *rincón* of Act II, Juan Labrador's principal administrative acts concern his arrangements for the marriage of his son.

149. Lope de Vega, *La Dorotea*, ed. E. S. Morby (Madrid, 1958), 85. Translation of "A mis soledades" by E. L. Rivers, *Renaissance and Baroque Poetry of Spain* (New York, 1966); see 235.

150. *Don Quijote de la Mancha*, 2:53–54. See my "Sancho Panza and Cervantes' Embodiment of Pastoral," *Literature, Culture, and Society in the Modern Age: In Honor of Joseph Frank*, Stanford Slavic Studies 4, no. 1:69–70.

CHAPTER 2. KING AND WARRIOR

1. Agustín Moreto's tidy, rationalistic *refundición*—written several decades later for a more comfortably established absolutism and court society and appropriately retitled in abstractions, *El valiente justiciero*—comes much closer to justifying the reading of the work as an unambiguous celebration of the triumph of law and the rise of the state. See below.

2. See Angel Sánchez, *La imagen del Rey don Pedro en la literatura del Renacimiento y del Barroco* (Guadalajara, 1994), 41. For a provocative analysis of the play's doubling procedures as supporting a "recuperación de la fama del rey," see Henryk Ziomek, "El despliegue semiótico en *El Rey Don Pedro en Madrid*," in *Crítica semiológica de textos literarios hispánicos*, ed. Miguel Angel Garrido Gallardo (Madrid, 1983), 2:277–283. For an informative review of the sixteenth-century efforts to restore Pedro's reputation, see Nancy F. Marino, "Two Spurious Chronicles of Pedro *el Cruel* and the Ambitions of His Illegitimate Successors," *La Corónica* 21 (1993): 1–22. For the origins of Trastamarist propaganda and the political agenda of Enrique II concerning questions of regicide, legitimacy, and elective monarchy, see Joaquín Gimeno Casalduero, *La imagen del monarca en la Castilla del siglo XIV: Pedro el Cruel, Enrique II y Juan I* (Madrid, 1972), 73–114. The ballads have been collected by Antonio Pérez Gómez, *Romancero del Rey don Pedro* (Valencia, 1954). See also W. J. Entwistle, "The Romancero del rey Don Pedro in Ayala and the 'Cuarta Crónica General,'" *Modern Language Review* 25 (1930): 307–326, and Anne J. Cruz, "The Politics of Illicit Love in the 'Pedro el cruel' Ballad Cycle," *ARV: Scandinavian Yearbook of Folklore* 48 (1992): 1–17.

3. *Empresas políticas: Idea de un príncipe político-cristiano*, ed. Q. Aldea Vaquero (Madrid, 1976), 362.

4. Ibid., 247–249, 389.

5. Juan de Mariana, *Historia de España*, ed. BAE, vol. 30 (Madrid, 1854), 483, 441, 500, 502, 503.

6. *El Rey Don Pedro en Madrid o El Infanzón de Illescas, Obras de Lope de Vega*, ed. RAE, vol. 9 (Madrid, 1899), 503. Subsequent page references are to this edition. For a thorough reconsideration of the problems in determining the authorship and date (1621–1626?) of the play and in establishing a "definitive" text from its manuscript versions and traditions, see Carolyn Bingham Kirby's critical edition, *El Rey don Pedro en Madrid y el Infanzón de Illescas* (Kassel, 1998), 62–112. Kirby concludes that the most probable author is Lope de Vega but admits that the attribution cannot be made with absolute certainty. See also her discussion of the "bipartite titles" of the drama and "the argument for a bipartite title for the primary tradition" of the play (53). Most of the theories that have been advanced regarding the problem have conceded at least a partial role to Lope. My argument is concerned with the political, historical, and monarchist issues raised by the play (in one of its versions) and is not dependent on any specific answer to the question of authorship. The most powerful imaginative development of the legendary "seas of blood" surrounding Castile's controversial medieval "law-giver" is undoubtedly Calderón's *El médico de su honra*. Even more striking than the pervasiveness of motifs and images of blood in this strange work is its transformation of blood into a language or symbolism. The king, whose antagonistic relationship with his anarchic brother Enrique (his historical slayer) resembles the doubling of Tello and Pedro in the earlier play, divests himself of his royal robes to prowl at night through the streets of his kingdom. Amid the shadows he discovers crowds of disorderly *valientes* and, disregarding all the recognized restraints on royal behavior, challenges them to single combat. He violently "pacifies" the lawless group and imposes on their "profession" the state's regulating "carta de examen," which he describes in grotesque terms as a certifying document that is "iluminada con su sangre." The official papers of the state apparatus are written, signed, and stamped in blood. The curious little interruption of the conscientious king's familiar *ronda* can be viewed as an effective symbolic condensation of the play's most fascinating ambiguity: its attempt to reconcile the old warrior rituals of violent self-assertion, blood-letting, and revenge with the proper implementa-

tion of power in the new "scientific" state. Similarly, Don Gutierre, who is King Pedro's parallel double as "héroe científico" and creature of the night, ornaments the doors of Seville with the bloody print of his avenging hand, which will be the heroic emblazonment of his escutcheon as "médico de su honra," and, in the culminating, horrific epiphany of the tragedy, displays his wife's bloody corpse, which the king describes as an "espectáculo que admira/Símbolo de desgracia." At this point the rising sun is metaphorically bloodied; the stars and the spheres, obscured; and an anonymous voice sings from the darkness of the approaching bloodshed at Montiel. The prophesied regicide is envisioned earlier in the play, when Pedro is cut by the famous dagger in a palace altercation with his brother and is paralyzed by a momentary vision of his own corpse "bañado en mi sangre." In other words, the reach of the enveloping bloodshed, which chroniclers, balladeers, and political theorists kept alive in Spain's historical memory, could not be greater: home, palace, city, kingdom, and universe are engulfed in what in the king's "infelice imaginación" appears as "diluvios de sangre." In the intricacies of its languages of blood and "science" and in its incorporation of political and historical complexities, Calderón's depiction of Pedro el Cruel is far closer to the royal protagonist of *El Rey Don Pedro en Madrid* than it is to the monarch of the source of his plot and honor conflict, Lope de Vega's *El médico de su honra*, whose Pedro is simply an ideal king and restorer of order. In both plays the ironclad rigors of an archaic and personal code of honor manage to reassert themselves against a casuistic, tenuously victorious rationality that governs and contains a new political world that would appropriate the code and transform it into a system of rational, legalistic, and pragmatic calculations of favors and gifts to be distributed by an unchallengeable power from above. For such statist efforts to transcend or "update" the warrior code and sublimate its violent individualism, see Saavedra Fajardo's *Empresas políticas*, Empresa 58, where honor, like money, is conceived as a system of rational and just differentiations and bonds, hierarchical distinctions, and reciprocal obligations. For the contemporary French legalist and theorist of the monarchist state, Charles Loyseau, honor is, like love, necessary if the world is to avoid slipping into chaos. However, it has nothing to do with force and cannot be legislated; it is to be gained by merit and maintained by gentleness. See *A Treatise of Orders and Plain Dignities* (1610), ed. and tr. H. A. Lloyd (Cambridge, 1994), ch. 1, "Of Order in General." Considered in the light of such views, *El Rey Don Pedro en Madrid*, in its struggle of king and man, *rey* and *don*, and its efforts to reconcile force, warrior heroism, and legislation, is certainly marked by an "archaic" political vision.

7. For the prominence of these prophecies at such triumphant moments of Renaissance epic literature, see my *Cervantes and the Mystery of Lawlessness* (Princeton, 1984), 44–46.

8. Moreto makes the Enrique–Tello connection much more substantial and historically coherent. The seeming redundancy of the prince in the early play is the result of its focus on the king himself and his "lower self," Tello, as the principal antagonists and embodiments of "cruelty" and lawlessness.

9. The role of the shadow and the extreme complexity created by the insertion of yet a third "double" or counter-figure to be integrated or "appeased" are all but eliminated by Moreto's much more controlled version. See below.

10. See B. Kriegel's discussion of the rise and function of the absolutist state and its monarchist system of concentrating, rationally regulating, and limiting political power by the rule of law. *The State and the Rule of Law*, tr. Marc A. LePain and Jeffrey C. Cohen (Princeton, 1995). For the Thomistic philosophical background of the view that the king obeys natural law as a "direc-

tive force" rather than a "coercive power," see Bernice Hamilton, *Political Thought in Sixteenth-Century Spain* (Oxford, 1963), 64–67. Hamilton cites Domingo de Soto: "The prince is not outside the community but is a member of it. . . . Human law is binding in conscience because it is derived from the eternal law through the natural law. . . . By the very fact that a prince makes a law, he becomes subject to it by the law of nature." The question is discussed with admirable lucidity by Stephen Rupp, *Allegories of Kingship: Calderón and the Anti-Machiavellian Tradition* (University Park, PA, 1996), ch. 2, "Kingship and the Law."

11. *Empresas políticas*, 238. Saavedra Fajardo's essay, in both its concepts and its elaborated central metaphor, the horse of state, is highly suggestive as a "commentary" on the political dimensions of the complex drama. See below.

12. Juan de Mariana, *Del Rey y de la institución real*, ed. BAE, vol. 31 (Madrid, 1854), 490–491; emphasis added.

13. For Quevedo, state reason, which generally serves the interests of tyrants, and dueling were among the first inventions of Satan. See *Política de Dios: Govierno de Christo*, ed. J. O. Crosby (Madrid, 1966), 172. Pedro's dismissal of books at this moment might suggest an enthusiasm, common among contemporary statesmen, for experience as opposed to theory as the basis for dealing with political matters (e.g., Richelieu: "There is nothing more dangerous for the state than men who want to govern kingdoms on the basis of maxims which they cull from books" [See J. H. Elliott, *Richelieu and Olivares* (Cambridge, 1985), 27]). His motives are, however, precisely the opposite of those of the early modern pragmatists. His hostility to bookishness and the culture of the *letrados* serving the new states is rooted rather in an archaic, aristocratic personalism.

14. The ambiguities troubling the climactic resolution of the political questions raised by the play are consistent with the kind of stifling of momentary openings to, or reminders of, an optimistic political vision represented by these powerful moments. For example, Enrique, the celebrant of monarchy and law, appears as a *deus ex machina*, an "angel fallen to earth," who respectfully hands over the king's lost dagger, participates in the festivities of the comedic restoration, and prompts Pedro's bizarre commentary on the unfolding events in terms of a reversal of the myth of Abel and Cain. All of this might point to an overcoming of the overwhelming futility of human history that, according to Augustine's account in the *City of God*, begins with Cain's murder of Abel. At the same time, however, the author makes clear in the portents surrounding the concluding festivities the appropriateness of the Cain-Abel myth in relation to the grim realities of fratricide and regicide that were historically to occur following Pedro's triumph as *justiciero*. Similarly the celebration of Pedro as the "rock" and his epiphany in Madrid are deflected from the comedic focus on lawgiving and benevolent judicial decisions and shifted to the acts of a sinner-king's humiliating submission before divine omnipotence and his atonement in laying the foundational stones of a convent. To appreciate the stifling turn toward theological absolutism, one might contrast the words of the optimistic political philosopher Saavedra Fajardo concerning the value and the rationality of law. "Sobre las piedras de las leyes, no de la voluntad, se funda la verdadera politica. Líneas son del gobierno, y caminos reales de la razón de estado" (The true politics is founded not on the stones of the will, but rather on the stones of the laws. They are the paths of governance, and the royal highways of state reason) (*Empresas políticas*, 230).

15. For the importance of the revival of Roman law in the expansion of political thought beyond the limitations of medieval Augustinian conceptions, see Quentin Skinner, "Political Philosophy," *Cambridge History of Renaissance Philosophy*, ed. C. B. Schmitt and Q. Skinner (Cambridge,

1988), 389–452, esp. 389–395, where Skinner cites Azo as a representative of the jurists' doctrine that would be central to all subsequent contractarian political thought. For the rationalizing effects of the revival of Roman law on changing conceptions of the king's official body, see Ernst H. Kantorowicz, *The King's Two Bodies: A Study in Medieval Political Theology* (Princeton, 1957), ch. 4.

16. For Aegidius's metaphysical exaltation of the monarch as replicating the rational and benign purposes of a comprehensible God, visible in a natural order of things, and as representing, as the best human being, a Christian-classical ideal of moral perfectioning for all citizens as individuals, see Wilhelm Berges, *Die Fürstenspiegel des hohen und späten Mittelalters* (Leipzig, 1938), 211–228. Ruling and legislative acts are in a sense a process of *imitatio* (see 217). For Aegidius's Aristotelian and Neo-Platonic roots, see esp. 216–220. Berges emphasizes the historical importance of this *speculum principis* and its conception of the king—*rex quasi semideus*—animating, unifying, and bringing fulfillment to the essential social body of human beings. For its wide circulation in manuscripts, translations, and commentaries throughout Europe of the thirteenth and fourteenth centuries, see 211: the *De regimine principum* was "the most widely disseminated mirror of princes in the Occident and in reality one of the most widely read books of the late Middle Ages." Aegidius's treatise was written in 1280 for Philip IV of France, was translated into Spanish around 1345 with a commentary by Fray Juan García de Castrojériz, and was presented to the infante, Don Pedro. For its probable appeal to Peter the Cruel in his political project of unifying a chaotically divided state under the figure of a king, see Gimeno Casalduero, *La imagen del monarca*, 73–152. On the importance of such a readable natural order, containing rational and moral models for human perfectioning, as king, citizen, family member, and individual, in Erasmus's entire program of Christian restoration, see my *Cervantes and the Humanist Vision* (Princeton, 1982), 157–184.

17. See J. A. Fernández-Santamaría, *Reason of State and Statecraft in Spanish Political Thought, 1595–1640* (Lanham, MD, 1983), 48–50; J. A. Maravall, "Sobre el pensamiento social y político de Quevedo," *Estudios de historia del pensamiento español* (Madrid, 1984), 3:255–321. The political pessimism marking such conceptions is memorably represented in Milton's treatment of the unmentionable Nimrod in his introduction of the "new," post-Edenic political order of selfness, pride, and power on earth: "One shall rise/Of proud ambitious heart, who not content/With fair equality, fraternal state,/Will arrogate Dominion undeserv'd/Over his brethren, and quite dispossess/Concord and law of Nature from the Earth;/Hunting (and Men not Beasts shall be his game)." Since, with the Fall, man subjected himself to unworthy powers within, God often subjected him from without to "violent Lords." "Tyranny must be." See *Paradise Lost*, XII, 24–95. In Milton's epic we find that political activity—deliberative councils, "parliamentary" gatherings and procedures, votes, strategies of resistance, and considerations of state reason—is an art that thrives in hell. The unruliness and "anarchical" tendencies of this "republican order" parody the solemnity of the absolute ruler, God, who dictates and resolves by proclamation from his heavenly throne.

18. See *Política de Dios*, 172, 165, 151. The pessimism of Quevedo's denunciations of the evils and corruptions of kings, tyrants, and ministers makes this work unusual in the tradition of the *De regimine principis*. Only Christ knew how to be a king. He "did not descend from heaven 'clothed with honor and majesty,' to quote Psalm 104," and among his most notable actions were those of an authoritarian ruler who punishes, reforms, and criticizes. Monarchs of the world are almost

unexceptionally evil and weak in character; tyranny is nearly universal. As for the regalia and the majesty, Quevedo asserts that the crown and the scepter are "trastos de la figura, embara-çosos y vacios" (trashy accoutrements of the role, awkward and empty stage props). See Richard Edwards, "*Govierno de Christo* and *Tyrania de Satanas:* The Differences between Parts I and II of Francisco de Quevedo's *Política de Dios*," *Bulletin of Hispanic Studies* 76 (1999): 605–626. Edwards notes that Part II of the treatise is dominated by "a brooding atmosphere of malevolence, violence and cruelty."

19. Erasmus's ethically centered, optimistic political treatise, *De institutione principis christiani*, draws not only on the Gospels and his own *Philosophia christiana*, but also on the political writings of Plato, Aristotle, and Cicero concerning such notions as the common good, the private versus the public and institutional aspects of political life, and the relations of political organization to the attainment of the good life by the members of the polis. For Quevedo the focus is almost exclusively on the actions and words of the only worthy king, Christ; his relations with the apostles; and the seemingly inescapable failures and corruptions of the courts of the world. While Erasmus, as Eberhard von Koerber put it, accepted the traditional Pauline doctrine that "all power is from God" and rejected traditional justifications of regicide, he concentrated on the ethical rather than the theocratic foundations of the doctrine and "combined Christian charity and the enlightened eudaemonic state purposes deriving from classical antiquity." See *Die Staatstheorie des Erasmus von Rotterdam* (Berlin, 1967), 75–76. Quevedo would appear to be moving in the opposite direction. For the unusual character of his *speculum principis*, see Carmen Peraita, *Quevedo y el joven Felipe IV: El príncipe cristiano y el arte del consejo* (Kassel, 1997), 41–45, and Maravall, "Sobre el pensamiento social y político de Quevedo," and Ariadna García-Bryce, "All the Court's a Stage: Performing Piety in Quevedo's *Política de Dios*," *Journal of Spanish Cultural Studies* 6 (2005): 271–285. For Augustine, "empires and states are neither the work of the devil, nor are they good and hence justified by natural law. Their origin is man's sin and their relative value the preservation of peace and justice." In general the "*Civitas Terrena* is governed by expediency, pride, and ambition" (K. Löwith, *Meaning in History* [Chicago, 1949], 168–169). See R. Villari's remarks on the obsession with obedience in the age and the programmatic efforts throughout Europe to discredit all traditions that might dignify the figure of the rebel—e.g., the civic humanist interest in the morally idealistic slayer of despots (viz. Brutus) and the medieval scholastic belief in the monarch's obligation to abide by the limitations of his "contractual" relations with the people, who have delegated sovereignty to him (viz. Mariana). Although anything but a theocrat, the conservative Hobbes would probably agree with Enrique de Trastamara's striking declaration of the uncontestability of the royal will; men's "duty is to obey the king's laws"; the "civil laws are God's laws, as they that make them are by God appointed to make them" (*Behemoth*; cited by Villari, "The Rebel," in *Baroque Personae*, ed. R. Villari [Chicago, 1995], 120). Villari states: "The objective was to overpower opposition and eliminate political criticism, to present the rebel as a common bandit, an outcast for his own personal reasons, and a deviant from universally recognized and accepted norms of behavior" (115). It might be said that Tello, King Pedro's antagonist and double, belongs to a gallery of rebels and individualists unmatched in any other period of literary history. But what is most interesting about nearly all of such condemned figures, from Shakespeare's Macbeth and Tirso de Molina's Don Juan to Milton's prototype of the creature that "refuses to serve," is their refusal to be bound by the confinements of their political determination. Nearly all of them manage to "steal the show." In

his classical (and now controversial) study of the origins and historical function of the theory of the divine right of kings, J. N. Figgis emphasizes that the seventeenth century was obsessed with obedience to the law: natural law, canon law, positive and customary law. The need to counter the chaos of accelerated historical change and the breakdown of established traditions made the desire to locate a stable foundation for authority intense. Law becomes in reality the site of sovereignty, and the divine aspects of monarchy ultimately, following the Stuarts, are transferred to the rule of law. See *The Divine Right of Kings* (Cambridge, 1914), 227–238. As Oestreich has pointed out, the obsession might explain the striking pan-European enthusiasm for Neo-Stoicism and the interest in such values as duty, self-control, military discipline, responsible citizenship, and inner or private freedom—the values that would establish themselves as the philosophy of the rising middle class. In various historical studies, Maravall has emphasized the obsession with chaos, order, and obedience in seventeenth-century Spanish society. Quevedo's reactionary political philosophy should in fact be seen as a practical effort to counter its most disorderly tendencies. As for the theater, Maravall insists that its depiction of the king is uncompromisingly absolutist: there can be no resistance; the law is "acción única y absoluta del monarca" (see above).

20. Discussing Enrique II's political problem in justifying his violent capture of the crown and establishing the legitimacy of a dynasty, Gimeno Casalduero notes Spain's traditional reluctance to embrace "European" traditions of tyrannicide—e.g., John of Salisbury and Thomas Aquinas, for whom justice and the common good were of paramount importance—and its tendency to cling to more conservative positions—e.g., the biblical and Augustinian view that the tyrant fulfills divine purposes and the Gregorian insistence on veneration of the figure of the ruler, regardless of his individual conduct. It should be noted that such veneration in fact marked the doctrines of Aegidius Romanus, the most important political theorist of the rising European state and its concentration of power and legislative authority in the single figure of the monarch. An informative survey of the theme of tyrannicide in Spanish Golden Age drama is available in A. Robert Lauer, *Tyrannicide and Drama* (Stuttgart, 1987).

21. *Teatro y literatura en la sociedad barroca*, 126.

22. *La imagen del Rey don Pedro*, 136–137.

23. For the metaphysical and political traditions informing such descriptions in Lope's theater—and specifically the utopian vision of the peasant world in the second act of *El villano en su rincón*—see ch. 1 above.

24. See Karl Vossler's brief description of the dramatic power of this strange figure, in whom "mischen sich die Mächte des Himmels und der Erde gewaltiger als in anderen Sterblichen" (the powers of heaven and earth are intermingled more grandly than in other mortals) (*Lope de Vega und seine Zeit* [Munich, 1947], 237–238). The "incidental" nature of specific historical backgrounds in such works as Shakespeare's *King Lear* and *Macbeth* comes to mind. In discussing the relations of the historical, ideological, and mythic contexts of literature, Northrop Frye writes: "As he goes on, Shakespeare tends to leave English history for the more remote and legendary periods of Lear, Hamlet and Macbeth, where the titanic figures of tragedy can emerge as they could not have emerged from the battlefields of Agincourt or Tewkesbury. In time these periods are more remote from us; in myth they are far more immediate and present." See *Words with Power* (New York, 1990), 58.

25. See my discussion of the conventions, effects, and popularity of contemporary miracle literature in *Cervantes and the Humanist Vision*, ch. 4.

26. For the prominence of horse depictions and the cult of Apollo in glorifications of monarchs, see P. K. Monod, *The Power of Kings: Monarchy and Religion in Europe, 1589–1715* (New Haven, 1999), ch. 7. For Bernini's ill-fated equestrian statue of Louis XIV as Apollo, mounted on a "rebellious" horse, see the epilogue below. For Gracián's unusual elaboration of this mythology, as well as a bibliography on its origins and spectacular Baroque orchestrations, see my "At the Threshold of Modernity: Gracián's *El Criticón*," in *Rhetoric and Politics: Baltasar Gracián and the New World Order*, ed. Nicholas Spadaccini and Jenaro Talens (Minneapolis, 1997), 3–70, esp. 32–33, 50–51.

27. One might recall Mariana's colorful account of the king's furious reaction to the notice of excommunication, delivered by a terrified papal legate, who immediately raced to a waiting boat in the Guadalquivir and barely escaped the pursuing king, who forced his frightened horse farther and farther into the river while thrashing about wildly with his sword. See *Historia de España*, 515. The dramatic power of the legendary association of Pedro's violence and domination with bestiality is exploited by Andrés de Claramonte at the opening of his play *De esta agua no beberé* (ed. A. R. López-Vázquez [Kassel, 1984], 71), where the king's indefatigability and his horse's voracity evoke the frightening figure of the legendary tyrant and torturer Diomedes of Thrace. For López-Vázquez's argument that *El Rey Don Pedro en Madrid* was authored by Claramonte, see his introduction to Fernando Cantalapiedra's detailed study of the subject, *"El Infanzón de Illescas" y las comedias de Claramonte* (Kassel, 1990).

28. *El príncipe perfecto, Obras de Lope de Vega*, ed. RAE (Nueva edición), vol. 10 (Madrid, 1930), 464, 466, 469.

29. See Francisco Javier Díez de Revenga, "Monarquía y mito en la España del Siglo de Oro: *El anfiteatro de Felipe el Grande*," in *El mito en el teatro clásico español*, ed. F. Ruiz Ramón y César Oliva (Madrid, 1988), 196–202. Citing Maravall, Díez de Revenga suggests that such festivals were organized in order to procure for the monarchy "the blind, stupefied, and irresponsible support of the masses." For Saavedra Fajardo's and Lope de Vega's encomiastic poems, see *El anfiteatro de Felipe el Grande*, ed. José Pellicer de Tovar, facsimile edition by Antonio Pérez y Gómez (Madrid, 1974), 17, 72. It is instructive to compare this document to the allegedly propagandistic contemporary drama of kings in order to avoid the simplifications and blindness to complexity that the facile application of Maravall's theories of a "directed culture" to the interpretation of Golden Age political drama has encouraged. One can suppose that plays such as *El villano en su rincón* and *El Rey Don Pedro en Madrid* elicited a more reflective and discriminating response in their audience than such spectacles of thrilling bloodshed.

30. In words relevant to *El Rey Don Pedro en Madrid*, Pellicer offers his king in each poem of the collection a trophy "que diga siempre esta hazaña, de que puede V. M. gloriarse, por averla conseguido, obrando por si con su acierto, i no con su poder" (that may speak forever of this deed, in which Your Majesty may take special glory for having achieved it through ability rather than power) (*El anfiteatro de Felipe el Grande*, n.p.). This is the root of the dilemma that torments King Pedro—manliness and individual prowess versus majesty. He is infuriated by Tello's remark: "Siempre en los reyes se teme/Más el poder que el esfuerzo" (In kings one always fears their power more than their courage) (489). Certainly the most enduring monument of this sort of propaganda is the Hall of the Realms in the Retiro Palace, which, in a magnificent celebration of Spanish monarchy, decorated its walls with depictions of the great hero of civilization's conquest of the chaotic forces of nature and instinct, Hercules.

31. For several versions of the romance, see Pérez Gómez, *Romancero del Rey don Pedro*, 144ff. The poems narrate the tormented king's encounter with dark portents of his tragic destiny: his slaughtered hunting hawk and a wild young shepherd holding a serpent, a bloody dagger, and a skull, judging the king's crimes and announcing his death. Lope de Vega describes Philip IV's confrontation of the bull in terms that would suggest an enactment of the fantasy of the hunt in the center of the government: "Trasladó su singular Destreza del Campo al Amphiteatro, y del Monte solo, al Espectaculo universal" (He transferred his unmatched skill from the country to the amphitheater, and from the lonely mountain forest to the universal spectacle [of the city]). It reveals the "bizarra disposicion" of its "heroico principe." Needless to say, the hunter's loss of direction and the association of the forest or rugged mountain wilderness of his wanderings with transgressive erotic desire were among the most popular motifs of the *comedia* (see Noël Salomon, *Recherches sur le thème paysan dans la "comedia" au temps de Lope de Vega* [Bordeaux, 1965], 468–469). For our purposes it is worth noting that the convention was frequently connected with the king's behavior (e.g., *El villano en su rincón*) and that it was a common target of moralist denunciations of the theater in the age in its lack of decorum and its degrading view of kings', queens', princes', and princesses' sexual behavior (e.g., the anonymous *Diálogos de la comedias* [1620]: "ya el rey que se perdió en la caza y topó una pastora a la cual buscaba" [cited in *Bibliografía de las controversias sobre la licitud del teatro en España*, ed. Emilio Cotarelo y Mori (Madrid, 1904), 225]; see Eduardo Forastieri-Brasci, "El decoro de los reyes con los bueyes en el teatro de Lope de Vega," *NRFH* 32 [1983]: 412–423). For an illuminating discussion of the hunting ethos in aristocratic culture, approached through Montaigne's analysis and critique of cruelty, see David Quint, *Montaigne and the Quality of Mercy* (Princeton, 1998), 49–65.

32. See "The Culture of the Baroque Courts," *Renaissance Essays* (London, 1985). Also see Monod, *The Power of Kings*, ch. 7.

33. *Empresas políticas*, 361–368. See also Jerónimo de Zeballos's comparison of the art of ruling to the taming of horses and lions; cited by Maravall, *Teatro y literatura en la sociedad barroca*, 14.

34. See Agustín Moreto, *El valiente justiciero*, ed. Frank P. Casa (Salamanca, 1971), 38–39.

35. Américo Castro, *Origen, ser, y existir del español* (Madrid, 1959), 59, 99, 114. The English word "grandee," in its Spanish derivation, bears witness to the distinctively Hispanic origins of this conception of personal dominance and value.

36. *Philip of Spain* (New Haven, 1997), 228–229. See Monod, *The Power of Kings*, 43: "After the coronation ceremony had died out in the fourteenth century, Castilian kings were neither consecrated nor crowned, and they possessed no regalia—no sceptre, no throne, no crown."

37. Teofilo Ruiz, "Unsacred Monarchy: The Kings of Castile in the Late Middle Ages," *The City and the Realm: Burgos and Castile 1080–1492* (Great Yarmouth, Norfolk, 1992), ch. 13, 109–144; see esp. 131.

38. One should recall Machiavelli's praise of King Fernando's sober understanding of the political uses of religion.

39. Cited by Ruiz, "Unsacred Monarchy," 133.

40. Ibid., 132–133, 144. For a discussion of the exceptional coronation ceremony of Alfonso XI and the relevant question of the conflict of monarchy and chivalry, one of the conflicts that, I suggest, underlie the ambiguities of the play's opening violent image of King Pedro, see Peter Linehan, "Ideología y liturgia en el reinado de Alfonso XI de Castilla," in *Genesis medieval del estado moderno: Castilla y Navarra (1250–1370)*, ed. Adeline Rucquoi (Salamanca, 1987), 229–243.

41. It is perhaps worth noting that Moreto clarifies the king's appearance and motivation at this moment in a way that narrows and intensifies the focus of the political context that I am describing: the king is frenziedly pursuing his rebellious brother Enrique (the erasure of *cruelty* and the displacement of the unsettling paradoxical convergence of valor and violence by an image of valor and justice are successful, but the "dimensión imperativa" cannot be escaped), whereas in the model, much more suggestive, psychological, and ultimately religious, the king's movements and intentions are unfathomable, and the complexities of his doubling are connected with a mysterious shade who is lurking in the background. Is the monarch seeking? Pursuing? Perhaps fleeing? Is he already being driven by a "centrifugal" energy that foreshadows his uncontrollable urges to "regress" from palace, law, and etiquette into the darkest of nights and the pure violence of the *campamento*?

42. Such seals, which Peter the Cruel adopted, expressed "le pragmatisme politique et l'ideal de la force," thus displaying "l'essence même de l'Etat Moderne." See Teofilo Ruiz, "L'image du pouvoir à travers les sceaux de la monarchie castillane," in Rucquoi, ed., *Genesis medieval del estado moderno,* 217–227, esp. 227. For the prominence of the royal horse in martial and secular rites in the continuation of Visigothic traditions in the Spain of the Middle Ages, see Ruiz, "Unsacred Monarchy," 125.

43. See Carol Bingham Kirby, "Observaciones preliminares sobre el teatro histórico de Lope de Vega," in *Lope de Vega y los orígenes del teatro español,* ed. Manuel Criado de Val (Madrid, 1981), 329–339.

44. See *Obras de Lope de Vega,* ed. RAE (Nueva edición), vol. 10 (Madrid, 1930), 450, 461, 478–479. For the education paradigm in Calderón's *La vida es sueño,* a work that, in its concern with disorder and violence, is much closer to *El Rey Don Pedro en Madrid* than Lope's *Príncipe perfecto,* see Everett W. Hesse, "Calderón's Concept of the Perfect Prince in *La vida es sueño,*" in *Critical Essays on the Theatre of Calderón,* ed. Bruce W. Wardropper (New York, 1965), 114–133.

45. For the importance of Julius Caesar's *Commentaries*—their translation from the Latin and their interpretation—in the education of young princes and kings such as Philip III and France's Louis XIV, see Fernando Bouza, *Corre manuscrito: Una historia cultural del Siglo de Oro* (Madrid, 2001), 294–303.

46. For a suggestive discussion of the metatheatrical elements of the drama in connection with artistic illusion and literary issues, see William C. McCrary, "Theater and History: *El rey don Pedro en Madrid,*" *Crítica Hispánica* 1 (1979): 145–167.

47. For the importance of violent personal assertion, the confrontation of rivals, and the shedding of blood in the crucial identity ritual for the aristocrat, see Kristen B. Neuschel, *Word of Honor: Interpreting Noble Culture in Sixteenth-Century France* (Ithaca, NY, 1989).

48. For the "civilized" redirection of pure power in the early modern period, see Norbert Elias's fundamental studies, esp. *Power and Civility,* tr. E. Jephcott (New York, 1982) and *The Court Society,* tr. E. Jephcott (New York, 1983). One can in fact refine on the reading of the play as historical allegory that I suggest above by viewing it as a dramatization of the "monopolization of violence" that the modern state had to achieve in its origins. See Max Weber, "Politics as Vocation," in *Essays in Sociology,* ed. H. Gerth and C. Wright Mills (London, 1970). See also Lawrence Stone, *The Crisis of the Aristocracy 1558–1641* (London, 1967).

49. See Neuschel, *Word of Honor,* ch. 3.

50. See "Of Custom," *The Complete Essays of Montaigne,* tr. D. Frame (Stanford, 1958), 85. Mon-

taigne emphasizes the oddity of the co-presence of these opposing estates within the unified state and their different respective functions (e.g., waging war versus administering the peace). For Montaigne and contemporary controversies concerning the duel and honor, see Quint, *Montaigne and the Quality of Mercy*, 70.

51. For the importance of this kind of emblematic scene in the conventional celebrative depictions of the monarch and the institution of monarchy in Golden Age theater, see Frank Casa, "The Centrality and Function of King Sancho," *Heavenly Bodies: The Realms of La estrella de Sevilla*, ed. Frederick A. de Armas (Lewisburg, PA, 1996), 64–75: "The audience is the dramatic device that the comedia employs to show the king in the exercise of his primary function, the dispensing of justice." In his principal role as the vicar of Christ, he carries out his most sacred duty. See also Frank Casa, "The Use of the Royal Audiencia in Golden Age Drama," *Segismundo* 43–44 (1986): 63–79. The spectacular scene in the theater's "discourse of monarchy" obviously reflected the rituals of the governing powers. In the creation of the national state, Joseph R. Strayer notes that "rulers gradually began to see that justice was something more than a source of revenue. It was a way of asserting the authority and increasing the power of the king or greater lords." See *The Medieval Origins of the Modern State* (Princeton, 1970), 29.

52. In this play King Pedro vows his allegiance as judge to "el Señor supremo" and his "ley católica"; he is severe but just in his treatment of a cowardly soldier and a morally lax victim of seduction; and he resolves the problems raised by a grotesque honor revenge with a lucidity and a "dark" prudence that look forward to Calderón's complex recreation of Pedro el Cruel in *El médico de su honra*. However, the peculiar statist concerns of *El Rey Don Pedro en Madrid* do not appear in Lope's play. See *Obras de Lope de Vega*, ed. RAE, 9:456–457, 471. Probably the most familiar and ingenious ambiguations of the traditional celebrative scene depicting this most august ritual activity of the ideal king lie in Shakespeare's drama, notably in King Lear's hallucinatory audience on the heath, where, as insane and raging *rex judex*, he offers his devastating condemnation of mankind's limitless vices and corruptions.

53. For the importance of education, literacy, and written documentation in the creation of the bureaucracies and the permanent, impersonal institutions on which the existence of the modern state was to depend, see Strayer, *On the Medieval Origins of the Modern State*, 24–25, 76–78.

54. See Walter Ong's studies of the distinctive ways of thinking and organizing experience produced by oral and print modes of expression and communication. Particularly relevant are his discussions of the affinities of orality and the agonistic and the numinous, features that, as I shall point out below, are fundamental in the drama's "recuperation" of Tello and the sublimity of his world. See *Orality and Literacy: The Technologizing of the Word* (London, 1982), and *Fighting for Life: Contest, Sexuality, and Consciousness* (Amherst, MA, 1981). More recently Neuschel has demonstrated the residual power of orality in the speech habits of the nobles of sixteenth-century France as revealed in the formulas of their written letters. See *Word of Honor*, ch. 4. Emphasizing the priority of "la oralidad y la gestualidad visual" in "el *ethos* aristocrático," Fernando Bouza points out that "if there is something that defines the noble estate in the Spanish court after 1550, it is the outspoken disdain for the orderly, regulated knowledge that is fundamental to the practice of letters" (*Corre manuscrito*, 203).

55. For the significance of the gift in the foundation of personal and social relationships in the culture of the aristocracy, see Neuschel, *Word of Honor*, 72–78, and Quint, *Montaigne and the Quality of Mercy*.

56. In his efforts to consolidate his kingdom and expand the machinery of central government, the historical Pedro el Cruel continued the financial reforms introduced by his father, Alfonso XI, increasing and regularizing taxation and evidently supporting the introduction of professional *contadores* and the techniques of accounting on which the development of the modern state and its treasuries depended. These reforms "led to the gradual abandonment of the Crown's reliance on seigneurial fixed contributions (in kind, labor, rents, or in combination) in favor of a more efficient and generalized cash-based system of indirect taxation linked to actual market conditions rather than traditional practices" (Clara Estow, *Pedro the Cruel of Castile: 1350–1369* [Leiden, 1995], 108, 123). See also Miguel Angel Ladero Quesada, *Fiscalidad y poder real en Castilla (1252–1369)* (Madrid, 1993). The obligations of state building would appear to be sources of the "misery of kings" in the drama's portrait of a conflicted monarch. As for the bond of Pedro and soldier celebrated by the scene, the historical record would indicate that the king frequently had difficulty in raising money for his major expense—the payment of his armies—and had to deal with the desertion of disgruntled soldiers. See Estow, *Pedro the Cruel of Castile*, 106ff.

57. Such oppositions and their ambiguities mark many of the most notable works of literature of the period. A famous example is *La estrella de Sevilla*, where monarchy and a statist, prudent, Machiavellian king are juxtaposed to an appealing Sevillian aristocracy. The king demands written documents; the noble scoffs at them as superfluous: "¡Yo cédula! ¡Yo papel! . . . Tienen los sevillanos las palabras en las manos." *Obras de Lope de Vega*, ed. RAE, vol. 9 (Madrid, 1899), 145–148. They are fundamental to Cervantes's entire literary production, from the early *La Numancia*, with its "pre-statist" manly warriors hopelessly up against the enormous power and technology of the "heroless" Roman army, to his late depiction of the appealing loner who sets out on an insane quest to restore an age of individual heroism, Don Quixote. See my observations below on Shakespeare's *Coriolanus*.

58. The nature of the dilemma, the difficulties confronting the king in his obligation to maintain control in the state, and the obliqueness of his recommendation of violent individualism anticipate Calderón's dramatic treatment of these matters and his very different resolution of them in his most famous honor drama, *El médico de su honra*.

59. See John Elliott's discussion of Charles V as a "virtuoso of political stagecraft," who, as heir to Burgundian traditions of court ceremony, was acutely aware of the ways in which "symbols could be deployed and manipulated for political effect" and the assurance of royal preeminence. "The Court of the Spanish Habsburgs: A Peculiar Institution?" *Spain and Its World: 1500–1700* (New Haven, 1989), 142–161.

60. See Saavedra Fajardo, *Empresas políticas*, Empresas 31, 43. See also R. Bireley, *The Counter-Reformation Prince: Anti-Machiavellianism or Catholic Statecraft in Early Modern Europe* (Chapel Hill, 1990), and Victoria Kahn, *Machiavellian Rhetoric: From the Counter-Reformation to Milton* (Princeton, 1994). For a revealing discussion of the "theatricality of power" and the "power of the theatrical" in the early modern state, with reference to James I's famous assertion, in his widely read *Basilicon Doron* (1603), that "a King is as one set on a skaffold, whose smallest actions and gestures al the people gazingly doe behold," see Steven Mullaney, *The Place of the Stage: License, Play, and Power in Renaissance England* (Ann Arbor, 1997), ch. 4. For Gracián's satirical treatment of the subject, see my "Gracián's Theaters of Nothingness," in *Sin fronteras: Ensayos de literatura comparada en homenaje a Claudio Guillén*, ed. D. Villanueva, A. Monegal, and E. Bou (Madrid, 1999), 215–229.

61. Mullaney clarifies the function of the gift in the symbolic economy of political and social systems based on primitive domination; see *The Place of the Stage*, 131. As is abundantly illustrated in epic and chivalric literature, as well as in historical chronicles, the "gift horse" is one of the most honorable rituals of bonding and homage.

62. In this scene characters speak of what is happening to them in terms of the conventions and effects of the drama. For example, the metatheatrical strategies of the controlling king are underscored comically in the dialogue of the aristocrat's accomplice in the crime, the *gracioso*, who in the conventional misogynistic discourse of his role, can see only tragic consequences in the king's impending comedic resolution of the drama, which of course would include his forced marriage to his peasant victim: "¿Quién creyera/Que el entremés de *un tejado*/Viniera a hacerse tragedia?" (Who would ever believe that the farce of *a tiled roof* [his rooftop rape escapade] would turn into a tragedy?) (497).

63. See *The Court Society*, 92. Tello is, of course, befuddled by the incomprehensible, non-personal presence of the monarch. He receives a lesson on the "ubiquity" of the official body of the king and reacts, as one would expect, with comic exasperation. "Don Tello: ¡Qué necio he sido en fiarme/Del Rey! Cordero: 'Cuando no lo hicieras,/La misma seguridad/Tuvieras dél en Illescas;/Que el Rey es gallo que canta/En todo lugar. Don Tello:¡Paciencia!" (Don Tello: How foolish I have been to trust the King! Cordero: If you didn't, you would be no more secure from him in Illescas; for the king is a cock that crows in every corner. Don Tello: Patience!) (496–497). See ch. 1 above: "The king is everywhere and everywhere is the king."

64. See Kriegel, *The State and the Rule of Law.*

65. In his most grotesque act of blasphemy, Tello punishes the village magistrates, who would defend the victims of his rape, with their official staffs. The staffs bear the king's insignia, represent his scepter, and symbolize his justice. "El, quebrando/Las varas en sus cabezas,/Les metió el Rey en los cascos" (Breaking the staffs on their heads, he stuffed the King into their skulls) (483).

66. Sebastián de Covarrubias Orozco, *Tesoro de la lengua castellana o española*, ed. F. C. R. Maldonado (Madrid, 1995), 529.

67. The "escape" to Aragon that concludes the intensely developed agon of the king and the noble is highly suggestive. In Spain's medieval history, Aragon is a kingdom famous for its freedoms; its traditions of local laws (the *fueros*); the independence and lawlessness of its nobles, who maintained their legal right to wage war on their own; its resistance to statist pacification and monarchical centralization; and the prominence of marginal elements in its population—e.g., Moriscos, Lutherans, Frenchmen, and bandits. From the period of Pedro's endless wars with the king of Aragon and his allies in the French nobility and in Pedro's own family to the period of the play's composition, with the defiance of Philip II by the Aragonese Cortes in their protection of the fugitive traitor Antonio Pérez, the kingdom of Aragon was associated with anarchy, individualism, and aristocratic privilege. In his study of the prevalent banditry and smuggling and the general ungovernability of the border areas of the kingdom in the final decades of Philip's reign, Jaime Contreras writes that "diversity was inherent in the old order (disorder) of things. The uniformity of justice and law could scarcely stand up to the disintegration, variety, and multiformity of that social aggregate. Despite the king's efforts, anarchy ruled everywhere and the expression of violence reached the extremes of the primitive. The 'rationality' of the king's justice and the administrative and regulative efficacy of the Holy Inquisition turned out to be fruitless, lost amid the numerous private channels that developed irregularly and chaotically in that society. Every-

body recognized the authority of the king, but nobody paid much attention to it" ("Bandolerismo y fueros: El Pirineo a finales del siglo XVI," in *El bandolero y su imagen en el siglo de oro*, ed. Juan Antonio Martínez Comeche [Madrid, 1989], 55–78). The symbolical encounter of Pedro and Tello is certainly to some extent determined by and reflective of such specific historical realities. For Philip II's pursuit of Antonio Pérez into Aragon, the kingdom's defiance—described as a "revolt"—and the crucial issues in the preservation of its "ancient liberties," see Kamen, *Philip of Spain*, 284–294.

68. Kamen, *Philip of Spain*, 214–218. One can see in the ghostly palace confrontation of Tello and Pedro the evolution of one of the most celebrated debates of medieval and Renaissance literature and social life—arms versus letters—the controversy over the respective merits of warrior (knight, soldier) and cleric. Here the ultimate phase is reached as clerk metamorphoses into bureaucrat, jurist, and ultimately king. What Lope could still refer to in 1603 in his *Peregrino en su patria* as a "contienda eternamente indefinida" appears to be reaching a firm resolution in the rise of the state and the bureaucracy. See Jean Marc Pelorson, *Les letrados: Jurists castillans sous Philip III: Recherches sur leur place dans la société, la culture et l'état* (Poitiers, 1980), 141ff.; also see Fernando Bouza, *Communication, Knowledge, and Memory in Early Modern Spain*, tr. S. López and M. Agnew (Philadelphia, 2004), 33–38. As Jacques Barzun puts it, "Bureaucracy is the 'monarchical' institution par excellence" precisely because "it works with ABSTRACTIONS," imposing a conceptual uniformity in the categories that radiate from its single, organizing center. As Tello rages to be noticed as a grand and *unique* person ("Yo soy Tello") among the indifferent papers, uniformed authorities, alienated spaces, and rigid automatons ("espetados" in their obsessive movements), he is in fact resisting the "onenesses" of the new order and challenging the very idea of "nation, twin of the monarchical" (Jacques Barzun, *From Dawn to Decadence: 1500 to the Present* [New York, 2000], 253–255).

69. In terms of the historical contexts and agendas of the drama, the relation of Tello, the invented figure, to the historical Enrique de Trastamara—the lawless aristocrat and regicide—is one of the most intriguing—and elliptical—aspects of the work. Tello associates himself with the Trastamara precisely in a moment of blasphemy, when he draws his sword in the palace in this developing scene. "Mi espada es ésta,/De quien aun tiembla Castilla,/Y de quien los reyes tiemblan./Ricohombre soy e Infanzón,/Y a la par de sí me asienta/El Conde de Trastamara,/Que es su hermano" (This is my sword, before which even Castile and its kings quake in fear. I am of the highest nobility, a *ricohombre* and an *infanzón*. The Count of Trastamara, the brother of the king, seats me at his side as an equal) (495). See my discussion above of Enrique's proclamation of the most conservative of divine right justifications of monarchy. Is the cathartic role of Tello in fact double, displacing and purging the violence of both royal agents in a bloody national past?

70. "La experiencia enseña, que ay otros demonios, que sin espantar, ni fatigar a los hombres (porque Dios no se lo permite, ni les da mano para ello) son caseros, familiares, y tratables, ocupándose en jugar con las personas, y hazerles burlas ridículas. A estos llamamos comunmente trasgos, o duendes" (Experience teaches that there are other demons who, without frightening or fatiguing men [because God does not allow it, nor does he give them a hand for it] are domestic, familiar, and approachable, occupying themselves in playing with people and playing ridiculous jokes on them. These we commonly call poltergeists, or 'duendes') (Benito Remigio Noydens, *Práctica de exorcistas y ministros de la Iglesia. En que con mucha erudición, y singular claridad, se trata de la instrucción de los exorcismos para lançar, y ahuyentar los demonios, y curar espiritualmente*

todo genero de maleficio, y hechizos [Barcelona, 1688], 254). For the text and the translation, see Hilaire Kallendorf, *Exorcism and Its Texts* (Toronto, 2003), 162.

71. "Piensa/que los reyes, sin espada,/Como médicos pelean" (Bear in mind that kings, like doctors, fight without swords) (498). For the contemporary ascendancy of court rationality and its instrumental character, see Elias, *The Court Society*. Perhaps the most powerful literary example of the superiority of the "scalpel" to the sword is Calderón's *Médico de su honra*, a work in which Pedro el Cruel's advocacy of the new rationality, embodied in his double, is untroubled by the ambivalences that distinguish *El Rey Don Pedro en Madrid*. The analogy of statecraft and medicine is common in Renaissance political theorizing in the Machiavellian tradition.

72. See Elliott, "The Court of the Spanish Habsburgs," 147–152.

73. Particularly interesting as a comical concentration of the system is *Dineros son calidad*, a play traditionally believed to be by Lope but recently attributed to Andrés de Claramonte (ed. A. R. Rodríguez López-Vázquez [Kassel, 2000]). (Arguments concerning its authorship focus on its supernatural elements seemingly shared by *El Rey Don Pedro en Madrid* and Tirso's *El burlador de Sevilla*.) Here we find the usurping queen Julia, who together with her minister, César, transforms the monarchic system methodically into a machine of gratuitous tyrannical exercise. She continuously asserts the royal prerogative—the "queen's pleasure"—by contemptuously ripping up documents of state. Meanwhile, the exiled daughter of King Enrique and heir to the throne is championed by the three sons of a loyal old courtier, who has been reduced to poverty and disgrace by the vicissitudes of political life. The wildly melodramatic plot contains angry contests for precedence in seating arrangements, extravagant equestrian images of royal splendor, and references to the injunction to look upon the king's face; there is a ghostly statue animated by the divine presence of the king and imaginatively resurrecting the traditional notions of the monarch's doubleness (or "two bodies"). In what one might view as a comedic inversion of *King Lear*'s so-called "comedy of the grotesque," the arbitrary cosmic powers (and of course their ruling dramatist) work things out happily for everybody: tyrants and villains are redeemed, victims are restored, and everybody eligible manages to get married. If there is an ultimate meaning to be found amid such theatrical flamboyance, it seems to be the cynical realization that the whole system of *calidad*—including the elaborate cult of monarchy—originates in and is driven by the all-too-human lust for money. Such effects are even more striking in one of Lope's most ceremonial displays of the cult of the king, *Carlos V en Francia*, a work that includes pages dedicated to the brilliant processional entries of the emperor in the cities of France and concludes with the display of a triumphal arch depicting Spain and France in an embrace, standing above its conquered enemies—Indian, Turk, and Moor—while receiving the blessing of the Pope. Amid such celebration the mysteries and charisma of the royal body and the royal activities and duties, solemnly presented in the Mirrors of Princes, become the occasions for light-hearted fooling and parody. For example, Leonora is smitten by the portrait of the king, Charles V, and is driven to insanity by a frustrated desire to sleep with him. He, the ideal king, easily resists the traditional temptation of the tyrant—"'Yo soy quien soy,' respondió" (123). She then approaches the French king, Francis I, and requests that he use his thaumaturgic powers to cure scrofula to assuage the burning fury of her love. Meanwhile, Francis honors Charles by making him king of France for the period of his passage through the country, and he acknowledges that he is eclipsed by the radiance of a new sun and remains nothing but an "ordinary man." The festivity can reach shocking extremes. For example, "transformed into a French king," Charles, in the ritual scene of bestow-

ing honors and *mercedes*, decides to reward a German warrior for killing thirty Spanish soldiers in the Battle of Pavia—a striking assertion of the cult of the king over nationalism—and in a comic articulation of the palace protocol concerning violence, dueling, and the majesty, which is taken so seriously in *El Rey Don Pedro en Madrid*, Charles claims that "a no ser quien soy,/a canpaña y me matara/con él" (177). The seriousness of royal celebration returns at the very end, and Charles acknowledges the impermanence of the comic pleasures that have dominated the royal spectacle. "Assí se passan, Leonor,/las humanas alegrías" (182). For an interesting reconsideration of Leonora's role as a figure of resistance in this play, see Elaine Bunn, "Negotiating Empire and Desire in Lope de Vega's *Carlos V en Francia*," *Hispanic Review*, 72 (2004): 29–42. Stephen Gilman has emphasized the farcical notes in *El Rey Don Pedro en Madrid*, suggesting that one is tempted to conclude that Lope saw national history as "esperpento." "The head thumping episode is sheer Punch and Judy." The climactic nocturnal duel is literally and figuratively "black comedy." See *"El rey don Pedro en Madrid y el infanzón de Illescas* as a Tragic Poem," in *Hispanic Studies in Honor of Joseph H. Silverman*, ed. Joseph V. Ricapito (Newark, DE, 1988), 235–245.

74. The conflicts and ambiguities that mark the entire sequence of scenes dramatizing the official activity of the monarch in Act II demonstrate a fundamental aspect of the historical ascendance of the state that political theorists of the period seemed generally incapable of grasping. Attached to traditional conceptions of governance centering on the individual prince, clinging to the *speculum principis*—distinguished by such influential medieval and Renaissance manifestations as Aquinas's *De regimine principum* (ca. 1265), Aegidius Romanus's *De regimine principum* (ca. 1287), and Erasmus's *De institutione principis christiani* (1516)—as the proper format for all political analysis, they continued, for the most part, to approach problems of state operations and maintenance in terms of the ruler's education and moral character, conspicuously failing to recognize that a primary quality of the complex new reality that had come into existence by 1500 was in fact its depersonalization of the mechanisms and operations of the governing apparatus. The restlessness and dissatisfaction in Pedro's experiences in his dramatic incarnation around 1620 are not to be taken merely as a register of a conservative yearning in Spain of the period for a vanished era of personal heroism and "manliness" but, in more general and suggestive terms, as an expression of a general alienation that the European subject was experiencing in his dawning consciousness that he now, at the "threshold of modernity," as it were, belonged to a political entity that, in its increasing complex operations, interventions, regulations, and controls, had little demonstrable interest in the reassuring bonds of human connection and "consubstantiality" that characterized medieval scholastic and contemporary organicist conceptions of the human being's political home. In his study of Spanish political thought of the Renaissance, J. A. Fernández-Santamaría notes that even so pragmatic and revolutionary a thinker as Machiavelli could not detach his analysis of state power from the conventional centralizing focus on the person, will, and virtue of the ruler and goes on to suggest that the political theorists of the Baroque, despite their evolving awareness that the state existed as an entity "finding its beginning and end, its *raggione*, within itself," could not escape an "almost frantic tendency . . . to concentrate on the ruler." His speculations regarding the anxieties underlying this limitation are certainly compatible with the historical insights suggested by the dramatic conflicts that trouble *El Rey Don Pedro en Madrid*'s effort at celebrative depiction of a major founder of the Castilian kingdom. The theorists' incapacity to achieve a proper sense of proportion in their obsession with the ruler, for Fernández-Santamaría, is the sign of a "desperate attempt to return to the anthropomorphism of

the past as a means of both arresting the alienation of man from the creature of his creation, and making more manageable the task of understanding the creative and ever-expanding capacities of the creature itself" (see *The State, War and Peace: Spanish Political Thought in the Renaissance: 1516–1559* [Cambridge, 1977], 247–250).

75. See, for example, Charles Aubrun and José Montesinos, "Peribáñez," *Lope de Vega: El teatro*, ed. A. Sánchez Romeralo (Madrid, 1989), 2:181–182.

76. See Covarrubias's discussion of "gigante," *Tesoro*, 588. The giant is a tyrant, a blasphemous "hijo de la tierra" who fails to recognize that there is a god above him.

77. *The Descent from Heaven: A Study in Epic Continuity* (New Haven, 1963), 10.

78. *Lope de Vega und seine Zeit*, 237–238.

79. Joseph Campbell, *The Hero with a Thousand Faces* (New York, 1965), 30.

80. In its introduction of a metaphysical foundation for the principal thematic conflicts of the play, Elvira's speech is comparable to the rustic symposium scenes of Lope's most famous drama, *Fuenteovejuna*, where a peasant heroine, menaced by a predatory, self-centered aristocrat, discourses with her comrades on Plato, Aristotle, the elemental chaos, the erotic bonds of a harmonious universal community, the importance of conformity of wills and mutual respect in love, the naturalness of married love and procreation, and the virtue of loyalty. In her exchange with the disguised king at the climax of the act, Elvira incorporates the most revolutionary theme of the other work. Honor, traditionally viewed as the reward for heroic deeds ("la dimensión imperativa de la persona") and exclusively the attribute of the rich and the powerful, belongs in reality only to the virtuous, regardless of social rank and the heroic blood of ancestry. "El honor es como el sol,/Que en todo lugar es bello,/Limpio, puro y luminoso:/Y ansí, en mí no tiene menos/Calidad que en el más noble" (Honor is like the sun, which is beautiful—clear, pure, and luminous—wherever it shines: and so, in me it has no less quality than in the noble of highest rank) (488). For the origins and persistence of the metaphysical system celebrated in such scenes in Lope's political theater, see Leo Spitzer, *Classical and Christian Ideas of World Harmony: Prolegomena to an Interpretation of the Word "Stimmung"* (Baltimore, 1963). For its corollary in Western political thought, see the following note.

81. In general the political drama of the Golden Age, as well as its neo-scholastic theorizing on the existence of the state, reasserts what Isaiah Berlin calls "one of the deepest assumptions of Western political thought," the doctrine, "scarcely questioned during its long ascendancy" from Aristotle and Plato to the time of Machiavelli, that there exists "some single principle which not only regulates the course of the sun and the stars, but prescribes their proper behaviour to all animate creatures. . . . At its centre is the vision of an impersonal nature or reason or cosmic purpose, or of a divine Creator whose power has endowed all things and creatures each with a specific function; these functions are elements in a single harmonious whole, and are intelligible in terms of it alone. . . . The idea of the world and of human society as a single intelligible structure is at the root of all the many various versions of natural law—the mathematical harmonies of the Pythagoreans, the logical ladder of Platonic Forms, the genetic-logical pattern of Aristotle, the divine *Logos* of the Stoics and the Christian Churches and of their secularised offshoots" ("The Originality of Machiavelli," *The Proper Study of Mankind* [New York, 1998], 312–313). While the scandalous indifference of Machiavelli to the existence or relevance of such metaphysical foundations in his account of state organization and exercise of power led to widespread denunciation, the cogency and clarity of his insights could not be overlooked as the absolutist

states came into existence and the disquieting realities of "state behavior" could not be satisfacto-rily comprehended by traditional systems of thought. The Spanish dramas that I have chosen to study are, in my opinion, most interesting because their traditionality is enriched and ambiguated by a revealing engagement with the most complex political issues of this moment of crisis and evolution in the history of Western political consciousness. In his discussion of such significant changes in *Philosophy and Government, 1572–1651* (Cambridge, 1993), Richard Tuck empha-sizes the displacement of the deeply rooted scholastic and humanist tradition and its Aristotelian-Ciceronian accounts of man's civic and political life by a *raison d'état* and a new humanism, centering on Tacitus's analyses of Roman government, reflecting the philosophical skepticism that rose in Europe in the late sixteenth century, and eventually leading to a renewed conception of natural law (e.g., Grotius).

82. A refusal to take note of this shift from the paradigm of Lope's most famous plays is striking in Marcelino Menéndez y Pelayo's detailed analysis of the work. Rejecting a "deeply entrenched prejudice" that attributes the authorship of *El Rey Don Pedro en Madrid* to Tirso or Claramonte, he insists that "to Lope and to Lope alone belongs the creation of the character Don Pedro and the virulent feudal tyrant, kidnapper, and violator of women, overthrown and crushed by the power of the monarchy or by popular retribution, or by both at the same time: it is the conflict that appears so many times in his theater, and always with marvelous literary prestige, from the Galician knight Tello de Neira, of *El mejor alcalde, el Rey,* to the Comendador of Ocaña in *Peribáñez* and the Comendador Fernán-Gómez de Guzmán in *Fuenteovejuna* ("Observaciones preliminares," in *Obras de Lope de Vega,* ed. RAE, 9:clxxi). None of these plays depicts the para-doxical symbiosis of king and "feudal tyrant" that distinguishes *El Rey Don Pedro en Madrid* and points to its most far-reaching historical, political, and ethical implications.

83. In the striking double vision that begins the play, we observe, to recall Nietzsche's writing on the Apollonian and Dionysian principles, a turn from an aesthetics of idealism, essentialism, ratio-nality, individuation, and love to an aesthetics of power, disintegration, intensity of feeling, and pathos. See Christian Lipperheide, *Die Ästhetik des Erhabenen bei Friedrich Nietzsche* (Würz-burg, 1999), ch. 1.

84. Elvira's vision of the universe, with its orderly distinctions and spaces, was widely reasserted and celebrated in the spectacularly successful contemporary creation epics (e.g., those by Du Bartas, Tasso, Acevedo, Milton). In my study "At the Threshold of Modernity," I argue that several of the major affirmations of the individual's freedom and creativity that we associate with the turn to modernity at this historical moment (Cervantes, Góngora, Gracián, Milton) were made in a self-conscious critical, but frequently conflicted or ambivalent, engagement with this order and its great Baroque genre. *El Rey Don Pedro en Madrid* incorporates such a "rebellious" voice in its "celebration" of monarchy, specifically in the king's rejection of his royal body. See my following observations on the "presence" of Góngora in the work.

85. Compare Góngora: "Pastor soy, mas tan rico de ganados,/que los valles impido más vacíos,/los cerros desparezco levantados/y los caudales seco de los ríos" (I am a shepherd, but so rich in flocks that I obstruct the emptiest valleys, I conceal the lofty hills, and I dry up the rivers' streams). *Fábula de Polifemo y Galatea,* in *Góngora y el Polifemo,* ed. D. Alonso (Madrid, 1961), 239. Tr. E. L. Rivers, *Renaissance and Baroque Poetry of Spain* (New York, 1966), 180.

86. One should note that Góngora's work was preceded by several literary recreations of the myth—for example, Stigliani's Italian poem *Il Polifemo* and Carillo y Sotomayor's *Fábula de Acis y*

Galatea. Lope developed the subject in the frightening giant lover Alasto in *La Arcadia* and would return to it in *La Circe.* On the popularity of the subject, see Arthur Terry, *Seventeenth-Century Spanish Poetry* (Cambridge, 1993), 142–144. A painting by Nicolas Poussin depicts the huge figure of the Cyclops, piping his love song while seated on and towering above a rugged mountain range bordering an Arcadian landscape. The violence and sexual fury of the gigantic defier of courtly decorum and "affect control" are emphasized in A. Carracci's two paintings dominating and framing the depiction of classical myths in the gallery of the Farnese Palace. Frustrated in the ineffectiveness of his courtship and his amorous song, the powerfully muscled gigantic body rises up parallel to the adjacent Mount Aetna and, nearly filling the entire canvas, hurls a huge boulder at the pitiful, cowering, and beautiful lovers while the volcano angrily flashes forth its eruption. See J. R. Martin, *The Farnese Gallery* (Princeton, 1965). For the social changes I would link with the popularity of the monstrous ancestor of the "authentic" and "spontaneous" romantic hero, see Elias, *The Court Society*, esp. ch. 8, "On the Sociogenesis of Aristocratic Romanticism in the Process of Courtization."

87. For the relations of the sacred and the sublime and visions and depictions of nature in the eighteenth and nineteenth centuries, see M. H. Abrams, *Natural Supernaturalism: Tradition and Revolution in Romantic Literature* (New York, 1973), esp. ch. 2, sec. 6, "The Theodicy of the Landscape."

88. See, for example, *Las soledades*, I, 189–218. The wandering protagonist—pilgrim-poet-reader—surveys a vast panorama from the "green balcony" provided by a soaring peak, "re-mapping" it imaginatively in a seemingly endless series of extravagant metaphorical transfigurations of a natural landscape that unfolds in sunlight, shadows, and mists beneath his gaze. The more complete analogue for the passage under discussion is Polifemo's declamation with its erotic motivation and hyperbolic bravado (*Polifemo*, sts. 49–63). His flocks cover valleys and obliterate mountain tops; his bees inhabit more hives than there are flowers in the fields; they "spin sunbeams on distaffs of gold"; he towers above the clouds that crown the mountains; and, before crushing his erotic rival, the beautiful Acis, he laments that situated on his immense rock, he can trace with his finger his misfortunes on the heavens. For the metaphysical, aesthetic, and literary implications of such images of "cosmic recreation," see my "At the Threshold of Modernity," esp. 27–28. For the classicist Juan de Jáuregui, Góngora's mountaintop landscape description and its paradoxical incorporation of a viewer's reaction to sublimity—"Muda la admiración, habla callando" (Wonder, speechless, speaks by going silent)—were incomprehensible acts of verbal violence: "¿Quién ha de sufrir tan descompasadas y molestas hipérboles?" (Who can bear such disproportionate and annoying hyperboles?) See "Antídoto contra la pestilente poesía de *Las soledades*," in *La batalla en torno a Góngora*, ed. A. Martínez Arancón (Barcelona, 1978), 178.

89. Unlike Tello (and of course Góngora's mysterious pilgrim), the most memorable of the many eccentric wanderers and navigators of chaos in Baroque literature are censured for their destructive, individualistic behavior, but all are generally associated with the creative imagination and a transgessive, "alien" artistic virtuosity—e.g. Milton's Satan, Tirso's Don Juan, Quevedo's picaro, and Alarcón's liar. In view of the interesting links between the violence of the *extraño* Tello and the intensity of the Gongoresque poetic order, it is worth noting that the hostility and anxiety that marked the long polemic stirred up in Spain by the circulation of *El Polifemo* and *Las soledades* repeatedly centered on the *extrañeza* of the Cordoban poet. For example, his first critic, Pedro de Valencia, noting his failed attempts at sublimity, urged him: "No se vaya, con pretension de

grandeza i altura, a buscar i imitar lo estraño, oscuro, ageno, i no tal como lo que a v.m. le nasce en casa" (You should not, in aspiring to grandeur and loftiness, seek out and imitate what is strange, obscure, alien, and exotic, unlike what is born for you at home). The sympathetic critic, following Longinus, allows that the poet must astonish his readers and "sacar a los hombres de sí," but he insists that he must "guardarse de estrañezas" and avoid trying to "estrañar con estruendo de palabras." See "Carta a Góngora en censura de sus poesías," in *Pedro de Valencia, primer crítico gongorino*, ed. M. M. Pérez López (Salamanca, 1988), 77–80. As for the association of violence and confusion with Góngora's language, the anxieties implied by the reactions of one of his principal adversaries, Juan de Jáuregui, are revealing: Góngora's diction and syntax are "violentos" and "trastornados" (jumbled); he refuses to create a "buen asiento" (solid base) and a proper "engaste" (setting) to stabilize and contain his acts of verbal violence; he has an extravagant predilection for "vocablos nuevos y extranjeros." The word that appears to disturb Jáuregui most in his classical enthusiasm for clarity, simplicity, and order is *errante*, a word that "is never to be found in Garci Laso." See "Antídoto contra la pestilente poesía de *Las soledades*," 186, 176, 168.

90. For the centrality of fear, power, unbounded will, and fearsome immensity in the experience and aesthetics of the sublime, see Edmund Burke, *A Philosophical Enquiry into the Origin of Our Ideas of the Sublime and the Beautiful*, ed. J. T. Boulton (London, 1958), 1:6–18; 2:1–13. Also see Abrams, *Natural Supernaturalism*, 101–102, and Lipperheide, *Die Ästhetik des Erhabenen bei Friedrich Nietzsche*, 15–20.

91. The regressive, tabooed character of the king's submission to the violent urge to triumph as a man is plainly indicated in Lope's festive engagement with the oppositions of man and majesty in *Carlos V en Francia*. Disturbed by the German soldier's boast that he had killed thirty Spaniards in the Battle of Pavia, the emperor reminds himself that kings are not simply men: "Pacheco, a no ser quien soy,/a canpaña y me matara/con él" (Pacheco, if I were not who I am,/to the field of combat,/and I would fight him to the death) (176–177).

92. *Coplas a la muerte de su padre*, ed. V. Beltrán (Barcelona, 1993), 161; tr. E. L. King, in A. Castro, *The Structure of Spanish History* (Princeton, 1954), 20.

93. Probably the purest and most penetrating dramatic exploration of this aspect of an obsolete aristocratic culture at this moment of transition in the European political and social worlds is what has been called "surely the strangest of all Shakespeare's thirty-nine plays," *Coriolanus*. While the hero's incapacity to understand a statist order is directed not at an institutional monarch, but rather at the lower social world of citizens, tribunes, bourgeoisie, and urban proletariat of republican Rome, in his representation of the "strangeness" of the archaic value system—its rootedness in naked force and manliness; its elation in the beauty of bloodshed; its intolerance of any reductions, compromises, or disguises of self; its disgust with pandering, flattery, and political rhetoric; its contempt for weakness and humility—Coriolanus has undeniable affinities with the double protagonist, the two *extraños* of the contemporary Spanish work. The Roman hero is sublimely beautiful in his most blood-streaked epiphanies: "Thou art left, Marcius./A carbuncle entire, as big as thou art,/Were not so rich a jewel" (I, 4, 54–56). He is "mantled" and "masked" in blood. The Roman "loves the painting in which he is smeared." In his world of single combat blood "more becomes a man/Than gilt his trophy" (I, 3, 36–38). All communities—state, family, army—seem to decompose around the isolated, proud warrior, who cannot really understand his preceptor Menenius's vision of the state in the organicist metaphor, endlessly repeated by the Baroque theorists of absolutism and state, of the body and its interdependent and mutually

nourishing members. His deepest ambition is revealed in his climactic resistance to his mother's supplications: "I'll never/Be such a gosling to obey instinct, but stand/As if a man were author of himself/And knew no other kin" (V, 3, 34–37). (As his seventeenth-century aristocratic Spanish descendents put it, "¡Soy quien soy!") Shakespeare's treatment of the "dimensión imperativa de la persona" is of course tragic and psychologically focused on the mother-son dependency relationship rather than on issues of male rivalry. It has no concern with the kind of uneasy reconciliation of statist and aristocratic values that the Spanish play enacts. However, each play, in its own way, represents a powerful dramatic depiction of the impossibility of maintaining in its purity the old warrior ethos of individualism in a modern world that demands either its assimilation in a drastically transfigured or sublimated form or its extirpation. For the "strangeness" of the play, see H. Bloom, *Shakespeare and the Invention of the Human* (New York, 1998), 584. For its examination of the aristocratic ethos, see A. Kernan, *Shakespeare, The King's Playwright: Theater in the Stuart Court, 1603–1613* (New Haven, 1996), ch. 7, and N. Frye, *Fools of Time: Studies in Shakespearean Tragedy* (Toronto, 1967), 56–59.

94. If the presentation of the "personalistic ethos" of the aristocratic warrior tradition is certainly inflated in the Gongoresque language of the *infanzón's* claims, it is nevertheless important to recognize its seriousness in relation to the profound historical oppositions that the play is mediating. Pedro *el justiciero*, who uses a paper rather than a sword to dominate his opponent, cannot fully stifle his own impatience with bureaucracy and written document. If we look at one of the most flamboyant of the numerous celebrations of aristocratic values and models in Lope's theater, *Los Ramírez de Arellano*, we discover that a sequence of ritualistic scenes distinguishing a perfect noble from a political, or "statist," king climaxes in the hero's refusal to make a request for a deserved reward in writing, handing the king a blank piece of paper and reminding him that the gifts of kings, like those of God, require no written communications and transactions. See *Obras de Lope de Vega*, ed. RAE, 9:591. One might recall Cervantes's comic treatment of these oppositions in the juxtaposition of Don Quixote's eloquent naked body, with its revealing somersaults, to the two written documents that Sancho receives in his embassy to Dulcinea, the "unsigned" chivalric epistle and the contractual agreement concerning the delivery of the knight's *merced*— the ass foals. See *Don Quixote*, vol. 1, ch. 25.

95. Gilman, "*El rey don Pedro en Madrid y el infanzón de Illescas* as a Tragic Poem." One of the characteristic deflationary comments of Tello's *gracioso* follows his bombastic claims to belong to the most exalted nobility of Spain: "No es solamente noble el dueño mío,/Sino origen de nobles tan añejo,/Que el vino de más rancio y de más brío/Puede en su antiguedad tomar consejo./Dispensa en cuatro grados de judío/Con su aliento no más" (My master is not just a noble, but in fact a source of nobles so mellowed by age, that the most ancient and hearty wine could take counsel in his antiquity. The smell of his breath alone dispenses with four degrees of Jewishness) (485). The "carnivalesque" degradation is based on the comic equivalence of noble and a personified wine and their sharing of anxieties regarding recognizable traces of Jewishness and "purity of blood."

96. Menéndez y Pelayo, in "Observaciones preliminares," finds a clarifying parallel in Lope's *Los Novios de Hornachuelos*, in the boastful *ricohombre* de Extremadura, Lope Meléndez, who spurns the king's invitation to the court, flaunts his Gothic lineage, boasts of his prowess with women, and describes his vast estate and wealth in hyperbolic terms. In its enumeration of the specific items he possesses, his speech matches in very precise terms the declamation of Tello that we

have examined. All of this is noted by Menéndez y Pelayo and used in an argument to prove that Lope is in fact the author of *El Rey Don Pedro en Madrid*, which is alleged to be "exactly" like its "earlier model." In my view the undeniable replications are most interesting because they vividly underscore the radical *differences* between the plays and the greater profundity of the later work. One initially encounters similar political themes and historical oppositions. In the first scene of *Los novios de hornachuelos*, Lope Meléndez and his servant Mendo engage in a political discussion. At issue is the origin of the state. Is it based on the rule of the strongest, who establishes order and maintains control through violence and fear? Or does the state rather, as the servant argues in an eloquent rejoinder, come into existence as a delegation of power and a compact for peace, aimed at achieving the permanent goals of the society of human beings—law, justice, and rationality? Lope, however, turns abruptly from the political theme. There is no ambivalence in his depiction of the aristocrat: he holds no attraction for the king; his territories undergo no elevating poetic transfiguration; his prostration is comical and instantaneous. The king's monarchism is neither explored analytically nor problematized. He is quite simply an idealized counter-figure to the rebellious aristocrat, with whom he shares the heroic blood of Pelayo's descendants. As king, he is "top Goth": he easily "controls the horse of Castile" (400); he goes in pilgrimage to the Virgin of Guadalupe, while his adversary journeys to the woman he would seduce; in his illness he is well aware of his humanity and its fundamental "nothingness" unless elevated to the royal body as an instrument of God; demonstrating that "el nombre rey/encierra en si gran secreto" (396), he defeats his antagonist instantaneously, by merely displaying his charismatic figure ("Señor, no más; vuestra vista,/Sin conoceros, da espanto" [396]), brandishing his sword and lecturing the aristocrat on how he established dominance over the monstrous nobles of Castile in a battle of mountains. As if struck by a lightning bolt, Don Lope instantly falls at the monarch's feet and allows him to place his foot on his head. The emblematic scene could stand as a parody of the climactic moment in the complex symbiotic relationship of king and warrior in *El Rey Don Pedro en Madrid*. At this point Act II ends and with it any gestures toward political philosophy and serious history. The simple differentiation of monarch and noble in social rank and in married status is the presupposition for an effective comedy of *enredo* and parallel *entremés* plot, complete with comic courtships; confused identities; misinterpreted letters; diatribes and comic inversions (e.g., "el rey es un gran judío"); slapstick violence; and, in an ingenious festive parody of the grand political themes initially insinuated, a climactic "pacification" of the chaotic nobles of Castile and a royal "unmarrying" of two betrothed couples whose members, in accordance with the dictates of the proverb of the title, cannot stand one another. See ed. BAE, vol. 41 (Madrid, 1857), esp. 396, 400.

97. See *Primera crónica general*, ed. NBAE, vol. 5 (Madrid, 1906), 311. Saavedra Fajardo places the "loor de España" in the mouth of the first Gothic king to enter the peninsula, Ataulfo. Exhorting his soldiers, he claims that the blood of the "valorous and constant" natives is a part of the immense national patrimony of Spain. Mixing their Gothic blood with it, they will satisfy the "appetite to dominate that powerfully resides in their hearts." "De ninguna parte mejor que desde España podéis aspirar al dominio universal" (From no place better than Spain can one aspire to universal dominion). *Corona gótica, castellana y austríaca, Obras completas*, ed. A. González Palencia (Madrid, 1946), 735–736.

98. See Augustin Redondo, "Les divers visages du thème (wisi)gothique dans l'Espagne des XVI

et XVIIe siècles," in *L'Europe héritière de l'Espagne wisigothique*, ed. J. Fontaine and C. Pelli-strandi, *Rencontres de la Casa de Velázquez* 35 (Madrid, 1992): 353–364.

99. Ibid., 358. See also Ricardo Arco y Garay: "It is clear that the desire for an ancient lineage became a craze in the period of the poet [Lope de Vega]" (*La sociedad española en las obras dramáticas de Lope de Vega* [Madrid, 1941], 465).

100. See José Antonio Maravall, *El concepto de España en la Edad Media* (Madrid, 1964), 315ff.

101. See Carlos Clavería, "Reflejos del 'goticismo' español en la fraseología del siglo de oro," *Studia philologica: Homenaje ofrecido a Dámaso Alonso* (Madrid, 1960), 1:357–372.

102. See Thomas Case, "Some Observations on the References to the Goths in the Dramas of Lope de Vega," *Revista de Estudios Hispánicos* 3 (1969): 67–91.

103. *El príncipe perfecto, primera parte, Obras de Lope de Vega*, ed. RAE (Nueva edición), vol. 10 (Madrid, 1930), 482.

104. Case, "Some Observations on the References to the Goths," 71.

105. *La pícara Justina*, ed. A. Rey Hazas (Madrid, 1977), 1:169. See Redondo, "Les divers visages du thème (wisi)gothique," 362.

106. Moreto's title, despite its "erasure" of the uncontrollable personalism of the double protagonists and its concealment of a disturbing paradox behind a benign abstraction that approaches allegory—*El valiente justiciero*—suggests that he may have understood the deeper moral and political implications of its articulation of oppositions.

107. *The State and the Rule of Law*, ch. 1. See ch. 1 above.

108. *Obras de Lope de Vega*, ed. RAE, vol. 7 (Madrid, 1897), 44–48. See Juan de Mariana, *Del Rey y de la institución real*, 472–477. For the Gothic tradition of elective monarchy, see Saavedra Fajardo, *Corona gótica*, 856ff.

109. See, for example, *La primera crónica general*, ed. NBAE, 5:283–300. In one of the most interesting projects to align the glories of the Gothic tradition and the achievements of the Habsburg kings, the *Corona gótica*, Saavedra Fajardo insists that Bamba was not raised "entre el arado y azadón (como algunos creyeron) sino a las cortes y palacios, siendo de la primera nobleza de los godos" (between the plow and the hoe [as some believe], but in courts and palaces, being of the first nobility of the Goths) (974–975). As he is one of the leading theorists of absolutist monarchy, his arguments are of particular interest for us. Exalted in the official iconography of absolutism—thoroughly displayed in his emblematic treatise on the Christian prince—Bamba becomes the ideal absolute monarch, the "heart" of the political organism, the illuminating sun present everywhere in its territories. He masters the techniques of arousing fear and respect in his subjects; he lectures his subjects on the dangers of dynastic ruptures; he counters the political astuteness and prudence, the wily machinations, the manipulative flattery and rhetoric of his great rival, the traitor Paulo. He "brandishes his sword" as he leads his troops into battle and inflicts exemplary punishments on the enemies of the state (see 982). Bamba's decisive victory in the siege of Narbonne is described at great length. It focuses not on the individual heroes of yore and "epic confrontations" of the great warriors, but rather on the maneuvers of a modern army in its mastery of "disciplina" and "ciencia militar" and in its use of the most advanced technology of the siege. In other words, unlike Lope's Bamba and unlike the drama *El Rey Don Pedro en Madrid*, Saavedra Fajardo's reinvention of the Goths has purged all anxieties of the anti-statist warrior ethos, as well as the pretentiousness, status consciousness, and pride in blood and class

that victimize Bamba. One senses his awareness of the paradoxical aspects of his project to "modernize" and appropriate the power of the Gothic myth in his pragmatic doctrines of statecraft: "No parezca a algunos que yo no debiera empezar de los godos, nación tenida por bárbara entre los griegos, que estudiaba más en la espada que en la pluma; porque, antes, mejor de ella que de la griega o romana se puede aprender la verdadera razón de estado, porque la más segura es la que dicta la razón natural" (Let nobody think that I should not have begun with the Goths, a nation considered barbarian among the Greeks, one that cultivated the arts of the sword more than the pen; because, quite the contrary, one can learn from the Goths better than from the Greeks or Romans the true state reason, because the most reliable is that dictated by natural reason) (706). Saavedra Fajardo insists that in their political expertise, the ferocious people who were driven by a "bloody appetite for dominating" (723) offer contemporary princes an ideal mirror in which they can discover their true identity as kings and correct blemishes revealed in themselves (706–707).

110. The assimilation of Goth and *villano* myths is striking in several of Lope's imaginative recreations of early Spanish history according to the patterns of fairy tale and romantic comedy. A remnant of Gothic Spain becomes, for Lope, the "green world of romance," with its marvelous adventures, usurped kingdoms, lost infants, fleeing heroines, sheltering caves, friendly animals, dazzling metamorphoses, and reassuring deliverances. Sturdy rustics of "good blood" turn out to be ideal lovers, loyal patriots, and in some cases dispossessed kings and founders of Spanish kingdoms. In *El príncipe despeñado* the widowed queen Elvira, bearing in her womb the "royal sun, the descendant of Pelayo," flees her menacing brother-in-law, the usurper, and after giving birth in a cave, encounters a man dressed as a wild beast who turns out to be another brother-in-law, this one benign. He introduces himself—"Soy aunque salvaje, un caballero. . . . Soy buena sangre, soy reliquia goda" (Although a savage, I am a knight . . . I am of good blood, I am a Gothic relic) —and assists her in her deliverance and the restoration of the infant king, displayed on stage in the final scene as all actors kneel in homage (*Comedias*, vol. 7, ed. M. Arroyo Stephens [Madrid, 1993], 954–955). See also *El testimonio vengado*, which opposes the sturdy, honest *villano* Goth—who, as exiled bastard son of King Sancho, has been brought up in a mountain world associated with fertility, purity, love, and poetry and must follow his destiny to liberate Spain—to the decadent, unruly Goth of the court—his scheming, ambitious half-brother García, who violates his father's prohibitions and calumniates the queen. The former defends his stepmother; defeats García in a duel; displaces him as her son in a symbolic ritual of birth; and in a sense "refounds" Spain by restoring its "cradle" in the mountains, the ideal world of the authentic *villano* Goths. See *Obras de Lope de Vega*, ed. RAE, vol. 7 (Madrid, 1897).

111. The drama attaches the most damaging of the tyrant's traditional sins—uncontrollable lust and the violent appropriation of the bodies of other human beings in the act of rape—to the king's antagonist. Nevertheless, in a comic aside a *gracioso* notes that Pedro loves all ladies with an undiscriminating appetite; Tello scornfully tells the victim of his rape that she need not seek redress from the king, since he has "learned from the royal example" (488); and there is a suggestion that the youthful Pedro's murder of the singer and chaplain was connected with an attempt to violate the sanctity of a nunnery and, of course, to abuse its inhabitants.

112. Pedro as "stone" opposes the centrifugal forces and metamorphoses of Tello-"earth's" expansive, mountainous landscape, traditionally the locus of homelessness, statelessness, lawlessness, titanic denial of natural order, and loss of self. His laying of the stone at the temple in Madrid—a his-

torical fabrication—can be viewed as the act of a god or a civilizer who, as it were, establishes a center that organizes the cosmos around it (see Mircea Eliade: *Das Heilige und das Profane: Vom Wesen des Religiösen* [Hamburg, 1957], chs.1, 2, and *Cosmos and History*, tr. W. R. Trask [New York, 1954], 12–21). One might compare the legendary rocks in the temple of Jerusalem, considered in Christian and Jewish tradition to be the center of the universe. For example, the Zohar tells that in creating the world, God "detached one precious stone from underneath His throne of glory and plunged it into the abyss. . . . That stone is called in Hebrew Shetiyah—Foundation" (cited by S. Greenblatt, *Marvelous Possessions: The Wonder of the New World* [Chicago, 1991], 161–162). Pedro is, of course, founding a *state*, and his various acts in Madrid—setting up his street tribunals, pronouncing judgments in his audiences, building official edifices, and displaying state power through rituals of execution and carefully choreographed revelations of the "official body"—should be understood as symbolic authorizations of the new order. See A. S. Keller, O. J. Lissitzyn, and F. J. Mann, *Creation of Rights of Sovereignty through Symbolic Acts, 1400–1800* (New York, 1938); also see Greenblatt's discussion of the official procedures for taking possession of lands for the crown in the period of the explorations of the new world (*Marvelous Possessions*, 55–58).

113. Menéndez y Pelayo, "Observaciones preliminares," cl; see *Obras de Lope de Vega*, ed. RAE, 9: cl-cliii. See also Vossler on the power of Pedro as a dramatic character: "He is surrounded by the aura of a tormented being, one racked by terror, suspicion, and anxieties, but at the same time he is a being who commands from within himself impressive resources of security, confidence, and wisdom" (*Lope de Vega und sein Zeitalter*, 237).

114. For the association of political policy and medical intervention in the new, pragmatic statecraft associated with Machiavelli and his descendants, see Berlin, "The Originality of Machiavelli"; Tuck notes that even in Mariana's influential, humanistic "mirror of the prince," we find that the Jesuit, "absolutely characteristically, accepted that a prince should use fraud and deceit *ex commodo*, though rarely, and as if for medicinal purposes" (*Philosophy and Government, 1572–1651*, 79). On the other hand, in traditional humanistic philosophy, there was a tendency (e.g., Salutati's *De nobilitate legum et medicinae* [1399]) to define the political arts in opposition to medicine as a practical scientific art concerning the natural rather than the human world. See Maurizio Viroli, *From Politics to Reason of State* (Cambridge, 1992), 75–76. The most familiar Spanish drama raising such issues is Calderón's *El médico de su honra*, where the protagonist and his king—Pedro el Cruel—bond as doubles in their application of a medicinal remedy to the "wounds" and "bloodshed" that an uncontrollable antagonist—the violent, spontaneous aristocrat Enrique—inflicts on the state and its society by pursuing his instincts. Both *El médico de su honra* and *El Rey Don Pedro en Madrid* present the king as a conflicted figure, bound by the laws and political codes of statism; forced to repress his violent impulses; compelled to maintain social order and reputation through cold rationality, calculation, and compromise—i.e., the metaphorical *medicina* that is so grotesquely literalized in the "physician hero's" bleeding to death of his wife and preservation of honor—and his triumph in both plays is surrounded by tragic portents of his ultimate failure in the impending fratricide at Montiel. As for the king's "confinement" and impatience in playing palace and political "games" to manipulate his fierce opponent in Act II of *El Rey Don Pedro en Madrid*—e.g., his set of "mousetraps," his "game of chess," his choreographed "*entremés*" and "*comedia de palacio*"—it is worth noting M. Spariosu's distinction, in his recent studies of the role and importance of play in civilization, between the

kind of play characteristic of rational and middle-class societies—rule-determined, non-violent, collaborative, skill- rather than chance-oriented—and that characterizing pre-rational and aristocratic societies—privileging chance, violent conflict, the thrill in the risk of dissolution, individualism, and force. In the palace, the frustrated Tello futilely calls for his confiscated weapons and is unable to "play his game." But it is clear that the exasperated Pedro too is in an unfamiliar playing environment, one that he must learn to accept and master. This is of course the space that Elias has associated with the rise of civilization. To understand this strange scene and specifically the king's struggle for self-control as he coldly manipulates and "educates" his opponent in a palace "chess game," we should note that Luque Faxardo argued that chess is a game that teaches leaders the importance of benevolent rule and recalled that its inventor, Xerxes, "queriendo refrenar la crueldad, y braveza de un tyranno, por exemplo deste juego le demostro que muy poco vale la Magestad del Rey sin fuerças" (desiring to rein in the cruelty and ferocity of a tyrant, through the example of this game, demonstrated for him that the Majesty of a King is of little value without forces) (*Historia general del hombre en que se trata del hombre en comun* [Madrid, 1589], fol. 167; I am grateful to Michael Scham for bringing this work to my attention). The protagonist's climactic plunge into darkness, disorder, and loss of identity as king is a momentary return to the games and value system of the self and culture he must abandon in donning the crown. See M. Spariosu, *Dionysus Reborn: Play and the Aesthetic Dimension in Modern Philosophical and Scientific Discourse* (Ithaca, NY, 1989). As for the official attempts to contain and aestheticize the thrill of bloodshed in connection with the heroic king, the "game" that usually appears as part of the discourse of monarchy in conventional plays is the relatively controlled ritual of the bullfight. Its presentation in *El príncipe perfecto* is of particular interest precisely because it successfully reconciles the two systems of value that come into conflict in *El Rey Don Pedro en Madrid*. A bull escapes, and while all flee, the king, finding that "la Real grandeza/No sabe salir de sí," slays the animal; "bathes the street in blood"; and offers his hand to be kissed in homage by his courtiers, who express admiration for a *hazaña* (deed of prowess) inspired not by "la ciencia" (science), but rather by "el ánimo" (courage). The momentary reversion to the traditional hierarchy of values—*grandeza* and manliness—is punctuated by its opposition to the new political values: "La diferencia se ve/En el ánimo y la ciencia;/Que donde no hay prevención,/Es el ánimo maestro" (One sees the difference between courage and science; for where there are no preventive measures, courage is the master) (*Obras de Lope de Vega*, ed. RAE, 10:469). See my observations above on Philip III's *hazaña* in shooting the bull.

115. If one is willing to allow that tyranny, in its purest form, can be understood figuratively as a "crowning" of the impulsive Don Juan Tenorio, J. E. Hartzenbusch's nineteenth-century intuition of the affinities of Pedro and Tirso de Molina's *burlador* is not unfounded. Pedro resists his destiny to be the "rock" of the new order and must be defeated and humiliated by his spectral persecutor, who like Don Juan's avenging stone guest has been a victim of the latter's lawless violence. In their action, setting, atmosphere (the *chiaroscuro* of the menacing darkness and fire), motifs of blasphemy and submission to a supreme God, conceptual oppositions and powerful symbols of the stabilization of will and state in stone, and intrusion of divine power in the handclasp that burns both "sinners," the two scenes in fact have much more in common than Hartzenbusch noted. Nevertheless, his attribution of the authorship of the whole of *El Rey Don Pedro en Madrid* to Tirso, made in his BAE edition of 1848 and generally accepted until Menéndez y

Pelayo's reconsideration of the evidence and restoration of its title to Lope in the "Observaciones preliminares" to his edition of 1899, remains unconvincing. In view of the similarity of elements that link both climactic scenes, is it not possible that Tirso's great climax, so often repeated in the history of drama and opera (and specifically its development of the motif of the "convidado de piedra," a motif that students of the play, to be sure, have clarified, along with that of the "double invitation," as precedented in European folklore [see F. Márquez Villanueva, *Orígenes y elaboración de "El Burlador de Sevilla"* (Salamanca, 1996), 52–56]) was inspired by *El Rey Don Pedro en Madrid?*

116. Thomas Scott's words clearly express the threat that the duel poses for the new state: "Now every man whether private or publique, is a member of the Commonwealth, wherein hee live's [*sic*], and soe hath noe *power of his owne body*, to dispose of it this or that way. . . . For any man to hazard his person in a single *Duell*, without manifest necessity, is to comit violence to the Commonwealth, and to rend a limbe from the same." Tuck cites the English clergyman's treatise *Vox dei*, written in the mid-1620s and reflecting the impact of the Tacitean political theorists of the period. See *Philosophy and Government, 1572–1651*, 115–116. See also Neuschel: "The most important function of the duel . . . was its almost mythic function as a representation of the noble's power of self-definition. The duel was not a form of political opposition in our sense (for that would be ridiculous); it was rather an act that extended beyond the moment to symbolize nobles' willingness to define themselves as distinct from the state that forbade them to engage in it" (*Word of Honor*, 207).

117. The recuperation of aristocratic values in the scene of metamorphosis might in fact recall the complexities of Calderón's controversial work. The latter was based on an actual event in 1535 that Golden Age chroniclers considered, as the "last duel in Spain," the occasion for Charles V's and the Papacy's decrees banning the custom. It ridicules, in farcical scenes and outbursts of overblown rhetoric, the excesses of aristocratic behavior—pride, self-involvement, violence, bluster, and the inclination for man-to-man combat. At the same time, the drama paradoxically reaffirms the illustrious character of the Spanish nobility and its traditions, climaxing in a beautiful, ceremonious judicial duel between "honorable" Aragonese gentlemen. Here too a king—in fact an emperor—Charles V, sanctions and then interrupts a duel and ultimately reintegrates the competing nobles into the service of the new nation-state. As Claude Chauchadis has argued, Calderón's treatment of the issue is misunderstood if one interprets such a work as either a Christian moralist condemnation of dueling or an archaic aristocratic celebration of cruel and violent codes of conduct and manliness. See "Las denuncias de la ley del duelo en *El postrer duelo de España*: Nuevo examen," in *La comedia*, ed. Jean Canavaggio (Madrid, 1995), 381–396, esp. 390ff. Guy Rossetti's important study of the play and its sources stresses its fundamental monarchist point of view and its criticisms of clandestine marriage and aristocratic dueling. See "Introduction," to his edition of *El postrer duelo de España* (London, 1977).

118. Pedro's final role and scenario as dramaturgic king might be clarified by reference to Philip II's explanation of his decision not to follow through on the frightening threat to go personally, as *justiciero*, to the Low Countries, "where heads had to roll." "The strategy, explained the wily king, was 'first to use the severity of justice, then afterwards use clemency and kindness.'" See Kamen, *Philip of Spain*, 119–120.

119. Cited by Estow, *Pedro the Cruel of Castile*, 259.

120. See Pérez Gómez, *Romancero del Rey don Pedro*, *Romances* 21 and 22, 187–190. The English version of 21 is by Sir Walter Scott. See J. G. Lockhart, *Ancient Spanish Ballads: Historical and Romantic* (New York, 1842), 118–119.

EPILOGUE

1. In this mid-century *refundición* the fundamental story of the model, the encounter of Diogenes and Alexander, and the paradoxical descent-ascent of the monarch through humanization and philosophical insight disappear. Troubling questions concerning royal power are circumvented by the creation of the villainous aristocrat-seducer as a *tirano* and a master of the erotic discourse (the *finezas*) of courtly love. The king's sonnet is cut out, and he ceases to speak plainly with the voice of Epictetus. The most radical impoverishment in the imitation is its failure to incorporate the provocations of Lope's doublings and symmetries (i.e., king-peasant, palace-*rincón*, royal banquet–forest symposium). In its final scene the "sabio monarca" must remind his guest at the table that "este exceso/No le hago aquí como rey, Sino como un caballero/Particular; que por vos/Derogo los privilegios/De la majestad, pues gusto/Que hoy seais mi compañero,/Porque, en mi sentir, no es rey/Quien de su gusto no es dueño" (I do not indulge in this excess as a king, but rather as an individual nobleman; for you I renounce the privileges of the majesty, for it is my pleasure that today you may be my companion, because, in my opinion, he who is not the proper master of his pleasure is not a king). His final counsel would seem to be a denial and condemnation of all that Lope de Vega achieved in creating his peasant-philosopher. "Porque al Rey concedió el cielo/Una virtud superior/Oculta, que los plebeyos/Sus secretos no penetran,/Y el enseñarle es gran yerro/Pues sabe mas que el vasallo/El Rey, cuando sabe menos" (Because heaven granted the King a superior, occult power, the common people cannot penetrate his secrets. And the attempt to instruct him is a great error; for the King, when he knows least, in fact knows more than the vassal). See Juan de Matos Fragoso, *El sabio en su retiro y villano en su rincón*, ed. BAE, vol. 47 (Madrid, 1858), 217–218.

2. See Rudolf Wittkower, "Vicissitudes of a Dynastic Monument: Bernini's Equestrian Statue of Louis XIV," in *Essays in Honor of Erwin Panofsky*, ed. Millard Meiss (New York, 1961), 1:497–531. See also P. K. Monod, *The Power of Kings: Monarchy and Religion in Europe, 1589–1715* (New Haven, 1999), 317–324, and Walter Liedtke, *The Royal Horse and Rider: Painting, Sculpture, and Horsemanship, 1500–1809* (New York, 1989), 18–35. I. Lavin has recently discussed the unconventional and "disturbing" features and effects of Bernini's sculptures of royal figures in connection with the rise of a reconstituted scholastic-classical political theory—emphasizing the virtue of ruler and community, the delegation of sovereignty from the people to the ruler, and the transcendental connections and responsibilities of the latter—to which the rising states and the Counter-Reformation and Jesuit establishment turned in order to resist the appeal of the secularist, materialist, and pragmatic political theory of Machiavelli. Lavin finds a revealing example of this political theory in the spectacular exequies for Duke Francesco of Este in the cathedral of Modena, where the catafalque and the church setting are transformed into a grandiose architectural panegyric of symbols, allegories, icons, and histories and where the deceased ruler is identified with the sun and the perfection of the Platonic idea. This kind of architectural panegyric was common in Spain's celebrative drama of kings. (See, for example, Lope's *Carlos V en Francia*, Act III.) As we have seen, such a royal frame provoked the iconoclastic Cervantes

to ridicule (see the introduction above). See "La imagen 'Berniniana' del ideal del Monarca Cristiano," in *Figuras e imágenes del Barroco: Estudios sobre el Barroco español y sobre la obra de Alonso Cano*, Varios Autores (Madrid, 1999), 27–48. It is not surprising that Bernini's highly individualized, unsettled, unallegorical, and "unframed" figures were unacceptable for the cautious politician who ruled France and that in this case the horse and rider had to be turned into something else—a representation of Marcus Curtius throwing himself into an abyss to save his country—and discreetly placed in the gardens of Versailles, where they remained until 1980.

3. Agustín Moreto, *El valiente justiciero*, ed. Frank P. Casa (Salamanca, 1971), 100.

4. See "Die klassische Dämpfung in Racines Stil," *Romanische Stil- und Literaturstudien* (Marburg, 1931), 1:135–268.

5. See Alexander Parker, *The Mind and Art of Calderón* (Cambridge, 1988), 241: "The presence of a king in a play, whether seen or just felt, was a strong sense of authority (of law and order, as we say nowadays) with all the connotations of justice and the moral law. . . . In the drama kings are at hand to hear complaints, to pass judgment, and to right wrongs."

6. The most famous witness for the new consciousness, as well as implicitly for a new literary form adequate to its expression, is Don Quixote, who in one of his most confident moments claims that he can be the peers of France if he so chooses.

7. "In the course of the seventeenth century there were only four years of complete peace. . . . 'This,' Fulvio Testi, Italian poet and military commander, wrote in 1641, 'is the century of the soldier'" (see Geoffrey Parker, "The Soldier," in *Baroque Personae*, ed. R. Villari [Chicago, 1995], 32). For the designation of the period as the "political century," see G. Oestreich, *Neostoicism and the Early Modern State* (Cambridge, 1982).

8. Friedrich Meinecke, *Machiavellism: The Doctrine of Raison d'Etat and Its Place in Modern History*, ed. D. Scott (London, 1957), 76. See Boccalini's commentary on Tacitus in *Bilancia politica*, ed. L. Dumay (Castellana, 1678), 1:504. See Maurizio Viroli's discussion of the seventeenth-century "triumph of reason of state" and its "dismissal of the language of politics as the art of the republic" that "goes hand and hand with the recognition that the world is bound to remain deeply corrupt. It was the exact reversal of the hopes and attitudes that had accompanied the golden era of civil philosophy, namely, that the moral identity of a people should, and could be different and better" (*From Politics to Reason of State* [Cambridge, 1992], 266–267). Lope's *El villano en su rincón*, while thoroughly monarchist in its conception of state organization and the foundations of political authority, nevertheless, in its ethicist approach to power and civic responsibility, its concern for the moral development of citizen and ruler and their reciprocal responsibilities, and its respect for the inviolability of the individual human being can be seen as a reassertion of the humanistic traditions underlying the "golden era of civil philosophy."

9. *La vida es sueño*, ed. C. Morón Arroyo (Madrid, 1991), 164. The translation in the epigraph and in the following citations is by E. Honig in *Calderón de la Barca: Six Plays* (New York, 1993), 339–340.

10. While deeply pessimistic, Calderón's political vision remains consistent with its Christian-scholastic foundations regarding the connection of man, creator, and cosmos in their shared rationality. If man's capacities have been severely diminished by the Fall, he is nonetheless not estranged in a dualistic universe. The chastened Basilio must learn that God's "finger" never writes lies, or *engaños*, in the "golden letters and ciphers" on the "blue papers" of the heavens (202). The enormous distance separating human beings and their omnipotent creator is put more

starkly in Calderón's miracle *comedia, La cruz en la sepultura.* Eusebio dismisses an astrologer in the following words: "Vete libre . . . que desde el suelo/no se ha de medir el cielo,/que es infinita distancia" (Go in freedom, for from the earth one cannot make measurements of the heavens, for the distance separating them is infinite). See *La devoción de la cruz,* ed. A. Valbuena (Madrid, 1963), 85. As in the case of the Moorish princess Fénix (see below), such distance and the stellar misreadings it encourages can lead not only to political miscalculation, violence, and humiliation, but also to metaphysical anxiety and despair.

11. K. Löwith's discussion of Augustine's arguments concerning divine omnipotence, providence, fate, astrology, contingency, chance, human history, and the "limited" scope of man's freedom is relevant to an assessment of the political implications of Calderón's most dramatic celebration *and circumscription* of the human will. Historical issues and movements will always remain in certain fundamental ways unpredictable. Divine purposes and interventions are incalculable. "There is indeed a common ground of fearful reverence and free submission to fate, or providence, in ancient antiquity [e.g., stoicism] and ancient Christianity [e.g., Augustine], which distinguishes both of them from profane modernity and its belief in progressive manageability." See *Meaning in History* (Chicago, 1949), 200. Also see R. Bittner's "Augustine's Philosophy of History," in *The Augustinian Tradition,* ed. G. B. Matthews (Berkeley, 1999), 345–360. Monotonous, uncontrollable change and continuing insecurity are the conditions of man's life in history, which will always remain non-transparent. "There is in principle no way to improve the way humans live in this world. It is all rotten from the root up" (*City of God,* 13.14). The most political activity and institutions can achieve is peace and security. As citizen, man must obey. "The point is that in the one history of the world there is so little that counts: creation, fall, redemption, judgement, that is all. The rest is waste." As has often been pointed out, *La vida es sueño* is contemporary with Descartes's *Discourse of Method.*

12. *El príncipe constante,* ed. Pablo Pou Fernández (Zaragoza, 1962), 75–79, 86. See Elida Maria Szarota, *Künstler, Grübler, und Rebellen: Studien zum europäischen Märtyrerdrama des 17. Jahrhunderts* (Bern and Munich, 1967), 123–139.

13. "In the *comedias* Calderón often dramatizes the failures of kings and princes who promote immediate political interests in defiance of legal and spiritual constraints; in the *autos* he defends true statecraft in theoretical terms and demonstrates its operation in the institutions and affairs of government. These two perspectives are complementary. Taken together, they present a comprehensive program for Christian monarchy, illustrated through the methods of example and counterexample" (Stephen Rupp, *Allegories of Kingship: Calderón and the Anti-Machiavellian Tradition* [University Park, PA, 1996], 10. See also 26–27, 31, 68–76).

14. For Calderón's political Augustinianism, see Joachim Küpper, *Diskurs-Renovatio bei Lope de Vega und Calderón* (Tübingen, 1990), 376–377. I would, however, disagree with Küpper's view that there is little to distinguish Lope from Calderón regarding the nature of man's political life.

15. For a concise review of the hard historical realities underlying the hagiographic treatment of the death of the prince—an example of "the Counter Reformation appropriation of history"—see Küpper, ch. 5. The ill-fated Portuguese expedition against Tangiers occurred in 1437, and the first historical account of its failure made no mention of Fernando's *constantia* and his refusal to hand over Ceuta to the victorious enemy. The prince, a sickly type, in fact suggested a monetary settlement by the Portuguese; the latter evidently failed to pursue the possibility expeditiously, and he was transferred to Fez, where he died in isolation. The chronicle, motivated by a hagiographical

agenda (in 1470 the canonization occurred), pointed out that the prince accepted the news of the death of the king, his brother, with the patience of Job; that he was admired by his Moorish captors, who embalmed his body for subsequent sale; and that as he was dying, he had a vision of the Virgin. In addition to this account, written by Frei João Alvares between 1451 and 1460, another document, a "testament," points to a developing ideological agenda: the continuing Portuguese imperial expansion can be justified by the need to avenge the "saint" and free Christian captives in the Moorish lands. The crusading hero that we find in Calderón's drama nearly two centuries later thus comes into being. Notable embellishments followed in the sixteenth century—e.g, Camoes associated Fernando with the Roman Stoic hero Regulus and his self-sacrifice for his country; in Román's updated Spanish version of Alvares's chronicle (1595), the prince refuses to be exchanged for Ceuta and embraces martyrdom, and any remaining hints of Portuguese political cynicism in the unfortunate affair become irrelevant. See also A. E. Sloman, *The Sources of Calderón's El Príncipe Constante* (Oxford, 1950).

16. As Wolfgang Kayser pointed out in his analysis of the design of the play, this technique drastically attenuates dramatic movement. There is a discrete quality, a completeness, in the respective roles of the hero, assembled "timelessly," as it were. The emblematic, lyrical, spatialized, and atmospheric effects are pronounced, whereas "dynamic" conflicts and intrigues of the customary *ordo successivorum* of drama are insinuated only to be dropped and ultimately to fade out. One notes the recurrence of motifs attached to the different roles, a procedure that intensifies the *ordo simultaneorum*, just as musical repetition becomes stasis. See "Zur Struktur des 'Standhaften Prinzen' von Calderón," *Calderón de la Barca,* ed. Hans Flasche (Darmstadt, 1971), 321–346. The affinities of the play with the *auto sacramental* have been noted by Entwistle (see E. M. Wilson and W. J. Entwistle, "Calderón's *Príncipe constante:* Two Appreciations," *Modern Language Review* 34 [1939], 207–222).

17. Fénix is not to be found in the historical sources of the play, and her literary ancestry—e.g., the Saracen temptress or beloved of the crusader, the pleasure garden of the romance and epic hero's diversion or captivity, the beautiful Moorish maiden of the Abencerraje tradition—offers few clues that account for her compelling combination of vanity, vulnerability, anxiety, erotic passivity, and sensitivity. Despite the "deliverance" and comedic marriage that concludes her destiny in the play, the resolution has the effect of an afterthought, a crude effort to tie up a loose end or deal with a fragment that has removed itself from the center of the play. She remains fundamentally elliptical, and her silences are functional; she is precisely unforgettable because she is nothingness, pure ephemerality in her opposition to the constancy of the prince. She in effect declares herself irrelevant. The early chronicle texts mention the kindnesses of a jailor's wife following the transfer of the royal prisoner to Fez but nothing that would suggest a portentous encounter with a powerful female. Lope de Vega exploited the material for a characteristic erotic *enredo*, focusing attention on the good Moor, Muley, who, along with Fernando, is pursued by a sexually voracious Moorish queen; converts to Christianity in admiration of Fernando; defies the law to feed the starving prince; kills the Arab torturer, whose cruelty is condemned by the Arab king; and escapes, with the aid of a sympathetically drawn Jew, to Portugal with Fernando's bones, accompanied by a converted Moorish maiden who, like the pagan Erminia in Tasso's *Gerusalemme liberata,* the age's most influential depiction of the encounter of Islamic and Christian worlds, has miraculous powers of healing. All of this includes disguises and identity confusions, lovers' quarrels, triangles and jealousies, as well as such standard theatrical devices as

listones and intercepted letters. In short, we find all the formulas and effects of Lope's inclusive *comedia de enredo* and no effort to develop the machinery of its oppositions into anything resembling Calderón's somber intensifications of metaphysical, theological, and cultural divisions and conflicts. Despite its ritualistic scenes, which include hieratic displays of the monarch and regalia at beginning and end, the struggles of loyal vassals to gaze on the ruler's face, celebrations of Spain's heroic history and imperial destiny, and an invocation of the "sangre ilustre de los godos," *La fortuna adversa* is marked by a strong ecumenical tone that continues to sound in the opening act of the later play, with its bonding of Muley and Fernando in "chivalric internationalism" and its invocation of Allah and the Christian God in the same breath. Undressed and degraded as a savage, Lope's prince, in his saintliness, earns the highest recognition by his Moorish captor: "para ser de Alá un amigo grande/no le falta otra cosa si ser moro,/que cierto fuera un santo de Mahoma" (in order to be a great friend of Allah, the only thing he lacks is being a Moor, for certainly he would be one of Mohammed's saints) (*La fortuna adversa del Infante Don Fernando de Portugal*, in Sloman, *The Sources of Calderón's El Príncipe Constante*, 183). We might recall at this point the conciliatory approach toward morality and human differences that dominated *El villano en su rincón*. And precisely at this point Calderón must turn decisively in a radically different direction from that pursued by his humanistic predecessor. Unlike the other two plays examined, in this case the doctrinaire reduction, or "correction," of the early work under the pressures of ascendant absolutism produces the profound and enduring masterpiece.

18. In his discussion of the dramatic design of the play, Wolfgang Kayser correctly noted in passing that Fénix's emblematic character, in its interaction with the protagonist, is marked by a specific "stylistic" quality, the highly artificial, controversial poetic language of the *cultistas*. He cites a brilliant insight by Hugo Friedrich concerning the general presence of the frequently criticized mannerism of Calderón's dramas: "It is precisely in this style that illusory beauty can come into full blossom, only then, in the ensuing actions, to wilt into somber disillusionment. The pomp and the restlessness of the flowery language appear to glaze over the nothingness but in fact seem designed as illusions, themselves 'put on,' to conceal the deceit of nothingness that is always present in beauty." See Kayser, "Zur Struktur des 'Standhaften Prinzen' von Calderón," 339; Friedrich *Der fremde Calderón* (Freiburg, 1955), 29. As the following makes clear, I agree fully with Kayser's interpretation of Fénix's "stylistic" role, but I would suggest that the play's subjection of man's literary creations to the searing insights of *desengaño* goes well beyond the notorious excesses of the Baroque lyric (see the following note).

19. It should be pointed out that the play's processes of "disrobing" reach well beyond the political and regal issues I am emphasizing here. Like several other masterpieces of Baroque art— e.g., *Don Quijote de la Mancha*, Lope de Vega's *La Dorotea*, Tasso's *Gerusalemme liberata*, and Milton's *Paradise Lost*—*El príncipe constante* is a work of remarkable literary self-consciousness and inclusiveness, incorporating numerous traditional poetic orders, worlds, and genres for critical examination, rejection, reframing, reaccentuation, or essential reconstruction. All of these works register what is perhaps the fundamental fact of this period in literary history: its transitional character and its struggle to find alternative paths amid the inadequate formulas—the "wreckage"—of exhausted literary traditions and models. Gazing anxiously on her own image in the mirror, Fénix immediately finds herself in incomprehensible ways "dis-adequated" and puzzled before her traditional role and identity in epic, pastoral, chivalric, and Moorish romance. One thinks of the differences that separate her from her most famous immediate prede-

cessor, Tasso's beautiful Saracen princess Armida, triumphantly holding her mirror linking the eyes of herself and the enthralled captive of her garden, the crusading hero Rinaldo. Meanwhile, Fernando finds himself withdrawing from the conventional paradigms of the heroes of epic and heroic romance, the "true citizens" of the literary worlds he initially inhabits. In his opening speech, following the storm at sea, the disturbing portents, and the perilous landing, he clearly reincarnates Virgil's Aeneas and Tasso's Gofreddo, piously exhorting his soldiers to seek glory in a community effort, to dismiss fearful portents, to trust in a providential power, and to dedicate themselves to the foundation and liberation of cities. In his next scene, he bestrides a fiery, nearly uncontrollable horse, bonded with an admired enemy warrior in a trajectory of lost direction and solitary bravery that bears him away from the city to a challenging other world of unpredictable adventure, sentimental love, captivity, and possible dereliction. Calderón appears to have shifted the fictional worlds of his hero and suddenly traces the literary career of the knight of chivalric romance, investing him with the virtues of the heroic individual adventurer. The challenging horse of instinct, power, chaos, and discipline that appears in so many dramas of kings and state here takes the shape of the wild horse of romance, bearing individual heroes on personal quests and adventures away from the centers and the duties of their collectives. The scene surrounds the prince with echoes of the literary traditions of the most famous Italian *romanzi* (e.g., the horse that Ariosto's hero, insane with love, drives to exhaustion and drags all over the continent and the horses that bear their riders away from the responsibilities of religious warfare at the central site of Jerusalem in Tasso's epic). See A. Bartlett Giamatti, "Headlong Horses, Headless Horsemen: An Essay in the Chivalric Romances of Pulci, Boiardo and Ariosto," in *Italian Literature: Roots and Branches*, ed. K. Atchity and G. Rimanelli (New Haven, 1976). For Ariosto's "celebration and critique of *cavalleria* as horsemanship and heroic selfhood" and his "poem-long imagery of horses reined and running mad," see A. Ascoli, *Ariosto's Bitter Harmony: Crisis and Evasion in the Italian Renaissance* (Princeton, 1987), 36. The prince's literary determinations are as dense as those of the maiden. The protagonist's double, a literal sharer of the wild horse, is modeled directly on a well-known ballad by Góngora—"El caballero de Orán." See Dian Fox, "A Further Source of Calderón's *El Príncipe Constante*," *Journal of Hispanic Philology* 4 (1979–80): 157–166. The ecumenical, "international" atmosphere of the romantic episode of heroic doubles is intensified by its assimilation of the age's most famous depiction of Moorish chivalry, gallantry, and sentiment, *El Abencerraje*. In the final two acts all of this changes drastically: the garden becomes a place of delusion and torment for the maiden; the beauties of her countenance are discovered to be veils hiding the reality of the skeleton within—the most grisly of the doubles dominating the design of this play; and the human aggrandizements of epic are exposed as embellishments of shabby political realities. The only literature that might maintain an adequate connection with reality in the kingdom of man would appear to be the book containing the final model for the prince—the quiescent, enduring, and humble figure of Job. In the final scenes of Calderón's play, the mantle of majesty is lifted and reveals the most eloquent "royal pronouncement" of the king's real body—*Memento mori*! For a fundamental study of the crisis in language and literature in Baroque culture, see L. Spitzer, *Die Literarisierung des Lebens in Lope's "Dorotea"* (Bonn, 1932). Also see my "Lope's Broken Clock: Baroque Time in *La Dorotea*," *Hispanic Review* 37 (1969): 459–490, and "Gracián's Theaters of Nothingness," in *Sin fronteras: Ensayos de literatura comparada en homenaje a Claudio Guillén* (Madrid, 1999), 215–229.

20. The astonishing, distinctively "Calderonian" conceit—the hollow of a beautiful princess's bed-

ding conceived as an "emerald grave"—is arguably the most poetically concentrated manifestation of the fundamental tension running through the entire play.

21. See Kayser, "Zur Struktur des 'Standhaften Prinzen' von Calderón."

22. "The *Civitas Terrena* is governed by expediency, pride, and ambition, the *Civitas Dei*, by self-sacrifice, obedience, and humility. The one is *vanitas*, the other *veritas*. The *Civitas Terrena* lives by natural generation, the *Civitas Dei* by supernatural regeneration; the one is temporal and mortal, the other eternal and immortal. The one is determined by love of God, even to the contempt of self; the other by love of self, even to the contempt of God. The children of light consider their earthly existence as a means of enjoying God; the children of darkness consider their gods as a means of enjoying the world. Thus history is an age-long contest between faith and unbelief" (Löwith, *Meaning in History*, 169–170).

23. Fernando's bewilderment, as well as the fundamental error in Fénix's failure to make an essential distinction between flowers and stars, is illuminated by a passage in one of Calderón's most powerful depictions of the madness of the political order and man's inherent lust for power, *La hija del aire*. The Satanic "princess of the air," Semiramis, subordinates all human feeling to the pleasures of tyrannical and cruel self-assertion and, in the tradition of the political Nimrod, builds towers and hanging gardens that reach the clouds and display the power that comes to her "from below." When overthrowing her "confusa monarquía" and bringing freedom and *desengaño* to Babylonia, the young prince, Irán, describes the perversity of the splendor of her soaring monuments in their mingling of flowers and stars. "Babilonia, república eminente/que al orbe empinas de zafir la frente,/siendo jónica y dórica coluna/del cóncavo palacio de la Luna,/adonde colocados tus pensiles,/al Cielo se han llevado los abriles,/y con sus flores bellas/a rayos equivocan las estrellas:/que vengo a ser tu invicto Rey, no dudo" (Babylonia, eminent republic that lifts its brow to the sphere of sapphire; the ionic and doric columns of the concave palace of the Moon, where, your planted gardens' Aprils have been borne to Heaven and with their rays of beautiful flowers counterfeit the stars: I do not doubt that I come to be your unvanquished king) (*La hija del aire*, ed. F. Ruiz Ramón [Madrid, 1987], 312).

24. For the subtlety with which Calderón invests this climactic symbolical encounter with psychologically complex and convincing human feelings of erotic attraction and anxiety, see Leo Spitzer's imaginative reading: "The Figure of Fénix in Calderón's *El príncipe constante*," in *Critical Essays on the Theatre of Calderón*, ed. Bruce W. Wardropper (New York, 1965), 137–160, esp. 148ff.

25. *El príncipe constante*, 124–125. The momentary ambiguation in the climactic completion of the prophesied exchange is intensified by a fleeting recovery of Góngora's poetic voice and an implicit plea for the beauty of the earth. Up to this point Gongorism has been conspicuous in its attachment to the flawed and insubstantial world of the Moors. Aside from its association with Fénix and her garden, its most notable appearance is in Muley's long romance describing his scouting mission on the Mediterranean. His account of the changing visual phenomena as he surveys the Christian fleet is a spectacular description of metamorphosing forms, dissolving boundaries, violent alterations in perspective, and confusing multiplications of objects and appearances. As the eye strains amid the light and shadow of this "natural painting" in an effort to render its assembly of phenomena determinate and to emerge from the "engaño" in which it finds itself, the ships become successively rocks, mountains, cities, monsters, clouds, squalls, and the gardens of a towering Babylon. While the prince certainly speaks in the grand style in his most

theatrical moments, his world, with the possible exception of his description of the horse in his early romantic adventure with Muley, is not marked by the transformative, metaphorical idiom characteristic of the controversial style of the Cordovan poet. One might appreciate its startling assertion at this moment of ascetic renunciation and Christian otherworldliness as an appearance of Góngora's Fénix, the mythic bird of the East that rises, in one of the most memorable epiphanies of *Las soledades*, in celebration of the inexhaustible energies and the eternally self-renewing beauties of the earthly order. This *fénix* is of course the dazzling symbol of flux and mutability, all that the *constant* hero would appear to disavow. For Calderón's characteristic association of the splendors of Gongorist metaphorics with the illusory and fallen nature of this world, see H. Friedrich's words above, note 18.

INDEX